D1282941

- The reliability models in use today were invented for use with analog systems. Because of built-in idiosyncrasies, these reliability models are of no direct utility in the digital case.

In short, each of these general approaches to software quality is not powerful enough to overcome the digital debacle.

To complicate matters, software that is "correct" can produce undesirable behavior when it is executed. This is especially likely when software behavior is analyzed with respect to the rest of the system in which the software resides.

There are two groups of problems that are likely to arise in the future of digital systems. The first class of problems relates to defective software. The second class of problems relates to defective software environments. Almost all software quality assurance methodologies attempt to address the first kind of problem. But it is misleading to limit the scope of the software quality problem to defects in software. What is required is an approach that can predict worst-case outcomes, regardless of whether such problems are triggered within the code or by the code's external environment.

Fault injection includes many approaches that are geared toward answering both questions. By using fault injection to analyze software, it is possible to prepare for worst-case outcomes. Fault injection provides an objective, scientific tool for assessing software.

This book builds on the fundamental fault injection concepts presented in Friedman and Voas's book *Software Assessment: Reliability, Safety, Testability.* That book provides an introduction to software fault injection suited for graduate students and technical researchers. This book takes a much deeper look at several real applications of fault injection. Each technique is explained with reference to real-world case studies where fault injection has made a positive contribution.

Software fault injection is a family of techniques that is only beginning to gain the recognition that it deserves. We believe these software measurement techniques will become the most important assessment technique of the coming decades. The real world is demanding more emphasis be placed on "product" and less emphasis on the no-longer-in-vogue "process" approach to software engineering. Process is well and good, but what really matters in the end is the product. The need for development organizations to apply modern software fault-injection techniques will only increase.

This book is the first to describe in practitioner's terms the unique benefits and challenges associated with fault-injection methods. These methods are not well understood by today's software engineering practitioner who thinks fault-injection methods are good only for "reliability estimation." Fault injection has much more to offer. It has the potential to address several of the most pressing problems that plague today's information systems. Fault injection can play a useful role in critical software life-cycle tasks such as: unit testing, integration testing, component off the

Preface

Software is digital, making software quality hard to ascertain. In the twinkling of a digital eye, a binary system can completely modify its state. Consider how easy it is for a computer to change 11110000 to 00001111 by flipping all the bits at once. This sort of thing is not so easy in an analog system where gradual state-change rules the roost. Unless there is a major accident, a car going due West at 80 mph cannot instantly "flip" to going due East at 110 mph. In continuous systems, there are certain historical guarantees about the immediate future. If a car is going due West at 80 at time t, then it is reasonable to expect it to be going something close to due West at some speed near 80 mph at t + epsilon. This assurance about what will happen next makes analog continuous systems inherently more predictable than discrete digital ones. This critical difference between digital and analog systems continues to delay the replacement of aging analog components by modern digital components. But analog components are nearing the end of their predicted lifetimes. A digital solution *must* be found.

For the past eight years, researchers have been exploring what, if anything, can be done to address this critical difference between analog and digital systems:

- Trying to exhaustively test a digital system is no solution. Exhaustive testing is usually computationally infeasible.

- Formal methods might help produce better digital code, but they can in no way guarantee what will happen when an analyzed program is placed in the messy real world. Formal methods have no way of proving what might happen in every possible environmental situation.

- A metric can usually say something about the structure of digital code, as long as the metric has been previously correlated with a particular code characteristic. Any such metric can be used to suggest whether the code under analysis has that characteristic even when estimating that characteristic is otherwise impossible. This helps, but it doesn't solve the problem.

Fault Injection: A Technology for the Future of Software Engineering . . .

"The next wave in the rapidly advancing field of software quality assurance"

> —Barry Preppernau
> Test Training Manager
> Microsoft

"Voas and McGraw have made the complex and esoteric subject of fault injection into something understandable and compelling. There's just enough theory here to educate without overwhelming, but the book is really for pragmatists. The authors have opened a whole new front in the war against bad software."

> —James Bach
> SmartPatent

"Based on the successful use of fault injection on prior and on-going programs, we are moving toward standardizing on this technique for all future software-intensive safety critical systems."

> —Larry James
> Senior Scientist
> Engineering & Technology Center
> Hughes Information Systems

"This is a fundamental technology that has no equal. The principles and specific methodologies have been greatly beneficial in increasing the efficiency and effectiveness of our software testing, especially in the area of high-reliability, high-availability systems."

> —Mike Friedman
> Hughes Electronics

For the Voases and the first Jack McGraw.

Publisher: Robert Ipsen
Editor: Marjorie Spencer
Managing Editor: Frank Grazioli
Associate Editor, Electronic Products: Mike Sosa
Text Design & Composition: North Market Street Graphics, Lancaster, PA

Designations used by companies to distinguish their products are often claimed as trademarks. In all instances where John Wiley & Sons, Inc., is aware of a claim, the product names appear in initial capital or ALL CAPITAL LETTERS. Readers, however, should contact the appropriate companies for more complete information regarding trademarks and registration.

Dr. Voas's work is partially supported by DARPA Contract number F30602-959C-0282 and NIST Advanced Technology Program Cooperative Agreement Number 70NANB581160. Dr. McGraw's work is partially supported by NSF grant number DMI-9661393 and DARPA Contracts number F30602-959C-0282 and DAAH01-97-C-RO95. The views and conclusions contained in this book are those of the authors and should not be interpreted as representing the official policies, either expressed or implied, of DARPA, NSF, NIST, or the U.S. government.

The version of software used in Section 7.3 is the UVA MSS experimental prototype, which is a version of the code that is not in any production system.

This book is printed on acid-free paper. ∞

Library of Congress Cataloging-in-Publication Data:
Voas, Jeffrey M.
    Software fault injection : inoculating programs against errors /
Jeffrey Voas, Gary McGraw.
        p.   cm.
    Includes bibliographical references and index.
    ISBN 0-471-18381-4 (cloth/CD-ROM : alk. paper)
    1. Fault-tolerant computing.   2. Computer software—Quality
control.   I. McGraw, Gary, 1966– .   II. Title.
QA76.9.F38V63   1998
005.1′4—dc21   97-26283
                                                         CIP

Printed in the United States of America.
10 9 8 7 6 5 4 3 2 1

Software Fault Injection: Inoculating Programs Against Errors

Jeffrey M. Voas

Gary McGraw

WILEY COMPUTER PUBLISHING

JOHN WILEY & SONS, INC.

New York • Chichester • Weinheim • Brisbane • Singapore • Toronto shelf (COTS) subsystems testing, security vulnerability assessment, system-level testing, system maintenance, risk assessment, and safety analysis. Space is devoted to each of these tasks. Software fault injection can also be combined with unusual testing environments to assess how robust systems are when rare events are fed into the software. Additionally, software fault-injection algorithms can be customized to address current "hot" problems such as the Year 2000 bug.

This book is intended to be useful to both practitioners and advanced students of software engineering. It is written at a level that should be easy to read by software engineers at all levels of experience. This book is also intended as a reference for those persons who are charged with overseeing the quality assurance programs of their organizations. This book will be particularly useful to persons concerned with the dependability, safety, fault tolerance, and security of their information systems. Fault injection can play a very important role for each of these problem areas.

Chapter 1 defines the current state of the art in software quality. This chapter explains where fault injection fits in with the many other less-potent software quality approaches. It details the differences between structural metrics and behavioral metrics, and explains the difference between static and dynamic approaches to studying software. Chapter 1 explains why digital systems are inherently unpredictable, and why we must assess high levels of uncertainty when we analyze such systems.

Chapter 2 presents both the history of fault injection and the requisite terminology and definitions for performing fault injection. Fault injection is a multiphased process that requires several key decisions by the practitioner. It is not a method that can be simply "thrown over the wall" to the masses as can many static software metrics. Forethought about where to employ fault injection, and what sorts of faults to inject, is a definite must. As a relatively new technology, fault injection introduces a number of new terms. The definitions given in Chapter 2 show up throughout the rest of the book.

Chapter 3 covers the fundamentals of fault injection. Fault injection requires attention to program inputs, program outputs, and all data states in between. Executing programs usually requires some sort of input, and the kind of input they get often determines their behavior. Inputs drive internal states, and internal states can be perturbed or changed by fault injection. Of course, in the end, the question is really: *What happens if we change this data state like this?* Answering this question requires close attention to program output. In later chapters, we customize the basic ideas presented in Chapter 3 for specific behavioral characteristics that we wish to predict (e.g., testability, safety, and security).

Chapter 4 delves into software mutation, a kind of fault injection that simulates programmer faults. Because of its computational complexity, software mutation has not been adopted for commercial use. But as desktop computers surpass the supercomputers of yesteryear, this excuse will become irrelevant. Software mutation may yet pay off as a potent analysis tool.

Chapter 5 describes the first fault injection case study—software testability assessment. In the late 1980s, Voas's first application of fault injection was to measure software testability. Applications of fault injection to domains such as software safety and security vulnerability analysis have their roots in this initial research. This chapter explains why faults hide during testing, and what fault injection can do to try to find where latent defects are most likely to remain. Software testing still remains one of the costliest phases of the software life cycle. Fault injection can make that phase more cost-effective. Testability assessment has three major components: propagation, infection, and execution. Together, these three components make up the PIE algorithm. Each piece of PIE is explained in Chapter 5, along with high-level algorithms for implementation.

Chapter 6 describes how testability techniques (that predict where faults are more likely to hide) evolved into techniques that can predict how external failures in the software's environment can impact software. This move makes fault injection instantly applicable to an essential problem—the problem of software safety. The move to encompass software's environment during analysis is a subtle yet fundamental distinction that has important implications for the information produced by fault injection. Fault injection, when modified in this way, offers important payoffs for problems associated with software failure, COTS components, and embedded systems. This chapter highlights several important real-world applications of fault injection and clearly explains the benefits of the approach. Chapter 6 introduces EPA, extended propagation analysis, for safety analysis.

Chapter 7 explains how EPA has been used to address real-world software safety problems. Software is quickly moving into safety-critical domains. It is now controlling not just trains, planes, and automobiles, but also nuclear power plants and surgical devices. This chapter details how EPA, in its commercial guise called SafetyNet, has been used to analyze train control code for the Bay Area Rapid Transit (BART) system, code for controlling the Magneto Stereotaxis System (MSS), and nuclear control code.

Chapter 8 describes current research exploring how the advanced fault-injection technique of Chapter 6, EPA, can be enhanced and then used as a software vulnerability measurement technique. This makes fault injection useful as a tool for computer security specialists. A software hazard and a malicious intrusion turn out to be different classes of "undesirable output events." That means if we can predict (using fault injection) how likely it is that hazardous outputs can occur, then we should be able to predict how likely it is that intrusion attempts can succeed. This chapter describes ongoing DARPA-sponsored research that has proven highly successful in its initial phases.

Chapter 9 describes how fault injection can be applied to several key problems in reuse and maintenance. In maintenance, the fundamental concern is how a change in one part of the code can affect other parts of the code. Many people claim that the bulk of the costs over the entire life of a software system reside in the maintenance phase. We show how fault injection can clarify the complex interrelationships between different computations and data within a piece of software. A related concern in software engineering is reuse. Software reuse is concerned with whether the original testing of a component might prove adequate given a new environment for the component. Fault injection reveals valuable insights for both maintenance and reuse.

Chapter 10 details several very new research areas that can be combined with standard fault-injection methods to make them even more powerful. Inverted and modified environments, as well as different classes of assertions, can all enhance fault injection. It is important to understand that external information fed into software directly affects its behavior. This chapter provides methods that make it easier to analyze how such differences in input affect software behavior.

Finally, and perhaps most important, Chapter 11 shows how to convince management of the utility of software fault injection. By this point in the book, you have learned how fault injection works and seen some real-world data. You probably see places where fault injection could help your organization. However, management is often skeptical of new software engineering techniques, and rightly so. Too many tool vendors and academics have promised silver bullet after silver bullet for too long. This chapter discusses a credible plan for convincing management to try fault injection. The method? Try fault injection on a pilot system and look carefully at the results.

Software development is a peculiar process, half science and half art. Now that software is doing things like controlling airplanes, the artsy part had better be backed by solid engineering practice. Consumers are no longer satisfied with code that "mostly" works. Quality and reliability are more important than ever before. Fault injection is a useful tool in developing high-quality, reliable code.

Software professionals find themselves living in interesting times (an ancient Chinese curse come true). Pressure from the Internet explosion is compressing development schedules like never before. At the same time, lawyers and insurance companies are becoming interested in software. The liability grace period we are all enjoying is about to come to an abrupt halt. Both of these factors can be addressed by fault injection. Because fault injection can be automated, it can fit into compressed schedules. Because fault injection is the state of the art in assessment, it can address liability concerns. The time to adopt this technology as your own is now.

Acknowledgments

This book represents the fruits of much hard work done by the dedicated employees of Reliable Software Technologies (www.rstcorp.com). Though the authors wrote the words you read, the ideas, algorithms, and experiments reported herein leverage the work of many others. We gratefully acknowledge the work that made this book a possibility.

RST is an excellent place to work. The stimulating research environment makes it easy to succeed. Nothing like being surrounded by smart people! Many RSTers helped with this book in many ways:

- Frank Charron (research associate and chief architect of the SafetyNet) developed the tool included in the CD-ROM and has been instrumental in designing, implementing, and experimenting with a number of essential research prototypes.

- Michael Schatz (research associate) created the HTML tutorial for the CD-ROM and is also heavily involved in the research projects covered in this book.

- Chris Michael, Ph.D. (senior research scientist) read the entire manuscript and helped improve it.

- Jeff Payne (CEO) helped cofound RST (and continues to drive its forward-thinking philosophy), read many chapters, and commented insightfully.

- Anup Ghosh, Ph.D. (research scientist) drafted some of the material included in Chapter 8 and is leading security research efforts at RST.

- Cathy Streightiff (office manager, ATP Division) provided administrative support.

- Rich Mills (director of development) made the computers behave when we were burning the CD-ROM.

- Ana-Marija Beskin (software test consultant) and Rob Craven (software engineer) put the CD-ROM through its paces.

We would also like to thank: Professor Jeff Offutt (George Mason University), Professor Jim Bieman (Colorado State University), and Lora Kassab (Naval Research Laboratory), for providing feedback on the manuscript.

Many thanks to those individuals who have kept our research programs alive at Reliable Software Technologies over the past several years. Without their support, a majority of the research discussed in this text could never have been carried out: Teresa Lunt (DARPA), John Faust (Rome Laboratories), Dolores Wallace (NIST), David Fisher (SEI), Michael Nowak (NIST), and Barbara Cuthill (NIST).

Wiley's staff once again did a super job with the book, taking our pathetic Word documents and properly typesetting them (we're going back to LaTeX guys). Thanks to Marjorie Spencer, a superb editor, for championing book number two. Also thanks to Frank Grazioli for being Frank.

Finally, and definitely most important, we're grateful to those who put up with us outside of the work environment. Amy Barley, babyman Jack, and the bean could hardly believe there was another book in the makings at home! Watch out, there may be more.

Contents

1   *Software Assurance*
Why Code Behavior Matters

1.1   Software Quality

Software quality is a function of time; it is not an easy-to-measure static quantity such as the number of lines of code. It is not possible to evaluate a program without running it and say much of interest about its quality. In that sense, analyzing software quality is akin to analyzing a physical system. For most physical systems, quality must be determined over some time period. A physical system's reliability—something closely related to quality—generally decreases over time. Consider the quality and reliability of a car. One can determine how reliable a car is only by testing it extensively over time.

Things aren't quite this simple, of course. There are several important differences between software quality and physical system quality that must be considered. Physical systems tend to degrade, meaning reliability almost never increases with age. A program, on the other hand, can turn out to be more reliable in the future than it is today—and this upward mobility in reliability can happen without any change to the program. How on earth could that be?

1.1.1   Software Behavior

Software behavior changes according to context. The same piece of code can be executed in many different environments. Because some environments may cause software to behave more reliably than others, it is possible to see how a piece of software could turn out to be more reliable down the road than it is today. Of course the opposite is also true—software may well be less reliable when it is used in a new environment than it was in its original environment. These two scenarios are both influenced by program modification. When software is modified over time, particularly when bugs are fixed, reliability growth models must account for incremental software improvement.

Software structure is often confused with software quality. Old-fashioned software metrics that traditionally measure visual characteristics of software flowcharts were once considered reasonable measures of software goodness. But software has moved significantly beyond flowcharts. Purporting to measure software quality without ever running it is silly. Eyeballing code structure is not a very productive exercise, however there is some evidence that structural complexity is related to defect density. Back in the days of punch cards, it was useful to make flowcharts, look at code before it was ever run, and do static analysis. In those days it was very expensive to run any code, reliable or otherwise. Now that computer time is cheap and plentiful, we should upgrade our code assessment techniques to match the technology.

The term *spaghetti code* refers to code that is wildly unstructured. Spaghetti code uses goto's for jumping into and out of loops, and into and out of code blocks. Spaghetti code can be very difficult to understand because it can be very difficult to follow its logic. Nonetheless, spaghetti code can be correct and reliable. That is, spaghetti code can be well-behaved. This is not to say that we condone the use of goto or that we think writing spaghetti code should be encouraged. It's just that we believe what code looks like is much less important that what code does.

Having correct code is only one piece of the software quality puzzle. Let's assume for the sake of argument that everyone believes software quality must be measured by watching a program run. If that's true, then it is critical to look at any and all aspects of execution that affect behavior. For many systems, human inputs are a key factor in behavior. There are other types of inputs to the system that must be considered as well. Programs read input from files, sensors, hardware peripherals, device drivers, and the like. The fact is that "goodness" of the inputs—something that can be captured and modeled statistically—can play a key role in the goodness of the software's behavior.

We don't want our claim about static and dynamic analysis to be taken too far. Sometimes it does pay to look at software by hand. Simply seeing a statement such as "while (5=5) do" immediately tells anyone who understands programming that the code fragment will never terminate. Infinite loops are rarely considered quality improvement features. These sorts of things can be found by software inspections and code reviews, both of which have shown to be useful in improving software quality.

Have you ever wondered why a piece of software purchased only three years ago is worthless today? Many three-year-old programs had good reliability when they were purchased, and most didn't undergo much change during their existence. Yet today, many three-year-old programs are as useless as washboards. Software's inherent plasticity helps to make software obsolete at a faster rate than almost any other modern product. When software plasticity mixes with a few months of calendar time, software becomes one of the most quickly depreciating capital investments extant. Reduced life expectancy is based on external factors outside the scope of the program itself. This is all because of things like the environment that a program runs in (including compilers and operating systems) and the hardware platforms that a program runs on.

Software evolves at a rate of approximately a minor new release every six months and a major new release every year. Incidentally, Internet time has only served to shorten these numbers. After several years, the utility of a piece of software previously found reliable borders on nil. Hence software quality is partially a function of how old a program is with respect to the age of its environment, including hardware and software.

If people could predict the future, they could predict how software would behave in future environments. Of course, true psychics probably don't need software in the first place. In any case, most people can't predict what software environments may look like tomorrow. This difficulty is compounded by two other problems: (1) ignorance of what is wrong with a piece of code today and (2) no knowledge of what possible inputs will be presented to a piece of code throughout its lifetime. The second problem could be considered one part of the problem of knowing what tomorrow's software environment will be.

Every piece of software has a *real* reliability rating; the problem is finding out what that rating is. Consider the reliability of program P to be the probability of failure-free operation in a fixed environment for a fixed period of time. The key to our definition is fixing the environment and fixing the time interval. For a given environment, A, and some time interval, X, P's reliability could be, say, 0.0. For another environment, B, over the same time interval, the reliability could be 1.0. Given our definition of reliability, the following problems crop up:

1. You almost never know the precise environment in which a piece of software will exist throughout its complete lifetime.

2. It is usually impossible to determine an oracle for the program; in other words, the method for determining correct outputs will almost certainly be flawed for some portion of the test cases.

3. Even if you were so lucky as to have perfectly flawless software, the software can't always produce desired outputs if some of its inputs become corrupted.

Our definition above rates the real reliability of a piece of code. Since we cannot compute this value precisely for the reasons we raised, software practitioners have invented two ways of approximating reliability—estimation and prediction. *Estimation* is the process of approximating reliability today. *Prediction* is the process of approximating reliability tomorrow.

When you turn on the eleven o'clock news and the meteorologist tells you the current temperature is 74 degrees Fahrenheit, that's actually an *estimate* of the true temperature, which might more accurately be 74.62745 degrees. When the meteorologist says that tomorrow's high will be 80 degrees, that is a *prediction* based on the best guess for what weather patterns will be in a particular geographic region. The prediction may even be partially based on today's temperature estimation. Tomorrow's real high temperature may be 82.98765 degrees. Weather prediction varies according to geographic region for obvious reasons. Moving the prediction area even a few miles in any direction can substantially change weather prediction. When that happens, the environment of the prediction is changing. Just as weather prediction is sensitive to this sort of geographical environment, software reliability prediction is sensitive to the executing environment.

Knowing all of the possible exact values of all program parameters in all possible combinations is hard, if not impossible. To get around this problem, we can assign probabilities to parameter values. Hopefully such probabilities reflect the key defining aspects of reality. This doesn't solve the problem cleanly however, because probabilities are often difficult to quantify accurately. One thing that makes such quantification hard is the amount of evidence required before an estimation is made. Sometimes we don't have as much information as we really need.

As an example, consider flipping a fair coin—a coin that in no way favors heads over tails. We all know the exact probability of getting heads: 50 percent. But what if we flip the coin 100 times and get heads only 45 times? Does that mean that our coin is not actually fair? Of course not! What this says is that based on a particular set of 100 tosses, heads appeared 45 times. If you were to continue flipping, say for one billion flips, you will probabilistically see the original measure of 45 percent approach 50 percent. Our example brings home the simple fact that the accuracy of estimations is based directly on the size of the sample. Sometimes a poor reliability estimation will result from a poor sample size. This problem is particularly acute for software reliability estimation to higher levels of reliability. It is also generally problematic for dynamic analyses based on repeated execution of a piece of code with different test cases.

Estimation is distinct from prediction. Some people treat them interchangeably, but they should not. This is not to say that estimates can't be used as predictors—they frequently are. For example, if you toss a coin 1000 times and 499 of those tosses result in heads, then you can predict that in the next 1000 tosses you should expect a similar outcome. Similarly, if the outside temperature at this moment is 50 degrees, you can predict that the temperature one hour from now will also be around 50 degrees, that is, if you know that the general atmospheric conditions are not unusually volatile. From a software standpoint, reliability estimation is often used as prediction. People estimate the reliability of their code by repeatedly executing it using scenarios that are their best guess of what the future will hold. This process results in an estimate of reliability. Given such an estimate, it is possible to predict with some accuracy that the future reliability of the code will be close to the current estimated reliability. There is plenty of room for error in such a process, but that's what people generally do today.

One common approach to the problem of predicting future scenarios is to hypothesize a set of different scenarios and estimate program reliability for each of them. After collecting a set of estimates, the worst reliability score can be selected, providing a conservative confidence that the future's reliability will be at least as good as if not better than this value.

Let's turn back to physical–world reliability models. One problem with applying traditional models that are based on how systems age for purposes of predicting reliability is that software does not suffer from physical decay as do hardware systems. Tires on a car wear out. Thus, a manufacturer can predict what the reliability of a tire is simply by subtracting the number of miles for which a tire has been used from the expected maximum distance that the tire can go. For software, no such metrics exist. There is no limit to the number of times that you can execute a program. A second, and possibly even more serious problem, is that software is digital and discrete, not analog and continuous. To get a better feeling for why this is a problem, consider the following analogy.

Suppose a cookie recipe tells you to bake cookies for 30 minutes at 300 degrees; and suppose you know that your oven does not work accurately. You know that your oven bakes slightly hotter than the temperature you set it for. Based on this knowledge, you decide to reduce the baking time by a couple of minutes. By adjusting the baking time, you are deviating from the precise directions. It is likely that your cookies will turn out okay, because baking is analog, not digital. The digital case is fundamentally different. Making even the slightest such deviation in a software system can result in absolute disaster. That's because software states that are close syntactically speaking, say, in Hamming distance, are far away semantically in actual behavior. This makes predicting how software will behave in the future a very tough cookie.

1.1.2 The Impossibility of Exhaustive Testing

Determining software quality would be easy if you could test a piece of code on every possible input and show that it produces the exact output that you want every time. This is known as *exhaustive testing*. What's being exhausted here is the input space, not all possible paths through the code. As we explain in more detail later, even if you could exhaustively test your code on all inputs and demonstrate absolute correctness, you still will not have demonstrated that your software is incapable of coming up with an undesirable situation. That fact may make you wonder whether correctness is what we want to build into our software. During the 1970s and 1980s, much research went into finding techniques to ensure software correctness. Unfortunately, this research never led to commercial-grade solutions. Building in correctness in general has been found to be impossible. Software engineers have instead turned to another software characteristic called *robustness.*

To give the reader a flavor for the kinds of resources that exhaustive testing requires, it is useful to look to the data. On average, it takes the software industry from one to four person-hours to generate a test case, test the code using the test case, and document the test results. Even if the program we are told to test involves only one 32-bit integer input, the number of individual test cases required for exhaustive testing is large. Costs can mushroom out of control. Unless the code under consideration is extremely trivial in terms of the number of individual test cases required, using exhaustive testing to ensure correctness is not feasible.

If testing were a viable solution and you could simply "test in" quality, then a company such as Microsoft, with its enormous assets and its tester-to-developer ratio of approximately 1:1, should exhibit very high quality. Bill Gates, Microsoft's CEO, acknowledges the problem:

> *Testing is another area where I have to say I'm a little bit disappointed in the lack of progress. At Microsoft, in a typical development group, there are many more testers than there are engineers writing code. Yet engineers spend well over a third of their time doing testing type work. You could say that we spend more time testing than we do writing code. And if you go back through the history of large-scale systems, that's the way they've been. But, you know, what kind of new techniques are there in terms of analyzing where those things come from and having constructs that do automatic testing? Very, very little. So if you know a researcher out there who wants to work on that problem, boy, we'd love to put a group together.* [Massachusetts Institute of Technology Distinguished Lecture Series 1996, Bill Gates Keynote Address, Wednesday May 30, 1996. http://www.microsoft.com/corpinfo/bill-g/speeches/internet/mit/mit2.htm]

1.2 Measuring Software

Software quality is not an all or nothing phenomenon—there are varying degrees of quality. Because of this, it is necessary to be able to measure software in order to know how good a particular program is. By knowing this, we can take appropriate steps to increase quality if we are dissatisfied with the results of the measurement.

1.2.1 Achieving Quality Is Easier Than Measuring Quality

Because many organizations have historically suffered from poor processes, "process improvement" has become a buzzword in the 1990s. The current trend in software quality is to measure the maturity of development processes and assume that the quality of the processes directly affects the quality of the code. Apparently, some number of years ago, the software community decided that measuring code quality was too difficult. Because of this, the process-implies-product approach was adopted.

Recently there appears to be a fairly strong shift away from the process-based paradigm. Many people are finding out the hard way that good processes do not always a good product make. In software quality, there are two distinct issues that must not be confused. Achieving quality means that the code will produce the outputs that we want. Measuring whether the code actually has this characteristic is another issue. Software fault injection was created to address both of these issues. If you observe undesirable behavior after applying fault injection, then a lower quality score will be assigned. Once a lower score is assigned, you have the ability not only to examine what in the code led to the lower score but also to improve the code.

A key goal in software measurement is that results be applicable to product improvement should deficiencies be discovered. Feeding information concerning quality back into the development life cycle is the only way to improve the development processes over time. Product quality measurement is a simple way to roughly gauge the goodness of the processes. The product can also be incrementally improved through a feedback cycle. An easy way to ensure product reliability improvement is to have a good set of measures. It is very satisfying for developers to watch as successive versions of their product receive higher rankings.

Counterintuitive though it might seem, it may actually be easier to develop high-quality software than it is to know that this has been accomplished. In most other engineering disciplines, it is far harder to build a quality product than it is to determine if a product meets quality requirements. Because defects in software are logical problems and not physical problems, assessing quality is much harder. Other than dynamic code execution, of which fault injection is a kind, static measurements of quality include code inspections and parsing/compiling tools.

Software is unique among manufactured products in many ways. One of the most interesting quirks is that software quality is assessed *after* the software is developed. Can you imagine building an airplane without any guess as to what its reliability would be before building it? Can you imagine building a bridge without doing an analytical assessment predicting the strength of the bridge? Of course not. In the physical world, a divide-and-conquer approach can be used during design and development. We build components, then subsystems, and finally entire systems, and we know throughout the development process what the quality of the product is at each stage.

In software, we can also apply a divide-and-conquer strategy, but we probably don't know what the reliability of the product is at any intermediate developmental stage. In the physical case it is possible to build in quality at each point of development. This is commonly done in physical manufacturing. In the non-physical software world, people commonly attempt to test in quality after development is complete. Software validation and verification (V&V) are the life-cycle processes geared toward developing and assessing quality. Using Boehm's terminology, software verification is a process of determining that we are building the product correctly; software validation is the process of determining that we are building the right product. Verification processes employed early in the life cycle can be used to achieve higher quality. Verification processes employed at the tail end of the life cycle can be used to measure quality. This book is about fault injection—a modern and successful verification process.

1.2.2 Direct and Indirect Measurement

Generally speaking, software fault injection is focused on predicting the future. It is not easy, because values for all parameters that may impact future behavior cannot be known until they have become part of the past. Hindsight vision is a clear-eyed 20/20; but foresight vision is often blind.

There are two distinct methods for measuring software quality—direct measurement and indirect measurement. *Indirect* measures of quality use metrics such as software testability (see chapter 5). Software can be correct, yet have a low testability score. *Direct* measures of quality require metrics for things such as reliability, performance, and availability. Examples of direct measurement processes include testing (assuming that quality is viewed as a behavioral characteristic) and software metrics such as McCabe's cyclomatic complexity and Halstead's information volume (assuming that quality is quaintly viewed as a structural characteristic). Other characteristics of software that can be directly measured include the number of lines of code or the number of function points. The lines-of-code metric is really geared more to a measure of productivity than to quality, yet many professionals believe that the greater the code size, the greater the inherent testing costs and the more problems that will crop up. In the case of large programs, if testing is harder to do because of size, it will be done poorly and the final product will be less reliable. If testing is based solely on attaining some coverage level, there may be some truth to this idea.

Software testing is perhaps the most widely recognized form of directly demonstrating that code satisfies the logic of a code specification. But what if the requirements say something vague, such as, "the code is expected to recover from problems that might occur if a human operator inputs the wrong sequence of commands." This is an impossibly hard characteristic to test for, because the possible combinations of all wrong commands is probably intractably huge. Worse yet, the ways that inputs can be combined may not even be defined. Fault-injection methods that can simulate combinations of corrupt data are ideal for indirectly but only partially demonstrating whether code meets the sort of vague requirement under consideration. We say "partially" because we cannot measure what the code does on all combinations, as that could be an infinite set. But for any classes tried, we can demonstrate compliance.

When software fault injection puts well-defined problems into your code that your code is expected to deal with correctly, but the code fails, this serves as a direct assessment of the quality of your code. When software fault injection puts less well-defined problems into your code—problems that may never actually occur in the software's real lifetime—and the code fails, this serves as an indirect assessment of the quality of the code.

There are two things that you must recognize before using fault injection as a tool. First, you must acknowledge that the characteristics of the code for which you are curious are behavioral in nature. Second, you must recognize that these characteristics cannot be directly estimated to any degree of precision. The reason that they cannot be directly estimated stems from the fact that many of the parameters that directly impact the behavior you want to measure are unknown, and they will be unknown until such time as you no longer care about the software in question. An example may clarify our reasoning. When a bridge is first built, it is not possible to know if some act of nature will someday destroy the bridge. On the day some government decides that the bridge is no longer useful and actually dismantles the bridge, it is possible to know that the bridge will not suffer from an act of nature. At this juncture, such information is no longer useful. The same sort of idea applies to software. For control software used in some manufacturing process, it is impossible to know whether someday either some human or some sensor will send in corrupt input that causes the software to fail in a catastrophic way. But on the day the software is taken out of service, the answer is both clear and irrelevant. The only reason you might be interested in such information is if future software systems are designed based on the observed behavior of old systems.

1.2.3 Structural Metrics

Reasons for measuring structural versus behavioral properties of a piece of code may not always be obvious. Why should it matter whether the code is 1000 lines or 100,000 lines long, as long as it has the correct functionality? Actually, there turn out to be some reasons, including the following:

- It takes more memory to store a bigger executable.
- Longer code will likely take longer to test.
- Longer code takes longer to document.
- Longer code is harder to inspect and debug.
- Longer code will almost certainly be harder to maintain.

In addition, it will be far more expensive to apply formal development methods. The current corporate average cost for one documented and tested line of code is $50. That means a longer program will cost more to develop. For these reasons, knowing the size of the code provides hints about potential costs of other processes that will occur during the life cycle. In particular, testing, debugging, inspections, documentation, and maintenance will all be impacted by code size.

People love to assign numbers in hopes of getting their arms around something nontangible. That is one of the reasons that software metrics have flourished. Suppose before testing begins, the question is raised as to how much time should be scheduled for unit testing. The first questions that should be addressed are: *How many units are there?* and *How large is the largest unit?* By starting with these questions—as well as some other facts concerning the types of unit testing desired and the goals of the unit testing—we can more comfortably make plausible predictions that shed light on the scheduling problem. The key word is *plausible,* because there is no guarantee that the eventual costs, even with sound answers to our size questions, will be similar to the predictions. However, if some given metrics tend to correlate with the process costs, then there is at least some empirical evidence that the metrics provide useful insights.

Many critics of software metrics point to the frequent result, from independent studies, that most software metrics essentially produce the same results as the lines-of-code metric, which naturally is the cheapest of all metrics to gather. An exception here is module cohesion, which does not correlate with code length at all. It is this seeming weakness in the actual value of the more complex metrics that has made many people skeptical about metrics altogether. Estimates of how difficult or expensive different phases of the software life cycle will be are the key applications of metrics. For example, simply knowing how hard your system will be to maintain in future years is often enough to determine whether to simply scrap an existing system in lieu of developing a successor from scratch. Metrics that assess the degree of coupling in the design of a system are sure candidates for aiding in such decisions.

1.2.4 *Static and Dynamic Analyses*

After you decide what characteristics of the code you wish to measure, you must decide how many resources you are willing to expend to collect the information. There are two options for collecting the information: *static* measurement and *dynamic* measurement. Static measurement does not rely on execution of the software. Dynamic analysis does. Executing software is not required in order to count the number of source lines of code in the file. Similarly, execution is not required for determining that some variable is used before it is defined—a compiler can tell you that. But estimating the reliability of a program that is expected to receive only odd integer inputs will likely require repeated, dynamic executions of the code with odd-integer inputs. In this particular case, suppose we know what the reliability of the software is on even inputs. What does that buy us? It's hard to say. Even if we know that 99.999 percent of the code executed for the even calculations is also used for the odd calculations, and we know that the code was completely reliable for many even calculations, these facts tell us very little about how reliably the code will perform on the odd calculations.

The key difference between static and dynamic analyses is that static analysis is a function of just the code, whereas dynamic analysis is a function of both the code and the inputs to the code. The following analogy serves to drive home the point: Would you purchase a new car based solely on looks, or would you insist on test-driving it first? Most people would prefer to give the car a few of their own inputs and see how it responds before making the purchase. After all, a new car might look great but have a highly defective engine. If your main interest lies in how software behaves, as opposed to how it looks, then it is vital that you take the time to specify what types of inputs you expect the software to experience. Without this information, quantifying and/or observing behavioral characteristics will be very difficult.

Another example of investigating behavior involves *profiling* a program to see where it spends most of its computing time. This almost always requires dynamic execution as well, with a rare exception being the ability to hand trace through the code in a manner consistent with what the program would do for specific input space partitions. Only if you know the likelihood with which inputs from specific partitions will be selected can you do a manual trace effectively. It's still very hard.

Possibly the greatest reason for employing static metrics instead of dynamic metrics is cost. Static measures are platform-independent, compiler-independent, and can often be calculated from very basic parsing technology. Dynamic metric tools are a completely different story. To get a flavor for some of the differences in computational costs for performing static and dynamic analysis, consider the different ingredients needed for each different approach. Static analysis requires only the source code. If you plan to analyze the source automatically, you will need what amounts to a fancy parser with the ability to collect information while the parser passes through the source. This will sometimes be a one-pass process, and other times it might involve multiple passes. All in all, parsing is not a particularly expensive procedure. (For now, we're ignoring the cost of building the parser.) It is true, however, that not all static analyses are automated. If you plan to analyze code manually using peer-reviewed software inspections, then there are no computational costs, only human costs. Incidentally, inspections are considered a static approach. Not surprisingly, the total costs associated with this sort of static, manual approach often outweigh the total costs of a dynamic, automated analysis, even with the computational costs considered.

The ingredients required for dynamic analysis differ from those needed for static analysis. This includes computational costs. Testing the code's reliability behavior is a good example of dynamic analysis. Doing so requires an oracle, an operational distribution, and thousands of successful, correct outputs in order to gain any confidence in the results. Dynamic analysis requires that the code be compiled and executed. Thus you need source code and a compiler. If you wish to analyze different internal phenomena occurring at specific places in the code, you need to put instrumentation in the code to collect the data. The instrumentation process can be accomplished automatically or manually, although doing this automatically requires a sophisticated tool. There are also other requirements: that test cases be created, that the instrumented source code be compiled, and that the executable code be run with the test cases. Depending on how extensive the instrumentation is, program execution may slow down by half or by as much as 500 times. Dynamic analysis has a clear scaleability problem that must be properly handled. If it takes a week to execute a program given a particular suite of test cases, and the instrumentation slows things down 100 times, then it will take two years to complete the results of the instrumented analysis!

One exception to this rule is software inspections. They are static analysis methods, yet remain quite expensive to perform. On the bright side, inspections are very good at defect detection, and thus are considered by many to be well worth their costs.

1.3 The Process and Product Debate

In software engineering, there are two different schools of thought concerning *what* should be measured. Some believe we should measure the quality of the processes used and thus provide a score for the maturity of the organization. Others firmly believe that the software is what should be measured. We have just discussed different forms of product measurement, and now wish to discuss more about the pros and cons in the process versus product debate.

1.3.1 Industry Process Standards

Most current best practices involve achieving or surpassing some numerical level with a given measure. Once we get a little deeper into the mechanics of software fault injection, we will discuss several different standards and measures related to safety-critical software and see how software fault injection can be applied toward complying with these measures. Commonly today, development organizations are forced to work under ridiculously tight schedules. As a result, many organizations are apathetic about using software development measures. Notable exceptions occur when clients contractually obligate adherence to particular standards and measures.

Standards for the development and validation of software can be broken into two classes: regulated standards and de facto standards. *Regulated* standards are rules sanctioned by some governing body. These rules are ratified by the members of a committee or working group appointed by an organization. For example, in the global nuclear-power community, there are a number of different international bodies charged with ensuring that software placed in a facility in country A is robust. That's because if it is not, then a problem at a facility in country A could very well drift over and contaminate a neighboring country. This is a primary example of how software is so critical that multiple countries must agree on its production, even though the software may be employed in only a single country. International bodies that oversee nuclear code include the International Atomic Energy Agency and the Nuclear Energy Agency.

Hundreds if not thousands of software standards are in existence today. The overabundance of standards has resulted in major confusion as to what standard or group of standards should be followed. The problem has become so critical that many developers disregard standards altogether, not only because of the confusion, but because of a general lack of proof that the standards provide a reasonable return on investment given the effort that must be undertaken to comply.

Even with all of today's standards, organizations such as the U.S. Food and Drug Agency (FDA) are still contemplating whether they will develop their own new standards or simply adopt portions of standards from other agencies (such as the FAA's DO 178B or several existing Defense Department standards). The FDA is also trying to figure out who might be subject to its standards should they be developed. Should it regulate the blood industry, pharmaceutical production facilities, medical devices, and so on? The unfortunate reality is that standards have proliferated to the point that they are coming to define an entire industry in and of themselves. It's quite possible to make a tidy living writing standards and attending standards meetings. Ironically, not one credential is required to undertake these activities. Then again, developing and/or validating software is a free-for-all activity, too. Such is the state of the standards community.

So what about the *de facto* standards? These are the standards in widespread use. They need be neither written down nor formally adopted by any regulatory body, but there is probably more evidence of their benefit than many of the regulated standards enjoy. You don't need to tell a developer to use a debugger or a memory leak detector. Such technologies have become the de facto standards of the industry. As new technologies prove their mettle across many diverse applications, you can expect them to be widely adopted as well.

1.3.2 Clean Pipes and Dirty Water

Can dirty water flow from clean pipes? Of course it can. Clean pipes can break, they can be attached to the wrong source, or the original water source may infuse dirty water into the pipeline. The complementary question is: *Can dirty pipes produce clean water?* Once again the answer is "yes," but that is less likely.

The analogy between water flowing from pipes and software flowing out from process standards is quite simple. Consider the original set of requirements to be the original water source and each successive process applied to the developing software to be the next link in the pipe. In this analogy, each link in the pipe is a process, and each process is geared toward either developing software or validating software. Certain processes may be reapplied during development, and the pipeline may contain distributed, redundant links. Eventually something exits from the pipeline. With a little luck, what exits will be quality software. The quality of the pipeline certainly impacts the quality of the code, but to what degree and at what cost varies. There is no guarantee that even the most superb software development processes will result in correct code.

"Software quality" has become a catchall buzzword for a huge family of methods geared toward either achieving better software or assessing how good software is. Each of these methods represents a different pipe link. There are various ways of integrating these links that make sense. Other combinations are nonsense. For example, putting a system-level testing link in front of the processes checking for ambiguous requirements is foolish.

Today's software quality methods can be generally divided into two camps: process-oriented or product-oriented. Process-oriented methods are focused more toward achieving quality than assessing it. Process-oriented standards include standards such as CMM, DO178-B, and ISO-9003, whereas product-oriented standards include software metrics and system-level testing. It is not uncommon for process-oriented standards to call for certain product-assessment methods to be performed, but these standards are more concerned with team infrastructure and interpersonnel communication than rigorous product measures. In terms of our analogy, product-oriented methods result in valves at different locations along the pipe where water quality is sampled, whether the protosoftware/water is defined in a design language, a specification format, or actual code. Any product-oriented methods that are specifically designed for software assessment will be clustered near the outflow of the pipeline, since in the earlier phases, code will not be available. Process-oriented methods attempt to ensure that the original requirements are clean, and that every transformation through the development cycle does not inject dirt. If the water is dirty at point A, then at a later point B, it will still be at least that dirty and possibly even dirtier, unless a filter is employed between A and B. Dirty water doesn't clean itself any more than incorrect software corrects itself.

Today's software process movement is a logical, evolutionary advancement that evolved from the unstructured, ad hoc software engineering methods used in the 1970s and early 1980s. The demand for systematic, repeatable methods with which to create more reliable software was only natural given the state of the practice at the time. The call was answered by dozens of different software development standards, even including manufacturing standards that were supposedly refurbished to account for software idiosyncrasies. Organizations such as the ECC have adopted such standards, not necessarily because the standards guarantee higher quality software imports, but rather as protectionist legislation to reduce software imports. The unfortunate effect of the process movement has been a point of view antithetical to the claim that clean pipes can produce dirty water. Software development processes are heavily based on manual effort and fallible software tools. Believing that clean pipes cannot produce dirty water amounts to accepting the position that flawed software tools and flawed human efforts will somehow offset each other and produce good software. Still, this myth lives on in the minds of both novice and expert software engineers, and behavioral software assessment continues to take a back seat to process improvement models.

Why is it that the software industry seems so preoccupied with quality processes instead of quality products? For a start, exhaustive testing of software is generally infeasible, testing software to high levels of reliability is intractable, and software-assurance models are often viewed with suspicion. Furthermore, the idea of doing things right from the outset has an intuitive flavor that is simply too alluring to challenge. Software practitioners face what appear to be insurmountable obstacles to accurately assessing software quality. Because of this, many professionals are either clinging to the outdated techniques of yesterday or have decided that software assessment is hopeless and have embraced process improvement as their best alternative.

It is not the case that to assess software quality, all that is needed is accurate reliability estimation. Because we can almost never know the true reliability of a piece of software, most software reliability models employ error history information to predict future failures. However different error-history–based reliability models often compute different reliability predictions for the same data, making it impossible to determine which model will be the most accurate for a specific system. This implies that the state of the practice in software reliability assessment is deficient.

Even direct measurement of software quality is less than practical. Consider that the testing effort required to establish a certain mean-time-to-failure (MTTF) with 90 percent confidence is at least twice that MTTF. Even ignoring all problems of test generation, test oracles, test-administration overhead, and the use of overspeed execution and parallel hardware for testing, it is difficult to see how more than about 10 tests/second for complex software could be performed. Current state of the practice is perhaps three orders of magnitude slower.

Many software assessment approaches focus on metrics. Over 100 software metrics are in widespread use today that measure mainly structural, static properties. However only a handful of approaches attempt to measure behavior dynamically. The key problem with structural metrics is that they do not capture the essence of software. Software defines a process by which an input is transformed into an output by a series of instructions. This transformation is the essential characteristic of the software. A program execution is a series of state transitions, where the final state contains the output. Exactly what effect a particular instruction has on the mapping between program inputs and program outputs is determined by the program's input distribution and the program's instructions. Structural metrics cannot capture this dynamic aspect of software behavior. This lack of connection with the behavior of the software makes structural metrics especially poor as software reliability assessors. Structural metrics are good, however, at quantifying such quality parameters as maintainability.

Software fault injection purposely "trips up" software in some manner during execution, and checks to see how that affects the software's output. Since fault injection operates on software, it is a pipe that lies near the exit of the pipeline, and in many cases will be the last pipe.

Software fault injection is not without limitations. The combination of problems that most information systems will experience during their lifetimes is intractable. Software fault injection simulates some of these events, and by doing so, it predicts how the software will behave in the future if these anomalous events were to occur. This affords a rough feeling for how software will behave when confronted with the remaining anomalies that were not simulated, since some of the behaviors will be similar. The entire process of fault injection involves lots of statistics and pseudorandom fault-injection methods. The actual process of instrumenting to inject anomalies is also quite complex. But the results can be most informative, particularly when you learn that your code doesn't handle problems quite as well as you thought it would. This information provides an immediate quality improvement opportunity.

Interestingly and somewhat ironically, while software fault-injection methods directly assess the behavior of code, they also indirectly assess the goodness of development pipes. By this, we mean that if software fault-injection methods find that software is intolerant either to internal faults or to anomalies that come from external sources (such as human factor errors, failed external hardware, or failed external software), then we learn that the software development processes failed to build in all necessary water-filtering mechanisms. Code must be designed with proper water-filtration systems to ensure that what comes out of a development pipe in the end is crystal-clear water. If software is incapable of producing the outputs we want under anomalous circumstances, then we cannot claim that the pipes produce only clean water. However, if over time we can demonstrate with the results of fault injection that the processes employed over and over again *do* result in clean water, this would provide real evidence correlating particular processes and software quality.

In summary, the quality of your pipes is only one part of the formula for determining the purity of your water. It is dangerous to believe otherwise. Sadly enough, people at the highest levels in governments and corporations have all swallowed the process approach, hook, line, and sinker. Process is fine, but in the end what matters is product.

Quality software does not fail often, and never fails in hazardous ways. Software development processes do not define software quality; software behavior does. Behavior is an intrinsic characteristic of software that can be viewed without regard to the software's developmental history. Before we can have faith in software standards and process models, it must be demonstrated that they have a quantifiable relationship to the behavior of the software produced with them. Parnas once said: "It seems clear to me that not only is a 'mature' process not sufficient, it may not even be necessary."

The current popularity of process-oriented assessment techniques is, in part, a reaction to the intractability of performing adequate software assessment. Unfortunately, the relationship between development processes and the attainment of some desired degree of product quality is not well established. This problem is particularly acute for formal methods: Performing the required processes does not give a quantifiable confidence that the software, when released, will have the required reliability. Testing measures the right thing—reliability—but it often cannot measure it to the desired precision. Process measurements are more tractable, but they measure the wrong thing.

1.3.3 Why Measure Product?

Software development always involves some manual effort. Manual effort introduces defects. Whereas ten years ago there was much hue and cry for defect-free software, today people accept defective software as a normal part of the game. This negative but probably accurate mindset has deeply rooted itself in the collective mind of the software industry and its clients. By and large, people are willing to accept buggy code as the norm, that is, as long as the buggy code is not going to alter their life catastrophically.

If the control software for a gas range does not ensure that the gas gets cut off when the pilot light goes out, then the endangered public is going to raise a stink. Most likely, something will occur similar to the outcry that ensued after Ford's decision not to recall its defective Pintos in the '70s—and rightly so. On the other hand, rebooting your personal computer once or twice a day is a nuisance, but it usually isn't a life-threatening proposition. Today's software systems are more complex than ever, but the time relegated to develop new systems is shorter than ever. The first thing to go when a development process starts to lag is testing. These facts almost guarantee that defective code will always be with us. Nevertheless, as software moves from performing peripheral tasks to performing critical tasks, our standard attitudes will be forced to adjust.

Software defects are only one source of problems impacting the behavioral quality of the code. Even correct software cannot always produce the outputs that we desire. Code can do undesirable things when given faulty data. In the real world, incorrect data being fed into software can result in unsafe situations.

The point of this anecdote is that most software systems today are dependent on information that comes in from outside. Such input may arrive in real time from an external source or perhaps be looked up in a database when required. Any corruption to this information can cause the output produced by the software to be undesirable, even if the output is "correct" in terms of the software's specification. Suppose, for example, that the correct output value is 2 for some input value 1. Further suppose for an input value of 2, the correct output value is 50. Now suppose that for some manufacturing process, an operator is to look at some gauge, read its value, and input that value to the software. The software output then feeds into some other processes in the plant. Consider the case where the software is correct, but the operator incorrectly inputs a 1 instead of a 2. The software will correctly produce the output, 2, but given the true state of the plant, this is not the correct value. Such a mistake may turn out to be equally disastrous to a case where the software mistakenly computed the wrong value. The moral of this story is that *any* external source of information on which the code operates must be viewed as a potential source of problems. All such external inputs have clear effects on the behavior of the software.

There is yet another important source of software-system problems that we address in chapter 8—malicious inputs. *Malicious inputs* are data deliberately input to software to try to cause it to fail in some manner consistent with the wishes of the attacker. Malicious inputs can be as hard to predict as any other act of terrorism. But software fault-injection methods are well suited to predicting how vulnerable software is to potential malicious input. Software usually makes no clear distinction between legal input, corrupt input, and malicious input. It uses all sorts of inputs equally. It should now be apparent that it is not enough to show simply that software exhibits correct behavior. Instead, it is necessary to show that software exhibits desired behavior, regardless of what input it gets.

1.4 Fault Injection and Software Assessment

Our need to be able to assess the quality of software under a variety of circumstances cannot be overstated. As you will see, fault injection is able to do this for a much broader variety of circumstances than any other V&V technique used today.

1.4.1 *Traditional Process Improvement*

Software fault injection is a strangely bipolar class of software validation processes. On one hand, fault injection is unlike traditional testing in many ways. On the other hand, fault injection has some similarities to statistical testing. In the end, software testing focuses on assessing correctness. Software fault injection focuses on determining how well or how badly a piece of software will behave under a variety of anomalous circumstances.

Traditional process improvement is not focused on software goodness or badness, but instead is focused on manufacturing process goodness or badness. The fallacious reasoning is very simple: Using good processes will produce good code every time. Instead of determining how good a piece of code is, process pundits go one step backward, and assess how good development processes are.

We are skeptical that processes, which are for the most part a hodgepodge of manual and automated procedures, are rigorous enough to automatically and reliably result in good code. Even the most rigorous processes, such as formal methods, can be improperly applied. Our point can be summed up in a simple statement: Just as clean water can come from dirty pipes, dirty water can come from clean pipes. The literature documents cases in which Level 1 SEI-CMM organizations develop code that is as good as code from Level 3 organizations. What does this say about the accuracy of the CMM? The purity of the final product should never be based solely on the quality of the pipes.

We are not against good software engineering processes, per se. In fact, we are staunch advocates. But we don't buy into the process-improvement hypothesis as an absolute truth. Instead, we believe that good processes and good product-assessment measures should be applied in concert to provide a proper mix of development and assessment technologies. It is not one or the other, but both, that must be applied.

In an ironic twist, product-assessment measures can validate the goodness of the development processes. For example, suppose that a set of development processes were applied to projects A, B, and C. Further suppose that a sound measure of quality was applied to these finished projects which demonstrated that the products were all of high quality. What is gained here is anecdotal evidence that the processes used for A, B, and C enabled quality products. If over time enough successful demonstrations like this are observed, then evidence will mount that cannot be easily refuted. If the reverse is true, however, and the products of good processes turn out to be very poor in quality, then the myopic focus on processes needs to be reevaluated.

Because software fault injection is itself a process—usually applied at the tail end of the development phase—it too can be improperly used. If improperly applied, fault injection can be useless or even harmful. Misinterpreted results can lead to false confidence. Of course this is true of other processes, the testing process in particular. If someone tests a program 100 times and claims the code is correct based on those few tests, while there are actually millions of other test cases never attempted, then clearly a misrepresentation of the results has happened. Ensuring that claims like those don't occur is virtually impossible. Education and training are the best preventatives that can be applied. However, if someone wishes to deliberately misinform a client or supervisor about what some results mean, stopping this is clearly not easy.

In 1996, Hughes Aircraft Company was involved in just such a case. Hughes agreed to pay $4.5 million to settle a civil lawsuit in which they were accused of falsifying quality-control tests on electronic parts used in various high-tech Pentagon weapons. The illegal activity allegedly happened during the late 1980s. The civil suit alleged that Hughes managers instructed employees to skip or alter certain tests and to submit bogus paperwork to disguise their activities.

1.4.2 Predicting Future Quality

Let's review what we have covered so far. We brought up several problems with static metrics. We discussed how hard it is to discover the key parameters needed to measure software quality. We explained why for most programs, testing to demonstrate correctness is not plausible; even if it were, that is not always the measure of quality we are most concerned with. We invoked the pipes-and-water analogy in order to emphasize the fact that perfect processes may well result in imperfect code.

What we want is a way to know how badly our code might behave tomorrow, given the code that we have in our hands today. Plumbing the depths of this fundamental unknown plagues the software industry with cost overruns and delayed product releases. Although not widely reported, the fear of what might happen tomorrow is a tremendous cost to the software industry. Most of the cost is likely due to overtesting that often occurs for safety-critical systems—excess testing that has little likelihood of detecting serious problems, but allows lawyers and developers to sleep more easily.

Even systems that are not safety-critical can receive unnecessary testing. Consider what you might do if you knew that the code you were about to give a customer had serious bugs in some particular feature, but you knew with certainty that the customer would never access that feature. Would you delay releasing the product to your customer in order to fix the bugs? Probably not, because in the case of your customer, the defects resides in what is effectively dead code. Few organizations that wish to succeed in business can afford to invest time and money in debugging code that they know will never be used.

Overtesting code to provide confidence that the code will not disappoint us in the future is not a good idea. Oftentimes, added test cases simply exercise the same regions of the code exercised by original test cases. Even if additional test cases did exercise more regions of the code, the problems that may arise in the future may not even be related to the code. Problems may occur because of the way that the code interacts with its environment. Thus testing won't help.

Will today's quality measures predict higher quality than will actually be found by users in the field? Have we only fixed and patched the code to the point that it works for our regression tests (coding to the tests)? If our input conditions step outside of the testing parameters, do we have enough information about how well the code will behave? And what about the environment that the software will reside in? Did we do a good enough job building operational profiles? Did we select enough test cases to have any confidence in our reliability estimates? Have we built in enough robustness and tolerance to handle problems that could attack our software from the outside world?

All of these questions are superseded by a larger question: *How will a piece of software behave in the future?* We can attempt to guess the parameters that will directly influence the software in the future, but will we get all of them? Can we get any of them right? Without some way of gauging what tomorrow holds, it is difficult to know how to develop and test a product today. All this implies that software engineering methods that help to predict software's future behavior in a large number of different circumstances are the key.

1.4.3 Fault Injection in the Physical World

The underlying theory behind software fault injection can be traced to other scientific and manufacturing disciplines, including automobile manufacturing and medicine. Automobile manufacturers crash-test hundreds of cars each year to test the susceptibility of their cars to various impacts: side-on crashes, head-on collisions, fender-benders, and so on. Of course, all car manufacturers model and simulate what is likely to happen using sophisticated computers. But real, physical crashes in the laboratory are needed to validate the predicted outcomes of the model. That's because a simulation might say that the bumper will not fall off if an impact is under 5 miles per hour, but until real impacts of 5 miles per hour and under are tried, under reasonable scenarios involving crash-test dummies, manufacturers cannot confidently know how resistant to impact their bumpers actually are. Thus testing serves two purposes: It provides confidence in the automobiles, and it provides confidence in the validity of the models and simulations. The latter is something that may prove useful in assessing future automobile designs.

Medicine is another field where the concepts of fault injection are readily employed. Scientists cannot confidently know the effect of various experimental drugs on humans without some experimentation on other mammals possessing similar internal and biological subsystems. They can hypothesize and analytically argue how they *believe* an experimental drug will affect an organism, for example by considering how similar chemical compounds affect that organism, but until a real live sample group receives the chemical and is monitored, key results and detrimental side effects cannot be accurately predicted. After new drugs are successfully field-tested on laboratory animals, it is then necessary to organize a statistically valid group of human subjects. One portion of this group receives the new drug, another portion receives a placebo, and occasionally other portions receive whatever the best current alternative therapies may be. Some participants must necessarily receive an ineffective placebo or existing therapies in order to have a baseline for comparison with the results of the new therapy. This provides a fair basis for determining exactly what a new drug does to human patients.

Automobile manufacture and medicine, though representative of fault injection in the physical world, are not the only kind of case. There are fields where our knowledge of the quality of a newly composed system is substantial enough that once the system is built, fault injection would not be appropriate. Mechanical engineers and architects have hundreds of years of experience building skyscrapers. It is unnecessary as well as impossible to build a real skyscraper and simulate an earthquake under it to determine its tolerance to earthquakes. The literally thousands of tall buildings that have been built throughout history, more than a handful of which have crumbled in natural disasters, have taught us how to predict a priori and with high confidence how fragile certain building designs are. Insurance companies rely on such information when underwriting policies. Engineers are so good at predicting how robust structures are that when things like the Kansas City Hyatt Regency Hotel walkway collapse [Hauck 1983] or the Los Angeles freeway collapse in 1994, which resulted from a 6.7 magnitude earthquake that hit Northridge, California, people are taken by surprise. Both such events were not supposed to happen since the two structures were expressly designed to handle the stresses under which they failed.

Another example where a design quality can be measured before the design is implemented is bridge engineering. Mechanical engineers know the tolerances and load capacities of bridges before they are ever built. How many people would show up for the testing of a new bridge if the Department of Transportation simply put out an announcement that said: "Please come help us test the new bridge. Load up your car with as many people as you can fit. Drive forward until your bumper is as close as possible to the car in front of you and put your car in park. Once parked, get out of your car and jump up and down vigorously. If the bridge survives after five minutes of jumping, return to your car and drive off when the car in front of yours starts moving." You might get a crowd for such event, but it would be mostly onlookers and possibly some suicidal participants. It is only because engineers understand physics and mechanical engineering so well that we can avoid such testing.

1.4.4 Fault Injection in the Virtual World

All this talk of the physical world is interesting since it shows how fault injection can be used in the real world and how it sometimes is not required. However, we're interested in software—a logical system. For logical systems that are free from physical laws, engineering principles are considerably less well understood. Logical laws govern computations. The good thing is that logical premises like negation and inference are easy to understand on a small scale and are thus amenable to proof of correctness. Although simple on a small scale, logical arguments built of simple premises and axioms become very complex very quickly as more and more propositions pile on one another. On a grand scale often required to solve real problems, this complexity defies our ability to confidently reason about logical systems. Because modern software systems are incredibly complicated and involve dynamic behavior, changing as time progresses, they have become more like complex organisms than like simple logical systems. Some researchers have taken notice of this analogy and have gone as far as to create an entire scientific discipline called Artificial Life [Langton 1995]. Such properties are interesting if you are studying living things, but living things are notoriously hard to predict. Without prediction we can't have true assurance.

As we've shown, fault injection is a well-understood tool in common use by many physical disciplines. The underlying concepts of software fault injection are not all that unusual or foreign. On the contrary, they are based on typical assurance processes employed in many successful engineering disciplines. Software practitioners want a tool that can aid in understanding how software behaves when it is stressed in unusual ways. As will become apparent, the key to gleaning useful results from software fault injection is to employ useful *unusual events.*

The main reason to employ fault injection is to assess the goodness of a design. For software, this boils down to assessing the goodness of the logic. If fault injection were unable to say something useful about quality, there would be no reason to employ it. Most traditional quantitative/behavioral methods of software quality assess the frequency of error-free output. Of these methods, testing is most commonly chosen, but testing can accurately assess probabilities of error-free output only in the .999 to .99999 range, which translates into probabilities of failure in the 10^{-3} to 10^{-5} range.

There are two different classes of software metrics: absolute and relative. Both classes are quantitative. On one hand, *absolute* metrics are numerical scores that present an estimate of a true characteristic of the code. A prime example of an absolute metric is the probability-of-failure metric. Another example of an absolute metric is the number of references to a particular variable in a program. A third is the number of lines of code in a program. Absolute metrics such as the number of lines of code involve no uncertainty. There is one and only one correct answer. However, most absolute metrics are based on parameters that contain some degree of uncertainty or variability. In such cases, absolutely determining what assumptions to make is a tricky issue.

On the other hand, a *relative* metric is a quantification of some code characteristic that cannot be directly measured. (These are sometimes referred to as *indirect measures*.) For example, measuring the difficulty of testing a program would result in a relative metric. There is no absolute and objective way to measure testing difficulty. Any answer will depend on multiple parameters, such as how thorough the testing is required to be. Many other software characteristics, including ease of maintainability, cannot be simply measured. According to our definition, these characteristics are always measured in a relative way. Putting any number to any of these characteristics often involves a fair amount of subjectivity. Most important, for the purposes of this book, software fault injection results in relative metrics.

One caveat about relative metrics: It becomes easier to fudge results when they are relative. Make sure you understand what a relative metric means as clearly as possible. Don't be duped by possibly useless but attractive-looking numbers. The fact is that metrics were oversold by early proponents. Some of the initial overblown claims didn't pan out, and this has left much of the software community skeptical. Nevertheless, relative metrics can provide useful information—if they are used wisely. Absolute metrics are not subject to many of the unfortunate characteristics of relative metrics; however, it is often impossible to determine a useful absolute metric. That leaves us with wise use of relative metrics as a logical result.

In general, people seem to be uneasy about placing quality numbers on software. People often say such interesting things as, "I love to see quality numbers, but I never believe them." Much of this distrust has its roots in the inherent unpredictability of digital systems. When analog systems are tested at the boundaries and work correctly, it is highly likely that they will work correctly for points in between. But for digital systems, this doesn't hold. Software might work correctly for all values except for one. So testing on the boundaries, even if you include many points in between, can fail to ferret out a failure point.

Fortunately, software fault injection is a process that transcends this debate over the validity of quality metrics. If you want to attach a number to the observed frequency that some event was seen to happen after fault injection is employed, you can do that. If, instead, you have no interest in particular frequencies, you can simply look at system output as a Boolean event; that is, if the event of interest ever occurs, then output TRUE, but if the event never occurs, output FALSE. Since the frequency with which an output event occurs after fault injection is not an absolute metric, any measure of frequency serves only as a "severity" indicator. That means, for instance, if some undesirable output event A occurs a mere 1 percent of the time, this is clearly less worrisome than if A occurs 99 percent of the time. Of course when human life is at stake, the mere fact that A happens at all may be the most important and revealing factor.

Ultimately, software quality is dependent on a huge number of unknown variables. Programmers are people, too, regardless of standard opinion to the contrary. That means there is some possibility that a programmer may be having a bad month due to marital problems. Or perhaps the development team charged with creating a critical module is mostly made up of new and inexperienced hires. All of these limitless intangibles can directly affect software quality. By its very nature, fault injection transcends these unknowns and is able to simulate problems that could occur during execution regardless of whether a development team is inexperienced or a developer is having personal problems.

Software fault injection can be used to simulate both programmer faults and the failures of systems external to the software, but connected to the software through interfaces. Much work in this area has occurred since the late 1980s [Segal 1988; Arlat 1990; Dilenno 1991; Arlat 1992; Avresky 1992; Echtle 1992; Voas 1992; Kao 1993; Rosenberg 1993; Solheim 1993; Clark 1995]. Metrics resulting from these approaches can be divided into two categories: (1) frequencies stating how often some particular output event came about due to an injected fault, or (2) simple Boolean results describing whether a particular output event ever happened.

The key applications of software fault injection described in this book include: sensitivity analysis (for testing purposes), mutation testing (for test case generation), safety/failure tolerance, and security/vulnerability analysis. Table 1.1 shows which classes of problems are simulated in each of these application areas.

It is critical to emphasize again that fault injection is not concerned with *why* a certain anomalous event may have occurred with respect to some executing code; all fault injection is concerned with what happens *after* an event simulated by fault injection occurs. If an injected event causes bad things to happen, we want to know about it. By taking this stance, we can avoid the trap of spending all of our time worrying about how realistic certain anomalies may be, and simply observe how those anomalies impact the software. In the end, it is software behavior that we're interested in.

Table 1.1 Failure Classes and Applications

	PROGRAMMER FAULTS	EXTERNAL CORRUPTIONS
Sensitivity	X	X
Mutation testing	X	
Safety failure tolerance		X
Vulnerability/security	X	X

1.4.5 Software Inoculation

Biological inoculation against disease has saved countless lives during this century. The ability to inject weakened strains of viruses and other harmful biological agents into an organism so the organism's immune system learns to recognize the attacker in the future is one of the most important breakthroughs in medical history.

Like biological inoculation, software fault injection forces strains of anomalous corruptions into software. In software fault injection, the goal is to see what happens when executing software finds itself in anomalous states. This information can be used in a variety of ways to make the code less likely to hide faults and less likely to propagate erroneous data states to undesirable output states. Thus it is fair to think of software fault injection as a means for inoculating code against the effects of anomalies. Software fault injection provides a way to isolate which types of anomalies software must be capable of defeating, and provides the opportunity to ensure that software behaves itself.

References

[Arlat 1990] J. Arlat, M. Aguera, L. Amat, Y. Crouzet, J.-C. Fabre, J.-C. Laprie, E. Martins, and D. Powell. "Fault Injection for Dependability Validation: A Methodology and Some Applications." *IEEE Trans. on Software Engineering,* 16(2):166–182, February 1990.

[Arlat 1992] J. Arlat. "Fault Injection for the experimental validation of fault tolerant systems." In *Proc. Workshop Fault-Tolerant Systems,* pp. 33–40, 1992.

[Avresky 1992] D. Avresky, J. Arlat, J.-C. Laprie, and Y. Crouzet. "Fault Injection for the formal testing of fault tolerance." In *Proc. 22nd International Symposium on Fault-Tolerant Computing,* pp. 345–354, 1992.

[Clark 1995] J. A. Clark and D. K. Pradhan. "Fault Injection: A Method for Validating Computer-System Dependability." *IEEE Computer,* pp. 47–56, June 1995.

[Dilenno 1991] T. Dilenno, D. Yaskin, and J. Barton. "Fault tolerance testing in the advanced automation system." In *Proc. 21st Int'l. Symp. on Fault-Tolerant Computing,* pp. 18–25, 1991.

[Echtle 1992] K. Echtle and M. Leu. "The EFA fault injector for fault tolerant distributed system testing." In *Proc. Workshop on Fault-Tolerant Parallel and Distributed Systems,* pp. 28–35, 1992.

[Hauck 1983] G. F. W. Hauck. "Hyatt-Regency walkway collapse: design alternates." *Journal of Structural Engineering,* 109(5):1226–1234, May 1983.

[Kao 1993] Wei-Lun Kao, R. Iyer, and D. Tang. "FINE—a fault injection and monitoring environment for tracing the UNIX system behavior under faults." *IEEE Transactions on Software Engineering,* 19(11), November 1993.

[Langton 1995] C. Langton. *Artificial Life.* Addison-Wesley, Redwood City, CA. 1995.

[Rosenberg 1993] H. Rosenberg and K. Shin. "Software fault injection and its application in distributed systems." In *Proc. 23th Int'l. Symp. On Fault-Tolerant Computing,* pp. 208–217, 1993.

[Segal 1988] Z. Segal et al. "FIAT—fault injection based automated testing environment." In *Proc. 18th Int'l. Symp. on Fault-Tolerant Computing,* pp. 102–107, 1988.

[Solheim 1993] J. A. Solheim and J. H. Rowland. "An Empirical Study of Testing and Integration Strategies Using Artificial Software Systems." *IEEE Trans. on Software Engineering,* 19(10):941–949, October 1993.

[Voas 1992] J. M. Voas. "PIE: A Dynamic Failure-based Technique." *IEEE Transactions on Software Engineering,* 18(8):717–727, August 1992.

2 Setting the Stage
History and Basic Definitions

2.1 History

Much work has gone into studying fault injection during the last ten years. You might be surprised to learn, however, that fault injection has been around much longer than that.

2.1.1 Early Pioneers

The earliest work in software fault injection can be traced to Harlan Mill's *fault seeding* approach which surfaced as early as 1972 [Mills 1972]. The original idea was to estimate reliability based on an estimate of the number of remaining faults in a program. This estimate could be derived from counting the number of "seeded" faults that were uncovered during testing in addition to counting the number of "real" faults that were found during testing.

In the model, N_1 faults are planted in a program already containing N faults, where N, of course, is unknown. The probability that exactly k of r faults that are caught during testing are of the seeded variety is given by:

$$q_k(N) = \frac{\binom{N_1}{r}\binom{N-N_1}{r-k}}{\binom{N}{r}}$$

The maximum likelihood estimate of N is thus given by:

$$N = \frac{N_1(r-k)}{k}$$

This equation gives us an estimate of the number of faults that currently exist in the program, under the assumption that existing faults in the program were not fixed during testing.

The next major milestone in fault–injection history was software mutation. This work is discussed more fully later in both chapters 4 and 5. *Software mutation* is the form of fault injection that actually modifies the syntax of the code. There are several different applications for the ideas of code mutation, including: test case generation, studies concerning test case effectiveness, and the possibility that mutation may someday be used as a way to build information systems that are strong enough to survive attacks from malicious users.

The underlying ideas behind fault injection are not new. There is much in the way of literature describing how to employ fault injection for hardware system validation, software testing, and hardware design validation [DeMillo 1978; Arlat 1990; Solheim 1993; Clark 1995]. Unfortunately, migration of these proof-of-concept ideas into practical methods for software validation has yet to happen. Concern over the plausibility of injected anomalies has held things up. It is much easier to be realistic when modeling something well understood. Unfortunately, this is not the case in software. In an integrated circuit, the failure classes are obvious: stuck-at-one, stuck-at-zero, and so on; but for a software system, the choices are not as simple, and in fact the number of different choices can be intractably large.

2.1.2 Fault Injection in Hardware Design Languages

The underlying ideas behind software fault injection have been applied to hardware prototypes, in particular integrated circuits, for many years. Given that electrical devices such as stereo amplifiers are made of many tiny transistors and capacitors, engineers are interested to see what impact the failure of a particular component has on the entire system. Like any reasonably complex system, stereos can be implemented in a large number of ways. Fault injection serves to elucidate possible design flaws and measure the robustness of a design. One example of fault injection as applied to building stereos is pulling a component out of the design. Another is deliberately replacing a working component with another of different design.

Integrated-circuit–based fault injection is far more common than software-based fault injection. Hardware-based fault injection employs such techniques as bombarding a system with ion radiation, mutating logic levels on external chip pins, and injecting voltage sags on power rails. The problem is that this analysis is performed only after the hardware systems are assembled. Obviously, if a logic error is discovered during analysis, the redesign and refabrication costs can be staggering. The easy lesson is that fault injection should be employed as early as possible, if it is to be cost-effective.

Not the types to miss such an important lesson, hardware engineers are more readily applying fault-injection techniques to logical designs *before* the systems are prototyped. It is much more cost-effective to apply fault injection to a hardware design description than to an expensive physical prototype. Hardware description languages (HDLs) were created to make hardware design more effective. In HDLs, signals communicate data between logical components and processes. Interestingly enough, HDLs are often very similar to programming languages. Furthermore, HDLs can be executed in software simulations in order to test hardware design behavior. In the end, the HDL that gets tested with fault injection *is* software! The upshot is, not only does the success of HDL fault injection have a valuable lesson to teach about software, but lessons from software fault injection are clearly applicable to HDLs. Many of the ideas we discuss in this book have been or could easily be successfully applied to HDLs.

In HDL fault injection, signals can be corrupted by using a *fault mask* and a *fault operation*. A fault mask represents those bits on which to apply the fault operation. If a fault mask covers bits 1, 3, and 5, and the fault operation is XOR, then a fault is injected simply by flipping the first, third, and fifth bits of the signal. For the most part, hardware fault simulation is based on the classical stuck-at fault. This assumes that when a component fails, from that point forward it always produces a "1" or "0" no matter what input it may get. In other words, under the stuck-at assumption, the model assumes that the functionality of a failed component does not change. Incorrect outputs propagate from stuck-at faults only when the output of a stuck-at component is the opposite of what it should be for some input.

Code mutation in an HDL design is an alternative form of fault injection. Code mutation requires that the logical component itself be modified, for example, making a NAND-gate into an AND-gate or vice versa. Just as is the case in software mutation, the number of possible replacements is very large. (Note that this number is very large for software systems, most of which are built using languages orders of magnitude much more complex than HDLs.) As the number of possibilities grows, so too does cost. As a result, HDL code mutation is generally not used. It is simply too expensive.

Signal corruption in HDLs is generally more powerful than code mutation anyway. Code mutation's effects can be effectively modeled by a single signal corruption; and a single signal corruption can be traced back to multiple mutants. (This is also true in the case of software.) If it can be shown that for some signal corruption the output is still desirable, then that amounts to showing a system is tolerant of a class of logical mutants.

Integrated circuit (IC) testability is a particularly interesting measure that employs fault injection. IC developers analyze the controllability and observability of the circuit. The idea behind IC observability is straightforward: the ability of a system to propagate problems to the outside, observable interface. *Controllability* is the ability to fix all points in a circuit to particular values, and then modify one or more of the fixed points to see what impact those modifications have on circuit output. The ability to observe can in this way be directly related to the ability to control. If it is very difficult to fix the points and toggle the interesting ones, then it will be difficult to assess the observability of a particular design.

Fault injection provides IC developers a way of assessing what types of faults the logic is likely to mask. By studying the potential for error masking, integrated circuit developers can better determine where to inject probes to analyze internal signals during testing. Consider the circuit shown in Figure 2.1 as an example. This circuit has five input signals, and one output signal. We can observe the effect on the output signal, H, of various fault classes injected throughout the circuit. For example, we could fix A, B, D, and E, and toggle C, to see what impact this has on H. If it is difficult to control A, B, D, and E, then the controllability is reduced, and hence testability is also reduced. Likewise, we could control C, D, and E, and toggle F, to see what a stuck-at fault at the A-AND-B–gate might cause. Or we could simulate a stuck-at fault at H, and see what impact that has later in the system. In summary, the ideas of inserting anomalies into an integrated circuit or IC design are central to the discipline of integrated circuit testing. Fault-injection testing of hardware is par for the course and is expected best practice.

Bear in mind that integrated circuit testing is still a very difficult and costly process, even using the fundamental fault injection concepts of controllability and observability. As the famous INTEL Pentium bug shows, testing is essential to ensure reliable hardware, but it is not always easy. Interestingly, the Pentium bug was not caught even with over 1 billion test cases. To confirm their predic-

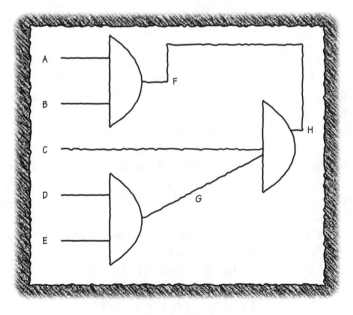

Figure 2.1 *Integrated circuit example.*

tions of the Pentium's failure rate, INTEL performed both mathematical modeling and experimentation. To validate their failure rate models, INTEL reported that it would have had to perform over 1 trillion test cases, something they did not do. The infamous INTEL Pentium bug reportedly cost the company a corporate write-off loss of $475 million against earnings. This was the projected cost to replace the approximately 4–5 million defective chips at no charge.

The lesson here is that testing, even testing a billion times, can be inadequate for particular forms of subtle logical errors. Logical faults, unlike physical faults that can be transient or intermittent, are permanent and deterministic, and for every test case that excites them, infects the software's state, and propagates that to the output, the software will fail. The question then becomes an issue of trying to force software testing to make this chain of events happen for each logical fault in the program during the test phase. As you will see later when we talk about software testability, one primary application of fault-injection technology—the role of testability assessment—is to find out whether software is likely to be hiding bugs like the one that caused the Pentium problem. If we can fine-tune software fault injection to localize those places where subtle bugs like the Pentium bug are likely to hide, then we can customize our validation and verification processes so as not to be fooled into missing subtle defects.

2.1.3 Low-Level Software Fault Injection

Historically, the first instantiations of fault injection for software show their roots in hardware fault injection. That is because the early models focus on low-level software as opposed to applications. They tend to do things such as tweak CPU register values and particular locations in memory. Though the focus of this book is fault injection for high-level software applications, it is still important to note related work on low-level software.

Many of the faults injected in low-level software are meant to simulate hardware problems. Commonly used mechanisms include time-out and exception/trap perturbations. In *time-out* perturbations, a timer expires after some preset time and triggers faults. This is accomplished by causing an interrupt signal, and requires a link directly into the system's interrupt handler vector. The time-out sort of fault simulation is good at simulating transient faults and intermittent hardware faults. *Exception/trap* perturbations work by injecting faults when a hardware or software exception is thrown. This kind of perturbation is less arbitrary than the time-out variety, because exceptions can be linked to particular system states. Once again, most exception/trap models used in low-level software analysis are directly tied to the system's interrupt handler vector.

By contrast to these low-level analysis techniques, the kind of software fault injection we are most interested in inserts new code into the application under analysis. This gives an experimenter fine-grained control over where and in what conditions faults are injected. The analysis is performed at run-time after the new code is compiled into the application being analyzed. So instead of perturbing a value in a register, code-insertion approaches can change particular variable values.

Examples of low-level fault injection tools include Ferrari (Fault and Error Automatic Real-Time Injection) [Kanawatti 1992], Ftape (Fault Tolerance and Performance Evaluator) [Tsai 1996], and Doctor (Integrated Software Fault Injection Environment) [Han 1995]. All of these systems are experimental systems developed in an academic setting. *Ferrari* uses the exception/trap method to corrupt registers and memory locations. It emulates data corruption. *Ftape* injects faults into CPU module registers, memory locations, and the disk subsystem. *Doctor* allows injection of CPU faults, memory faults, and network communication faults. It uses all three of the techniques previously outlined and can be applied to application-level software. A more detailed overview of these systems can be found in [Hsueh 1997].

2.2 Basic Definitions and Relations

2.2.1 *Fault Injection as Nontraditional Testing*

If you stand far enough away and squint, software fault injection can be viewed as a kind of testing; albeit not testing in the traditional sense. Traditional testing seeks to ascertain whether some implementation meets its stated requirements. To do this requires a definition of what the correct outputs should be. Without such information, it is not possible to determine whether software is defective.

Fault injection is generally incapable of determining correctness. That is because anomalies are injected into the code, and, in the end, the program is run in an altered state. That means it is impossible to assert that the code *itself* produced incorrect output; however, it would be appropriate to assert that the *modified* code produced incorrect output. What fault injection is capable of demonstrating is what sort of outputs the software produces under anomalous circumstances. Often fault injection will simulate scenarios that are so bizarre that no person ever would have thought of worrying about what the software does in those cases. It follows that since no person ever will have thought of such anomalies, requirements may not exist stating what expected output events should occur. It is still both interesting and important to see what happens.

Good software engineering practices, as well as good practices in other disciplines such as safety engineering, attempt to predefine what should occur for as many anomalies as can be thought up and fleshed out. Given a set of these anomalous conditions, testing can be used to ensure that the software or other system handles the problems appropriately. This allows testers to see what the software does with the standard problems the developers foresee. Fault injection, on the other hand, often tests the software to see what it does under unreasonable—sometimes even stupid—conditions. If the results of testing in such conditions also turn out to be stupid, nothing is lost other than the effort involved. But what if the results from asking stupid questions are not stupid but instead result in serious answers and shed light on program behavior? In that case, fault injection has demonstrated that the software is highly sensitive to the problems that it was forced to deal with, and the software has failed to sufficiently handle the problems.

The form of traditional testing most closely related to fault injection is probably stress testing. *Stress testing* is the process of seeing how performance degrades as system workload requests increase. It would not be improper, then, to think of fault injection as *torture testing,* with the torture being the anomalous conditions that are thrown at the software as it executes.

Fault injection can be used to probe many key characteristics of software. In this book, we focus on six.

1. Safety
2. Failure tolerance
3. Vulnerability
4. Timing faults
5. Maintainability
6. Reusability

All of these characteristics can be measured using customized fault-injection techniques. As you will see, software fault injection can augment and enhance almost any activity in the software life cycle that occurs once the code exists. Because information discovered through fault injection has proven exceptionally beneficial, current research investigates how much earlier in the life cycle the technique can be pushed. For example, if we have state-based models for a system, can we apply fault injection to them? From a theoretical standpoint, the answer is "yes," but from the standpoint of building an automated tool, the question remains open.

We have one result from which we can reasonably extrapolate. Electrical engineering has been successful at employing fault injection in hardware designs for years. Hardware designs are essentially detailed models of the circuitry. It is our goal someday to be able to apply fault injection techniques to software design models in the same fashion as is done for hardware. This will allow software practitioners to assess design robustness earlier than ever before.

2.2.2 Absolute Correctness Is a Red Herring

The first thirty years of software engineering was driven by the desire to develop correct software. Correct software may be a laudable goal, but it is also generally unattainable. In any case, just what correctness means is not as set in stone as it may seem at first blush. The main point is simply this: Though software can be shown to be correct, its "correctness" is always determined relative to something (like a set of test cases), and that something may well be flawed. If the something is flawed, but the code implements it properly, the code is still technically correct. But what good is it if correct code is developed on flawed assumptions? Consider another angle on this issue: cases in which incorrect software meets the needs of users. Is it worth the effort to make such software correct? Together, these two questions boil down to the same issue: Is correct code what we *really* want?

The software engineering life cycle, whether you prefer to think of it as a spiral model or a waterfall model, is simply a series of semantics-preserving transformations of decreasing abstraction and increasing information density. Starting with the most information-rich part of the life cycle—the code itself—we can work backward to the requirements. The code will undoubtedly be richer in information than the design or the specification. The design will be richer in information than the specification, and the specification will contain more information than the requirements. Starting at the requirements and working your way back up, if any information is lost in successive phases, then some requirement will probably have been lost along the way. This almost certainly implies that the likelihood of ending up with correct code will have been compromised. The goal is to minimize the introduction of incorrect information at transformation points between phases.

Ensuring that all transformations between phases are handled properly does not fully address the undesirable output problem. As we argued earlier, even correct output can sometimes be undesirable. It is often the case that spending valuable resources to build correct code serves as a decoy to what you really want: acceptable outputs, even when unacceptable circumstances arise. Given the complexity of today's software, and given that correct software is not always what we want anyway, it is our contention that less emphasis should be placed on correctness, and more emphasis should be placed on building robust systems that can adapt to aberrant behavior.

These issues are made murkier by the somewhat unclear relationships between different measures of software quality. For example, failure tolerance means that acceptable output will be produced, but being failure tolerant does not imply correctness. Turned around, neither does correctness imply failure tolerance. Nor does correctness imply safety. Once again the reverse is true: Safety does not imply correctness. Apparently, correct software can be unsafe and intolerant to failures! Is that good?

An example may serve to clarify this point. Suppose that when some system is in state *X,* the software is supposed to receive an input *I,* and when it receives *I,* the software produces result *K.* Further, suppose that *K* is the correct, safe result. And suppose that when the system is in state *Z* and the software receives input *J,* the software produces a correct, safe result of *M.* But suppose that when the software is in state *X,* somehow an input of *J* is presented to the software. *M* is the correct, safe output for *J,* but *M* is not necessarily safe in system state *X.* The question is whether it is fair to blame the software for producing an output that is unsafe given the current system state. Traditional software engineers would not blame the software for this glitch, and would walk away from the problem saying that the software did its job correctly. Safety engineers might not be so generous, and would argue that the software has created an unsafe output, and should thus be blamed. Regardless of viewpoint, an undesirable output has occurred for the system, even though the software did produce a correct output. Correct software does not guarantee Utopian behavior.

2.2.3 Defining Some Terms

Software verification is the "process of evaluating a system or component to determine whether the products of a given development phase satisfy the conditions imposed at the start of that phase" [IEEE 1983]. *Software validation* is the "process of evaluating a system or component during or at the end of the development process to determine whether it satisfies specified requirements" [IEEE 1983]. Software fault injection is more of a software verification process than a software validation process. It can, however, be used to validate the satisfaction of certain sets of conditions.

A *fault* is a defect in the program, usually difficult to pinpoint. To count as a fault, something must cause at least one input to result in failure. The reason that faults are often very difficult to pinpoint is because faults can rarely be isolated to a single cause. Some simple faults, such as forgetting to increment a counter, can be easily localized. But these are the exception, not the rule. Faults of this nature are sometimes termed *single-point faults.* Most faults turn out to be a series of mistakes scattered throughout a program. Together, these mistakes compose "the fault"; and all of them must be executed for some test case in order for the software to fail. These types of more complex problems are termed *distributed* faults. Obviously they are impossible to isolate to any single place in a program. From a fault-injection standpoint, simulating distributed faults is a nearly impossible task, not simply because of the combinatorics, but because the individual problems comprising a distributed fault interact in a way that causes a specific erroneous event, not just a bunch of random corrupted events. Ten random corrupt events may have no impact on the program whatsoever, but ten different corrupt events may come together as a single corrupt event and cause the program to fail. Being able to build enough intelligence into fault-injection mechanisms to simulate distributed faults reasonably remains an unattainable goal. Fortunately, there are some workarounds to this problem. These are discussed in subsequent paragraphs.

Single-point faults usually occur in individual software code statements. We need a way to isolate different types of code operators when we apply fault injection to source code. For the sake of simplicity, we consider a *location* in a program to be any statement that alters the flow of control or modifies the value in some variable. For example, the statement "if (a>5) then" modifies control flow, it counts as a location. Any looping control mechanism also counts as a location. An assignment statement such as "a=5" and an input statement such as "read(a)" are also both locations.

The state of the program between two sequential locations is termed a *data state*. A data state includes the state of all programmer-defined variables, and fully determines where the flow of control goes next. Precisely knowing every value for each variable in a data state turns out not to be important during fault injection. What is important is the ability to access particular values of interest in order to replace them.

Software testing is the process of determining whether software meets its defined requirements. Software testing comes in many flavors, based on a number of different perspectives. *Structural testing* seeks to ensure that code is exercised. *Functional testing* seeks to ensure that the functionality of the code is correct. Another way to partition testing techniques is according to whether source code is considered during test case generation: *Black-box testing* does not consider the source code; *white-box testing* does. Testing techniques can also be separated according to how much of a system they consider at a time: *Unit testing* techniques consider only smaller units (including individual functions); *system testing* tests the entire system as a single function composed of any number of subcomponents. Under each of these broad types of testing, there are a variety of individual techniques that attempt to ensure that different characteristics are satisfied. For example, *branch testing* is a form of unit, structural, white-box testing. *Specification-based testing* is a kind of functional, system-level, black-box testing. There are even techniques that exist to satisfy a cross section of these different partitions. For example, boundary-value testing can be a cross between domain testing, which is black-box, and structural testing, which is white-box.

A program having no faults is *correct*. An *error* is a mental mistake made by a programmer that results in a *fault*. Note that the terms fault and error are frequently misused—something we will try to avoid. The *input value space* is the set of all possible input values to the program. The size of a fault (termed *fault size*) is the number of inputs in the input space that execute a particular fault and result in failure. Fault size is usually reported with respect to all inputs in the input value space and includes the likelihood that bad inputs are selected.

An *input distribution* is the probability density function (*pdf*) over each element in the input value space. That means an input distribution defines the likelihood of selection for every member of the input value space.

The *output value space* is the set of all possible output values of the program. Note that this space may differ from the desired output value space, according to the specification. For example, the specification might say that no output values can exceed 100. But suppose that the program is capable of producing a value of 101. In this simple example, the output value space of the software includes the value "101" even though it should not in principle.

Observability is the probability that a failure will be noticeable in the output space. In practice, a simple file compare between two output files will inform us that something anomalous has occurred. An *oracle* is a predicate on input/output pairs that checks to see whether the desired behavior f has been implemented correctly by some function g. Formally speaking, oracle $w(x, y)$ is true iff $f(x) = y$. The quality of the oracle and its ability to detect faults is directly dependent on the level of observability and detectability exhibited by program failures.

Oracles come in two types: human and automated. *Human* oracles are experts that can examine an input, its associated output, and then determine whether the program delivered the correct output for the particular input. *Automated* oracles perform exactly the same task, but do so automatically. Typically, oracles are only "partially automated." Most regression tools come with this sort of functionality.

Detectability is the probability that a failure will be observable and that the oracle will be "smart" enough to detect the failure. This has proven to be a serious problem in *n-version programming* voters for floating-point calculations, something we detail in chapter 6. To get a flavor of the problem, consider whether 97.12345 is "the same" as 97.123449.

Software failure is the occurrence of an output value that does not meet the requirements for the input value. For software to fail when it is incorrect, there must be sufficient levels of observability and detectability. Our interests in fault injection are not whether faults exist and programs fail per se, but whether programs are capable of producing certain types of output failures.

In the software engineering community, there is much disagreement over whether software failure is random in nature. If software failure isn't unpredictable, it can have a believable number attached to it. Such an exercise turns out to be hard, specifically when the software rarely fails. It should be obvious why software that fails often can have failure-frequency numbers assigned to it. That leaves the cases where the software either never fails or almost never fails. It turns out that the people who are most vocally opposed to the idea that software fails with any regularity are usually the same people that oppose quantitative measures of quality. These people would rather qualify the goodness of the *processes* used to develop the software, ignoring the software itself.

One of the most important concepts in software fault injection is the idea of an anomaly. Anomalies can occur at two main levels: (1) internally in the program states, and (2) externally in the output space. When we mention anomalies throughout the book, we refer to internal program state corruptions. We define an *anomaly* to be some event, either static or dynamic, that appears to have the potential to alter software behavior through the alteration or corruption of some internal program state value. It is important to make this distinction between whether an anomaly actually does alter behavior or whether it simply appears to do so. To know for sure whether an anomaly alters program behavior requires testing on each possible anomaly—something that is impossible to do. Even if we do try some anomaly, and it has no impact on program behavior, then we have only discovered that the corruption was not problematic under some well-defined set of circumstances. That means under a different set of circumstances the same anomaly may turn out to be problematic. To further complicate matters, all of this is fundamentally affected by the definition of what an impact on program behavior might be. For example, some anomaly may cause some program to slow down substantially. In some cases, this might not matter, but in a real-time system, any slowdown might be disastrous. Obviously, the more closely we can force simulated circumstances toward those expected in real life, the better we can extrapolate from our results in order to predict the future.

Anomalies are events that corrupt internal states. A fault is a preanomaly event that, if executed and given some set of inputs, will corrupt the state of an executing program. The sequence of events necessary for a program to fail because of a particular fault is as follows: Inputs force faults that corrupt internal states; corrupt states propagate to failures. This model of how faults cause failure has been referred to as the fault/failure model [Morell 1988; Voas 1989]. Put succinctly:

1. An input must *execute* a fault.
2. The fault must *infect* data state after execution.
3. Infected data states must *propagate* to the output.

If any of these three events does not occur, the fault will remain hidden. Note that the events are temporally dependent on one another: You cannot have infection if execution does not occur, nor can propagation occur without infection. Propagation, infection, and execution make up the PIE model of testability described more fully in chapter 5.

There are three approaches for thwarting the effects of software faults: elimination, avoidance, and tolerance. *Fault elimination* is the responsibility of testing. *Fault avoidance* is a development issue, and hopefully occurs during the requirements, specification, design, and coding phases. *Fault tolerance* is a property of the software, and must be designed into the software. Software is said to be fault tolerant when it is able to produce acceptable results even though it is faulty. In chapter 5, we delve more deeply into the role that software fault injection can play for assessing fault tolerance.

We still haven't got the whole picture. That's because software faults are not the only type of anomaly. Anomalies can originate from any information source that feeds a program: hardware error, human error, and software failures in other modules. Furthermore, anomalies are not necessarily always bad. There are many classes of anomalies that are not problematic. Since the definition of "problematic" is plastic, any determination of the goodness or badness of an anomaly is hard to pin down. Fault injection simulates anomalies, injects them, and observes their relative impact on a program. It is up to the user of fault injection to define what constitutes problematic output. In other words, a user must decide upon and then define what impacts are bad and what can be safely ignored.

In the remainder of this section, we define a host of different metrics for determining how likely a program is to fail and when a program is likely to fail. We begin with the standard definition of *software reliability*. Software reliability is the probability of failure-free operation of a computer program for a specified time in a specified environment, D [Musa 1987]. By contrast, the *probability of failure* (*pof*) is the probability that program P will fail on the next selected input according to some environment, D. D includes both the program's input distribution and other factors, including but not limited to the operating system, the compiler, and the particular processing chip. Software reliability and probability of failure are closely related ideas provided that they are measured with respect to the same environment. There is, however, a subtle difference:

- Software reliability is defined with respect to some period of time.
- Probability of failure is time-independent. High probability of failure suggests low reliability and low probability of failure suggests high reliability.

Using simple transformations with parameters such as *mean-time-of-a-program execution,* a probability of failure can be converted into a reliability estimate. Likewise, given a reliability estimate and a mean-time-per-program execution measure, a probability-of-failure estimate can be calculated.

As noted earlier, many computer scientists have backed away from endorsing quantitative measures of software quality. That's because they place little faith in quality metrics. Many people think that though reliability is a nice characteristic to quantify, in the end the numbers cannot be trusted. This lack of confidence has multiple causes. The two main causes rest on the belief that the levels of precision for probabilities of failure in the 10^{-5} and lower range cannot be trusted, and the fact that given a fixed set of parameters, many different reliability models give different reliability estimates. There are further complications that are beyond the scope of this book; however, we feel compelled to mention one problem that plagues direct probability of failure estimation. This problem occurs when a program never fails during the time when the direct probability of failure parameter is being quantified. Let's make this concrete: If a program fails 1 percent of the time, then you can roughly say that the probability of failure is 0.01. But if the program does not fail at all in 10,000 trials, what is the resulting probability of failure? The pof is 0, *only* if the 10,000 trials include *all possible inputs* to the code. If all inputs are not covered, then it is possible that the code will fail on the 10,001st trial. It might fail on the 10,002nd trial, too.

The probability of failure of a program is a function of the subset of inputs from the input value space that produces software failure. This set is sometimes referred to as the *fail set* [Musa 1987]. Reliability is a function of the failure intensity of the software. *Failure intensity* is defined to be the number of failures per unit time. That means failure intensity is approximately equivalent to the unconditional probability of failure in one unit of time. Failure intensity can be calculated as the derivative with respect to time of the mean value function of failures. The *failure rate* is approximately the conditional probability of failure in one unit of time, assuming that there have been no previous failures in the given unit of time. The probability of failure parameter can be used to calculate the failure rate.

In addition to failure intensity, another way to discuss how damaging some type of failure will be involves assigning different *failure severity* ratings to software outputs. For example, in the FAA DO-178B's software standard, different classes of failure are identified as: catastrophic, serious, and major. Ranking failures allows for a way to focus resources on eliminating more severe fault classes, that is, those fault classes that will lead to the more serious classes of failures. In disciplines such as software safety, hazardous classes of failures are separated out from other failure classes, and the goal is to develop software that is incapable of producing the hazardous varieties. Since the elimination of all faults from software is unrealistic, employing failure-severity analysis can be quite cost-effective.

A *failure interval* is the time that elapses between two successive failures. This can be calculated given the probability of failure and the mean time to execute an input. *Fault density* is the ratio of the number of faults in a program to the number of instructions in the program. Finally, the *fault exposure ratio* is the rate at which faults result in failure for a program. The fault exposure ratio can be used to calculate both a failure rate and a probability of failure.

For systems made up of different subsystems that interact, the concept of fault tolerance is particularly important. *Fault tolerance* traditionally refers to the level of assurance that the failure of one subsystem will not cascade (propagate) causing the failure of others. Fault tolerance is usually implemented via redundant components that are placed in parallel. Each of these redundant components must in no way negatively affect the behavior of its counterparts. Software is considered failure tolerant if and only if:

1. The software is able to compute an acceptable result even if the software suffers from logic problems.

2. The software, whether correct or incorrect, is able to compute an acceptable result even if the program itself receives corrupted or malicious incoming data during execution.

Fault tolerance and failure tolerance are similar, with the key difference being that fault tolerance is geared toward demonstrating that a failure in subsystem A cannot cause subsystem B to fail, whereas failure tolerance is concerned with whether a failure in A or B can cause a particular undesirable output from the system as a whole. Much of this book is geared toward demonstrating how fault injection can measure to what extent systems and subsystems are fault-tolerant and failure-tolerant.

References

[Arlat 1990] J. Arlat, M. Aguera, L. Amat, Y. Crouzet, J.-C. Fabre, J.-C. Laprie, E. Martins, and D. Powell. "Fault Injection for Dependability Validation: A Methodology and Some Applications." *IEEE Trans. on Software Engineering,* 16(2):166–182, February 1990.

[Clark 1995] J. A. Clark and D. K. Pradhan. "Fault Injection: A Method for Validating Computer-System Dependability." *IEEE Computer,* 28(6):47–56, June 1995.

[DeMillo 1978] R. A. DeMillo, R. J. Lipton, and F. G. Sayward. "Hints on test data selection: Help for the practicing programmer." *IEEE Computer,* 11(4):34–41, April 1978.

[IEEE 1983] *IEEE Standard Glossary of Software Engineering Terminology,* IEEE Std 729-1983. IEEE, 1983.

[Han 1995] S. Han, K. G. Shin, and H. A. Rosenberg. "Doctor: An Integrated Software Fault-Injection Environment for Real-Time Systems," *Proceedings of the Second Annual IEEE International Computer Performance and Dependability Symposium,* pp. 204–213, IEEE, 1995.

[Hsueh 1997] M. Hsueh, T. K. Tsai, and R. K. Iyer. "Fault Injection Techniques and Tools." *IEEE Computer,* 30(4):75–82, April 1997.

[Kanawati 1992] G. A. Kanawati, N. A. Kanawati, and J. A. Abraham. "FERRARI: A Tool for the Validation of System Dependability Properties." *Proceedings of the 22nd Annual International Symposium on Fault-Tolerant Computing,* pp. 336–344, IEEE, 1992.

[Mills 1972] H. D. Mills. "On the statistical validation of computer programs." IBM Federal Systems Division, Gaithersburg, MD, Red. 72-6015, 1972.

[Morell 1988] L. J. Morell and J. Voas. "Infection and Propagation Analysis: A Fault-Based Approach to Estimating Software Reliability." Technical Report WM-88-2, College of William and Mary in Virginia, Department of Computer Science, September 1988.

[Musa 1987] J. D. Musa, A. Iannino, and K. Okumoto. *Software Reliability Measurement Prediction Application.* McGraw-Hill, 1987. ISBN 0-07-044093-X.

[Solheim 1993] J. A. Solheim and J. H. Rowland. "An Empirical Study of Testing and Integration Strategies Using Artificial Software Systems." *IEEE Trans. on Software Engineering,* 19(10):941–949, October 1993.

[Tsai 1996] T. K. Tsai and R. K. Iyer. "An Approach to Benchmarking of Fault-Tolerant Commercial Systems." *Proc. 26th Ann. Int'l. Symp. Fault-Tolerant Computing,* pp. 314–323, IEEE, Los Alamitos, CA. 1996.

[Voas 1989] J. Voas and L. J. Morell. "Fault Sensitivity Analysis (PIA) Applied to Computer Programs." Technical Report WM-89-4, College of William and Mary in Virginia, Department of Computer Science, December 1989.

3 Fault-Injection Fundamentals
Implementing Anomalies for Inputs, Outputs, and Everything in Between

3.1 The Three Fundamentals

The essential concepts underlying fault injection parallel the core concepts of computation itself. *Computation* in its purest form is a transitioning of inputs to outputs, where intermediate states are created throughout the process as subcomponents of the software execute. Subcomponents include such structures as code statements, functions, modules, objects, and so forth. Fault injection is simply the act of adding a transition and watching to see what effects the added transition has on the output of the system. Figure 3.1 provides a simplistic representation of the computation process and its parts: inputs, outputs, code subcomponents, and internal data states.

In this simplified process, fault injection can be applied to inputs, code subcomponents, and data states—all for the purpose of seeing what happens. The effect can be seen in lots of different places, including the output of the program and data states inside the program. Whenever a piece of code, its input information, or its internal states are modified, an anomaly is said to have been injected. Since the purpose of fault injection is to answer the question, "what if?," it may also be necessary to build monitoring mechanisms that see what effect a fault injection has. It is important to do this testing in a real operating environment. By performing fault injection, we can take a global view of the anomaly impact on complete software systems instead of a purely local view. That is, we get more from the process than simply a view that only monitors a program internally or at prespecified program output points.

3.1.1 Inputs

The requirement to have legal software inputs to use during the fault injection process cannot be overstated. *Legal* inputs refers to all members from the input value space, that is, those inputs upon which the software is expected to work

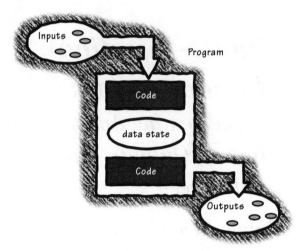

Figure 3.1 *Inputs, outputs, and data states.*

correctly. When we apply fault injection directly to code and its internal data states in order to modify them in some way, we must use legal inputs or the results lose their meaning. The value added by using valid and likely-to-happen inputs cannot be overstated.

Results that we collect after execution of the fault injection instrumentation are directly biased by the inputs employed. Meaningful inputs are particularly useful if we are collecting metrics concerning frequencies of particular output events. It is even preferable to have legal inputs when the inputs themselves are the target of the fault injection process. The idea is to corrupt legal inputs and find out what happens. Interesting results can still be obtained when we employ nonsense inputs, particularly for applications such as security assessment. But in terms of most of the other applications of fault injection, this is not true. Nonsense input values provide little value for statistical results collection, even though from a Boolean perspective, they can sometimes provide interesting insights.

Another reason to use valid inputs is that it makes possible the job of deciding which output events to classify as undesirable. It might even be useful to run a set of normal inputs to determine baseline behavior.

Inputs can come from many sources; they can be generated from the expected operational distribution, generated directly from the specification, simply generated at random, or generated with respect to domain knowledge such as domain boundaries. Unless we carefully select the inputs, the results from fault injection may be too biased to be of value.

Input to software typically comes from input files, humans, or sensors. These are the obvious cases, but even information returned from an operating system call must be considered input. A call looking up the current date and time returns input to the calling software. If we were to run a date-calling program randomly at any time of the year, then any value returned would be equally as likely as any other. If we executed the program only on certain days or at certain times, however, then there would be a way to pare down the input space. For more on this issue, see the Year 2000 problem discussion in chapter 9.

From a safety-critical perspective, probably the most troubling of all inputs are rare-event inputs. These are those members of the operational input value space that are very unlikely to be selected. Here, *rare* refers to the likelihood of being selected, and not some other unusual characteristic. For example, the input value space might be all positive integers except for one possible negative value, but if that negative value is the most likely value to get selected, then it is not considered rare.

It is possible to find rare-event input values given a mathematical description of the likelihood that any individual member of some input value space will be selected. All that is required is to invert this description, sample from it, and select from among the least-likely input values. This assumes, of course, that the original distribution has a high variance. If the only inputs available are in input files and there is no frequency description, it may still be possible to build an input description from the files, which is sometimes referred to as curve-fitting data. If curve fitting proves successful, then the resulting description can be inverted. The process of curve fitting files and then inverting the distributions is very difficult, and for most applications will not be possible. Later in the book we demonstrate the benefits of using rare but legal inputs during fault injection.

3.1.2 Outputs

Inputs are a very important ingredient in the fault-injection process, but an even more important ingredient is software outputs. We must take care to ensure that the output events are well defined enough that outputs of interest can be tracked. It is possible to see what happens successfully only if we know what to look for.

Watching for particular output events requires the software fault injection process to have an appropriate level of observability. Although observability was defined in chapter 2, it is worth restating here: *Observability* is a characteristic of code that allows problems in the program to manifest themselves in the output. There will be applications where observability of the code alone is not enough. In these cases, we will also have to concern ourselves with the observability of the environment in which the code operates. In the final analysis, it is best to consider observability as a combination of the observability of the code and the observability of the environment.

If a program neither produces any output nor has any impact on the environment, then the code has zero observability. If a program has no observability whatsoever, then it is obviously completely useless, unless, of course, the program is the bitbucket—implemented as /dev/null in UNIX. If, on the other hand, the program has "printf" statements immediately following every statement in the code which serve to output the results of every computation, then the program has very high observability. Increasing observability is the approach used by debuggers. In a debugger, the user is allowed to manually look at values stored by different variables in order to see where a computation goes awry. With no observability during fault injection, we could never hope to answer the fundamental fault injection question, "what if?," which would render fault injection impotent.

The issue concerning what constitutes an output event and which output events should be monitored ultimately control the amount of value that can be realized through fault injection. Suppose we improperly define some event that we are interested in so that it boils down to tracking whether the output of the program ever results in a "0." In our example, what we should have been monitoring for is whether the output ever results in a "−1." Since we are monitoring for the wrong thing, any results that we get concerning the output of "0"s are ultimately useless.

There will also be cases where all we need to determine is whether the outputs from a piece of software differ after fault injection is applied. In this case, we are not looking for certain output events, but rather whether the fault injection causes any discernible difference in the output events. In other cases, all we will be interested in is whether internal states show the effect of fault injection that occurs at some earlier point in the program. Finally, in yet other cases, we will be concerned with specific output events; for example, whether the value of some variable is outside of some range. All of these concerns share a common thread in that they are all related to the level of observability of the software.

There are yet other forms of output that we must consider as well. Just as some system calls can result in input to a program, any call from the application software to the operating system is an output event. Although these are not what we typically think of as outputs, they are events that have the potential to change the state of the machine in which the application is executing. It is therefore necessary to consider them valid output events. In security analysis, we may be concerned with attempts to remove a specific file from some directory.

There are two fundamental approaches to monitoring output events:

1. Monitor whether *any* deviation occurs in the output, which requires that another version of the code be executed as a baseline in which fault injection does not happen.

2. Monitor for a *specific* type of output event, such as an output value that is outside of some range.

To perform the first type of observation, one approach is to dump all of the output of the two different programs—original and fault-injected—to different output files and then compare the files. Of course, this assumes that the file format and the comparison program can handle all of the different possible representations of file data. This can be hard when output contains characters that cannot be printed.

In our previous security-related example (file removal), it is critical to check to see if the call actually succeeds for the two different programs, fault-injected and normal. These types of outputs are not so easy to check, because once the first program executes this command (whether it is the original or fault-injected) and succeeds in removing the file, the file will not be there for the second program executed! We must anticipate side effects such as these and handle them properly in order to do a fair comparison.

Performing the second type of observation, checking for a specific output event, does not require execution of an unmodified baseline version of the code. What it requires instead is an assertion-like computation that takes in the output event and checks it against an assertion. By contrast with the baselining approach, the monitoring approach to output observation is usually less expensive computationally, since complete execution of the code without fault injection is not needed. The assertion approach does, however, require that the assertion-like language be built into a tool or at the very least that there exists some searching facility (such as UNIX's grep) to apply to the output to see if certain values or character strings were produced.

Definition of a class of output events to monitor will greatly impact how useful and valid fault injection results are. If you define too broad a class of output events, then your answer to "what happens if" is likely to be "too much to deal with"; if you define a tight, narrow class, then your answer to "what happens if" is likely to be "apparently nothing." Suppose we define some output event of interest to be TRUE if some variable is greater than 0. This broad class of possible numbers is much larger than if we defined some output event as TRUE only when the variable is equal to 100. Suppose it turns out that the variable is set to 50. In the former case this would be flagged, whereas in the latter case it would not. Since propagation from the injection points to the output is what we're keeping an eye on, the definition of output events is of critical importance.

There is an interesting class of programs that essentially have no definable output. What, for instance, is the output from an operating system or a system daemon? These programs are meant to run continually, and deciding just when an output may have occurred is very difficult. For dependability reasons, Parnas suggests that safety-critical programs such as these be turned off or reset from time to time, so that any nasty side effects that build up through program-state corruption over time are halted. Suppose we have a program that just sits and reads in data and never produces any output until some event of interest is observed.

Here, determining the output of the software is difficult, because there might literally never be any. For these types of programs, it will be necessary to define "artificial" output points before fault injection is employed. Then we can determine whether fault injection has in any way affected the state at these points.

3.1.3 Propagation

When program states transition into other states and the information in an initial state directly impacts the information in the successor state, we say *propagation* has occurred. Propagation is a key factor directly linked to observability. Programs that tend to propagate problems through themselves into their output tend to have high observability.

Propagation can be measured at several different levels. It can be measured in the output of the software; it can be measured in the operating system or environment state; and it can be measured at any intermediate point between atomic source operations throughout the code. To measure propagation requires a formal language capable of monitoring events at any of these different levels across the total state of the executing system.

There are three different places in the code where we might be interested in observability: the system level, the application level, and the output level. (See Figure 3.2.) Placing assertions in the software at each of these levels will engender greater understanding of what is occurring during execution. From a testing perspective, each of these points presents an opportunity to build programs that do not hide away their errors.

3.1.4 Atomic Operators and Data Spaces

Fault injection can be applied either directly to code or to the data states that are created during execution. Before tackling this topic, however, it is important to distinguish what constitutes a data state in relation to code operators.

Code operations are simple atomic actions that can be formalized as follows: Beginning with the program in some state X, exercising an atomic action leaves the program in some state Y after which the next atomic operation can be executed. In a program state Y, lots of information concerning the status of the scope, the program stack, the values of programmer-defined variables, the next instruction to be executed, and so forth, are available. There will be cases where it is useful to include the input value used in the program execution, thus creating some particular data state out of the set of every possible data state. But we'll address that later. A data state is typically limited to include only those data units that hold the values of the programmer-defined variables as well as the program counter. In this case, what we mean by program counter is not the same as the

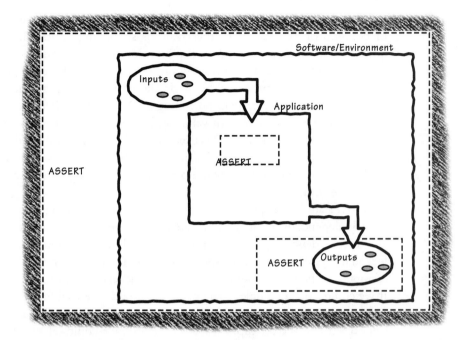

Figure 3.2 *Three different levels of assertions.*

traditional machine code program counter but is instead the program's control flow indicator that points to the next source instruction to be executed. A programmer has direct access to this counter through the conditional expressions written into the code. Because of this, it is often meaningful to direct fault injection against control flow to see what effect that has.

In the software testing community, people have taken both sides in the argument as to whether incorrect control flow necessarily relates to incorrect outputs. This issue is debated under the moniker *coincidental correctness.* The question is this: What is the likelihood that a program can get on the wrong path yet still result in a correct answer? If the probability is small, then hiding control flow faults is a problem that we can essentially ignore during test-case generation. If the probability is large, then we will need specific test cases whose job is to expose control flow problems. Intuition leads many to believe that incorrect control flow should be an easy problem to detect, but unfortunately this has never been conclusively shown, suggesting that maybe it isn't easy to detect. Furthermore, it has been argued that events, such as taking one more or one less iteration in a loop, do not matter much in terms of program behavior. Because of these and similar counterexamples, and because this issue is specifically tied up in the intricacies of particular programs and specifications, the issue is still open.

Interestingly enough, however, we can use fault injection to force the results of conditional expressions to reverse, thus simulating control flow errors. By doing so, we can begin to address this question with additional evidence.

An example of a data state is shown in Figure 3.3. In this example, we posit a simple input space represented by single-dimensional integers. The output space is also made up of one-dimensional integers. Notice that after the first statement is executed, x holds the read-in value, and the next instruction to be executed is instruction 2. After statement 2 is executed, we see that x still has the same value, variable a is now defined, and the next instruction to be executed is number 3. In this case, we did not include the original input value (1) in the data states, but clearly we could have.

A data state is a snapshot in the state of an executing program. A data state is directly dependent on the place in the code where the snapshot is taken and it is also directly dependent on the input that started the execution. If we were to collect all unique data states for a specific point in the code that could ever occur for all inputs to the system, we would have what is termed a *data space* for that point. If we could store a complete data space, we could delete all of the code executed prior to that point, assuming that we could never reach it again, and simply consider the data space the input space. In the end, we could select a data state from the data space, and begin execution from there.

Every data space and every source statement in a program represent *injection points*. An injection point is a place in the software where instrumentation can be added that alters the syntax and/or the semantics of the original software.

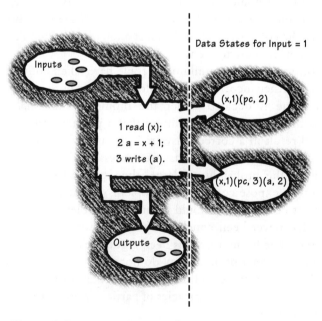

Figure 3.3 *Data state example.*

Now that we have defined what we mean by data space, we can look further at what statements are candidate injection points. At the assembly and object levels, any operation would be an injection point. At the source level, we typically consider any condition that affects control flow or any statement that affects values of programmer-defined variables to be injection points. Function calls, return statements, and constant declarations are also injection points.

Data states have a property referred to as dimensionality. Most complex programs will have data states of such extreme dimensionality that they must be pruned or otherwise pared down. Sometimes this involves pruning even what is considered important data-state information. It is a good idea to prune things like dead variables since their value can no longer impact computation. Keeping such things around is a waste of overhead. For our purposes, applying fault injection to such variables can result in only one outcome: learning that the fault injection did not impact the code as it executed.

3.2 Anomalies

The most fundamental concept behind fault injection lies in the notion of *anomalies*. Anomalies are simply unexpected events, and here we will begin to discuss the issues involved in deciding how to simulate anomalies as well as how to observe anomalies. We do this to ensure that our results will be significantly reflective of future problems that could occur.

3.2.1 Theorizing about Anomaly Spaces

Three pieces of information are required before fault injection can begin:

1. Where do software inputs come from?
2. Where in the software are the mechanisms to handle the outputs?
3. What events (either internal or external) do we want to watch for—that is, what are we observing?

Other information that we will need concerns input distributions and test suites to sample from.

For most systems, the space of possible problems that could manifest themselves in a program's state during the software's lifetime is effectively *infinite,* as represented in Figure 3.4.

We refer to this as the "All Problems" space. By gradually decomposing this space, we can isolate those portions that will be useful during fault injection. Besides being infinite, this space is *unknown:* The set of all problems that might arise during the life of the software cannot be enumerated. Because of this, we

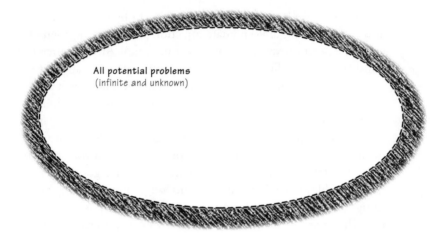

Figure 3.4 *All problems that the software could experience during its lifetime.*

need to classify and partition different parts of the space that share similar properties. We partition the space in order to isolate those problems that can and should be simulated using either syntactic mutation or data–state mutation. To begin, let's consider the partition that represents the problems caused in the data states by logical faults that are already resident in the program. (See Figure 3.5.) This theoretical move is plausible because logical faults exist internally.

The "All Problems" space continually changes whenever the environment that the software operates in changes. The internal partitions change, too. Suppose

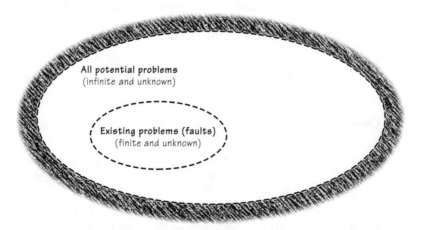

Figure 3.5 *All existing faults in the program.*

that in some part of the code there is a conditional statement, and in the TRUE branch there is a faulty computation. If the input distribution of the code is such that the TRUE branch cannot be exercised, then that code is dead, dynamically speaking. Following the IEEE definition of what constitutes a fault, statically dead code cannot be faulty code, though what is dynamically dead differs according to inputs used. If we apply a different distribution to the same program and there exists at least one test case that *does* execute the faulty code, then a fault does exist in the TRUE branch. For purposes of our space, the "Existing problems (faults)" space will not contain anomalies for this fault if the environment for the program is such that it will not allow the TRUE branch to be exercised.

The preceding partition is created by real faults and can be finite or infinite in size depending on the input value space. The members of this partition are still unknown. If we knew where the faults were, we could simply opt to fix the faults and thereby shrink the partition. Keep in mind that if the program is correct, this space is empty. Because we are looking at the problems created by faults instead of the faults themselves, we can ignore precisely what the faults are. Recognize that fault localization is very difficult. To understand why, consider that for any specification there are an infinite number of syntactically distinct correct programs that implement it. For each unique correct program, there are an infinite number of incorrect versions that can be derived from any correct version, as shown in Figure 3.6.

Given one specification, there are N correct implementations of that specification. For correct implementation 1, there exist K faulty versions. It is fair to think of the K versions as K mutants of the correct version. Because of this, distinguishing what *the* fault is can be subjective. For example, when incorrect version 1-1 is compared to correct version 1, we will likely have a very different syntactic perception of what is wrong than when we compare incorrect version 1-1 to correct version 2. We must determine what truly counts as a fault with respect to the correct version that is the "closest" syntactically to the incorrect version. The problem is that most of the information we put in our picture does not exist. What is likely to exist in the real world is only a specification and one version of the software.

In the case shown in Figure 3.7, we do not know which side of the dividing line—between correct and incorrect—the implementation is on. If we look at the problem of fault localization in terms of errors instead of faults, this problem is easier to remedy. Recall that an error is a mental mistake made by the programmer, whereas fault is the syntactic representation of that error. For this reason, software-engineering techniques such as fault-based testing are difficult to implement, because it is impossible to demonstrate via proofs an absence of all possible fault classes.

The partition of the "All Problems" space representing programmer faults does not require simulation if we wish to use fault injection for applications such

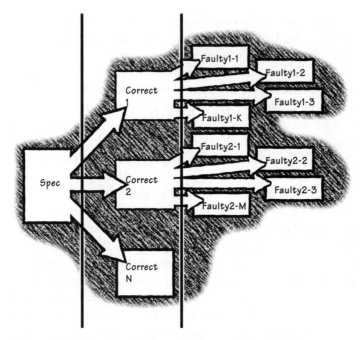

Figure 3.6 *One specification, and an infinity of different incorrect programs.*

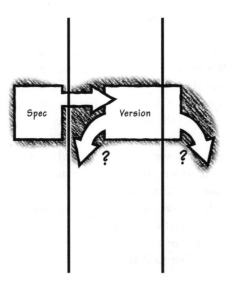

Figure 3.7 *Having a version, and not knowing if it is correct.*

as safety and failure tolerance. For applications of fault injection such as safety and failure tolerance, determining what effect programmer faults will have on the safety and failure tolerance of the software can be done by repeatedly testing the software to see how large these logical problems are and how they affect the software's output. But, as you will see for applications such as testability, simulating programmer faults can be very useful.

The next partitioning of the "All Problems" space isolates those anomalies that could attack the system from outside of the software. (See Figure 3.8.) These problems might arise from human factor problems; problems with the operating system or computer hardware; and problems from other sensors or software systems such as databases upon which the software depends for inputs, files, and so on. In short, this partitioning represents all external factors that are not related to faults in the code that could somehow manifest themselves in the state of the program. As you would expect, this partition is again infinite, but unlike other partitions this partition is partially known. That's because for some of these classes of problems, it is possible to know the incoming failure signatures, or modes. If some input signal device fails, it might return all "1"s or all "0"s to the software. This is easy to simulate. Likewise, if some call to the operating system is known to return a null pointer when it fails, that too is a problem that can be easily simulated.

The second partition represents all external problems that *could* occur. We can theoretically divide this partition further into a third and fourth group: those external problems that *will* occur in the future and those that *will never* occur. Once again, the inability to know what the future will hold will not allow us to make this partitioning in practice. It is nevertheless a meaningful exercise to differentiate these two classes in our minds even if we cannot dif-

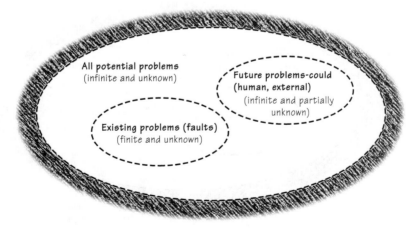

Figure 3.8 *External problems that* could *occur.*

ferentiate them in practice. An interesting thing to note here is that the partition representing those problems that will occur is of *finite* size. This is because there are only so many problems that the software can experience, since its life cannot last infinitely long. After all, if the software experiences or contains too many problems, we would probably just decide to shelve it or otherwise discontinue its use.

There is an important class of problems that requires both corrupt inputs from the external world *and* embedded faults in order to produce an anomaly. This class of problems can be assigned to either of the two partitions already mentioned. For our purposes, we assign such a problem to the external-problems-that-could-occur partition.

And now for the point of this whole exercise. Unless we are concerned with testability measurements, the problem space that we ideally want to use fault-injection mechanisms to simulate is the partition of external problems in the future that *will* occur. (See Figure 3.9.) Of course, since that space is clearly an unknown black box, simulating only its members will be impossible in practice. In the end, the best that can be done is to simulate as many anomaly classes associated with the "All Problems" space as possible, with limited or no knowledge concerning what partition they belong to.

The goal of chapter 6 is to discuss methods for simulating as many members of the internal circle as possible—representing future problems that *will* occur—and make economic sense. In Figure 3.10, we show the anomalies that actually do get simulated by randomly sampling from the "All Problems" space in the large darkened oval. In this particular case we've hit pay dirt because the darkened oval of injected anomalies completely subsumes the future-problems-that-will-occur

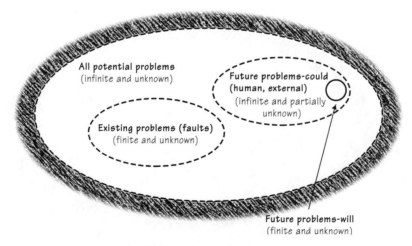

Figure 3.9 *External problems that* will *occur.*

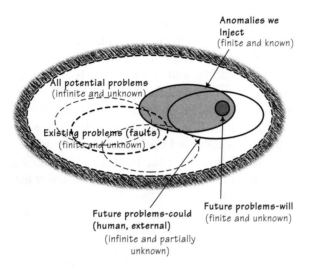

Figure 3.10 *Simulated anomalies randomly selected from all subspaces.*

circle. This is the Utopian dream of fault injection. In the nonperfect real world, we could just as easily have missed simulating the future-will circle completely, as demonstrated by the two dashed-line ovals we have included.

At this point, the obvious question is whether the results we spent all those cycles gathering are of any value if we inadvertently avoided covering the inner circle during anomaly simulation. In this case we will have only simulated external events that were never going to happen during the software's lifetime. The issue is this: Can simulating anomalies that are never going to happen still produce information that can help predict future undesirable behavior?

A recent research result published by Christoph Michael supports the idea that information learned from simulating *any* anomaly can still be useful for a better understanding of what to expect from specific anomalies [Michael 1997]. Michael has been studying homogeneous propagation. *Homogeneous propagation* occurs when several different forms of state corruption impact the same program variable at the same injection point for the same test case, and all of these state mutations exhibit the identical propagation behavior. That means that either all of the corruptions propagate, or none of them do. If some propagate and some don't, we say that the program suffers from *nonhomogeneous* propagation.

Results by Michael tested homogeneous propagation on three programs:

1. A back-propagation connectionist network

2. A module from an auto-pilot

3. A large computer game (nethack)

In each program, 20 data-state mutations were made on the value of each variable appearing on the left-hand side of an assignment statement. This was done for one execution of the back-propagation network, five executions of nethack, and 500 executions of the auto-pilot. In the back-propagation program, homogeneous propagation occurred for 84 percent of the variables. For nethack, 84 percent of the variables showed homogeneous propagation on all five test runs. For the auto-pilot, 46 percent of the variables showed homogeneous propagation on all 500 test runs, and another 37 percent showed homogeneous propagation on at least 95 percent of the test runs. Thus, only about 5 percent of the variables showed homogeneous propagation on fewer than 95 percent of the test runs.

What this research result shows is that software systems appear to have fairly consistent propagation behaviors once an anomaly is introduced into the program's state. This suggests that the behavior that a program will exhibit for an anomaly from the inner circle will often be similar to the behavior that the software will exhibit for an anomaly outside of the circle. Thus, even if we fail to customize our fault injectors to mimic future, undesirable events, simulating random anomalies from anywhere in the large oval can still produce meaningful predictions. That is good news for fault injection.

3.2.2 Using Software Standards to Partition the "All Problems" Space

In each of the applications we discuss later in this book, the types of output events that we must monitor will need to be specialized. Monitoring for file movement might be legitimate in a security effort, but monitoring for the same event in an avionics program might be a complete waste of effort. Just as there is a need for appropriate output monitoring functions, there is a need for appropriate anomaly injections.

It is becoming more common for software standards to spell out certain classes of internal anomalies and output behaviors that must not manifest themselves during execution. The problem here is that as soon as some event is specifically spelled out in a standard, it will become the only anomaly that developers will concentrate on. Once such an anomaly has been mitigated, developers will decide that they have applied enough preventative measures. Simply protecting against one specific anomaly—for example, lightning hitting a nuclear power plant at the same time that a jumbo jet crashes into it—might not be enough protection for the situation involving lightning, a jumbo jet, and a tornado. This can become a nightmare for standards.

We have explained which anomalies should be simulated in the ideal case: those in the circle of anomalies that *will* occur in the future. But since that partition is unknown, we need to turn to different sources for guidance on what to simulate. There are myriad different ways to isolate the anomalies that we should simulate with fault injection. One quick way is to follow the guidelines provided in software standards. Such standards provide this information by listing specific problems that must be protected against. If we simulate these events and undesirable outputs occur, then we have not properly protected against such problems. If, on the other hand, bad outputs do not occur, then it is likely that we have protected against such problems. The only problem with many of these standards is that they list the fault classes that should be protected against, but fail to list any specific external events that might cause the code to misbehave. As we pointed out earlier, it is the role of testing to determine the impact of the resident faults, since there is no need to simulate (via injection) problems that are already there.

If guidance from software standards is not available, it is left to the developer to best decide what problems to simulate based on his or her knowledge of the system. Here, we briefly look at two recent software standards and the types of anomalies that they spell out as events that must not occur.

For software standards to be effective, they must relate in some way to software output behavior. For standards to take hold in practice, they must be objectively shown to improve quality, not simply be touted as a "good thing to do." When a measure of quality suggests good software, that measure has also indirectly assessed the effectiveness of software processes employed during development. Standards are successful only when the software developed using them has better behavior. Behavior-based measurements can act as a check on claims about process improvements.

Fault-injection techniques can be applied to assessing software compliance with standards in two ways:

1. Determine if a software standard generally results in higher-quality software
2. Demonstrate that a particular piece of software satisfies a standard

Next, we demonstrate how applying fault injection can empirically mitigate concerns stated in two safety-related software standards, one from NASA and the other from Underwriters Laboratories.

The recent NASA Interim Report NSS1740.13 introduces a software safety standard that states that the Code Safety Analysis phase of development must:

> *Identify potentially unsafe states caused by input/output timing, multiple events, out-of-sequence events, failure of events, adverse environments, deadlocking, wrong events, inappropriate magnitude, improper polarity, and hardware failure sensitivities, etc.*

This NASA requirement essentially mandates a forward trace after anomaly injection occurs to determine whether unsafe outputs can be produced by said problems. Fault injection is capable of simulating instances of each of these potentially dangerous events and determining the impact on the output. Here, fault injection can aid in empirically demonstrating that the software product satisfies this requirement. The ultimate goal, of course, would be if the results of fault injection show that all output states reached by injected faults are safe outputs. Although something like this is not a proof that unsafe states can be produced by related but different instances of these anomaly classes, it is at least a demonstration that the anomaly classes used in simulation have no negative safety considerations. One key thing to realize is the clause we pulled from the standard spells out neither any specific developmental procedures nor any validation procedures that must be used. Fortunately, fault injection makes it possible to assess how effective such procedures actually are.

What then does our fault-injection scheme say about the effectiveness of the safety-critical development processes employed? For a critical system in which hazard analysis is almost certainly performed at some level of rigor, programming language firewalls will almost certainly be the key design scheme for protecting critical code sectors from noncritical code sectors. Incidentally, another option that is recently gaining favor is the application of software wrappers. Fault injection can empirically demonstrate whether these design-for-safety processes, such as static fault tree analysis, actually do adequately protect the critical regions of the code; that is, simulated fault injection can test whether in some real product the development process has produced correctly partitioned code. As fault injection successfully validates families of products, an archive of evidence can accumulate that validates the quality of the processes that created them.

Underwriters Laboratories' Standard UL1998 entitled *Safety-Related Software* also describes undesirable events [UL1994]:

> These requirements [UL1998] address risks that may occur as a result of faults caused by software errors, such as the following: . . . b) Coding errors, including syntax, incorrect signs, endless loops, and the like; c) Timing errors that can cause program execution to occur prematurely or late; d) Induced errors caused by hardware failure; e) Latent errors that are not detectable until a given set of conditions occur; . . .

The NASA standard talked about showing whether unsafe states could be produced by certain undesirable internal events. In this standard, we again see the need for a forward trace from the injected anomalies to the output to see what forms of risk are engendered. Fault injection can once again demonstrate the risks and impacts of most if not all instances of these classes of problems in the same manner as described for NASA Interim Report NSS1740.13. This is possible by careful customization of the fault-injection mechanisms. As in the previous case, if fault injection were to show repeatedly that software products from development process A had sufficiently low risks according to UL1998, then evidence is accumulated that A is a good process to employ.

One interesting side note: Although Underwriters Laboratories has finalized this standard, they have yet to produce an equivalent list of recommended techniques to better enable their clients to satisfy these concerns. Without this information, this standard is difficult to enforce in any systematic manner.

3.2.3 *Simulating Distributed Faults*

We mentioned earlier the difficulty in simulating distributed faults via fault injection. The crux of the problem involves combinatorics. Simply put, there are infinite combinations of ways to simulate these problems. Fortunately, all is not lost. Certain methods of fault injection can be used to simulate the effect of distributed faults without simulating each individual part of the distributed fault.

Suppose that four program variables, *A, B, C,* and *D,* are all improperly calculated by the programmer, and together they are the components making up a distributed fault. Any input that fails to execute the code that computes values for all four of the variables will fail to flush out this error. Suppose that at some point in the program there is a call:

```
x := f(A, B, C, D)
```

If we have failed to simulate incorrect computations affecting *A, B, C,* and *D,* which will almost certainly be true, then we cannot know what impact the distributed fault will have. But almost certainly, this distributed problem will ultimately cause *f* to fail, causing *x* to be corrupted. So by simulating a failure of *x,* we can get fairly close to simulating a failure of *f* due to the failure of the computations on *A, B, C,* and *D.*

Program slicing can also play an important role in this approach. That's because we can slice a program and see which variables interact and which ones do not. Distributed faults will be valid only when this interaction exists. If the interaction does not exist in the static case, then the set of all possible locations at which to simulate a distributed fault contains at least one location that is irrelevant to the distributed fault.

3.3 Implementation Issues

Conceptually speaking, the ideas behind fault injection are quite intuitive. But when it comes time to actually implement those ideas, suddenly many questions are raised and the process starts looking less than straightforward. Here, we begin to address some of these implementation-specific issues.

3.3.1 When to Apply Fault Injection

Fault injection can be applied to source code as soon as it exists. Unlike traditional testing, however, fault injection is best applied as the code matures and is getting close to being a stable entity. Traditional testing is more adaptable and can be applied either to somewhat "raw" code in order to find defects or to fairly stable code to assess quality. When testing is used to find defects, it is said to be employed in a development capacity.

Fault injection can be costly, and doing it all over again every time a new version of the program is declared is undesirable from a cost standpoint. Broad rules of thumb for deciding whether code is ready for fault injection include:

1. The code compiles.
2. The code is deterministic; that is, it returns the same output for the same input.
3. The code does not include infinite loops or, if the code runs continuously, there is at least some reasonable way to determine when one run of the code ends and the other begins.

3.3.2 Pseudorandom Number Generation

Pseudorandom number generation plays a pivotal role in software fault injection, similar to the role that random test-case generation plays in software testing. In software testing, test cases are usually selected at random after the program has been shown to work properly for specific, deliberately chosen test cases. In fault injection, randomness is applied at several different levels: In some cases fault injection relies on random selection when deciding which mutations to employ; random selection is often used in deciding which injection points or locations to use, if we cannot use fault injection for all injection points in the program; and fault injection often employs random selection when mutating the values in data states.

Randomness is necessary because of the uncertainty that comes along with trying to predict the future by playing "what if" fault-injection games. If there is no uncertainty, then simulating uncertainty via pseudorandom number generation is absurd. But if there is no uncertainty, there is no need to predict, and fault injection is rendered obsolete. Pseudorandom number generation provides a sound way to study the effects of hypothetical events that can be as close to or as far from real, future events as we desire.

Fault-injection mechanisms that are applied to data states can create a wide variety of simulated state errors by using a pseudorandom number generator. In our own fault-injection work, we use the Lehmer pseudorandom number generator with a fixed initial seed described in Park and Miller [Park 1988]. To mutate data states, we actually insert the necessary code to cause a state mutation, which we call a perturbation, into the program under analysis. We do this by inserting a source-code module containing the pseudorandom number generator into the code under analysis and place a call to this module from the location where we want a data state perturbed.

When replacing an existing value with a new value, there are essentially two options:

1. Sending the module the current data-state value and asking it to return a replacement data-state value that is based on the original value

2. Simply asking for a replacement value, without any regard for what the original value was

Care must be taken, however, to ensure that the replacement value is different from the original value. If this is not ensured, then no state corruption may actually have occurred, no propagation can occur, and no real work has been accomplished.

Random selection of replacement values can be applied to a wide variety of data types. Numeric data is the easiest to mutate; however, it is possible even to perturb pointers in structures if this is a realistic concern. In later chapters, we explain the customized manner in which we mutate data states for the specific type of fault injection being applied. For some forms of data-state replacement for security analysis, it might make sense to simulate a vulnerability that makes no sense whatsoever in terms of a safety-critical system. Likewise, among safety-critical applications, there may be a wide variety of different state mutations that we are interested in, depending on the domain in which the software operates. For example, there might be one class of corruption that makes more sense for nuclear applications than it does for avionics applications.

Possible random distributions for data-state mutation include all continuous and discrete distributions. In practice, people more often use a uniform distribution because of a lack of overwhelming knowledge as to which distribution is best or even if a "best" exists. Fortunately, the use of a uniform distribution yields encouraging results.

One very important consideration here deals with the notion of "repeatability" after fault injection is used. Given the exact same scenario—where scenario refers to the program, program inputs, fault-injection mechanisms, and the same initial random number seed used by the fault-injection mechanisms—the results from this scenario should never change from run to run. In other words, the results from fault injection must be deterministic for fixed, identical experiment parameters. Of course, a change as seemingly minor as using a different seed will have drastic effects on system behavior. As the number of trials grows, the deviation in the results should vary less. This is why we can safely disregard worrying about which particular random seed to start with.

3.3.3 *Instrumentation*

Intrusive versus Nonintrusive Approaches

Collecting information about what is occurring internally in software as it executes requires some form of instrumentation. That means instrumentation is a prerequisite for fault injection because we are interested in finding out what happens to software once faults are introduced. An analogy may be helpful in understanding the purpose of instrumentation. If you decide to tap your neighbors' telephone line, one method is to find the wires that go from the street to their residence, splice a second set of wires to their lines, and feed this newly spliced line into your home. After you do that (an activity that we don't recommend), you will have performed the needed instrumentation to tap your neighbors' telephone. With a little amplification, you should be able to monitor their calls.

Instrumenting software is a very similar idea. Just as you would need a splice to tap your neighbors' phone, you need some mechanism to collect data internal to software—data that probably exist for only a nanosecond or a microsecond in the machine. To be successful, the mechanism must know the precise instant at which to capture the information. There is no more obvious way to do this than to insert additional software code at the exact point in the original code where the desired information is accessible. This additional software code, called *instrumentation,* is responsible for collecting the data, processing it, and holding it until some later time. All of this requires additional code and some new data structures be added to the original code. Sometimes instrumentation simply communicates information outside the original program in such a way that another system can process it. Other times, instrumentation includes data-storing capability.

One fundamental decision that must be made before fault injection is employed is the issue of just how the instrumentation of the code will take place. There are two alternatives: intrusive and nonintrusive. *Intrusive instrumentation* is the process of adding code to the program under analysis that will collect the data and process it. This new code will be executed along with the original code after it is compiled in. The purpose of the new code is to allow collection and storage of the results that we are seeking. The easiest way to do this is to add new code, though sometimes this may not be possible.

In real-time systems, however, adding code to collect results can be problematic, because the CPU cycles required to perform the instrumentation processing can throw off the original timing behavior and thus skew the outputs that the code would have normally produced. If the additional code is extensive, it may expand the size of the original program to two or more times its original size. Just like the timing trouble, this can be particularly problematic for embedded systems, where the amount of available memory is almost always pretty small.

The nonintrusive approach is really misnamed; that is, *nonintrusive instrumentation* still requires something be added to the code to communicate the raw data to the outside world. The key is to add only very small nonintrusive taps. The nonintrusive method is generally so inexpensive in terms of extra time and space requirements that the somewhat misleading terminology has caught on.

Patil and Fisher [Patil 1995] report an implementation of nonintrusive instrumentation for the purposes of memory leak detection. By using a *shadow processor* that actually executes the instrumentation, which is simply a processor that sits in the background communicating with the main program being analyzed, they are actually able to detect memory leaks that will occur on the main processor *before* the main processor suffers from them. Although their approach does not employ instrumentation that performs fault injection per se, it appears as though their approach is generic enough to be used for fault injection with little modification to the main process. What is most interesting from their findings is the extremely small overhead to the main processor. The communication costs between the main and shadow processors reportedly slow the main process on the order of 10 percent or so. This finding suggests that nonintrusive instrumentation for fault injection might be even more applicable to real-time systems than is generally thought presently.

Source Code versus Object Code Instrumentation

We briefly described in chapter 2 why mutating HDL code is easier than mutating most programming languages. Simply stated, this is because HDLs offer far fewer replacement options. In programming languages, our choices will be similar in nature, but there will be many more of them. For example, in an HDL we might wish to replace an AND-gate with an OR-gate, while in some programming language we might wish to replace a "+" with a "-". An important difference between the two is that in the software case we may wish to consider simulating bad input data. This is rarely considered in integrated circuit testing. In a circuit with 10 pins, the number of different inputs is 2^{10}, and the circuit will likely be tested on all of these different input combinations. These 2^{10} inputs make up all of the legal inputs, and exhaustive testing can be feasibly performed. By this reasoning, smaller instruction sets make smaller the possible ways that fault injection can be applied.

On computers, source code never actually gets executed; machine code does. The number of different instructions at the machine level is smaller than at the source level, particularly since many source instructions get translated into many different machine instructions. Therefore, an interesting question presents itself concerning whether the fault injection should occur at a higher level or at a lower level. Source-code versus object-code instrumentation presents an interesting conundrum. This book and its techniques are focused on source code instrumentation, but we must acknowledge how these two approaches differ and address the associated tradeoffs.

In the FAA's guidebook for the development of software on airborne systems [FAA 1992], there are very specific requirements mandating that test cases be created according to the structure in the assembly code, and not be based on the structure of the source code. This is because there are many people who do not trust the integrity of the compilation/translation process. As we all know, validating compilers is very difficult, if not completely impossible. Airborne system code represents a key safety–critical domain where the U.S. Government has put its weight behind the premise that compilers do weird things, and they want the avionics code that comes out of the compiler and put aboard the aircraft thoroughly exercised. Since the possibility exists that there will be paths through the machine code that do not get exercised even though the source code is thoroughly tested, they mandate this extra level of assurance.

The process of compilation from source code to executable code takes a source code program of size X lines and creates an object code file of size AX instructions, where $A > 1$. What this means in terms of instrumentation is that at the source level, certain operations are atomic that are nonatomic at the object level. This translates into many lesser atomic operations at the object level than there are at the source level. For example, suppose you had

```
if (A = B) then
    A := A + 1
else A = A - 1;
```

in your source code. These three source operations would translate to something resembling the following in assembly, before then being translated to object code:

```
        LOAD   A   R1
        LOAD   B   R2
        CMP    R1  R2
        JMP    20
        DEC    R1
        JMP    21
    20  INCR   R1
    21  STOR   R1  A
        next instruction
```

As you can see, there are many more opportunities to instrument the low-level information than there are at the higher levels. By more opportunities, we simply mean that there exist more locations in the code at which to place injection instrumentation. At the assembly level, we can do things like poll to find out what information is in a particular register. That means we could, for instance, corrupt the contents of a register without corrupting a memory cell. Or we could corrupt a jump address. Many of these options simply do not exist at the source-code level, meaning that there is no way to corrupt the source code in order to cause identical semantic effect.

One thing to consider here is that it can be hard to collect meaningful information about what is happening at the source-code level by instrumenting the lower levels. This is, in part, because today's compilers (for machines such as the PowerPC) use highly complex methods during translation. What this means in the end is that you actually need decompilation capability that takes executable code back to source code in order to say what is happening at the higher level based on information collected at the lower level. Access to decompilers is certainly rare. Given the fluid nature of the industry, around the same time decompilers become available for some platform, manufacturers end up switching to a different scheme. The moral here is simple: You can collect information about what is happening at the source-code level from instrumenting the object code, but this process is compiler/machine-specific and, depending on what is being observed, very expensive. If, for example, you are trying to observe which source-code branches are exercised from doing instrumentation on the object code, you will need to follow every jump through the object code. This means you will need to instrument every jump in the object code. After you collect all of that information, you still must be able to properly map it all back to the source conditions, which for some short-circuiting languages can be quite a task. For higher levels of coverage, such as Meyer's multiple condition coverage [Meyers 1979], mapping back from instrumented object-code jumps to source will almost always be impossible.

A further consideration here involves what application of fault injection you are instrumenting for. If you are trying to simulate different classes of programmer faults, then instrumenting at lower levels incurs the risk that you will inject anomalies that cannot be mapped to programmer faults and hence exhibit completely different behaviors. This clearly would defeat the purpose of performing the fault injection. If you were instead interested in simulating different classes of errors introduced by compilers, then instrumenting at the lower levels would make perfect sense. What if the compiler fails to improperly terminate a repeat loop, and allows it to loop one too many times? What does that mean with respect to the machine-code implementation? If you were interested in testing the compiler itself, you might wish to step up a level and instrument the source code for the compiler, in order to get a flavor for how likely the compiler is to hide faults.

In summary, simply having more injection points at which information can be collected does not necessarily imply that instrumenting at the lower levels is more desirable. The application and purpose of the results must be considered as well.

Fault Injection for Interfaces

Code is not the only place where it makes sense to apply fault injection. For very large systems, we will almost certainly not have the option of applying source code at the statement level, and instead will be forced to inject anomalies into the interfaces between software components. When an anomaly is injected into the interface carrying information away from component X, and no anomalies are injected into the interface that carried information into X, this has the effect of simulating a failure of X.

This idea of injecting anomalies into interfaces also enables us to get away from the idea that fault injection must be applied only when there is source code. This allows us to treat a software component as a black box and ignore the code inside of the component altogether. For systems that are composed of commercial-off-the-shelf (COTS) components, as well as for legacy systems for which source code is not available, this capability will be the only way that we can assess where in a system anomalies can start a cascade of problems that ultimately lead to undesirable outputs. Further, with component-based software quickly becoming a driving force in the marketplace, driven by reuse as the predominant goal, we must be willing to accept that more and more of our applications will contain calls to code about which little is known. By simply having the ability to simulate failures of this alien code, we will be better able to assess its impact on our system should the code prove defective.

There is one large problem with applying this idea for systems for which source code is not available—that is, a "correct" definition of what the outputs of the system are. Recall our claim that system calls and other side effects are technically outputs from the software. If we cannot know whether such events occur inside the black box, then the effects of fault injection on them cannot be monitored. This is both an observability problem as well as a problem for anomaly injection. Put another way, if we don't know about an interface that feeds in information, we cannot send corrupt information in to determine its impact. Similarly, if we don't know about an interface that sends out input, we lose access to a potential observation point. This is why for COTS and legacy systems that do not clearly define all their interfaces to the outside world, the notion of observing and controlling is limited.

Current wisdom in software engineering has started to limit the likelihood of software components injecting corruptions into the exit interfaces by applying a technique known as wrapping. A *wrapper* is simply a software filter that takes the output data that a component was planning to return, and allows only certain types of output to actually exit. This reduces the likelihood that information will leave one component and negatively impact another component. Essentially, this is just another form of information hiding or decreasing observability.

How Often to Inject Anomalies into Loops

With data-state mutations, the decision concerning when to apply data-state mutation during loop execution for a single test case critically affects the results. Looping constructs allow multiple iterations across the same code. The question is, during which iteration or iterations should mutation be applied? If an injection point is placed in a loop that iterates three times, then we can inject on any of the following combinations of iterations: (1), (2), (3), (1, 2), (1, 3), (2, 3), (1, 2, 3). Note that if we do decide to inject on more than one execution of a location, the injector affects the same variable or combinations of variables in the data states on each iteration.

Part of this question can be answered by considering the type of real anomaly that is being simulated. If we are simulating a hardware failure sending in a corrupted signal, and we know that when the device fails it sends in all high bits, then we can best simulate hardware failure by sending in high bits on all iterations. In this case, it is reasonable to assume that input will continue to be corrupted the same way in a continuous manner until the hardware device is repaired. Thus it is plausible to apply the injection mechanism each time a read from the hardware device is called. But even if we do not have all this device-specific knowledge, it turns out to be a good idea in general to apply the injector on each iteration. This works on the assumption that once some subcomponent starts acting up, it is likely that it will continue to act up.

3.3.4 Propagation

Forward and Backward Analyses

Dynamic fault injection is generally a forward analysis process. Forward approaches start from some point in the code and trace toward points in the code that will be executed at a later time. At any point along the trace, execution can be halted and the state can be analyzed. This forward (in time) trace allows us to analyze the sequence of events from time t_0 as far forward in time as we want, even all the way to the output space of the program. Keep in mind that some location in the code may be executed at a later time than a geographically subsequent location even though it may be syntactically closer (location-wise) to the initial statement. What that means is location in time and not location in space is what is important.

The purpose of doing a forward analysis is to see how events unfold in time. In a forward analysis, we hypothesize a starting state, and then move forward in time to see what other states or events result. Not too surprisingly, in a backwards analysis, we do the reverse. We hypothesize some event or state at time t_n to see what prior states would need to occur at time t_{n-x}.

The key problem with rolling backwards is *nondeterminism*. The issue is this: If, when going forward, state A and state B both result in state C after some operation occurs, then which way do we go when going backward from state C? Do we go to state A? Or should that be state B? This problem can be alleviated by first doing a forward trace and storing information about each data state created along the way. This allows an easy mapping of later events to earlier ones.

In terms of fault injection, backwards nondeterminism is not a problem, because in fault injection we will always know what event was hypothesized (fault classes were injected). Therefore we will know the start and end states of the process. From such information, we can cluster all initial states that led to a particular end state, and begin to classify them. Such information can be particularly useful for building recovery mechanisms to boost fault tolerance.

Slicing

After defining the input space of interest, and deciding what output events to watch for, the next issue is deciding what parts of the program to instrument in order to perform the fault injection. Slicing is a technique that can provide valuable, cost-effective solutions here.

Program slicing comprises a set of decomposition techniques based on extracting those statements that are relative to a particular computation in the program. Program slicing prunes the set of computations associated with a particular program behavior as much as possible. The benefit of slicing is that it isolates a (hopefully) small set of statements with respect to some computation. Since such statements can be scattered throughout code and are difficult to find manually, automated slicing can decrease costs. The key applications of slicing are program debugging, testing, and software maintenance, but other applications have been proposed as well.

The original type of slicing proposed by Weiser [Weiser 1984] has come to be known as static program slicing. Several variants of this idea have been proposed, including: (1) program dicing, (2) dynamic slicing, and (3) decomposition slicing. To perform static slicing, you must first build a flow graph of the program. A slicing criterion for a program slice is a tuple $<I, v>$, where I is a statement in the program and v is a subset of the program's variables. A slice is computed on v at statement i. A program slice of some program P for some tuple $<I, v>$ is a new program P' obtained by deleting zero or more statements from P such that the values of all variables in v are the same when I is executed for both P and P'.

Slicing is a very valuable technique from a propagation standpoint. Suppose that you have the following program:

```
1 junk(n,x)
2         int    n;
3         float  x[];
4{
5         int    I,w;
6         float  sum,avg;
7         x[1] = 4;
8         w = 0;
9         sum = 0;
10        avg = sum/n;
11        printf("avg=%f",avg);
12}
```

For the criterion <12,avg>, our slice would be:

```
1 junk(n,x)
2         int    n;
4{
5         int    I,w;
6         float  sum,avg;
7
9         sum = 0;
10        avg = sum/n;
11        printf("avg=%f",avg);
12}
```

This static slice shows all computations that have any potential effect on variable *avg* at some point in the program. What this shows is that variable *w* and array *x* have no impact on *avg*. This information defines where problems can originate and propagate from and where they cannot. So, for instance, if *w* and *x* are in any way incorrectly defined or are the wrong type of structures, those problems will in no way adversely affect *avg*.

Static slicing can clearly benefit fault injection, because it can show whether injecting at point A in the code can ever have an impact at point B. If static slicing shows that A cannot impact B, then injecting at A and observing at B is useless. Dynamic slicing can benefit fault injection even more. Dynamic slicing was introduced to reduce the size of static slices. After all, just because a set of statements has the potential to affect some computation, whether they do is directly dependent on the input used. Dynamic slices are computed from a program trajectory or execution trace for some input. A dynamic slicing criterion for a program that is executed on input x is a 3-tuple (x, I^q, V), where I^q is the qth instruction in the program trajectory and V is a subset of program variables. When programs include arrays, dynamic objects, and structures, the size of dynamic slices can be much smaller than for static slices [Marciniak 1994]. If we have a set of inputs that we plan to use during fault injection, and we compute the dynamic slices based on those inputs and observe that certain computations are not relevant to those slices, then we immediately know where fault injection need not be applied and observations for the impact of the fault injection also need not be considered. So in short, dynamic slicing can refine further the results of static slicing before fault injection is actually applied.

This brings up an interesting point that relates static events to dynamic events. Dynamic events are always a subset of static events. Static events are defined relative to all possible scenarios, but to make all such scenarios happen requires very large numbers of inputs. If some such inputs are exceptionally rare, then certain behaviors that appear to be possible from a static perspective turn out to be realistically impossible at run time.

3.3.5 Statistics and Result Collection

After fault injection is performed and the raw data are collected, the next major task is to dig through the results. If fault injection has been employed liberally throughout the code, there will be a large amount of resulting data. It is therefore necessary to collapse that information into a more manageable and, hopefully, more compressed format. Imagine the pile of information that would result from corrupting some data space one million times at one million locations! There is no need for each individual result relating whether propagation to some successor data space occurred. An easy solution is to collect and organize the information in the form of statistics or probability estimates. Instead of having one billion results, this might result in one million, or even one. A good example of how things could boil down to just one result might be a statement saying that the output event of interest occurred 45 percent of the time. This one result thus provides a probability estimate.

Each probability estimate has an associated confidence interval, based on a particular level of confidence desired and the number of test cases used, n. The computational resources available when fault injection is performed will determine how large n can be. For example, for 95 percent confidence, the confidence interval is approximately $p \pm 2 \ \mathrm{sqrt}(p(1-p)/n)$, where p is the sample mean. Since the n's used in such algorithms are expected to be large, $2 \ \mathrm{sqrt}(p(1-p)/n)$ will likely be insignificant. Unless p is close to 0 or 1, for $n = 10^4$, $2 \ \mathrm{sqrt}(p(1-p)/n)$ is approximately 0.01; for $n = 4 \times 10^4$, $2 \ \mathrm{sqrt}(p(1-p)/n)$ is approximately 0.005.

Because of its dependency on randomness, fault injection can suffer from qualitative errors. As a result, confidence intervals play only a minor role in attaining confidence in probability estimates. When we say *qualitative error,* we mean that fault-injection methods may have been employed incorrectly. An example is using complex mutants, such as removing huge blocks of code, when what should have been used are simple mutants. (See chapter 4.) In such a case, the statistics gathered may well be right, but the processes employed for gathering those statistics were wrong. Unfortunately, such a qualitative error renders results meaningless.

Software fault injection plays what-if games by employing code- and data-state mutants. Our confidence in the value of these games' results should not rest on 95 or 99 percent confidence intervals. Instead, we can be confident in results that have been shown experimentally to reflect the effect that actual anomalies cause. Fault injection is only as good as the anomalies simulated, test inputs used, and observability points defined. If these things are wrong, then tight confidence intervals will not be enough to make the results meaningful.

It is worth repeating the following tenet of fault injection for emphasis: Any frequencies that are collected are valid only with respect to the test vectors employed. If test vectors change drastically, fault frequencies probably will, too. Hence it is prudent to employ as accurate a test distribution as possible when statistics are collected.

3.4 Summary

The first three chapters provide the fundamental background that will be relevant throughout the remainder of the book. The family of software fault-injection techniques is relatively new, and because of this quite a large set of new terms have been developed. The underlying ideas behind fault injection, however, are very intuitive. If you understand that fault injection is a dynamic process that instruments a piece of code with software mechanisms for causing code- or data-state changes, then executes the code to see what happens after anomaly injection, you have successfully grasped the fundamentals.

References

[FAA 1992] Federal Aviation Authority. "Software Considerations in Airborne Systems and Equipment Certification." 1992. Document No. RTCA/DO-178B, RTCA, Inc.

[Marciniak 1994] J. Marciniak. *The Encyclopedia of Software Engineering.* Wiley, 1994.

[Meyers 1979] G. Myers. *The Art of Software Testing.* Wiley Interscience, 1979.

[Michael 1997] C. C. Michael. "On the uniformity of error propagation in software." In Proceedings of the 12th Annual Conference on Computer Assurance (COMPASS '97). Gaithersburg, MD, 1997.

[Park 1988] S. K. Park and K. W. Miller. "Random Number Generators: Good Ones are Hard to Find." *Communications of the ACM,* 31(10):1192–1201, October 1988.

[Patil 1995] H. Patil and C. Fischer. "Efficient Run-time Monitoring Using Shadow Processing." In Mireille Ducasse, ed., *Proc. of the 2nd International Workshop on Automated and Algorithmic Debugging.* St. Malo, France, 1995.

[UL 1994] Underwriters Laboratories Inc. *Safety-Related Software,* January 1994. Standard for Safety UL1998, First Edition.

[Weiser 1984] M. Weiser. "Program Slicing." *IEEE Transactions on Software Engineering,* SE-10(4):352–357, July 1984.

4 Software Mutation
Invasive Injections Simulating Programmer Faults

4.1 Getting the Most from Software Testing

Software testing is an important and critical enterprise that helps make up a sound software engineering program. There are literally hundreds of software testing techniques, ranging from memory leak detection to multiple condition coverage. But in terms of computer science theory, software testing suffers from several undecidable problems (e.g., test data generation for coverage, mutant equivalence, and whether a program will terminate and produce output). One root of the problem is that it is impossible to determine whether a program will halt during testing. Clearly, if one of many tests takes forever to compute, testing will never end. As if that weren't enough, it is also theoretically impossible to exhaustively test many kinds of programs. That's because there are so many possible states the program can be in, driven by different inputs and internal logic, that testing all possibilities would take more time than has gone by in the universe so far—13 to 14 billion years by the latest scientific estimates. The third major problem that software testing must deal with is that in order to know whether a program is doing the right thing—computing the right answer, for example—you have to know what the answer was supposed to be. Theorists call the answer-giving mechanism an *oracle*. But automated oracles are often impossible to create, and human oracles are often wrong [Ammann 1994]. After all, if you're using a computer program to solve a problem, it is likely that you don't know the answer to the problem you're solving.

What we're left with once we take all these theoretical problems into account is the problem of good test-case generation. We can't test everything, so the key is to test as intelligently as we can, not to just throw as many test cases as possible at the problem. Also, testing with enough test cases for high levels of assurance is generally infeasible. Demonstrating one failure per X hours of execution requires approximately $10X$ hours of testing [Bertolino 1995]. Even though we know of all these problems, software testing is still the predominant method for assuring confidence in software before release.

Software testing comes in many guises: There's dynamic black-box testing with an oracle, for example. The most basic distinction among types of testing breaks things down into black-box versus white-box testing. *White-box* techniques take into account the actual code making up the software when selecting test cases. *Black-box* techniques do not. That means *specification-based* testing and *requirements-based* testing are both classes of black-box techniques. No actual code is considered in these kinds of testing. In black-box testing, input is fed into a program and the output is checked. What goes on inside the program (the black box) is unimportant.

The other kind of testing is white-box. We have already mentioned the size problem in today's modern software. Software systems are huge. Because there is so much code in large systems, white-box approaches based on taking the code into account are usually applied only at the subsystem level, and not to complete systems. There's simply too much code to take on. White-box testing also suffers from another basic problem: It can be helpless when trying to detect some very serious classes of problems, including *missing code faults.*

Some people erroneously believe that software testing tests just software. In reality, software testing can also involve testing software specifications and requirements. If you can create an oracle that is able to ascertain correct behavior from incorrect behavior, and is not directly based on the requirements or the specification, then software testing can actually reveal errors in earlier phases of the life cycle. In reality, this typically requires a human-variety oracle. Ironically, software testing sometimes reveals errors in the oracle! Errors found at the level of requirements and specifications are often expensive, because their discovery leads to redesign. But the earlier in the software life cycle they are discovered, the better. Errors that creep all the way to a final product are the most expensive of all.

In its most typical instantiation, fault injection is a white-box type of analysis. Using fault injection to mutate program syntax makes use of the source code, and is in this sense a white-box technique. Injecting faults via code mutation is a fairly straightforward process, theoretically speaking, when source code is available. From a practical standpoint, however, code mutation can be a very difficult process to implement. The benefit of having access to source code is that it gives instant access to logical layout and data structures. But fault injection can be used in a black-box way as well. When fault injection only corrupts inputs before they go "into" the box, it is being used in a black-box way.

Software testing is usually employed for one of two reasons: reliability assessment or fault detection. During standard reliability testing, failures are observed and counted, but no fault eradication takes place. When software testing is employed for fault detection, the idea is to fix the faults after failures are observed. A combination of these two approaches has evolved that is known as *reliability growth* testing. Reliability growth testing assesses interfailure rates (between failures) after fixes are employed. This activity provides some level of confidence that fixes actually solve any problems that are discovered without introducing new problems.

Before software mutation was invented, the earliest code modification technique for studying the code behavior was introduced by Harlan Mills in 1972. Mills's method was called *fault seeding*. Its goal remains to assess reliability [Mills 1972]. In this reliability estimation technique, a known number of faults are purposefully placed into the code, thus the term *seeding*. The total number of seeded faults uncovered during testing, as well as the total number of indigenous faults uncovered are then tracked. Using combinatorics and the maximum likelihood technique, the total number of faults resident in the code can be estimated from the two numbers, indigenous and seeded fault counts. From that, the reliability of the code is estimated.

Our main job in this chapter is to present a software test-case-generation approach to finding tests that thwart fault hiding. This chapter walks the reader through a listing of Ada83 mutant operators developed for mutation testing under a NASA-sponsored effort. Mutation testing was one of the earliest applications of software fault injection and is important because it adds value to testing by suggesting test cases that are more likely to find defects.

Code mutation was an early form of software fault injection. Mutation testing was once an early application of code mutation. Mutation testing attempts to see how good test cases are at detecting injected anomalies, which in this case involve mutated code. The idea is to change the code in a well-defined way and see if you can detect the difference between the changed code's behavior and the original code's behavior. The key issue in mutation testing is what it means for a test case to "detect" an injected anomaly. Certainly if the output of the program is modified because of an injected anomaly, then the test case allows the tester to know that the injection has taken place (i.e., the injection has managed to propagate all the way through the code). But waiting to see whether a mutation propagates is computationally costly, because after the fault injection has taken place, the tester has to wait and see what outputs result before determining if the test case detects the injection. This form of mutation testing has been termed *strong mutation testing*.

To reduce these computational costs, Howden proposed another type of mutation testing, *weak mutation testing,* that looked to see only if the state that was created immediately after the mutant was executed is different from the "same" state created in the original nonmutated code [Howden 1982]. If these states differ, then the test case is said to have detected the injection. Of course the main issue here is whether test cases that detect injections at the first data space are as good and useful as test cases that force propagation all the way to the output. If so, then once test cases are found that cause the first data space to be altered, those test cases would also cause the output to be altered, meaning we could get high-observability test cases at a very low cost. It is not clear how much water the hypothesis holds, and the debate about weak and strong mutation has never been fully resolved. As a compromise to these two extreme positions, Woodward and Hennell [Woodward 1980] propose *firm* mutation testing, where at some injection point between the mutant and output space, detection of a corrupt data state means that the test case has detected the problem. To our knowledge, probably for purely practical reasons, people that use mutation testing tend to employ only the weak variant. Firm mutation and strong mutation testing have never caught on.

4.2 Code Mutation versus State Mutation

There are two basic places to inject anomalies in software: (1) into code, and (2) into the data states that are created during execution. Source-code mutation considers what syntax currently exists, and based on that, modifies that syntax in different ways. Source-code mutation is expected to create mutants that are semantically different for at least one input to the code. Without this requirement, the entire process is a waste of effort. There may, however, be other reasons for creating populations of syntactically diverse programs that are semantically identical.

Source-code mutation suffers from a form of intractability similar to exhaustive testing. When code is syntactically modified, the resulting code is termed a *mutant*. There are potentially an infinite number of mutants that can be made from any original statement in the program, not to mention the infinite number of mutants that can be made from a mutant. To address this problem, different levels of mutation are defined. Taking an original source code statement and mutating it results in what is called a first-order mutant. When a first-order mutant is then mutated, the resulting mutant is called a second-order mutant, and so on. Lower-order mutants are typically referred to as *simple* mutants, and higher-order mutants are called *complex*.

Data-state mutation (DS mutation) chooses as its target either the complete data state or some subset of it. Based on that, data-state mutation substitutes a new data state for the original data state. Looking back to HDLs and their use of a fault mask and a fault operation, we see that DS mutation is essentially signal corruption for hardware designs. DS mutation can occur at any place in the code where it is legal to place an assignment statement. Part of a data state can be replaced in one of two ways, either based on the data being replaced or not. Use of current information in the data state as a basis for the replacing information requires the current information in question to be defined. This sort of DS mutation is done by using the original value as a statistical mean of some numerical distribution and selecting a replacement in the neighborhood of the mean. If a replacement is attempted and the original data is undefined, then some random value can be used to replace the missing definition.

To determine what impact a particular mutant will have on a program, the mutant must be executed. If there is no way to reach the mutant code given some input, then there is said to be no impact on the mutant for that input. Just for the record, there are fault-injection approaches that can force a program to get on the "wrong" path in order to increase the coverage attained for a particular input [Bieman 1996]. If it is impossible to exercise a mutant for input, assuming that we do not force coverage, then the mutant code and the original code are both dead.

For DS mutation this is still a problem, since to mutate a data state, the original state must have been created by some input. So in both cases, regardless of whether the fault-injected section is reached, the impact of the mutations is none. It is important to note that seemingly identical results have a different interpretation when the fault-injected section is reached and executed, and the impact is still none. Believe it or not, we are aware of instances in which testing personnel have tried to use unreached fault-injection mechanisms as a demonstration of critical characteristics such as robustness. To avoid this misunderstanding, tools should be careful to explicitly describe when no impact is observed because of a lack of reachability. Reliable Software Technologies' SafetyNet tool has this capability.

The rules for what constitutes a mutant are well-defined in the Mothra toolkit [DeMillo 1988]. Mothra employs 22 mutation operators for the Fortran-77 language. These operators are fairly simple. This simplicity turns out to be both the boon and the curse of syntactic mutation approaches in general. On the upside, simplicity means that the operators are quite straightforward and easy to understand, implement, and instrument into code. On the downside, because of their simplicity, such operators lack a real sense of representativeness. In other words, it is not guaranteed that mutants will behave the ways real faults behave.

Let's make this concrete. What does replacing one operand with another operand really mean in terms of the likelihood that a programmer will ever actually make this mistake? What does replacing one variable reference with a reference to another variable really teach us? That is, what information can we confidently learn from doing such a thing? Mutants are in no way equivalent to the original code, and if the code there is wrong, it is probably wrong in a different way than can be captured by the mutant. Even if the code is wrong, then the mutants will be based on wrong code. Sillier still, what if the mutant that gets selected actually turns incorrect code into correct code? The point here is that code mutation that tries to simulate programmer faults appears in the extreme to be a futile, intractable process. However, Daran and Thevenod report that simple mutants may not be as useless as the preceding questions might suggest [Daran 1995]. In fact, they have discovered that simple mutants exhibit behaviors that are not that dissimilar to the behaviors of actual faults. Thus, although the underlying theory seems to be weak, in practice the theory appears to work.

This entire fascination with mutants, and in particular, how best to make meaningful mutants can be traced back to the work of DeMillo et al. [DeMillo 1978]. They put forth a theory called the *competent programmer hypothesis* which asserted that good programmers will write code that is within a few keystrokes of what is correct. From this hypothesis, the argument can be made that simple mutants that were just a few keystrokes off of the original would be similar in nature to typical programmer faults. The result of Daran and Thevenod is, of course, just one finding, but to date, it is certainly one of the more provocative findings with respect to source-code mutation and its plausibility as a method for simulating program defects.

Turning to today's objected-oriented, distributed systems, it is clear that there has not yet been enough research and experimentation with mutants. No one knows what mutants might be reasonable in such a system. It is well known that some of the nastier faults to isolate are those associated with timing issues. Thus mutants that simulate timing problems are a very reasonable class to consider; though little work has been done in this area. Another issue that has not been fully addressed yet is the language-dependency issue concerning mutants. For example, what would a reasonable mutant be for a Pascal source statement such as: "a = a + 1;" versus the same statement written in C++. Would the set of reasonable mutants change? Some languages, such as C, allow side effects. The fact that you can write a conditional such as:

```
if (K = b == 5) then
```

allows not only for control flow changes but also for the side effect assigning a value to variable *K*. How do these statements interact with mutation?

Three other key source code mutation issues include:

1. What is the relationship between how a mutant looks and how it behaves?

2. Should mutants be injected that are syntactically incorrect with respect to the source language? (What if they are syntactically correct but will result in run-time errors?)

3. How can you determine if a mutant is only syntactically different from the original and not semantically different?

Software behavior is a combination of many factors: which particular data states are created, what paths are exercised, how long execution takes, what outputs are produced, and so forth. Because software behavior has so many factors involved, trying to quantify it is a difficult undertaking.

The first issue here of the relationship between how a mutant looks and how it behaves is difficult to measure at a purely syntactic level, since any mention of behavior automatically suggests some dependency on what inputs will be executed. The same mutant can behave very differently for one set of inputs versus another. More complex syntactic mutants can have a smaller effect on program behavior than simple mutants have. Because of these and other reasons, it is nearly impossible without far too much analysis to predict how a mutant will behave by simply observing it.

The second issue as to whether mutants should be injected that are syntactically incorrect with respect to the source language is more easily resolved from a conceptual standpoint, yet less easily resolved from an implementation standpoint. First, it should be clear that we do not want mutants that are syntactically illegal in the source language. But it is okay if we introduce mutants that result in a run-time error. In fact, for some systems, this is the behavior we may be interested in observing, and hence injecting mutants that force a run-time error is okay. The complicated issue, however, is what result a run-time error has on the overall results processing for the other fault injection mechanisms. For example, if a run-time error for some mutant Y causes the results to be lost from some other mutant X, then this behavior must be trapped before the operating system loses mutant X's information. This problem is undesirable when the instrumentation approach that is used compiles all mutants into a single program, as we discuss later. In that case, when the program containing all mutants is run, a run-time error from one mutant can cause the results obtained for other mutants to be lost, unless some intermediate results are collected and written out from time to time. A quick answer is to trap key signals before execution aborts.

Our third concern as to how you can determine if a mutant is only syntactically different from the original is undecidable, and is frequently referred to as the "mutant equivalence problem." If for all inputs the behavior of a mutant is identical to that of the original code, then the mutant is in no way a simulation of an anomaly class, and must be ignored. The mutant equivalence problem has been a fly in the ointment of *mutation testing*—a test-case generation criterion that attempts to find "good" test cases, where goodness is based on whether a test suite can distinguish all mutants from the original. This activity cannot occur if as little as one equivalent mutant has been generated until the equivalence problem is resolved. The problem stems from the necessity for some person to manually determine equivalence. When there are thousands of mutants that appear on the surface to be equivalent—because so far no test case has been able to differentiate them from the original—this task is far too burdensome, and somewhat defeats the purpose of ever using mutation as an approach to generating good fault-detecting test cases. In this case, the best that can be done is to ignore such mutants and simply use those test cases that detected the other mutants.

One DS mutation, which in an HDL is analogous to signal corruption in integrated circuit testing, can potentially simulate a much larger class of anomalies than can one code mutant. For example, suppose that at some data state we change the value of some integer variable from 50 to 100. This corruption could potentially be independently caused by a handful of mutants, but by causing only one data-state mutation, we get the equivalent fault-injection power for all of those possible mutants. Although we do not yet have a good theory for exactly why, other than the preceding argument, data-state mutation seems to be more powerful than injecting code mutants and executing the code until the end to see what happens. There seems to be some grain of truth in the idea that DS mutants have more power than code mutants.

4.3 Compiling or Interpreting Mutants

An early source code mutation system, Mothra, was developed for Fortran and used an interpreter. In Mothra, mutants were generated and executed in a loop. (A demo of Mothra can be found on the CD-ROM.)

It is well known that interpreted code is performance-inefficient when compared to compiled code. Thus, compiled mutants present obvious advantages. The PiSCES Mutation tool from Reliable Software Technologies compiles all mutants into a single executable for execution efficiency reasons. This requires multiple mutants to be associated with a single statement. All the mutants can be executed either in parallel or perhaps sequentially on different runs. For example, suppose that we have the sequential code:

```
x = a + b;
c = c + d;
```

An approach that implements weak mutation testing on the second statement involves adding some instrumentation, resulting in the following code:

```
x = a + b;
if (a+b) <> (a-b) then mutant1 detected
if (a+b) <> (a*b) then mutant2 detected
if (a+b) <> (b-a) then mutant3 detected
if (a+b) <> (b+b) then mutant4 detected
c = c + d;
```

The next step is to compile the entire mutant block into a complete instrumented executable. Obviously the code grows substantially during instrumentation. That can be a problem. If there are 1000 statements in the original code, and the average number of instrumentation lines per statement is 20 (that is, there are 20 mutants per line), then the code becomes at least 20 times larger.

Another problem with this approach crops up in languages with side effects. If a particular mutant causes side effects, they may well affect the next mutant in the block or even the remainder of the program. In this case, a sophisticated approach to instrumentation must be employed that effectively rolls back the side effect from mutant X before mutant X+1 is executed. Clearly this is expensive to implement, but necessary. Lets roll back ourselves to a previous example:

```
if (K = b == 5) then
```

In this case we can't do the obvious and create a mutant block like this:

```
if (K = b ==5) <> (b = K ==6) then mutant1 detected
if (K = b ==5) <> (K = c ==5) then mutant2 detected
if (K = b ==5) <> (K = b > 5) then mutant3 detected
```

because variable *K* will be continually changed between mutant comparisons of supposedly equivalent output behavior. What is needed is an approach that does not allow a side effect to affect other mutants in the block.

One nice side-effect-elimination mechanism for code mutation is used by the Generic Coverage Tool (GCT) built by Brian Marick. The basic mechanism works as follows: if <expr> is a C or C++ expression, it can be replaced by:

```
(tempvar = <expr>, tempvar)
```

without changing the semantics of the program. Here tempvar is a temporary variable that is specific to the expression. After all of the expressions have been so modified, weak mutation can be performed by comparing the mutated code to temporary variables. This prevents the original expressions from being evaluated, and thus it prevents side effects. Note that certain constructs, like assignment statements and certain address references, need to be given special treatment with this approach.

You might be tempted to think that only those expressions that might contain side effects should be treated in this way. Not true. If we made temporary variables for all subexpressions other than those containing only a single variable or constant, the computational savings obtained by not having to reevaluate the expressions during weak mutation analysis more than makes up for the extra effort needed to create the variables in the first place.

If implementing side-effect rollback seems too complex, a simpler but less efficient approach is to wrap each mutant program as a separate component—you can think of a program as a procedure or function—and then compile one huge program with all components in it. One of the components in this huge program will be the original program. Then for each input, simply call the original function, and then call each mutant, and finally compare the output of each function to the output of the original to see if the mutant produced a result that is different from the original. For programs of scale, this will almost certainly overwhelm the compiler. Thus although this approach is easier to implement, it will provide many unsolvable run-time and compile-time problems.

4.4 Assembly and Object Language Mutation

To our knowledge, little research has been performed on the application of mutation to languages below the source level. Certainly, this fact alone does not suggest that the fundamental ideas of mutation cannot be applied to assembly or object code.

From a practical standpoint, one key problem that will continue to keep vendors from attempting to build a commercial low-level mutation tool is the huge number of different assembly languages used in industry. To be frank, there are simply too many assembly languages in existence. But a low-level mutation tool might be appropriate for Java byte-code since it is platform-independent.

From a theoretical standpoint, it is somewhat unclear as to what mutation at a lower level would actually mean. Unless code were explicitly developed in assembly (something that is becoming less common), low-level mutation would be a means of simulating faults inserted by the translator from source-code to assembly. If the mutant classes at the lower levels could be mapped back to programming faults at the source level, that too might be useful, but it is not clear that this is the best way to simulate programmer faults. Consider what it would mean if certain low-level mutant classes could never be mapped back to fault classes at the source level. That is, what would it mean to collect information about how an assembly program behaves through mutation analysis when the mutations do not in any way reflect fault classes at the source level? There could well be some very useful information uncovered through such a process, regardless of whether a mapping to higher-level faults existed. But separating the signal from a very large amount of noise will be so difficult that it renders the analysis imprudent.

4.5 Creating Mutation Operators

Traditional software testing, whether at the unit level or the system level, follows the process shown in Figure 4.1, iterating many times through it.

Mutation expands on the usual approach by adding a "test-case goodness" step to the procedure. Figure 4.2 is a simplified diagram of the mutation testing process. Here, an input must first differentiate code that has been mutated from the original code. Then that input is used to test the original code against the oracle. Note that if the first comparison evaluates to false, then the second comparison will not be done for that particular input. That's because the input apparently exhibits little ability to expose faults.

Figure 4.2 schematically shows how mutation testing works. Simple source code transformations, called *mutations,* are introduced into the program by *mutation operators.* Each mutation produced by a mutation operator results in a *mutant program.* Note that a mutant program is not necessarily an incorrect program. For example, replacing one variable reference with another reference, where the variable that was originally referenced was correct, does not result in an incorrect program if the two variables always have the same value at the given location in the code. A mutant is *killed* by a test case that causes the mutant program to produce "altered" output. That is, if the mutant doesn't behave like the original under some input, it is killed. A test case that kills a mutant is considered to be effective at finding faults in the program, and the mutant(s) it kills are not executed against later test cases. Over time, inputs are added to the final test set if they kill a mutant. *Equivalent mutants* are mutant programs that are functionally equivalent to the original program and therefore cannot be killed by any test case. Determination of equivalent mutants is usually done by hand since it is a hard problem. The goal of mutation is to find test cases that kill all nonequivalent mutants. Any test set that does so is said to be adequate relative to mutation.

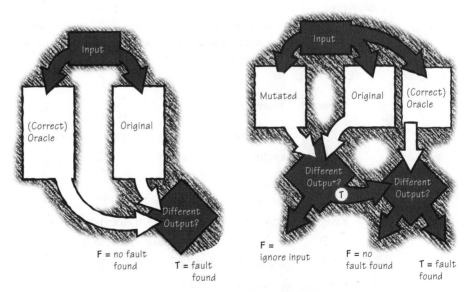

Figure 4.1 *Basic testing process.*   **Figure 4.2** *Mutation testing process.*

Out of this process comes a mutation score for a given test set. The mutation score is the ratio of the number of dead mutants to the number of nonequivalent mutants. This score measures the adequacy of the test case set. Recall that there are divergent ideas about what it means to kill a mutant and just what "altered" output is. These differences result in two subbranches of mutation testing called weak and firm mutation testing.

Mothra [DeMillo 1988] was one of the first important mutation testing systems. It is a public-domain program that can be found on the Net. Mothra operates on Fortran-77 source units. It automates the process of mutation testing by creating and executing mutants, managing test cases, and computing the mutation score. Mutation operators are represented as a set of rules that describe syntactic changes to elements of the program. Mothra can be obtained via anonymous ftp at isse.gmu.edu and is found in the file /pub/mutate/Mothra.tar.Z. Alternatively, Mothra can be found on this book's CD-ROM.

The complete set of mutation operators used by the Mothra mutation system is shown in the following table [King 1977]. These were derived from studies of programmer errors and correspond to mistakes that programmers typically make. These mutants thus enforce common testing heuristics, such as execute every statement. This set of mutation operators represents more than ten years of refinement through several mutation systems. The operators in the Mothra mutation set not only require that the test data meet statement and branch coverage criteria, extreme values criteria, and domain perturbation, but they also directly model many types of errors. Each of the 22 mutation operators is represented by the three-letter acronym shown on the left. The "array reference for array reference replacement" (AAR) mutation operator, for example, causes each array reference in a program to be replaced by each other distinct array reference in the program. These are powerful operators. Nevertheless, Jeff Offutt, Mothra's creator, and his colleagues have speculated that there are further modifications that could greatly improve this set, for example, "*selective mutation*" [Offutt 1996].

Type	Description
AAR	array reference for array reference replacement
ABS	absolute value insertion
ACR	array reference for constant replacement
AOR	arithmetic operator replacement
ASR	array reference for scalar variable replacement
CAR	constant for array reference replacement
CNR	comparable array name replacement
CRP	constant replacement

CSR   constant for scalar variable replacement

DER   DO statement end replacement

DSA   DATA statement alterations

GLR   GOTO label replacement

LCR   logical connector replacement

ROR   relational operator replacement

RSR   RETURN statement replacement

SAN   statement analysis (replacement by TRAP)

SAR   scalar variable for array reference replacement

SCR   scalar for constant replacement

SDL   statement deletion

SRC   source constant replacement

SVR   scalar variable replacement

UOI   unary operator insertion

Although mutation is a good unit testing technique, existing automated technologies for implementing it tend to be too slow for practical situations. Mothra is a research system that was built merely to demonstrate the concept of mutation analysis and to provide a laboratory for basic research on mutation [DeMillo 1988]. But in many ways, Mothra represents the state of the art.

Mothra uses a code interpreter to work, which partially explains its slowness. It operates as follows:

1. Mothra parses a test program into an intermediate form.

2. Mothra applies the 22 mutation operators to create program mutants.

3. A set of test cases is supplied to the system.

4. Each test case is interpreted on the original program under test and the outputs are saved.

5. Each test case is next interpreted on every live mutant program. If the output of a mutant differs from the original, then that mutant has been shown to be incorrect and is eliminated (killed). The tester is provided with a mutation score that indicates the percentage of mutants that are killed.

6. Any test case that did not kill at least one mutant is deleted.

7. The tester examines the output of the remaining test cases on the original program. If an output is incorrect, testing stops until the program is corrected.

8. The tester examines each remaining live mutant, and does either of the following:

   a. creates a test case to kill it

   b. decides that the mutant is equivalent to the original program and can be eliminated

9. Steps 3 through 8 are repeated until all mutants are either dead or declared equivalent, the tester is satisfied with the mutation score, or testing resources are exhausted and killing additional mutants is too expensive.

The mutation operators are designed to ensure a high level of fault detection by the test cases. The tester is guided toward high-quality test cases by the mutants, each of which remains alive and under consideration until a test case is submitted that detects the fault(s) represented by the mutant. Although mutation testing is usually performed using all mutation operators, a tester can select a less stringent testing criterion by using a subset of the operators. If, for example, an organization requires extended branch coverage, the tester can satisfy that criterion by using the appropriate mutation operator subset.

There are two cost-intensive manual steps involved in this approach to mutation: step 7, where the tester examines the outputs of the test program; and step 8, where the tester must determine whether each mutant is equivalent or killable. Step 5 incurs the most computational cost, where thousands of slightly differing versions of the program must be executed dozens of times.

To make this concrete, consider using this approach to test a 30-line function with 1000 mutants. This job requires hours of execution time on a high-end UNIX workstation, and several more hours of human time, mostly spent determining equivalent mutants. Given the complexity and size of today's software, where 30-line programs are in short supply, it is clear that unless these numbers can be improved by several orders of magnitude, mutation testing will never be adopted in practice.

Another publicly available weak mutation testing tool called the Generic Coverage Tool (GCT) has been written by Brian Marick. The GCT works on program units coded in C. Unlike Mothra, GCT performs only weak mutation testing. This freeware UNIX tool is unsupported. You can ftp a free copy of GCT by following the directions found in the file: ftp://cs.uiuc.edu/pub/testing/GCT.README.

At one time, Reliable Software Technologies (http://www.rstcorp.com) made available a commercial mutation testing tool called the PiSCES Mutation Testing Tool. But due to poor demand in the marketplace in applying mutation testing, the company has since discontinued offering it for sale. The tool contained both a strong mutation testing capability and a weak mutation testing capability for C programs and modules. This tool used a schema-based approach to compiling and executing mutants. PiSCES supported only a subset of the mutation operators that were shown in the Mothra operator table. Although this dilutes the theoretical power of the tool, it made the tool applicable to much larger systems. The tool reduced the complexity and computational demand of mutation testing by avoiding the creation of mutants that are extremely easy to kill. We talk more about the idea of trivial kill in subsequent sections. The tool was based on the C mutant operators recommended in [Agrawal 1989]. Two drawbacks of the tool were: (1) no mutant equivalence detection whatsoever, and (2) no help in generating static constraints that can be evaluated to find inputs to kill mutants.

4.6 Ada83 Mutation

Earlier, we defined the different mutation criteria (weak, firm, and strong) and basic terminology for talking about the complexity of one mutant versus another. Now, we walk the reader through a listing of Ada83 mutant operators developed by Reliable Software Technologies and Dr. A. Jefferson Offutt of George Mason University. These mutation criteria date to 1993, ancient history in the fast-paced world of computer science. To date, no tool has been built that implements the operators defined in the research described in subsequent paragraphs.

We include this information to give you a realistic sense of how to develop more complex mutants or even mutants for new languages such as Java. Each language introduces its own peculiarities and complexities. The exercise of moving mutation from Fortran-77 [King 1977] and C to Ada83 helps shed light on these complexities.

To develop a theoretical basis for Ada mutation, it was necessary that these key issues be addressed:

1. How to test programs that use strong typing and information-hiding mechanisms

2. How to test memory mechanisms such as dynamic data structures and static, long-lived data storage structures

3. How to test complex control mechanisms such as exception handling and tasking

4. How the use of concurrent processing affects the applicability and feasibility of mutation testing

Although mutation testing has been applied to several diverse languages, the Ada programming language presented many new features, both syntactic and semantic. In both GCT and Mothra, these issues were absent. Developing plausible mutants for Ada83 required taking these issues on. However, most of the mutation operators for other languages turn out to be meaningful for Ada, with appropriate changes in the names. We'll stick to the new features since they provide interesting insights into mutation. Another issue that came up was the difference that weak and strong mutation makes. This choice has a strong effect on certain mutation operators. There are certain mutant operators that will almost always cause the *weak* condition (i.e., the infection condition) to occur, but not necessarily the *strong* condition (i.e., propagation to the output space).

4.6.1 *Syntactically Incorrect Mutants*

A *stillborn* mutant is a mutant that is syntactically illegal. The number of possible stillborn mutants depends on the strength of the type checking. A *trivial* mutant is a mutant that is killed by almost any test case. Any practical Ada mutation system will need to avoid generating stillborn mutants as often as is possible, and a well-designed set of operators will avoid most trivial mutants. Although avoiding stillborn mutants requires more care on the part of the developer and more analysis on the part of the mutation system, it results in fewer Ada mutants and thus in turn reduces the cost of mutation testing.

For a program P, mutation testing produces a set of alternate programs. Each alternate program, P_i, known as a mutant of P, is formed by modifying a single statement of P according to some predefined modification rule. These modification rules are called *mutation operators*. The syntactic change itself is called the mutation, and the resulting program is the mutant program, often simply referred to as the mutant. The original program plus the mutant programs are collectively known as the program neighborhood, N, of P [Budd 1982].

This section defines one set of mutation operators for the Ada83 programming language. Many different sets could have been generated depending on the complexity of the set desired. The set we include here is just one possible set that serves as a real-world example. It is by no means the only possible set of operators! These operators cover the complete Ada83 language as defined in the Ada83 Reference Manual [DoD 1983]. This is distinct from an earlier published report on Ada83 operators defined by Bowser; which did not cover the entire language [Bowser 1988]. Additionally, the operators defined by Bowser were designed with limited Ada83. As a result, the operators we cover are significantly more extensive than the earlier set.

We organize our mutants differently than others have done in the past. In particular, the operators are separated primarily on the basis of what type of lexical elements are modified.

This approach gives us five types of operators. Mutation operators within these groups have reasonably uniform semantics and rules for applications. Also, the number of mutants produced are on the same order of magnitude for each of the operators within our types. That is important for use in estimating potential costs of mutation. We include the coverage operator specifically for those interested in branch coverage testing strategies. It may seem odd to use an advanced fault-based, fault-injection approach for a testing criterion as simple as coverage, but it is important to realize that this can be done.

The five types of mutation operators for Ada83 are:

1. Operand replacement operators (30 operators)
2. Statement operators (14 operators)
3. Expression operators (14 operators)
4. Coverage operators (4 operators)
5. Tasking operators (3 operators)

A total of 65 operators is defined in the following subsections. Following that, we present all 65 Ada operators in one comprehensive table, shown with the correlated Fortran and C operators, if any exist.

4.6.2 Operand Replacement Operators

Each operand replacement operator starts with the letter O. There are 30 operand replacement operators. These operators cause each operand to be replaced by each other syntactically legal operand. There are five kinds of operands in Ada83:

1. Variables
2. Constants
3. Array references
4. Record references
5. Pointer references

Although in Ada83 there is no real difference between record and pointer references, separate operators are defined so as to have uniform definitions. Replacing these five kinds of operands results in 25 operators. The 25 simple replacement operators are all uniform and merely replace one type with another. There are four additional operators for three structured types (OAN, ORF, ORN, OPN) and one additional operator for variable initialization (OVI):

1. **OVI:** Variable initialization elimination.

    Definition: Eliminate the initialization part of each variable initialization.

2. **OAN:** Array name replaced by an array name.

   Definition: Replace just the array name in an array reference by other array names when the base types are the same, and the index types are the same.

3. **ORF:** Record field replaced by a record field.

   Definition: Replace a record field reference by another field name of the same record when the second field is of the same type.

4. **ORN:** Record name replaced by a record name.

   Definition: Replace just the record name in a record reference by other record names when the field names and types are the same.

5. **OPN:** Pointer name replaced by a pointer name.

   Definition: Replace just the pointer name in a pointer reference by other pointer names when the field names and types are the same.

The 30 operand replacement operators are:

Operand Replacement Operators

OVV	Variable replaced by a variable
OVC	Variable replaced by a constant
OVA	Variable replaced by an array reference
OVR	Variable replaced by a record reference
OVP	Variable replaced by a pointer reference
OVI	Variable initialization elimination
OCV	Constant replaced by a variable
OCC	Constant replaced by a constant
OCA	Constant replaced by an array reference
OCR	Constant replaced by a record reference
OCP	Constant replaced by a pointer reference
OAV	Array reference replaced by a variable
OAC	Array reference replaced by a constant
OAA	Array reference replaced by an array reference
OAR	Array reference replaced by a record reference
OAP	Array reference replaced by a pointer reference
OAN	Array name replaced by an array name

ORV	Record reference replaced by a variable
ORC	Record reference replaced by a constant
ORA	Record reference replaced by an array reference
ORR	Record reference replaced by a record reference
ORP	Record reference replaced by a pointer reference
ORF	Record field replaced by a record field
ORN	Record name replaced by a record name
OPV	Pointer reference replaced by a variable
OPC	Pointer reference replaced by a constant
OPA	Pointer reference replaced by an array reference
OPR	Pointer reference replaced by a record reference
OPP	Pointer reference replaced by a pointer reference
OPN	Pointer name replaced by a pointer name

Several notes are warranted here:

1. The strong typing rules of Ada83 drastically reduce the number of mutants of this type that are generated as opposed to Fortran-77 and C.
2. It is reasonable to mutate initializations (only OCC).
3. It is reasonable to mutate references of enumerated types.
4. Do not mutate types.
5. Do not mutate declarations.
6. Do not mutate CASE constants.
7. Do not mutate loop parameters on FOR statements (it is a declaration).
8. Variables that are of a type that is declared externally and private are considered to be scalar.
9. The following named objects are considered to be CONSTANT and are mutated using OVC, OC★, ORC, OAC, and OPC:

   a. Objects declared with the keyword CONSTANT
   b. Loop parameters
   c. Parameters of class IN

4.6.3 Statement Modification Operators

Each statement modification operator starts with the letter S. There are 13 statement modification operators. These operators modify entire statements and modify the control structures of Ada83. The relevant control structures are:

1. BLOCK
2. CASE
3. EXIT
4. FOR
5. GOTO
6. IF
7. LOOP
8. RAISE
9. RETURN
10. WHILE

We summarize the operators in the following table, and then discuss each operator in greater detail.

Statement Modification Operators

SEE	Exception on execution
SRN	Replace with NULL
SRR	Return statement replacement
SGL	GOTO label replacement
SRE	Replace with EXIT
SWR	Replace WHILE with repeat-until
SRW	Replace repeat-until with WHILE
SZI	Zero iteration loop
SOI	One iteration loop
SNI	N iteration loop
SRI	Reverse iteration loop
SES	END shift
SCA	CASE alternative replacement
SER	RAISE exception handler replacement

1. **SEE:** Exception on execution.

   Definition: Replace the first statement in each basic block with:

   ```
   RAISE mut_trap;
   ```

   mut_trap is a mutation-defined exception. The mutant number needs to be given to the handler, which can be in the local procedure or the main program. It is recommended that the mutant call a subroutine:

```
Except_on_Exec (42);
```

which then raises the exception.

Do not replace if elimination of the statement would result in a compile-time error, for example, if the statement is the only RETURN in a function. SEE should be applied to statements and block statements. For example, applying the SEE mutant operator to the following structure will result in four mutants:

```
WHILE (e1) LOOP
        IF (e2) THEN
          s1;
        ELSE
          s2;
        END IF;
        END LOOP;
```

Mutant 1: Except_on_Exec (n);

```
Mutant 2: WHILE (e1) LOOP
            Except_on_Exec (n);
          END LOOP;
```

```
Mutant 3: WHILE (e1) LOOP
            IF (e2) THEN
              Except_on_Exec (n);
            ELSE
              s2;
            END IF;
          END LOOP;
```

```
Mutant 4: WHILE (e1) LOOP
            IF (e2) THEN
              s1;
            ELSE
             Except_on_Exec (n);
            END IF;
          END LOOP;
```

2. **SRN:** Replace with NULL.

    Definition: Replace each statement with the statement NULL.

The replacement should be done according to the rules of the SEE mutation operator, except that the replacement should be done on each statement, not each basic block. Do not replace if elimination of the statement would result in a compile-time error, for example, if the statement is the only RETURN in a function.

3. **SRR:** Return statement replacement.

   Definition: Replace each statement in a FUNCTION or PROCEDURE with RETURN.

   For parameterized RETURN statements (in functions), replace each statement with every RETURN that appears in the function. Do not replace RETURN statements. Do not replace if elimination of the statement would result in a compile-time error.

4. **SGL:** GOTO label replacement.

   Definition: Replace each GOTO label with all other visible, legal labels.

   The innermost sequence of statements that encloses the target statement must also enclose the GOTO statement (note that the GOTO statement can be a statement of an inner sequence). Furthermore, if a GOTO statement is enclosed by an ACCEPT statement or the body of a program unit, then the target statement must not be outside this enclosing construct; conversely, it follows from the previous rule that if the target statement is enclosed by such a construct, then the GOTO statement cannot be outside.

5. **SRE:** Replace with EXIT.

   Definition: This operator replaces statements within loops with EXIT statements. There are three variations:

   a. Replace each statement in a loop with EXIT;
   b. Replace each statement in a loop with an EXIT name; for each named enclosing loop.
   c. Replace each statement in a loop with each EXIT WHEN . . . ; that appears in the loop.

   If there is only one statement in the loop, this change would be equivalent to SRN, so do not generate.

6. **SWR:** Replace WHILE with repeat-until.

   Definition: Although there is no explicit repeat-until statement in Ada, the construct is commonly built using a LOOP and an EXIT.

Using the incorrect kind of loop is a common programming mistake. The format of the change is:

```
ORIGINAL              MUTANT

WHILE (e) LOOP        LOOP
     .           .
     :           :
END LOOP;             EXIT WHEN NOT e;
                      END LOOP;
```

7. **SRW:** Replace repeat-until with WHILE.

   Definition: This is the opposite of SWR. The format of the change will be:

```
ORIGINAL              MUTANT

LOOP                  WHILE (NOT e) LOOP
     .           .
     :           :
EXIT WHEN e;          END LOOP;
END LOOP;
```

Rather than applying this operation only to loops where the EXIT WHEN statement is the last statement in the loop body, it is applied to all EXITs in the loop.

8. Definite loop mutations.

   We have four goals for mutating definite loops (FOR).

   a. Bypass the loop entirely (zero iterations).
   b. Cause the loop to iterate once (one iteration).
   c. Cause the loop to be iterated more than once (N iterations).
   d. Cause the loop to be executed in reverse (reverse iteration).

   The first three goals are satisfied by introducing a new loop counter for each loop. For a loop i, associate the counter *loop_i_count*. *loop_i_count* is initialized to zero before the loop begins. It is incremented by one each iteration through the loop.

   a. **SZI:** Zero iterations

      Definition: After the loop, if *loop_i_count* $= 0$, then RAISE Mut_Trap;

b. **SOI:** One iteration

> **Definition:** After the loop, if *loop_i_count* = 1, then RAISE Mut_Trap;

c. **SNI:** N iterations

> **Definition:** After the loop, if *loop_i_count* > 1, then RAISE Mut_Trap;

d. **SRI:** reverse iteration

> **Definition:** Add the keyword REVERSE to the loop if it is not there, remove it if it is.

9. **SES:** END shift.

> **Definition:** Move each END statement up and down one statement. This applies to END statements occurring in BLOCK and LOOP statements, but not CASE statements and subprograms.

10. **SCA:** CASE alternative replacement.

> **Definition:** First, each case statement alternative with multiple choices is separated into alternatives where each alternative contains only one choice. A range (e.g., 5 . . . 20) is considered to be only one choice. Next, substitute each statement sequence with each other sequence in the CASE statement. Do not mutate choices.

```
Example:
CASE Var1 is
      WHEN A | B => statements_1;
      WHEN C  => statements_2;
      WHEN OTHERS => statements_3;
END CASE;


This case statement creates 8 mutants:

CASE Var1 is
      WHEN A  => statements_2;
      WHEN B  => statements_1;
      WHEN C  => statements_2;
      WHEN OTHERS => statements_3;
END CASE;
```

```
CASE Var1 is
      WHEN A   => statements_3;
      WHEN B   => statements_1;
      WHEN C   => statements_2;
      WHEN OTHERS => statements_3;
END CASE;

CASE Var1 is
      WHEN A   => statements_1;
      WHEN B   => statements_2;
      WHEN C   => statements_2;
      WHEN OTHERS => statements_3;
END CASE;

CASE Var1 is
      WHEN A   => statements_1;
      WHEN B   => statements_3;
      WHEN C   => statements_2;
      WHEN OTHERS => statements_3;
END CASE;

CASE Var1 is
      WHEN A   => statements_1;
      WHEN B   => statements_1;
      WHEN C   => statements_1;
      WHEN OTHERS => statements_3;
END CASE;

CASE Var1 is
      WHEN A   => statements_1;
      WHEN B   => statements_1;
      WHEN C   => statements_3;
      WHEN OTHERS => statements_3;
END CASE;

CASE Var1 is
      WHEN A   => statements_1;
      WHEN B   => statements_1;
      WHEN C   => statements_2;
      WHEN OTHERS => statements_1;
END CASE;

CASE Var1 is
      WHEN A   => statements_1;
      WHEN B   => statements_1;
      WHEN C   => statements_2;
      WHEN OTHERS => statements_2;
END CASE;
```

11. **SER:** RAISE exception handler replacement.

   Definition: For each explicit RAISE statement, replace the name of the exception by other exceptions. Replace programmer-defined exceptions only by other programmer-defined exceptions, and built-in exceptions by other built-in exceptions.

4.6.4 Expression Modification Operators

Each expression modification operator starts with the letter E. There are 14 expression modification operators. These operators modify expression operators and entire expressions. The operators are summarized in a table, and then discussed in detail.

Expression Modification Operators

EAI	Absolute value insertion
ENI	Neg-absolute value insertion
EEZ	Exception on zero
EOR	Arithmetic operator replacement
ERR	Relational operator replacement
EMR	Membership test replacement
ELR	Logical operator replacement
EUI	Unary operator insertion
EUR	Unary operator replacement
ESR	Subprogram operator replacement
EDT	Domain twiddle
EAR	Attribute replacement
EEO	Exception on overflow
EEU	Exception on underflow

1. **EAI:** Absolute value insertion.

    Definition: Insert the unary operator ABS in front of every arithmetic expression and subexpression. Do not mutate if the expression can be statically determined to be greater than or equal to zero. For example, this can be determined for the following cases:

    a. Constants

    b. The type is a nonnegative subtype of Integer (for example, Natural or Positive)

    c. Loop variable where the lower bound is greater than or equal to zero.

    Do not mutate if the change will make a discrete range in a FOR statement have a NULL range (this would be equivalent to an SZI mutant). Also, do not mutate CONSTANTS (this would be equivalent to a EUI mutant).

2. **ENI:** Neg–absolute value insertion.

   Definition: Insert −ABS in front of every arithmetic expression and subexpression. Do not mutate if the expression can be statically determined to be less than or equal to zero. For example, this can be determined for the following cases:

   a. Constants
   b. The type is a negative subtype of Integer

   Do not mutate if the change will make a discrete range in a FOR statement have a NULL range (this would be equivalent to an SZI mutant). Also, do not mutate CONSTANTS (this would be equivalent to a EUI mutant).

3. **EEZ:** Exception on zero.

   Definition: Insert the subprogram Except_on_Zero in front of every arithmetic expression and subexpression. Except_on_Zero(E); raises EEZ_Exception if E is 0, else it returns E. Do not mutate if the expression can be statically determined to be not equal to 0. For example, this can be determined for the following cases:

   a. Constants
   b. The type is a subtype of Integer that does not include 0 (for example, Positive)
   c. Loop variable where the range does not include 0

4. **EOR:** Arithmetic operator replacement.

   Definition: Replace each binary arithmetic operator (+, −, *, /, MOD, REM, **) with each other binary arithmetic operator that is syntactically legal. Note that:

   a. MOD and REM are only defined for Integer types
   b. ** requires the right operand to be Integer
   c. * allows Fixed Point and Integer to be mixed
   d. / allows Fixed Point on the left and Integer on the right

5. **ERR:** Relational operator replacement.

   Definition: Replace each relational operator with each other relational operator that is syntactically legal.

   $<$, $>$, $\geq$, $\leq$ are defined for only scalar and discrete array types.

6. **EMR:** Membership test replacement.

    Definition: Replace each IN with NOT IN and each NOT IN with IN. Note that this operator is subsumed by the CDE operator and should not be used if CDE is being employed.

7. **ELR:** Logical operator replacement.

    Definition: Replace each logical operator (AND, OR, XOR, AND THEN, OR ELSE) with each other logical operator. AND, OR, and XOR are defined for Boolean expressions and one-dimensional arrays of type Boolean.

8. **EUI:** Unary operator insertion.

    Definition: Insert the unary operator − in front of each arithmetic expression and subexpression. Note that the unary operator + is the identity operation.

9. **EUR:** Unary operator replacement.

    Definition: Replace each unary operator (+, −, ABS) with each other unary operator. Expressions should be fully parenthesized, since ABS has higher precedence than + and −.

10. **ESR:** Subprogram operator replacement.

    Definition: Replace each function and subroutine name with each other function or subroutine name that has the same syntactic signature and comes from the same package. Also replace with = and /= if the signature is appropriate (= and /= are implicitly defined for all types). Do not consider the parameter class in the signature comparison.

```
Example:
Package Matrix Specification:


    Matrix_Type ...
    "+" (M1, M2: Matrix_Type) RETURN Matrix_Type;
    "*" (M1, M2: Matrix_Type) RETURN Matrix_Type;
    "<" (M1, M2: Matrix_Type) RETURN Boolean;


Matrix Use:


    A, B, C : Matrix_Type;
      .
      :
```

```
C := A + B;  ==> mutation ==> C := A * B;
.
:
IF (A < B) ...  ==> mutation ==> IF (A = B) ...
            ==> mutation ==> IF (A /= B) ...
```

11. **EDT:** Domain twiddle.

   Definition: Each innermost expression (operand: constant, variable, array reference, record reference, pointer reference) is twiddled, that is, modified by a small amount. For each operand, the modification produces two mutants, one where the modification is in a positive direction, the other in a negative direction. This amount depends on the type:

Type	Modification
Integer	+1 and −1
Float	*1.05 and *.95
Fixed Point	+Delta and −Delta
Character Types	T'SUCC and T'PRED
Enumerated Types	T'SUCC and T'PRED

   The twiddle must not create a value out of the range for that type. For example, if X is of type Natural and has the value 0, the mutant −1 is not generated.

Other important considerations about the EDT mutant operator are:

- Do not twiddle array subscripts—most changes would cause an out-of-bounds failure.
- Do not mutate if the change would result in mutant that is equivalent to another twiddle on the same expression (for example, (X+Y) ==> ((X−1)+Y) and ((X+1)+Y), but not (X+(Y−1)) and (X+(Y+1))).
- Do not mutate loop parameters if the change would result in a NULL range (this would be equivalent to an OCC mutant).

12. **EAR:** Attribute replacement.

   Definition: Each attribute is replaced by each other syntactically legal attribute. Attributes are defined in Appendix A of the Ada Reference Manual.

13. **EEO:** Exception on overflow.

    Definition: Insert the subprogram Except_on_OverFlow in front of every arithmetic expression. Except_on_OverFlow(E) raises EEO_Exception if the expression results in an overflow, else it returns the value of the expression. Do not mutate if the expression can be statically determined to not overflow. For example, this can be determined for the following cases:

    - Constants
    - Loop variable

    It might be possible to allow the Ada run-time system to detect overflow problems, and define a handler for the overflow. The Ada reference manual, section 4.5.7, paragraph 7, says:

    > *If the result overflows, NUMERIC_ERROR should be raised, but will not necessarily be raised. That is, it is not strictly required.*

    The Ada reference manual, section 13.7.3, says:

    > *If an overflow occurs, and there is no NUMERIC_ERROR, T'MACHINE_OVERFLOWS is FALSE, else TRUE.*

    But this does not make sense for two reasons:

    - The value for T'MACHINE_OVERFLOWS seems to be backwards.
    - NUMERIC_ERROR is not required because detecting overflow is hard in some situations. But setting this attribute requires overflow to be detected.

14. **EEU:** Exception on underflow.

    Definition: Insert the subprogram Except_on_UnderFlow in front of every arithmetic expression. Except_on_UnderFlow(E) raises EEU_Exception if the expression results in an underflow, else it returns the value of the expression. Do not mutate if the expression can be statically determined to not underflow. For example, this can be determined for the following cases:

    - Constants
    - Loop variable

4.6.5 *Coverage Operators*

The previous operators do not cover the branch coverage criteria [Myers 1979] as do the Mothra operators. Separate operators must be defined expressly for this purpose. This is so the tester can explicitly choose to cover one or more of the branch coverage criteria, without having to use other operators.

The coverage criteria considered are based on the following definitions:

Definition: A *Condition* in a program is a pair of algebraic expressions related by one of the relational operators $\{>, <, =, \geq, \leq, \neq\}$.

Conditions evaluate to one of the binary values TRUE or FALSE and can be modified by the negation operator NOT.

Definition: A *Decision* is a list of one or more conditions connected by the two logical operators AND and OR and used in a statement that affects the flow of control of the program. Decisions represent branches in the control flow of the program.

Statement Coverage (SC) requires that every statement in the program be executed at least once. Decision Coverage (DC) requires that every decision evaluate to both TRUE and FALSE at least once. DC is also known as branch testing and all-edges [White 1987]. Condition Coverage (CC) requires that each condition in each decision evaluate to both TRUE and FALSE at least once. Decision / Condition Coverage (DCC) requires that each condition in each decision evaluate to both TRUE and FALSE at least once, and that every decision evaluate to both TRUE and FALSE at least once. DCC combines DC and CC. Modified Condition / Decision Coverage (MC/DC) requires that every decision and every condition within the decision has taken every outcome at least once, and every condition has been shown to independently affect its decision. Multiple-Condition Coverage (MCC) requires that all possible combinations of condition outcomes in each decision be covered, that is, the entire truth table for the decision has been satisfied. MCC is also known as extended branch coverage [White 1987].

Four Ada operators cover these coverage criteria. Each coverage operator starts with the letter C. The four coverage operators are summarized in a table, and then discussed in detail. The SEE operator satisfies statement coverage, so it is not included in the coverage operators set.

Coverage Operators

CDE   Decision coverage

CCO   Condition coverage

CDC   Decision/condition coverage

CMC   Multiple-condition coverage

1. **CDE:** Decision coverage.

   Definition: Each decision must evaluate to both TRUE and FALSE. Replace each decision by TRUE and FALSE.

2. **CCO:** Condition coverage.

   Definition: Each condition must evaluate to both TRUE and FALSE. Replace each condition by TRUE and FALSE. Note that there will be some redundancy; this can be reduced by having the mutation system suppress certain mutants.

3. **CDC:** Decision/condition coverage.

   Definition: Decision/condition coverage combines decision and condition. The CDC operator simply turns on CCO and CDE. We define it separately as a convenience.

4. **CMC:** Multiple-condition coverage.

   Definition: All combinations of conditions must be exercised separately, which yields, for a decision with n conditions, 2^n combinations. Another way of stating the MCC requirement is that the entire truth table for the decision must be covered.

4.6.6 Tasking Operators

Three Ada operators specifically cover tasking. Each coverage operator starts with the letter T. The tasking operators are summarized in a table, and then discussed in detail.

Tasking Operators

TEM   ENTRY statement modification

TAR   ACCEPT statement replacement

TSA   SELECT alternative replacement

1. **TEM:** ENTRY statement modification.

   Definition: Each ENTRY call is modified just as procedure calls are modified by the ESR operator. Replace each ENTRY call name with each other ENTRY name that has the same syntactic signature and comes from the same task.

   Also replace conditional and timed entry calls by simple entries.

2. **TAR:** ACCEPT statement replacement.

   Definition: Replace entry names by other visible entries of the same time.

3. **TSA:** SELECT alternative replacement.

   Definition: Each SELECT alternative is modified just as the CASE statement is modified by the SCA operator. First, each SELECT statement alternative with multiple choices is separated into alternatives where each alternative contains only one choice. Next, substitute each statement sequence with each other sequence in the SELECT statement.

4.6.7 Comparison of Ada, C, and Fortran-77 Operators

This section contains a table that relates our Ada83 mutation operators with the previous operators for Ada [Bowser 1988], the C [Agrawal 1989], and Fortran-77 operators [King 1977]. In our comparison tables, the character ~ means that there is no corresponding operator.

Operand Replacement Operators

Ada83	Description	C	Fortran-77
OVV	Variable replaced by a variable	Vsrr	svr
OVC	Variable replaced by a constant	Vsrr	csr
OVA	Variable replaced by an array reference	Vsrr	asr
OVR	Variable replaced by a record reference	Vsrr	~
OVP	Variable replaced by a pointer reference	Vsrr	~
OVI	Variable initialization elimination	~	~
OCV	Constant replaced by a variable	Ccsr	scr
OCC	Constant replaced by a constant	Cccr	src
OCA	Constant replaced by an array reference	~	acr
OCR	Constant replaced by a record reference	~	~
OCP	Constant replaced by a pointer reference	~	~
OAV	Array reference replaced by a variable	Varr	sar
OAC	Array reference replaced by a constant	Varr	car
OAA	Array reference replaced by an array reference	Varr	aar

OAR	Array reference replaced by a record reference	Varr	~
OAP	Array reference replaced by a pointer reference	Varr	~
OAN	Array name replaced by an array name	Varr	cnr
ORV	Record reference replaced by a variable	Vtrr	~
ORC	Record reference replaced by a constant	Vtrr	~
ORA	Record reference replaced by an array reference	Vtrr	~
ORR	Record reference replaced by a record reference	Vtrr	~
ORP	Record reference replaced by a pointer reference	Vtrr	~
ORF	Record field replaced by a record field	VSCR	~
ORN	Record name replaced by a record name	~	~
OPV	Pointer reference replaced by a variable	Vprr	~
OPC	Pointer reference replaced by a constant	Vprr	~
OPA	Pointer reference replaced by an array reference	Vprr	~
OPR	Pointer reference replaced by a record reference	Vprr	~
OPP	Pointer reference replaced by a pointer reference	Vprr	~

Statement Modification Operators

Ada83	Description	C	Fortran-77
SEE	Exception on execution	STRP	SAN
SRN	Replace with NULL	SSDL	SDL
SRR	Return statement replacement	SRSR	RSR
SGL	GOTO label replacement	SGLR	GLR
SRE	Replace with EXIT	SBR	~
SWR	Replace WHILE with repeat-until	SWDD	~
SRW	Replace repeat-until with WHILE	SDWD	~
SZI	Zero iteration loop	~	der
SOI	One iteration loop	~	~
SNI	N iteration loop	SMTT	~
SRI	Reverse iteration loop	~	~
SES	END shift	SMVB	~
SCA	CASE alternative replacement	SSWM	~
SER	RAISE exception handler replacement	~	~

Expression Modification Operators

Ada83	Description	C	Fortran-77
EAI	Absolute value insertion	VDTR	ABS
ENI	Neg–Absolute value insertion	VDTR	ABS
EEZ	Exception on zero	VDTR	ABS
EOR	Arithmetic operator replacement	ORAN	AOR
ERR	Relational operator replacement	ORRN	ROR
EMR	Membership test replacement	~	~
ELR	Logical operator replacement	OBBN	LCR
EUI	Unary operator insertion	Uuor	UOI
EUR	Unary operator replacement	Uuor	~
ESR	Subprogram operator replacement	~	~
EDT	Domain twiddle	VTWD	crp
EAR	Attribute replacement	~	~
EEO	Exception on overflow	~	~
EEU	Exception on underflow	~	~

Coverage Operators

Ada83	Description	C	Fortran-77
CDE	Decision coverage	Oior	lcr
CCO	Condition coverage	~	ror
CDC	Decision/Condition coverage	~	lcr, ror
CMC	Multiple condition coverage	~	ror, lcr

Tasking Operators

Ada83	Description	C	Fortran-77
TEM	ENTRY statement modification	~	~
TAR	ACCEPT statement replacement	~	~
TSA	SELECT alternative replacement	~	~

An analysis of these tables shows that the number of new operators for Ada83 that were not in Fortran-77 is 37, and the number of new operators for Ada83 that were not already in C is 20. This is a result of the increased richness of the Ada83 language over earlier Algol-like languages that did not include advanced features such as tasking.

4.7 Selective Mutation

Mutation testing, even for a simple language like Fortran-77, can be quite expensive in terms of the number of mutation operators that must be applied. The six most populous of Mothra's 22 mutant operators account for 40 to 60 percent of all mutants created. Recent experimental research indicates that of the 22 mutation operators used by Mothra, 17 of them (including the six most populous) seem to be in some sense redundant; that is, test sets that are generated to kill only mutants generated from the other 5 mutant operators are very effective in killing mutants generated from the 17. *Selective mutation* is an approximation technique that selects only mutants that are truly distinct from other mutants. In experimental trials, selective mutation provides almost the same coverage as nonselective mutation, with significant reductions in cost.

Selective mutation is an idea originated by Jeff Offutt (George Mason University) among others. The basic idea stemmed from two observations: (1) mutation, in its current implementation in Mothra, was too inefficient in terms of performance, and (2) much of this inefficiency came about as a result of redundancy in the mutants used.

To better understand this redundancy, consider the following statement:

```
x := x + 1
```

Valid mutants using the CRP operator here might be:

```
x := x + 2    Mutant 1
x := x + 3    Mutant 2
x := x + 4    Mutant 3
```

and so forth. Note, however, that an input that kills Mutant 1 will kill the others. So why even make the others to begin with? Why not make one from this class, and possibly make another such as:

```
x := y + 1    Mutant 4
```

from the OVV class? The point here is that a set of test cases that can kill one mutant from (Mutant 1, Mutant 2, Mutant 3) and kill Mutant 4 is better than a set of test cases that can only kill the members of (Mutant 1, Mutant 2, Mutant

3). This thinking leads to the following reformulation of the 65 Ada83 mutant operators—and significant savings in terms of testing resources.

Results indicate that the mutation operators that replace all operands with all syntactically legal operands add very little to the effectiveness of mutation testing. Additionally, the mutation operators that modify entire statements add very little. The five selective operators for Fortran-77 are:

1. **ABS,** which forces each arithmetic expression to take on the value 0, a positive value, and a negative value
2. **AOR,** which replaces each arithmetic operator with every syntactically legal operator
3. **LCR,** which replaces each logical connector (AND and OR) with several kinds of logical connectors
4. **ROR,** which replaces relational operators with other relational operators
5. **UOI,** which inserts unary operators in front of expressions

We next list the mutation operators for Ada83 that should be included in the selective set. We will leave out all operand replacement operators and most of the statement operators. Most of the expression operators are included in the selective set. Because we have no experience to draw on with respect to the tasking mutation operators, they must remain as in the original list. Further experimentation is needed to verify whether these are really necessary.

Expression Modification Operators

EAI	Absolute value insertion
ENI	Neg-absolute value insertion
EEZ	Exception on zero
EOR	Arithmetic operator replacement
ERR	Relational operator replacement
EMR	Membership test replacement
ELR	Logical operator replacement
EUI	Unary operator insertion
EUR	Unary operator replacement
ESR	Subprogram operator replacement
EEO	Exception on overflow
EEU	Exception on underflow

Coverage Operator

CMC	Multiple condition coverage

Tasking Operators

TEM   ENTRY statement modification

TAR   ACCEPT statement replacement

TSA   SELECT alternative replacement

4.8 Summary

Chapter 4 has described software mutation testing, and has provided an overview of the types of decisions that must be made when developing a set of mutant operators for a new language. Mutation testing has never caught on in the commercial marketplace, namely because there has never been a commercial tool that was efficient enough to perform this computationally intensive analysis. The key to someday having access to a commercial mutation-testing tool for test-case generation lies in additional evidence being provided that software mutation does make reasonable approximations to the types of errors that real programmers make. Although that evidence has been publicized, it has still not calmed the fears of many that mutants just do not capture the essence of reality, and hence the test cases are no better than other less-expensive approaches to unit testing, such as structural testing.

Software mutation techniques were some of the earliest fault-injection techniques, and their purpose was to find test cases that could warn about code mutations. In this chapter, we looked at how mutation operators could be designed for the Ada83 language. Until a tool is built and these mutation operators are put into practice, we cannot know how plausible these operators are.

Because you can easily show that mutation subsumes coverage, no one argues against mutation testing being better than basic forms of structural testing. The problem for mutation testing is the nonexistence of commercial tools to perform it in addition to the semantic equivalence problem. Until these problems are adequately addressed, even though mutation is a key form of fault injection, as a tool for generating "better" test cases, its acceptance as a general "best" practice may never occur.

References

[Agrawal 1989] H. Agrawal, R. DeMillo, R. Hathaway, Wm. Hsu, Wynne Hsu, E. Krauser, R. J. Martin, A. Mathur, and E. Spafford. "Design of mutant operators for the C programming language." Technical report SERC-TR-41-P, Software Engineering Research Center, Purdue University, West Lafayette, IN, March 1989.

[Ammann 1994] P. E. Ammann, S. S. Brilliant, and J. C. Knight. "The Effect of Imperfect Error Detection on Reliability Assessment via Life Testing." *IEEE Transactions on Software Engineering*, 20(2):142–148, February 1994.

[Bertolino 1995] A. Bertolino and L. Strigini. "On the use of testability measures for dependability assessment." *IEEE Trans. on Software Engineering*, 22(2):97–108, August 1995.

[Bieman 1996] J. M. Bieman, D. Dreilinger, and L. Lin. "Using fault injection to increase software test coverage." *Proc. of the Int'l. Symposium on Software Reliability Engineering*, pp. 166–174, October 1996.

[Bilsel 1983] S. Bilsel. "A survey of software test and evaluation techniques." Technical report GIT-ICS-83/08, School of Information and Computer Science, Georgia Institute of Technology, Atlanta, GA, 1983.

[Bowser 1988] J. Bowser. *Reference Manual for ADA Mutant Operators.* Software Engineering Research Center, Georgia Institute of Technology, Technical Report Number GIT-SERC-88/02, February 1988.

[Budd 1982] T. A. Budd and D. Angluin. "Two notions of correctness and their relation to testing." *Acta Informatica,* 18(1):31–45, November 1982.

[Daran 1995] M. Daran and P. Thevenod-Fosse. "Software error analysis: a real case study involving real faults and mutations." *Proc. of the ACM SIGSOFT ISSTA '95,* pp. 158–171, 1995.

[DeMillo 1978] R. A. DeMillo, R. J. Lipton, and F. G. Sayward. "Hints on test data selection: Help for the practicing programmer." *IEEE Computer,* 11(4):34–41, April 1978.

[DeMillo 1988] R. A. DeMillo, D. S. Guindi, K. N. King, W. M. McCracken, and A. J. Offutt. "An extended overview of the Mothra software testing environment." *Proceedings of the Second Workshop on Software Testing, Verification, and Analysis,* pp. 142–151, Banff, Alberta, July 1988. IEEE Computer Society Press.

[DoD 1983] *Reference Manual for the Ada Programming Language.* ANSI/MIL-STD-1815A-1983. United States Department of Defense, 1983.

[Hamlet 1977] R. G. Hamlet. "Testing programs with the aid of a compiler." *IEEE Transactions on Software Engineering,* 3(4), July 1977.

[Howden 1982] W. E. Howden. "Weak Mutation Testing and Completeness of Test Sets." *Trans. on Software Engineering,* 8(4):371–379, July 1982.

[King 1991] K. N. King and A. J. Offutt. "A Fortran language system for mutation-based software testing." *Software—Practice and Experience,* 21(7):685–718, July 1991.

[Mills 1972] H. D. Mills. "On the statistical validation of computer programs." IBM Federal Systems Division, Gaithersburg, MD, Red. 72-6015, 1972.

[Myers 1979] G. Myers. *The Art of Software Testing.* Wiley Interscience, 1979.

[Offutt 1996] A. J. Offutt, A. Lee, G. Rothermel, R. Untch, and C. Zapf. "An Experimental Determination of Sufficient Mutation Operators." TOSEM, April 1996, 5(2):99–118.

[White 1987] L. J. White. "Software testing and verification." In Marshall C. Yovits, ed., *Advances in Computers,* pp. 335–390. Academic Press, Inc., 1987.

[Woodward 1980] M. R. Woodward, D. Hedley, and M. A. Hennell. "Experience with Path Analysis and testing of programs." *IEEE Trans. on Software Engineering,* 6(3):278–286, May 1980.

5 Software Testability
Ferreting Out Faults with Pie

5.1 Defining Testability

Software testability is a characteristic associated with a program that is based on the premise that different programs have different abilities to allow or disallow existing faults to be detected at test time. In addition to the ability of the code to reveal problems during test, the ability of the selected test cases to detect problems is also an integral part of the software's testability. If software could be made to "wear its faults on its sleeves" during testing then a majority of the problems associated with faulty software and overbudget V&V programs would disappear [Hamlet 1993]. Thus this chapter is devoted to understanding fault injection techniques that help overcome the difficulties associated with traditional testing as it is currently used for fault detection. We won't be concerned with testing for reliability per se, though in the final analysis the techniques we cover could be useful for ensuring that the true reliability of the software grows. What we will do is predict where faults are likely to hide via software fault injection. If we can provide techniques that tell where testing will turn out to be unsuccessful at fault detection, then we can plan appropriate countermeasures such as test-case modifications and other V&V techniques.

This chapter is devoted to a fault injection–based technique called *Sensitivity Analysis* that employs fault injection methods to predict where in the code test cases will be incapable of revealing errors. This activity provides another way of saying how good the test cases are. Interestingly enough, sensitivity analysis is closely related to mutation testing (chapter 4) in its approach and employs many of the same underlying ideas. The distinction between the two techniques lies in their different purposes and their different methods for anomaly creation and injection.

Software testability is a vague, abstract characteristic that is generally defined in one of two ways. The "process difficulty" definition considers a program's testability to be a measure reflecting the inverse of the amount of testing effort required. Such a measure obviously depends on what testing approach (meaning how the test cases are selected) is chosen. Under this definition, the more effort testing takes, the lower the testability, and vice versa. That means if it is very difficult to perform branch coverage testing on a given piece of code, possibly because many of the branches are difficult to exercise, then the code will have low testability.

In contrast, the second perspective on software testability aims to measure the "effectiveness" of software testing. By this definition, software's testability is a measure of the likelihood that existing faults will be made observable by a given testing scheme, Q. Note that if Q is the operational profile and testability is low, this implies that the software has high reliability. The way software behaves with respect to Q determines the software's testability, and there are no limits on the ways in which Q can be generated. That is, Q can be generated either according to a white-box or black-box approach. The only thing that matters is to what extent Q is likely to disclose existing faults. So as you can see, unlike concrete software measures such as lines-of-source code, a perspective on software testability such as this can be quite hard to visualize and hard to develop an intuition for, and thus software testability is quite an abstraction.

For purposes of completion, we also mention one variant of the effectiveness definition of testability that was recently proposed by Bertolino and Strigini [Bertolino 1995]. They include a measure of the goodness of the oracle in their definition for testability, which was deliberately left out by Voas in his definition [Voas 1992b]. This move turns testability into what we earlier called *detectability*. To do this, Bertolino and Strigini use "guessed at" Bayesian failure rates as parameters that are needed to quantify testability. The problem with Bayesian prior estimates is their spurious trustworthiness.

There is no correlation between the two definitions of testability: process difficulty versus effectiveness. That is because though it might be very difficult to perform the testing, which results in low testability by the first definition, the likelihood of faults being observed may well be very high, which results in high testability by the second definition. Or the converse might hold: It could be easy to perform the testing, but the likelihood of faults being observed might be low.

Of course, the standards community has weighed in on the testability definition problem. The IEEE Standard ANSI/IEEE Std. 610.12-1990 defines testability as:

> 1. *the degree to which a system or component facilitates the establishment of test criteria and the performance of tests to determine whether those criteria have been met, and*

> 2. *the degree to which a requirement is stated in terms that permit establishment of test criteria and performance of tests to determine whether those criteria have been met.*

The U.S. Department of Defense's standard 2167A defines the testability of requirements as:

10.3.2 Testability of requirements. A requirement is considered to be testable if an objective and feasible test can be designed to determine whether the requirement is met by the software.

Although 2167A does not talk about software in particular, it does talk about the testing process. From that standpoint, the 2176A standard is concerned with "process difficulty."

For better or worse, the word *testability* has seen a recent upsurge in usage. In combination with the current popularity of maturity models, it was only a matter of time before a testability maturity model was invented. Indeed, David Gelperin of Software Quality Engineering in Jacksonville, Florida, was the first to enter the fray with a testability maturity model. In his model, he defines testability as the ability to perform cost-effective testing. To measure this, he created the following scorecard for assessing testability. To calculate testability maturity levels, add up the scores and divide by the number of questions answered.

	RARELY OR NEVER	SOMETIMES	USUALLY OR ALWAYS
Tester-Friendly Product Information			
1.–2. Effective strategies for acquiring information about:		(circle one)	
product requirements or intentions	1	1.5	2
product usage patterns	1	1.5	2
3. Requirements testable in content and structure	1	1.5	2
Understandable Risks			
4. Use of automated defect tracking	1	1.5	2
5. Effective strategies for determining dangers in application (failure-impact) and product (fault-likelihood)	1	1.5	2
Increased Visibility and Control			
6. Visibility and control issues detailed in requirements	1	1.5	2
7. Functional design includes visibility and control mechanisms	1	1.5	2
8. Use of code execution tracing	1	1.5	2
Cooperative Testing			
9. Effective communication into and cooperation with development	1	1.5	2
10. Test-sensitive resource allocation and task planning	1	1.5	2
11. Effective software configuration management	1	1.5	2
12. Test-sensitive change control	1	1.5	2

	RARELY OR NEVER	SOMETIMES	USUALLY OR ALWAYS
Cost-Effective Regression			
13. Effective testware configuration management	1	1.5	2
14. Regular preservation and reuse of test suites at multiple levels	1	1.5	2
15.–17. Detailed knowledge of relationships between:			
product states and functions	1	1.5	2
product functions and design components	1	1.5	2
design components	1	1.5	2
18. Test objectives traced to cases and procedures	1	1.5	2
19. Loosely coupled test cases and procedures	1	1.5	2
20. Use of automated support for test execution and result evaluation	1	1.5	2
SEI CMM Level (if known): _____ **TMM Level*:** _____			

To calculate your TMM Level, add up the scores for all of the questions and divide by the total number of questions answered.

Notice how most of the last three perspectives on testability—from the IEEE, the DoD, and a commercial software quality training association—take the "process difficulty" perspective. This is clearly the pervasive perspective in the industry and is likely to remain that way for years to come. But that does not make it the most useful perspective. After all, if the process difficulty perspective were so meaningful, why does industry have so much trouble figuring how much testing to do and what kind of testing to do?

In case it isn't obvious, we think the testing effectiveness view of testability is much more useful than the process difficulty view. You may wonder what any of this has to do with fault injection. It turns out that fault injection can play an important role in measuring our favorite kind of testability. More on that in a moment.

We would be remiss if we didn't readily acknowledge that the "process difficulty" perspective can be quantified much more cheaply without fault injection. The best way to measure that perspective on testability is by using traditional structural metrics such as number of lines of code and cyclomatic complexity. Although we won't spend any more time fretting about process difficulty, it is still useful information for some software engineering concerns such as cost estimation. Without believable cost estimates for the resources needed to perform testing, testing is likely to be underprojected, poorly defined, and poorly planned. The end result will probably be a lower-quality product. The problem—and our main beef—is that making testing easier to perform does not in any way imply that the testing will detect more faults. The great challenge is really to make testing easier while at the same time generating test cases that are likely to make faults observable. Later, we see how software fault injection can help us with this problem.

5.2 Reliability versus Testability

Before we begin, let's take a quick look at the relationship between testability (using the "effectiveness of testing" perspective) and *reliability.* There are some interesting relationships between testability and software reliability as shown in Table 5.1.

First, if software is truly correct and thus 100 percent reliable, then the effectiveness of the test cases at revealing faults becomes irrelevant. No matter how good the test cases are, they will not reveal faults, even though they might actually have enough power to do so. Second, if software meets some required level of reliability, regardless of how the reliability is measured, then test-case effectiveness is again irrelevant. After all, who cares about those last few faults if the code is good enough?

Thus, testability is more important for defect removal and the isolation of potential fault-hiding spaces than it is for reliability assessment. Testability nonetheless has an important relationship to reliability. Ultimately, the smaller the bugs in a program, the more reliable the software will be. Bug or *fault size* is a measure of how many different inputs cause the program to fail because of the bug as well as the frequency that those inputs are selected. Smaller bugs cause lower testability scores. The key relationship between testability and making software reliable is forcing testing to detect existing defects. How can you fix what you don't know is broken? Even though testing takes place at the tail end of the software-development cycle (which also happens to be the most costly end), testing is a key process in developing more reliable software. A critical result of software failure being uncovered during testing is that a debug-and-fix phase can be invoked. Believers in reliability growth models (as opposed to reliability decay models), hold that more "test-debug-fix" effort results in more reliable software. *High* testability suggests that if the code is incorrect, it should have fairly large faults, and hence be less reliable. *Low* testability suggests that if the code is incorrect, it should have higher reliability, as the fault sizes should be lower.

Table 5.1 Reliability versus Testability

	CORRECT	HIGH RELIABILITY	LOW RELIABILITY
High Testability	Do not care	No	Yes
Low Testability	Do not care	Yes	No

5.3 Fault Tolerance versus Testability

Another interesting comparison worth noting compares testability to fault tolerance. We brought this up in chapter 2, but is still worth repeating here. Fault tolerance deals with software's ability to hide problems—specifically, the effects of faults. Testability deals with the ability of software to reveal the existence of faults by failing during testing. In this sense, testability is the opposite of fault tolerance. If software is capable of hiding problems, then it has high fault tolerance, but low testability. If software is capable of revealing problems, then it has high testability, but low fault tolerance. For software systems that are critical, it is generally accepted that high fault tolerance in the deployed system is preferable to low fault tolerance. However as we see later, it is possible to have high testability during test time and low testability during the operational phase for the same program by having two different versions of the code. For this reason, one must be careful to design programs to have high testability during V&V and low testability during operation.

Interestingly, software probes, or what are termed as "assertions," can play a very useful role for both testability and fault tolerance. Software assertions test the internal states of programs and check for various types of states whose manifestation reveals that a problem has somehow entered in the software's state. These assertions can be used during testing to increase testability, and they can also be used as fault-tolerance warning triggers that tell the software that it needs to recover to another state since the current state is corrupted. Also, as we see later, there are a class of specialized assertions that can also perform recovery after they detect a problem, and so in that capacity, they do much more than merely produce warning.

5.4 Testability Anomaly Spaces

The Ada83 mutant operators described in chapter 4 provide a good foundation from which to begin talking about what anomalies to simulate in order to measure testability. In Figure 3.5 (found in chapter 3), we showed that the problems represented by existing faults did not need to be mimicked by fault injection because these anomalies were already resident in the code. This is true, but a problem arises because the extent of the existing fault subspace is unknown. The code may not be correct and yet the actual faults may have no impact on the output of the program. At least if the code is failing during test, then we know it is not correct and we can expect debugging to be applied. The hope in this case is that no new faults will be introduced during debugging. But if the code is not failing during test, then we must determine why this is if we are to halt testing with a confidence that ending testing was the proper thing to do.

Even if the code is not failing during test, that alone does not prove correctness, unless every possible input is considered. In fact, when code does not fail during test, the question changes from "will the code fail on these inputs?" to "why didn't the code fail on these inputs?" Ironically, the first of these questions is much easier to answer. When the first question is answered with a "no," we are left with a much harder second question.

Formulating an answer to the second question is difficult. There are two answers, but only one is correct:

1. The code did not fail because it is correct.
2. The code did not fail because the inputs are poor at revealing the particular defects in the code.

The difficulty associated with the second case is that the inputs are unable to reveal the existing defects. The obvious solution is to find inputs that *will* reveal those defects. Doing this, however, requires knowledge of what the defects are!

So what are we left with? We need the program to fail to determine whether it is correct, but when it doesn't, we need to know what the faults are in order that we are able to find the appropriate test cases to make it fail (so that we then know that it is not correct). This is a clear catch-22. In any case, even if we knew where the faults were, it is undecidable in general which particular test cases will make the code fail. This problem is not directly solvable.

There are alternative V&V approaches that can be applied that address the problem of fault isolation, such as formal verification and code inspections. Of course, if they also fail to detect faults, we still do not know whether the code is faulty or correct. Furthermore, formal verification is generally too difficult to perform on complete systems, and hence is applied only sparingly in earlier life-cycle phases, say, at the unit level.

Although there are many applications for fault injection technology, we also advocate the use of fault injection for finding an answer to the problem of why testing is not resulting in failures. Fault injection will be used to mimic the behaviors that programmer faults would exhibit. We will use the test cases that the testers plan to employ, apply code mutation and state mutation, and in doing so develop a road map of the software's behavior. This road map can pinpoint those regions that demonstrate a tolerance for hiding injected anomalies. An attempt will be made to deliberately inject anomalies that are believed to be difficult a priori for testing to detect. If this turns out not to be the case (and the anomalies are easily spotted), we will be pleasantly surprised about the "effectiveness" of the testing.

Recall that in mutation testing, mutants were deliberately employed that were not equivalent. At the same time, mutants were not specifically created to be hard to kill. In our current situation, however, we'll do just the opposite. We want mutants that are hard to kill, because our ultimate aim is a thorough "testing of the testing." Further, recall that selective mutation only attempts to weed out mutants that would fall prey to test cases that other mutants already fell prey to (due to the fact that such mutants are essentially "equivalent"), because such mutants end up recommending the same test case. By deliberately using mutants that are harder to kill, we will increase the benefit from using mutation for testability purposes.

In terms of data-state mutation, it is unclear as to how to force alterations of the state that are harder to observe. In the next section, we look at different methods of perturbing data states; however, the issue remains an open research question.

It seems reasonable to tackle the difficulty-to-detect issue by looking back at the reason for employing fault injection to detect software's fault-hiding ability in the first place. The original problem was that exhaustive testing with all test cases was generally not possible. That problem fades into thin air when testing does result in failures (i.e., the test cases are executing faults, causing infected states, and propagating them out) but is exacerbated when failures are not observed.

Programs that hide their "dirty laundry" are known as *fault tolerant*. This characteristic is naturally very desirable, provided that it holds over all inputs. But it is extremely lousy if it only holds for the test cases selected during testing! Recall that the definition of a fault requires that there be at least one test case for which "the fault" is exercised, infects the internal state, and propagates that problem out into the software's output. For example, if some piece of faulty code is always exercised by every test case fed into the software and the program states are always corrupted by those test cases, but not a single one of those corrupt states propagates, then that piece of code is *not* incorrect, that is, not faulty. By the official definition for what is and what is not correct, there is no fault there.

By employing fault injection to hypothesize that a fault exists in the code at some place, we can see how often a hypothesized fault gets exercised, alters program states, and propagates the altered state to the output. If we play these "what-if" games enough, and if the hypothesized faults are good imitators of real programmer faults (particularly if they also have the characteristic of being small), and if such events occur frequently, then we have an alternative means for addressing the problem of successful, nonexhaustive testing.

5.5 Fault Injection–Based Testability: The PIE Algorithm

Testability can be defined in such a way as to be useful for estimating things like the number of test cases needed, testing stoppage criteria, and estimates of the smallest-size fault that could exist in the program. To address these needs, testability will be implemented as a probabilistic measure relating to the behavior of the code, not simply how the code looks. We will quantify testability measures in the range (0, 1]. Several different algorithms and their numerical results are the focus of this section. In later chapters, we talk more about how to apply these algorithms.

One could argue that high testability measures reflect high software quality. But software quality is such an amorphous and generally ill-defined goal that today we have over 1000 software metrics attempting either to quantify the processes used to develop code or quantify the code itself [Zuse 1990]. The desire to say something mathematically precise about software, as opposed to using some vague, subjective, hand-wavy criteria, has led to this explosion in the number of available measures. This metrics explosion hasn't helped much, though. Because too many of the metrics are of little or no value.

It is not our purpose here to argue for or against the value of software metrics. Instead we want to demonstrate a group of conceptually simple metrics that we feel are valuable indicators of the likelihood of faults to hide during testing. These metrics are statistical. That means all of the limitations associated with gathering statistics for small sample sets apply. We will step through three basic algorithms that all collect their information in an efficient manner. These algorithms have been described in detail in *Software Assessment: Reliability, Safety, Testability,* where they were called the PIE model [Friedman 1995]. The three algorithms (Propagation, Infection, and Execution) are all based on repeated executions of the software. Two of the three use fault-injection methods. The main costs of the two fault-injection algorithms stem from the need for repeated executions of the software program for each fault injection location under analysis. We will present some alternate algorithms, which in the end sacrifice accuracy in the results in order to make the costs of collecting the testability metrics more reasonable.

One interesting aside: It is reasonable to consider the raw numbers produced by the three PIE algorithms as stand-alone metrics. As you will see, there is a lot of numerical data output from the algorithms. Each and every probability estimate says something about the likelihood that faults will hide during testing at a specific point in the code. Together, their power is formidable indeed.

5.5.1 *Propagation Analysis*

Propagation analysis is the most expensive of the three PIE analyses, with Infection analysis also costing slightly more than Execution analysis. Currently, there is no tool, either commercial or research prototype, that can handle hundreds of thousands of locations for the propagation analysis algorithm given in [Friedman 1995]:

Original Propagation Analysis Algorithm (P)

1. Set **counter** to zero.
2. Randomly select a data state that occurs after location l according to D.
3. Perturb the data state for some variable a and continue execution; also perform a different execution using that data state without perturbing it.
4. Compare resulting outputs; if different, increment **counter.**
5. Repeat steps 2–4 $N - 1$ additional times.
6. The propagation estimate for variable a at location l is **counter** divided by N.
7. Perform steps 1–6 for different variables.
8. Perform step 7 for different locations in the code.

This algorithm requires $2XN$ executions of the program, where X is the number of locations under analysis. If $X = 100,000$, $N = 1000$, then the program must be run 200 million times. This is not a feasible number of test runs for most programs. Clearly there is some need for a revised algorithm which we will now provide. But before we do, the reader may wonder whether PA can ever be made more practical than mutation testing. We believe that the answer is yes, because PA does not suffer from the equivalent mutant problem which is undecidable. Thus we believe in the future that PA will be practical in some form for very large systems.

If the code base is millions of source statements and if the number of test cases being used is significant, we will face a daunting cost problem when using the algorithm just described. For this reason we have developed a less-expensive alternative algorithm. It is possible to modify the propagation process by giving up statistical accuracy in order to make the algorithm plausible for very large systems.

If we apply the following revised propagation analysis algorithm, where 30 percent of the locations are removed from L after the first x1 test cases are employed, and then 50 percent of the locations are employed after (x1+x2) test cases are used, then the 200 million executions can be cut to 78 million. And by simply changing the threshold of t1 = 1, and therefore increasing the 30 percent score to 75 percent, the 78 million program executions decreases to 29 million.

Revised Propagation Analysis Algorithm

1. Let $L =$ the set of all locations in the program to receive analysis.
2. For each location l in L, set **counter**$_l$ to zero.
3. Set these constants: x1 = 10, x2 = 90, x3 = 900, t1 = 5, t2 = 10.
4. Find x1 test cases selected according to D that cause l in L to be exercised.
5. For each of the x1 test cases do

   a. Perturb the data state of some program variable a that exists and has a value immediately after location l, and continue execution of the program; also perform a different execution of the program using that data state without its being perturbed.

   b. Increment **counter**$_l$ each time the resulting outputs from the perturbed and unperturbed runs differ.

6. if **counter**$_l \geq$ t1 then

   $L = L - l;$

   score$_l =$ **counter**$_l/$x1;

7. Perform steps 4–6 for each l in L.
8. Find x2 test cases selected according to D that cause location l in L to be exercised.
9. For each of the x2 test cases do

   a. Perturb the data state for some variable a that occurs immediately after l, and continue execution of the program; also perform a different execution of the program using that data state without its being perturbed.

   b. Increment **counter**$_l$ each time the resulting outputs from the perturbed and unperturbed runs differ.

10. if **counter**$_l \geq$ t2 then

    $L = L - l;$

    score$_l =$ **counter**$_l/$(x1+x2);

11. Perform steps 8–10 for each l in L.

12. Find x3 test cases selected according to D that cause l in L to be exercised.

13. For each of the x3 test cases do

    a. Perturb the data state for some variable a that occurs immediately after l, and continue execution of the program; also perform a different execution of the program using that data state without its being perturbed.

    b. Increment **counter**$_l$ each time the resulting outputs from the perturbed and unperturbed runs differ.

14. score$_l$ = **counter**$_l$/(x1+x2+x3);

15. Perform steps 12–14 for each l in L.

In this revised algorithm, score$_l$ is the *propagation estimate* for location l and whatever variable was perturbed at l.

Perturbation Functions

In the revised propagation analysis algorithm, steps 5a, 9a, and 13a are the most pivotal computations. The validity of the results from the algorithm is dependent on the software functions injected into the code to corrupt (perturb) the internal states. Here, we discuss the considerations that must take place before those steps are implemented.

This section focuses on taking digital information stored in a program's data states, or in the input information read in by the program, and transforming it into unique new information. Here, "unique" refers to the fact that the semantic meaning and representation of the new data is different from the original data.

There are three different schemes for perturbing digital data states:

1. Flip one or more bits of data, without regard for what the semantics are of the resulting data value.

2. Perturb the current value such that the new value is a function of the original value and the new value represents meaningful data.

3. Simply ignore the original value completely and assign some new, randomly selected value that is not a function in any way of the original value.

We discuss all three of these approaches in this section, but it is important to remember that the goal is to automatically create information that could well have been created by programmer error.

To modify data, we use software functions called *perturbation functions*. Perturbation functions are embedded software instructions that take in the data to be modified as a parameter and return the new value. When fault injection is being applied to source code, the perturbation function code is compiled right in with the original functionality; this is referred to as "intrusive" instrumentation. In some cases, a perturbation function simply returns a value when called, one that can be fixed or randomly selected, and does not consider incoming information when generating the return value.

Perturbation functions change the data that the program has access to, without changing the code itself. We will begin by giving code for several "bit flipping" perturbation functions, and then go on to provide code for several perturbation functions that modify data at higher levels of abstraction.

The perturbation function, flipBit, flips any memory bit (or bits) from 0 to 1 or vice versa. In the following perturbation examples, we assume integer data types for reasons of simplicity. All of these mathematical routines can be easily adapted for other data types, such as floats and strings. We can also perturb pointers or pointer-based structures by randomly replacing one legitimate pointer value by another active pointer value, or by setting a pointer to null.

The first argument to function flipBit is the original value that we wish to corrupt. The second argument is the bit to be flipped; here we assume little–endian notation. The corruptions generated by flipBit simulate programmer flaws, human factor errors, design flaws, and corruptions coming into a software module from other external sources.

Function flipBit can be written in C as shown next and then linked with the executable. Note: The ^ symbol represents the exclusive-OR operation in C and the << operator represents a SHIFT-LEFT of y bits. Also, ~ represents the bitwise negation operator.

```
void flipBit(int *var, int y)
{
*var = *var ^ (1 << y));
}
```

Examples of the different perturbation functions that can then be created by calling flipBit include:

1. all bits high:
    ```
    void allBitsHigh(int *var)
    {
        *var = ((int)~0);
    }
    ```

2. all bits low:
    ```
    void allBitsLow(int *var)
    ```

```
       {
             *var = ((int)0);
       }
```

3. random bit patterns:

```
   void randomPattern(int *var)
   {
         *var = lrand48(); /* where lrand48() returns */
                      /* a pseudo-random integer */
   }
```

4. off-by-one:

```
   void offByOne(int *var)
   {
         if (lrand48() & 1) /* add 1 if random integer is
         odd */
            *var = *var + 1;
         else            /* otherwise subtract one.    */
            *var = *var - 1;
   }
```

5. *n* random bits flipped, $(n \geq 1)$:

```
   void flipNbits(int *var, int n)
   {
         int bits = 0;    int bitPos = 1;
         int i,j,k;     int xbit;

         for (i = 0; i < n; i++)   /* set n bits in the
         integer "bits" */
         {
           bits |= bitPos;
           bitPos <<= 1;
         }
         for (j = 0; j < sizeof(int) * 8; j++)   /* shuffle
         the bits */
         {
           xbit = lrand48() % (sizeof(int) * 8);
           if((!!(bits & (1 << xbit))) != (!!(bits &
           (1 << j))))
           {
             flipBit(&bits, xbit);
             flipBit(&bits, j);
           }
         }
         for (k = 0; k < sizeof(int) * 8; k++)
           if (bits & (1 << k))
               flipBit(var, k);
   }
```

The first perturbation function is responsible for causing all bits in a memory cell to contain "1". The second perturbation causes all bits in a cell to contain "0"s. The third perturbation function forces random assignments of "0"s and "1"s to the memory cells. The fourth perturbation function only increases or decreases the value of an integer data value by one. The fifth perturbation requires that the user decide which bits in a memory cell should be flipped, and then does the flipping.

Let's take a deeper look at the role of perturbation functions and what the issues are involved with building them. For testability, the key role of perturbation functions is to mimic in the data states the forms of corruption that real programmer faults would cause. Since we do not know what the real faults are (if we did, we would be able to test for them directly), we must consider what types of anomalies are the most likely to occur on account of programmer faults. We call these anomalies potential programmer faults.

Potential programmer faults relative to some program location comprise the set of faults that are considered to have a likelihood of occurring greater than some predetermined threshold. Since this set of faults will in general be unknown, in the discussion that follows we consider a set of common faults to be the set of potential faults. For instance, at a program location which increments a counter, a potential fault might be an omission of the location. On the other hand, inserting a compiler at the location is a ridiculous fault. Often, common faults involve changing existing values. Central to the idea of modifying an existing value is the idea of a perturbation interval. A *perturbation interval* is a distribution specifying the range of values that the set of potential faults at a given location can generate. Perturbation intervals are a function of the preceding data space and the set of potential faults. Although the set of potential faults at a location may be infinite, reasonable limitations can be placed on this set by determining membership within the set according to impacts on values. Perturbation function parameters contain the information relating to the desired impact on a variable in a data state. These parameters can be adjusted according to requirements. Intuition suggests that the wider the interval, the more likely it will be that the software is put into a state so different from the original state that propagation must occur. But this is not always true. A preliminary discovery by Michael termed *homogeneous propagation* explains why this is so [Michael 1997]. This was discussed in chapter 3.

A perturbation function will often be a parameterized function that is used to corrupt data states. Parameters to the function include the current value of the program variable being altered. The perturbation function outputs a new value in the range specified by the perturbation function parameters. If the perturbation function were to produce the same output value as the input value, no failure propagation is possible, and such a perturbation function would have added no value for us. In this case, the failure propagation estimate will be biased. If the perturbation function always reproduces the original value, the failure propagation estimate would be zero. In practice, the type of function used produces random values based on the input value, a perturbing distribution, and the perturbation function parameters. The perturbing distribution will in general be a random distribution, and the perturbation function parameters are the parameters to the perturbing distribution.

One trick to improve the efficiency of this process is to determine at the outset whether the variable being perturbed is actually a variable whose value from that point forward is used by the program. If a variable is perturbed and is found no longer to have any impact on the program, then it may be that a location where a fault may be hiding has been found. If the variable is actually being used by the program, this is true. But more often than not, what has really happened is that a perturbation function has been applied to a *dead* variable, or rather, a variable that should be dead. Thus not only is the result meaningless but computation resources were wasted. For this reason an important first step to apply before propagation is to determine liveness versus deadness on all program variables at all locations in the software.

Liveness and deadness are not the only key issues for efficiency. The issue of deciding which live variables to perturb at specific points in the code is critical as well. Suppose that you have a statement, "x = x + 1." Immediately after this location, it would be meaningful (assuming that x is live) to perturb x, because that simulates a class of potential faults in the expression "x + 1." This does not mean that it would not be meaningful to perturb other variables at this point in the code (since perturbing variables other than x does simulate *missing code faults*), but if resources are limited, it makes the most sense to perturb only those variables being affected at a single location, including side effects that might be occurring.

A dual concern exists in determining nonconstant perturbation functions: The first problem is to determine the perturbation distribution; the second problem is to determine the parameters encoding the perturbation function itself. The remainder of this section addresses a scheme for the second problem under the assumption that the perturbation distribution is uniform or equilikely. This scheme can be generalized to a nonuniform two-parameter perturbation distribution.

Possibilities for nonconstant perturbation distributions include all of the continuous and discrete random distributions. The perturbation function newvalue(x) := equilikely(trunc(oldvalue(x)*0.6)}, trunc(oldvalue(x)*1.40)) is an example of a discrete distribution that perturbs a value by substituting an equilikely random value somewhere in the interval of 40 percent less to 40 percent more than the original value. As defined, this function includes the possibility of returning a newvalue(x) = oldvalue(x). The following code avoids this. There are two things to point out about the following code fragment: If the value being perturbed is zero, either a negative random value or a positive random value is returned, and if "constant1" and "constant2" are so close to 1.0 that the while loop does not exit normally, the loop is forced to halt after five iterations. (In such a case, the input value is either increased or decreased by "random.") Note that the call to "random" is a call to the random number generator which generates a real value between 0.0 and 1.0. In our research, we use the generator that is defined by Park and Miller [Park 1988].

```
function perturb(x: real;): real;
var newvalue:            real;
constant1 :              real;
constant2 :              real;
counter :                integer;

begin
constant1 :=/*0.0 < constant1 < 1.0*/
constant2 :=/*constant2 > 1.0*/
newvalue := x;
if (x=0.0) then begin
   if random < 0.5 then
      newvalue := random
   else
      newvalue :=-random
   end
else
begin
counter := 0
  while (newvalue = x) do begin
    newvalue:= uniform(x*constant1, x*constant2);
    counter := counter + 1;
    if (newvalue = x) and (counter=5) then begin
       if random < 0.5 then
          newvalue := x - random
       else
          newvalue := x + random;
    end
  end;
end;
perturb := newvalue;
end;
```

The choice of a perturbation function is fundamental. If the impacts of the potential faults being simulated are expected to make modest changes to the value, and each of these changes is likely, then equilikely(trunc(oldvalue(x)*0.9), trunc(oldvalue(x)*1.1)) or equilikely(trunc(oldvalue(x)*0.95), trunc(oldvalue (x)*1.05)) are reasonable choices. If the analysis is performed with parameters that produce a smaller range of values, then a more conservative estimate of propagation results.

Even if the fault causes a smaller range of values than anticipated, there is uniform sampling from the points occurring in the smaller interval.

5.5.2 Infection Analysis

Here is the original Infection analysis algorithm from the PIE model. Once again we discuss application of a cost-saving method based on the one used earlier in the execution and infection algorithms. The infection analysis algorithm is responsible for injecting mutants and then determining how often those mutants alter the state of the software:

Original Infection Analysis Algorithm

1. Set **counter** to zero.
2. Create a mutant M of location l.
3. Execute the location l and mutant M on a randomly selected data state that occurs before l according to D.
4. Compare resulting data states, if different, increment **counter.**
5. Repeat steps 3 and 4 $N-1$ additional times.
6. The infection estimate for mutant M at location l is **counter** divided by N.
7. Perform steps 1 through 6 for different mutants.
8. Perform step 7 for different locations.

Revised Infection Analysis Algorithm

1. Let L = the set of all mutants of the program.
2. For each mutant M at location l, set **counter**$_{lM}$ to zero.
3. Set these constants: x1 = 10, x2 = 90, x3 = 900, t1 = 5, t2 = 10.
4. Find x1 test cases selected according to D that cause l in L to be exercised.
5. Execute the location l and mutant M on each of the x1 test cases. Compare resulting data states, if different, increment **counter**$_{lM}$ for each test case in which they are different (for a maximum score of x1).

6. For each mutant M in L do

    if **counter**$_{lM}$ ≥ t1 then

        $L = L - M$;

        score$_{lM}$ = **counter**$_{lM}$/x1

7. Find x2 test cases selected according to D that cause l in L to be exercised.

8. Execute the location l and mutant M on each of the x2 test cases. Compare resulting data states, if different, increment **counter**$_{lM}$ for each test case in which they are different (for a maximum score of x1+x2).

9. For each mutant M in L do

    if **counter**$_{lM}$ ≥ t2 then

        $L = L - M$;

        score$_{lM}$ = **counter**$_{lM}$/(x1+x2)

10. Find x3 test cases selected according to D that cause l in L to be exercised.

11. Execute the location l and mutant M on each of the x3 test cases. Compare resulting data states, if different, increment **counter**$_{lM}$ for each test case in which they are different (for a maximum score of x1+x2+x3).

12. For each mutant M in L do

    score$_{lM}$ = **counter**$_{lM}$/(x1+x2+x3)

In this algorithm, score$_{lM}$ is the *infection estimate* for location l and mutant M.

Mutation Spaces

The space of all unique programs, either correct or not, that implement a binary search on a 10-element array is infinitely large. Given any selected program from that space, A, there is another program, B, from that space that is syntactically X keystrokes away from being identical to A. The number of keystrokes one program is away from another is one way to define how mutated one program is with respect to the other. Because this space of unique programs is infinite, the number of different mutations that can be made from one member of the space is infinite. Fortunately, for testability predictions, not all members of this space are of interest to us, and we discuss here how to prune that space.

It is ideally preferable for fault injection to employ only those mutants that rarely alter data states. From a practical standpoint, this is not possible. Here's why. For a mutant to alter an internal data state only rarely, it is critical to consider where in the program the mutant is injected and what inputs are used. Note in the following example how radically different the impact of the same mutant (x div c) is at locations 4 and 200:

```
1      c = 29999;
2      b = 2000;
3      c = 30000;
4      a = x div b;
       :
       :
100    b = 40;
       :
       :
200    y = x div b;
```

This mutant is much more likely to alter the state at location 200 than at location 4. Without knowing something about *what* the semantics are at the location where the mutant will be injected and having information about the inputs that the program receives, it is impossible to say a priori whether a mutant will be harder to observe. In this simple example, we did not concern ourselves with the inputs coming into the code. But it is easy to think up examples where the same mutant for a fixed location is difficult to observe for certain classes of inputs and even harder for other input classes.

Because of this difficulty, one approach will be to start by using the basic mutation operators that were outlined for Ada83 and then customize these operators for other languages. Trying to predict statically how difficult a particular mutant operator will be without considering the environment where it will be injected is fruitless.

Relating Parameterized Perturbation Functions to Mutants

Whenever a data-state value is modified from within its perturbation interval using parameterized perturbation functions (for example, changing the value of 50 to 75, or changing 50 to 30) this modification represents an *offset* of some amount x. Since the purpose of data-state mutation is to simulate the effects of programmer faults on the state, the question becomes: "What programmer faults does an offset of x simulate?" This is an important question, because if the answer is none, then the offset created by the perturbation function has not accurately performed its function.

We could, of course, employ mutations for propagation analysis if we chose to. That is, instead of employing perturbation functions, we could inject code mutations, and if they infected, we could look to see whether propagation occurred. Actually, this is similar to what happens during strong mutation testing, where the mutants are considered killed only if propagation to the output space occurs. We don't advocate this, because the relationship between mutants and actual programmer faults is very uncertain.

By employing parameterized perturbation functions, two things are accomplished. First, there is randomness to what offsets are actually employed. Not until the analysis is run is it known how great the offsets are, because the degree to which a specific value is changed with respect to the perturbation interval depends on the current value of the seed used by the random number generator. We know the perturbation interval ranges, but we will not know how the offsets will actually distribute until execution with test cases begins. If we hardwired mutants into the code such as '+ 1', we can know exactly how much our offsets will be before we run the analysis, which in this case, is off by one. Second, each offset potentially corresponds to a wide variety of syntactic mutants. This means an offset of 30 may be achieved through a handful of unique mutants of some statement *l*. But an offset of 30 may also be achievable by groups of distributed programmer faults. So a perturbation function applied at a particular location has the additional capability to simulate the manifestation of problems spread throughout the code even though it is applied at a single point in the program.

In summary, the advantages of using perturbation functions for propagation analysis are as follows: Perturbation functions provide randomness, are capable of simulating the effects of different classes of mutants for a single statement, and are capable of simulating the effects of problems that are nonlocal to the point in the code where they are injected.

5.5.3 Execution Analysis

Finally, the simplest algorithm from the PIE model:

Original Execution Analysis Algorithm (E)

1. Set **counter**$_l$ to zero.
2. Increment **counter**$_l$ each time location *l* is executed; make sure that **counter**$_l$ is incremented at most once per input, hence if *l* is repeatedly executed for the same input, counter is only incremented once.

---

3. Execute the code with N test cases selected according to D. (D is the testing distribution.)

4. The *execution estimate* for location l is **counter**$_l$ divided by N.

5. Perform steps 1–4 for all locations in the code.

The simplest way to implement this algorithm is to instrument every single location in the code that is under analysis in a single instrumented version of the program, and then handle the bookkeeping of the results by a separate process that monitors the executing instrumented version of the software. So then at every location in the program, we have probes that are looking at whether a location was executed, and if so, the probes are incrementing the appropriate counter for that unique location.

Of the three algorithms from the PIE model, the execution analysis algorithm is the least computationally expensive. Nevertheless, if the code base is millions of source statements and if the number of test cases being used is significant, we can still face a daunting cost problem when using the algorithm just described. We can address this problem via a similar algorithmic revision to the ones we proposed earlier for propagation and infection.

Note that if the number of locations that receive this analysis is small, N is less than 1000, and a single program execution is fairly quick, then this algorithm, in its original form, will be fine as it stands. In this case there is no great benefit derived from using the following alternative algorithm:

Revised Execution Analysis Algorithm

1. Let $L =$ the set of all locations in the program to receive analysis.

2. For each location l in L, set **counter**$_l$ to zero.

3. Set these constants: x1 = 10, x2 = 90, x3 = 900, t1 = 5, t2 = 10.

4. Execute the program with x1 test cases according to D.

> for each l in L do
>> Increment **counter**$_l$ each time location l is executed
>
> for each l in L do
>> if **counter**$_l \geq$ t1 then
>>
>> $L = L - l;$
>>
>> score$_l =$ **counter**$_l$/x1

5. Execute the program with x2 test cases according to D.

> for each l in L do
>> Increment **counter**$_l$ each time location l is executed
> for each l in L do
>> if **counter**$_l \geq t2$ then
>> $L = L - l$;
>> score$_l =$ **counter**$_l / (x1+x2)$

6. Execute the program with x3 test cases according to D.

> for each l in L do
>> Increment **counter**$_l$ each time location l is executed
> for each l in L do
>> score$_l =$ **counter**$_l / (x1+x2+x3)$

There are several options for implementing this algorithm. One option involves several different compilations of the instrumented program, with instrumentation for the **counter**$_l$s compiled in only for the locations that exist in L in steps 4, 5, and 6. This method then would require three separate compilations of the program for L at the beginning of step 4, L at the beginning of step 5, and L at the beginning of step 6. Also, it will be necessary to know what the existing **counter**$_l$ is for those ls in L at the beginning of step 5 and step 6, so that the final score$_l$ is correct. Another option would be to add additional instrumentation that does a check to see if a location has been eliminated from L, and if so, then does not bother to increment the appropriate counter. This approach would eliminate the need for multiple compilations of the instrumented version, but performing all of those checks concerning whether a location is still in L could be as expensive as, if not more than, the original execution analysis algorithm. Hence this alternative may not provide any cost savings. And finally, a third option can be derived from the first option, where we employ the idea of three separate compilations, except that we do not require that we know what the existing **counter**$_l$ is for those ls in L at the beginning of step 5 and step 6 so that the final score$_l$ is correct; and each time, we rerun the first 10 or 100 test cases with each newly instrumented version of the program. This third option is likely to be the approach that is the easiest to implement and that provides the most cost savings.

This algorithm terminates Execution analysis on a location that has already shown a fairly good ability to be exercised. A prime example of this is the first statement in a program. That statement will get executed every time, so why run thousands of test cases through the program and collect information about how likely that location is to be exercised? That is, the execution estimate will be 1.0 after 10 test cases, it will still be 1.0 after 100 test cases, and it will be 1.0 after 1000 test cases. So why continue on this way with more and more test cases?

Given the values used in the alternate algorithm for constants t1 and t2, if after only ten test cases, five or more test cases exercise a particular location, the algorithm will discontinue assessing the frequency with which that location is exercised and spend those resources on other locations that have received less or no exercise. We justify this move by hypothesizing that locations exercised frequently by the initial test cases will also get exercised frequently by latter test cases. Of course this might not always be true. But to save resources, this is a risk worth taking. We are willing to sacrifice some statistical confidence in order to make the algorithm more tractable for larger systems.

5.5.4 *Understanding the Results of PIE*

Results from the original and cost-savings PIE algorithms we have presented are easy to understand at a gross scale: Larger scores are better, smaller values are worse. Results indicate how a program will likely reveal faults during testing. That means we do not necessarily care how the program behaves after fault injection has occurred; what we're actually interested in is the general trend. Although our results are simple statistics, their benefit derives from their predictive capacity, which can tell us how successful testing will be at detecting faults.

Note that the PIE algorithms produce a large number of scores for the different analyses and different locations. Collapsing the huge piles of information into a concise package is necessary.

Doing so ensures that the user of the information is not overwhelmed by the sheer volume of information provided. Methods for extracting the essential results from the three algorithms and collapsing these results into a more general testability metric are given in [Friedman 1995] and [Voas 1990].

5.5.5 *Using PIE to Generate "Better" Test Cases*

Recall from chapter 4 our discussion on using syntactic mutants to determine which test cases were better at revealing faults. We made that determination according to whether test cases could kill off any of the "live" mutants that still needed to be differentiated from the original code. Given that Infection analysis and Propagation analysis are two separate analyses that taken together are very similar to strong mutation testing, then we can take the scores from Infection analysis and Propagation analysis and use those scores to build test cases that are more likely to enforce the second and third conditions in the fault/failure model.

Also, Execution analysis can help us decide whether we are achieving enough test coverage from the test cases that we are employing. For example, if we have a test suite, yet we have locations with 0.0 execution analysis scores, then we are immediately alerted to the situation that some of the source code statements have not been exercised. This immediately tells us that additional test cases need to be generated.

Voas and Miller [Voas 1992b] have proposed an approach to ranking test suites and building test suites with test cases that are more likely to reveal faults using the scores derived from the PIE technique. Their approach is based on creating a score of a particular test case based on:

1. The number of locations that the test case exercised
2. The number of data-state infections that were created based on the syntactic mutants used during infection analysis
3. The number of injected data-state mutants that actually propagated all of the way to the output of the program

Once a particular test case is assigned a numerical score, then a suite of test cases can be ranked in comparison to a different suite of test cases. To do this, simply take two suites of test cases, each with an equivalent number of test cases, and all of the scores of the members of each test suite, and compare the totals for the two suites. The suite with the higher score has demonstrated a greater ability to enforce the three conditions of the fault/failure model for that program when PIE was applied. So that test suite should be the suite used during testing if the purpose of testing is to ferret out defects.

5.5.6 *PIE versus Formal Verification*

PIE is an empirical, dynamic technique that is anything but a formal method. In fact, its employment of randomness, and thus a lack of formality in how it does fault injection, may actually contribute to its success.

But like testing, PIE is limited in terms of the amount of analysis that can be performed due to computational limits. Similarly, one formal method, *formal verification,* is also limited in terms of the size of source code about which it can formally verify certain behavioral properties. Although experts disagree concerning what this threshold is, it is generally regarded that programs greater than 10,000 lines of code in size are not candidates for formal proofs of correctness via automated theorem-proving machines. And certainly no human can prove correctness manually for any program near that size.

PIE then is a technique that can be used to better suggest where formal verification is prudent in a large system as well as suggest where testing is sufficient and thus formal verification should not be applied. For example, if PIE were applied to a system and certain components of that system were found to be "untestable" by the current testing scheme, then those portions of the software would be ideal candidates for formal verification. Likewise, if other portions of the system exhibit excellent fault-revealing potential from testing alone, then those are regions that should be skipped for formal analysis and should experience testing alone.

Our point here is that the combination of testing and formal verification can be happily married via the use of a technique like PIE. Almost all persons in software engineering are now willing to acknowledge that there is no silver bullet technology for developing high-quality software. High-quality software can be achieved only through a blend of different techniques that are exploited for what they are designed for and not forced to perform tasks for which they are not designed. The PIE approach can highlight those regions of the code where testing will be beneficial and, in doing so, will find those regions where an approach such as formal verification, code inspections, or software assertions should be considered (see chapter 10).

5.6 Timing and Ordering Fault-Injection Mechanisms

Next we look at a variety of classes of timing faults, including the problem of events failing to occur or incorrect events occurring at the wrong time. Real-time embedded systems demand that precise events occur at precise times. The original PIE model addressed specific events (computations) and whether they produced the correct output for sequential systems but did not address the many issues related to certain events doing certain tasks at certain times. In real-time-sensitive systems, these events also depend on the timing of other tasks completed elsewhere in the system. For languages that support concurrency, such as Ada, fault-injection perturbation functions that simulate timing faults in processors become a necessity. Languages such as VHDL also require this capacity. That's because timing constraints are a part of the logic of the computation, and timing faults are a major source of errors that cannot be easily detected during testing.

The approach described next enhances the PIE fault-injection methods to handle parallel/distributed timing situations. Perturbing time yields an unexpected result: Not only can we predict the impact that timing faults will have on the output, but we can also find out whether the source code itself has timing faults. This "testing" capability is unique to the parallel/distributed domain and is not directly applicable to sequential systems. So, parallel/distributed perturbation functions can be employed to predict the sensitivity of parallel/distributed software systems to timing delays as well as identify where actual timing faults exist in the code. Debugging software is easiest when a fault causes software to fail often—that's because each failure furnishes new information about the fault. This information (hopefully) helps locate the fault so that it can be repaired. The most difficult faults are those that rarely cause the software to fail. That's because such faults provide very few clues as to their nature and location.

The parallel/distributed fault injection model begins just as the sequential testability model did—by first differentiating injection locations (in each of the different tasks) that are candidates for instrumentation. We will consider the same classes of constructs "locations" in the parallel/distributed model as we considered in the sequential model. In the sequential model, locations were sequentially numbered from the beginning of the program to the end: $l_1, l_2, \ldots, l_N$. In the parallel/distributed model, the numbering system is similar but slightly more complex. The concurrent system will be viewed as a collection of distinct tasks. Within each of these tasks, locations will be numbered in the same way as they were numbered in sequential programs. If we have M tasks, each with 100 locations, we would have a total of $100M$ distinct locations denoted as: $l_{t1,1}, \ldots, l_{t1,100}, \ldots, l_{tM,1}, \ldots, l_{tM,100}$. Note that in the concurrent domain, a perturbation occurs to a single variable, just as in sequential propagation analysis.

In the sequential PIE model, propagation was defined as "differing output." In the concurrent domain, propagation is viewed similarly: Propagation occurs in a concurrent system when the output of the perturbed case is different from the output of the unperturbed case. Propagation is not checked at the end of a task, but rather at the end of a system execution. That means even though tasks produce output that affects the system's output—unless, of course, the task is producing output that is ignored by the rest of the system—consideration of whether propagation occurred is not made until the system completes an execution.

Note that the definition of what constitutes differing output can be seen in distinct ways. In addition, the definition must be pinned down for each specific application. In the sequential model, testability analysis might include something like a tolerance within which two outputs would be considered identical for a given problem domain (e.g., two outputs within 0.01 real units of each other would be deemed equivalent). With parallel/distributed systems, the question of equivalent outputs can become more complex. For example, the order in which output results are produced may or may not be significant, depending on the application. For applications where the order is not significant, the PIE analysis must perform a relatively sophisticated analysis of two system-output traces before declaring any two outputs equivalent.

In a parallel/distributed system, most program variables are defined by the programmer, meaning they are statically declared or dynamically allocated. Time is a variable of parallel/distributed systems that a programmer has partial control over, but not total control over. When a programmer codes an inefficient algorithm, for example, the programmer is explicitly controlling time (in a wasteful way). Deciding to include a command such as sleep() is another way for a programmer to control time explicitly. However if a multitasking processor is executing another task in the background for an unanticipated user, the programmer has no control of the situation, and the programmer's application is at the mercy of the operating system. In this scenario, the machine and the programmer jointly share control of the processor and thus share control of time on that processor.

To account for the possibility of either the programmer or the machine itself affecting the time at which instructions are executed, three classes of system variables can be identified:

1. Variables that can be explicitly and completely controlled, such as statically declared variables, are termed *manipulable*.
2. Variables that can be controlled by the system alone are *nonmanipulable*.
3. Variables that a programmer has some control over, but not total control over, is termed *partially manipulable* (these variables are by definition somewhat manipulable and somewhat nonmanipulable).

Processor time is partially manipulable.

The reason for distinguishing these classes is that perturbation functions must be parameterized differently for manipulable and partially manipulable variables. Variables that are partially manipulable are perturbed in a manner that reflects those faults that a programmer could cause. Other kinds of perturbations include those that reflect errors caused by the operating system or the machine itself.

The time when a task completes is affected by many different factors, including processor speed, work load on the system, assigned operating system priorities, and communication overhead. Programmers are taught to consider these possibilities and insert software mechanisms (synchronization primitives) to allow for the speed variability that takes place in concurrent processing. Since parameters such as speed variability can be thought of as hidden inputs to the system, the output of an incorrect parallel/distributed systems can be nondeterministic. The stochastic properties must be recognized because these systems can produce different outputs for the identical user-supplied input. Such hidden inputs affecting speed variability cause output nondeterminism when a programmer fails to guarantee that time variability does not affect the computation, even though the system is theoretically deterministic. Unknown and unpredictable factors (including processor speeds and other hidden inputs) cause the confusion. If all parameters affecting the execution of a parallel system for a specific input could be controlled, identical output for a given input would always be guaranteed. This is not realistic. The goal in parallel/distributed programming is to synchronize shared variables so it is impossible for timing anomalies to cause failure.

Propagation of a time perturbation reveals the existence of a timing fault. In such a case, differing output occurs in multiple runs. Perturbing time and observing output also directly reveal information about the degree of difficulty that will be encountered during system testing, since timing faults can be the hardest to reproduce and detect.

A distributed system built on a network typically uses message-passing mechanisms (although there are documented approaches to building a shared address space on top of such message passing) to allow distributed tasks to concurrently execute and communicate. SIMD processors typically operate in such a way that multiple versions of an algorithm are executed in lockstep on a set of processors, while manipulating different sets of data. SIMD is useful for quickly solving problems that have a defined structure. MIMD processors, using either message passing or shared memory to operate on a set of independent tasks executing on multiple CPUs, are often considered the most general parallel architecture.

Detection of timing problems in parallel/distributed systems via fault injection is more amenable to MIMD architectures than it is to SIMD architectures. SIMD machines tend to execute instructions in a *lockstep* manner that makes it nearly impossible for timing to become a problem. In addition, the use of a single instruction path makes the code look sequential and allows us to operate on most SIMD constructs as if the system were running on a single CPU.

MIMD architectures are more likely to contain synchronization faults. Given a two task system, t_1 and t_2, we have three time-rollback possibilities:

S1. Slowing t_1 by Δ_1

S2. Slowing t_2 by Δ_2

S3. Slowing t_1 by Δ_1 and slowing t_2 by Δ_2

You can easily show that S3 is a special case of S1 and S2. To perform roll-forward on this two-task system, we again have three possibilities:

F1. Speeding up t_1 by Δ_1

F2. Speeding up t_2 by Δ_2

F3. Speeding up t_1 by Δ_1 and speeding up t_2 by Δ_2

F1 is implemented by S2, and F2 is implemented by S1. F3 is implemented by slowing t_k by Δ_3, where $k = 1$ if $\Delta_1 \leq \Delta_2$, and 2 otherwise.

When we consider a larger system of n parallel tasks (where $n > 2$), an explosion in the combinations of processors that could be slowed down occurs. For instance, in a 3-processor architecture, the possible combinations of processors that could be slowed are given by the following sets: $\{(1), (2), (3), (1, 2), (2, 3), (1, 3), (1, 2, 3)\}$. Given n tasks executing in parallel, then the number of combinations for slowing down i of the tasks is given by:

$$\frac{n!}{(n - i)!i!}$$

The number of ways of slowing all possible sets is:

$$\sum_{i=1}^{n} \frac{n!}{(n - i)!i!}$$

This is the upper bound on the number of combinations of task rollbacks that could occur for simulating distributed time faults on an n task concurrent system. Since the upper bound allows for the case of n items taken n at a time (which we have already shown to be a special case of the others), the true number of combinations is:

$$\sum_{i=1}^{n} \frac{n!}{(n-i)!i!} - 1 = 2^n - 2$$

As n increases, this number of combinations grows dauntingly quickly. Further, if different random values for each Δt_k and random locations within a task where rollback can be forced are included in the combinatorics analysis, the potential schemes for simulating timing faults become effectively infinite. Thus to be practical, the number of possibilities to be simulated must be limited.

Time can easily be perturbed on a processor by syntactically injecting a mechanism such as sleep(Δt_k), where Δt_k is based upon a random variable. This provides a means of perturbing time a random amount, much as is done in the perturbation functions of the PIE model. Δt_k should be based on how long the task normally takes to execute.

Timing errors can occur among tasks executing in parallel, or between a program and one or more external systems with which the program is supposedly communicating in real time. (We discuss the first of these anomalies when we address out-of-sequence events.) For now, we consider only timing errors. Timing anomalies in real time can result if an input or output event occurs either later than expected or sooner than expected. The first case can be simulated by inserting a delay in front of the input or output event:

```
Put(x);
```

would be modified as follows:

```
perturbed_delay(12);
Put(x);
```

where perturbed_delay is a function that permits us to selectively delay, or fail to delay, at the point where it is inserted. The number 12 given as an argument to perturbed_delay is used to tell the function which code location it is being called from. In the preceding example, there are at least 11 other locations in the code where delays or other perturbations can be selectively inserted; the example shows the twelfth. The function perturbed_delay will delay only one location during any one execution of the code, so that we will know which location is responsible if a timing anomaly causes a fault.

The actual code for perturb_delay is as follows:

```
procedure perturbed_delay(id: integer)
begin

if id = perturb_target then
        delay(standard.duration(perturb_time));
end if;
end.
```

perturb_target is a global value identifying the location to be delayed. This procedure is actually simplified somewhat; the actual implementation will be synchronized with a task that obtains perturb_target from a driver process that repeatedly executes the component while perturbing different locations.

Another interesting perturbation function simulates *wrong events*. For example, if a program's normal flow of execution during testing causes the wrong event to take place, the event's effect can be assessed by observing the outcomes of the tests. If the effect of a wrong event cannot be assessed through simple random testing, it follows that the program did not follow the flow of control that would have resulted in the wrong event. Therefore, to simulate wrong events, program control-flow is modified. This is done by changing the conditions associated with conditional executions, loops, accept statements, and so on. The conditional

```
if <condition> then
        <sequence of statements>
end if;
```

might be changed to, for example:

```
if boolean_control(12) xor ( <condition> ) then
        <sequence of statements>
end if;
```

As previously, the parameter 12 indicates that this is the twelfth conditional statement that is a candidate for this form of perturbation, and this parameter is used to control which one of several possible perturbations is actually activated. The function Boolean_control is simply:

```
function Boolean_control(id: integer) return boolean

begin
if id = perturb_target then
        return TRUE;
end if;

return FALSE;
end;
```

Since Boolean_control and the original condition are exclusively or'd, the Boolean condition in which the control is embedded takes on the same value that it would take on if there were no code instrumentation and the function returns FALSE. If the Boolean_control returns TRUE, the value of the Boolean condition is the opposite of what it would otherwise have been. perturb_target is a global variable, and the actual implementation of the function will contain code that ensures the value has been initialized before it is used.

Another interesting timing problem occurs when events are out of sequence. Two program events are out of sequence if they fail to occur in the order given by some specification. These faults can come about as the result of race conditions between tasks; this type of fault can be simulated by inserting code to delay the input/output activities of certain tasks with respect to those of other tasks. For example, if the code

```
Put (x * y);
```

appears in the code, it can be perturbed as follows:

```
perturbed_delay(12);
Put (x * y);
```

where perturbed_delay is the function already described. It is also possible for there to be an unexpected sequence of events within a single software module. The simulation of this type of anomaly is identical to the simulation of wrong events, and the argument we have made for wrong events also holds for this type of out-of-order events.

The next class of failure that we will be interested in simulating is failure of events to manifest. We define the *failure of an event to manifest* to be a condition in which a program event should occur but does not occur. The simulation of these events is similar to the simulation of wrong events. Instead of simply perturbing the flow of control, we modify it so that a particular condition cannot be true. The conditional

```
if <condition> then
        <sequence of statements>
end if;
```

will, for example, be changed to:

```
if not Boolean_control(12) and ( <condition> ) then
        <sequence of statements>
end if;
```

The function Boolean_control is the same one that was described earlier when wrong events were discussed. When perturbation for location 12 is activated by making Boolean_control return TRUE for that location, the condition in the if statement is always FALSE.

Deadlock is another serious type of time-dependent event. Deadlock results when two or more tasks compete for two or more resources, and each obtains exclusive use of only a fraction of the resources needed to continue. No task can continue without the others completing, and thus no task can ever complete. This is analogous to a sequential system becoming trapped in an infinite loop. Deadlock is only one class of timing fault. Deadlock faults can be simulated by halting individual tasks by injecting delays in order to see how the other tasks are affected. This can be simulated by inserting what amounts to an infinite delay:

```
loop
        delay 60.0;
end loop;
```

To detect deadlock, static analysis of the data flow patterns can be employed.

If a time perturbation affects the output of the entire system, what does that indicate about the system? In previous discussions of the PIE testability model, a propagation to the output caused by a perturbation to some variable *a* suggested that if *a* were ever incorrect (with respect to an assertion for what *a* should be), it is expected that the system would produce incorrect output during testing. Perturbing time and observing differing output reveal even more in the parallel/distributed domain: A timing perturbation that propagates reveals the existence of a timing fault in the system. This is not the case with other classes of perturbations. When a simulated timing anomaly propagates, we have direct evidence that the programmer has not properly synchronized the program. In summary, unlike PIE for sequential systems, fault injection on timing in a parallel/distributed environment can detect otherwise hard-to-catch timing faults.

5.7 Miscellaneous Parameters Affecting Testability Analysis and Mutation Testing

Several different user-controlled parameters impacting the results of testability analysis and mutation are worthy of mention.

There are two parameters that can be manipulated to affect the results from the testability algorithms just described as well as the test cases recommended by mutation testing: (1) the number of test cases used, and (2) the ordering with which the test cases are selected. Mutation testing is affected by both of these, while sensitivity analysis is affected mainly by (1), although the test scheme employed can be thought of as the parameter that orders the sequence of inputs used.

It should be obvious that if few test cases are used during mutation testing, then it is more likely that mutants will remain live. If few test cases are used during PIE, confidence in the accuracy of the estimates decreases. Further, if confidence intervals are ignored for such estimates, then it is possible that one test case could force all conditions of the fault/failure model to hold at all locations, thereby producing a testability score of 1.0. Finding such a test case will, however, almost certainly be a needle-in-a-haystack search that is not worth attempting. But nonetheless, there are people who will attempt this search purely to make it appear as though the testing that they performed had a high likelihood of finding faults, and their testability score of 1.0, created from the usage of one test case during testability assessment and during testing, provides the evidence they need to argue their absurd case.

5.7.1 Few Test Cases

From time to time, a Propagation analysis limitation arises when a user of fault injection is limited by access to a very few test cases when the analysis is run. As has already been stated, the number of test cases employed directly affects confidence in the statistical results. As an example, suppose that a system has only ten known system-level test cases, there are no input distributions, and there is no way to generate additional test cases. The confidence in the results will be weak when we employ the $p \pm$ rule with $n = 10$. (See chapter 3.) What, if anything, can be done here?

One obvious suggestion is test-case reuse, provided that anomaly reuse does not occur as a result. What we mean can best be explained by example. Suppose that at some place in the code, test case 1 causes the value of variable x to be 100. When we perturb x, we change the value of x to some random value, a. We could have made a different value modification to the value b (where $a \neq b$), or possibly to c (where $a \neq b \neq c$). The point here is that we are still using the same test case, but many different anomalies are being derived from the state of x created by that test case. Hence instead of having a different anomaly for each test case, we might have 10 different anomalies tried per test case. If for 10 test cases we were able to generate 100 anomalies, then we will have truly tried 100 different anomalies, and we should be able to gather statistics based on 100 different trials, not simply 10.

One note of caution here, however. There appears to be a statistical dependency between the propagation behaviors of different faults injected in the same place for the same input [Michael 1996]. That biases any statistical probability estimates. Hence, although we could still gather statistics based on 100 different trials using 10 test cases, it may not necessarily be true that we can assume that the total sample size was 100. It will likely need to be some number less than that, but hopefully greater than 10.

The reason that our algorithms show probability estimates as a function of the number of test cases is that we will usually be able to sample enough different test cases that we will not have to reuse them. But when necessary, we can reuse test cases by creating different internal anomalies from them. By doing so, our propagation algorithm changes to the following algorithm, which assumes that there are only a maximum of x1 test cases available:

"Few Test-Cases" Propagation Analysis Algorithm

1. Let $L =$ the set of all locations in the program to receive analysis

2. For each location l in L, set **counter$_l$** to zero.

3. Set these constants: **successes$_l$**=0; perturbs = 100. This value is arbitrary, and can be bumped up or down depending on resources; also, the algorithm can be gradually stepped along like the Revised Propagation Analysis Algorithm, where perturbed states stop being created if propagation is always occurring from the early perturbed states.

4. For each of the x1 test cases do

   a. Set Perturbed_Set = $\varnothing$

   b. For I = 1 to perturbs do

      (1) If the test case executes l, perturb the data state for some variable a that occurs immediately after l such that the perturbed state is $\notin$ Perturbed_Set

      (2) Increment **successes$_l$**

      (3) Continue execution of the program.

      (4) Perform a different execution of the program using the original data state without its being perturbed.

      (5) Increment **counter$_l$** each time the resulting outputs from the perturbed and unperturbed runs differ.

      (6) Add the perturbed data state created in (1) to Perturbed_Set.

5. if **successes$_l$**; $\neq 0$ then score$_l$ = **counter$_l$**/**successes$_l$** else score$_l$ = 0.

The problem of few test cases can also persist for Infection analysis as well as for Execution analysis, however this algorithm for reusing internal states will not be applicable to those analyses.

5.7.2 Test-Case Ordering

The effect of test-case ordering should not be great on testability analysis using the PIE algorithms, provided that many test cases are employed. But the ordering of the tests for mutation testing may have a significant role on the size of the eventual test suite that is generated. One method proposed in [Offutt 1995] aims to reduce the size of a mutation test suite while still retaining the same level of mutation adequacy. We begin by describing the hypothesis as to why the ordering can bias the size of a mutation-adequate suite. We then present the method [Offutt 1995] to sidestep this bias.

It has been conjectured that the amount of fault-revealing ability provided from a mutation-adequate test set may be less than it could be, given the number of test cases in the set. This rests on the idea that many test cases wind up in the set solely because they are generated early on by the generation criteria that order the sequence in which they are fed to the mutants. This hypothesis, however, has never been formally proven. The conjecture that a mutation-adequate set may be bloated in terms of the number of inputs that it has suggests that the set could have fewer members and still retain mutation-adequacy. If the conjecture is true, then it should hold for other unit-testing schemes such as single-statement coverage and data flow testing. Finding a cost-effective algorithm for pruning the size of a test suite could result in enormous cost savings.

The hypothesis here is that the random seed—or whatever other scheme is used to start generating test cases—may play a larger role in the size of the mutation-adequate set, and what its members are, than is desirable. Ideally, we want the size of the set to be based only on how difficult the mutants are to kill, not on something as silly as which initial seed is fed to the test-case generator. If the conjecture is true, then even though we will have a mutation-adequate set Z of size X after performing mutation testing, there may be a subset of Z of size $X - y$, where $y \neq 0$, that is also mutation-adequate. If a mutation-adequate test suite is all that is required, then there is no justification for letting the test suite be larger than necessary.

Offutt et al. devised a suite-pruning method for NASA and applied their technique to several different testing criteria [Offutt 1995]. Let's explore their approach. The savings, as demonstrated in their limited experiments, were quite large—up to 40 percent. Of course, if 40 percent of a test suite is removed, then you would expect that the test set will not be as good at detecting faults. They noted that the purpose behind their pruning algorithm was to reduce suite size while preserving the mutation-adequacy criteria. This move will not necessarily preserve the fault-detecting ability of the full suite.

Assume you have a set of test cases T with some reasonably high mutation score for a program, and T has size N. A minimal test set is the smallest subset of T that achieves the same mutation score. Since test case effectiveness depends on the order in which the test cases are executed, we need to run all orderings of the test set to find the minimal test set.

This problem collapses to a *minimal set cover problem*. Each mutant is covered by a test case that kills it. Thus, to find the minimal test set that satisfies the mutation criterion, we need to find the smallest set of test cases that covers the mutants. This is an NP-complete problem [Garey 1979]. Although NP-complete problems cannot be solved completely, good approximate solutions can usually be found using heuristics.

By changing only the order in which a set of test cases is fed into an automated mutation tool, we may well change the size of the resulting set. Suppose we have two test cases and three live mutants. If test case 1 kills mutants 1, 2, and 3, and test case 2 kills only mutant 2, then if test case 2 gets selected right before test case 1, and all three mutants are live, test cases 1 and 2 will be entered into the set. But if test case 1 is tried first, it will be the only member of the set.

Test-data-generation strategies for mutation orders N inputs into a sequence $S = \langle s_1, s_2, \ldots, s_N \rangle$. These inputs are fed into the mutants of a program P, in sequence, with the goal being for the inputs to cause as many mutants as possible to fail. When mutants fail, or are killed, by input s_1, the mutants are removed from the set, and input s_{i+1} is fed into the set of remaining mutants. As the tests are executed, the set of mutants is continually shrinking, until either all mutants are killed or the remaining mutants appear to be impossible to kill off.

Assume that the cardinality of test suite M is K. For input s_1, M is a complete set, and hence there are K opportunities for s_1 to cause a member of M to fail. If s_1 kills p mutants, then the most mutants that s_2 has the opportunity to kill is $K - p$. If s_2 kills g mutants, then the most mutants that s_3 has the opportunity to kill is $K - p - g$. Thus, the earlier in the sequence that an input occurs, the more likely it is that the input will kill a mutant. This implies there is a degree of luck involved, which can strongly affect the mutation testing process. We would like to decrease the process without relying on luck.

In the following example, test case 1 ($X = -1$, $Y = 5$) executes $Statement_2$ and $Statement_3$, test case 2 ($X = 5$, $Y = 5$) executes $Statement_1$ and $Statement_3$, and test case 3 ($X = -1$, $Y = -1$) executes $Statement_2$ and $Statement_4$. Consider the program and test where $Statement_1$ through $Statement_4$ are arbitrary statements. If the test cases are submitted in the order given, then all three test cases are required to cover all four statements. On the other hand, executing the test cases in the order $\langle 3, 2, 1 \rangle$ mean then that only test cases 3 and 2 are needed to cover the statements.

```
IF (X > 0) THEN
        Statement₁;
        ELSE
         Statement₂;
        END IF;
        IF (Y > 0) THEN
         Statement₃;
        ELSE
         Statement₄;
        END IF;
```

This hints that the *first* members of S may not be particularly good at killing mutants, but rather: (1) they were lucky enough to have been selected early, and (2) they had the opportunity to kill the "easy" mutants. This shows that it is possible and practical to reduce the effect of the luck factor while also reducing the size of the final set of inputs.

Offutt et al. [Offutt 1995] produced a series of algorithms for decreasing the impact of the ordering of the test cases and found that for their small study they were able to reduce the number of test cases needed to kill off the same number of mutants by around 30 percent. If the testing target was some test criterion such as statement coverage, the set could be reduced in size by up to 50 percent. Note that the results were for fairly small programs; it cannot be expected that similar savings will always result from this technique. The three main test suite reduction procedures are as follows:

> **Forward procedure.**   In the forward procedure, we have a test set T of size N that is ordered in some sequence, and run all the test cases against the mutants in forward order. That is, if $seqT = \langle t_1, t_2, \ldots, t_N \rangle$, we run in the order $t_1, t_2, \ldots, t_N$. Then dispose of all the ineffective test cases, leaving a (possibly) smaller set T_f of size N_f.

> **Reverse procedure.**   In the reverse procedure, we have a test set T of size N in some sequence, and run all the test cases against the mutants in reverse order. That is, if $seqT = \langle t_1, t_2, \ldots, t_N \rangle$, we run in the order $t_N, t_{N-1}, \ldots, t_1$. We then dispose of all the ineffective test cases, leaving a smaller set T_r of size N_r.

> **Inside_out procedure.**   In the inside_out procedure, we have a sequence $seqT = \langle t_1, t_2, \ldots, t_N \rangle$, with size N, and run it from the middle test case to both ends. If N is an odd number, we run in the order $t_{(N+1)/2}, t_{(N+1)/2-1}, t_{(N+1)/2+1}, \ldots, t_1, t_N$; if N is an even number, we run in the order $t_{N/2+1}, t_{N/2}, t_{N/2-1}, \ldots, t_1, t_N$. We then dispose of all the ineffective test cases, leaving a smaller set T_i of size N_i.

Given the previous three basic procedures, Offutt et al. defined 12 reduction heuristics that were combinations of these basic procedures. They collectively called these the *ping-pong heuristics,* since they all involve some sort of bouncing from one end to the other of the sequence of test cases. Their philosophy behind the heuristics was simple—try to maximize the difference in the ordering of the test sets. Since the first test case will always kill at least one mutant, you can think of the mutation process as applying a very weak filter to that test case. The last few effective test cases, however, are executed with only a few mutants still alive, and you can think of the filter as being very strong. Thus, it is fair to assume that the last few test cases are in some sense "better" than the first few test cases. The ping-pong heuristics they applied in their experiments were:

1. forward–reverse
2. reverse–forward
3. forward–inside-out
4. reverse–inside-out
5. reverse–forward–inside-out
6. forward–reverse–inside-out

Offutt et al. observed that the first inputs selected during mutation testing killed a disproportionately large number of mutants, as compared to later inputs. For instance, the first few inputs may kill off 50 percent of the mutants, while it may require thousands of later inputs to kill another 40 percent of the mutants. This suggests that some members of M are "easy targets," and practically any input could kill them. This is why the first inputs of S will appear to have a powerful ability to kill mutants, when in reality they may have very little ability in general.

In summary, these heuristics are interesting ways to decrease the size of a set of mutation-adequate test sets while preserving the mutation adequacy. Many would argue against ever decreasing the size of a test suite, because even though a member of the set might not appear to be adding value beyond what the other members appear to be adding, it is possible that test case is doing something useful that we are not able to measure; hence deleting it is detrimental to the value of the overall suite. The goal here is not to answer this criticism but rather to demonstrate that random test-case selection is biased heavily by the initial seed, and there are ways to lessen the impact of this situation.

5.8 Summary

Fault injection has long been viewed as a way to assess the goodness of testing. It can also be used as a way to improve the quality of the test cases generated. Other than reliability estimation, the key application of testing is fault detection, and by using simulated faults in the absence of knowing where the real faults are, we can learn much about the likelihood that no faults are hiding if testing never results in an output failure.

This chapter has focused on software testability measurement via the PIE model. Software testability approaches such as the PIE approach came along after software mutation testing techniques and demonstrated that data-state mutations were another key form of fault injection that could benefit software testing. By studying how data corruptions propagate, we learn much about the goodness-of-the-test cases and whether testing should be employed or whether we should look to other approaches, such as formal verification, assertions, or code inspections, to detect faults. In addition, we have demonstrated a variety of different perturbation functions and guided the reader through the considerations that must be made when perturbation functions are created.

Finally, we looked at several phenomena that can bias the results and efficiency of fault injection, specifically, the number of test cases used when PIE is performed and the order in which test cases are generated (by mutation testing). In both of these situations, these seemingly unimportant parameters cannot be summarily dismissed. The approach outlined for thwarting the effect of pseudorandom test-case generation is applicable not only to mutation testing, but also to other unit testing approaches, such as branch, statement, and condition testing. We have provided workarounds for both of these scenarios; however, neither is totally satisfactory.

References

[Bertolino 1995] A. Bertolino and L. Strigini. "On the use of testability measures for dependability assessment." *IEEE Trans. on Software Engineering,* 22(2):97–108, August 1995.

[Friedman 1995] M. Friedman and J. Voas. *Software Assessment: Reliability, Safety, and Testability.* Wiley, 1995.

[Garey 1979] M. R. Garey and D. S. Johnson. *Computer and Intractability: A Guide to the Theory of NP-Completeness.* Freeman and Company, New York, NY, 1979.

[Hamlet 1993] R. Hamlet and J. Voas. "Faults on Its Sleeve: Amplifying Software Reliability Assessment." Proceedings of the ACM SIGSOFT Int'l. Symposium on Software Testing and Analysis, pp. 89–98, June, 1993.

[Michael 1997] C. C. Michael. "On the Uniformity of Error Propagation in Software." In Proceedings of the 12th Annual Conference on Computer Assurance (COMPASS '97). Gaithersburg, MD, 1997.

[Offutt 1995] J. Offutt, J. Pen, and J. Voas. "Procedures for Reducing the Size of Coverage-based Test Sets." In *Proc. of 12th Int'l. Conf. on Testing Computer Software,* Washington, D.C., June 1995.

[Park 1988] S. K. Park and K. W. Miller. "Random Number Generators: Good Ones are Hard to Find." *Communications of the ACM,* 31(10):1192–1201, October 1988.

[Voas 1990] J. Voas and L. Morell. "Applying Sensitivity Analysis Estimates to a Minimum Failure Probability for Software Testing." In *Proc. of the 8th Pacific Northwest Software Quality Conf.,* Portland, Oregon, pp. 261–271, October 1990.

[Voas 1992a] J. Voas and K. Miller. "The revealing power of a test case." *Journal of Software Testing, Verification, and Reliability,* 2(1):25–42, May 1992.

[Voas 1992b] J. M. Voas. "PIE: A Dynamic Failure-based Technique." *IEEE Transactions on Software Engineering,* 18(8):717–727, August 1992.

[Zuse 1990] H. Zuse. *Software Complexity: Measures and Methods.* DeGruyter, Berlin, 1990.

6

Software Safety
Hiding Faults with EPA

In chapters 4 and 5, we focused our discussion on anomalies that were based on approximations of the types of faults that programmers would potentially make. We discussed both software mutants and perturbation functions that mimicked either the appearance or behavior of traditional programmer faults. This chapter is also concerned with anomaly simulation, but instead of focusing on potential programmer faults, we focus on *data-related* events that crop up during execution. This may well be the most exciting application of fault injection to date.

Different software reacts very differently to anomalous data–related events that arise during execution. In other words, different software have different tolerance of such corruption. This chapter broadens the types of problems that we simulate to encompass different types of corrupt states that the program could potentially experience. We are still interested in simulating the effects on internal states that programmer faults have, but we will modify the way we decide whether fault injections are impacting software behavior.

Recall from the PIE algorithms in chapter 5 that the baseline benchmark for deciding whether a corrupted state affects program output was determined by running another version of the software without the corrupted state. This provides a baseline from which we could say whether the corrupted state had an effect on the software's behavior. In the analyses described in this chapter, we do not require a version of the software to be run without the injected corruption. Instead we develop a quasi oracle (really nothing more than a postcondition) about acceptable output behaviors. If a program produces an output that violates the postcondition after experiencing fault injection, then we will declare that the injected corrupt data state does have an effect on the software's output, and that the software is not tolerant to that problem. (This is not entirely true, as the original behavior without fault injection also might have violated the postcondition, but to save the expense of having to execute the software without injection to determine this, we will not execute a version without the injection.) If the postcondition is not violated after the software experiences fault injection, then the software will be deemed tolerant to that anomaly. The reason we use a postcondition is that there are often particular classes of failures which are *acceptable,* and we should be able to safely ignore them.

Just as the fault-injection algorithms in chapters 4 and 5 were based on instrumenting source code, the algorithms we provide here also require instrumentation of the source. The analyses described in this chapter and in chapter 8 will be of interest to those involved in critical software systems. Although what is or is not a "critical system" is often debated, a critical software system here is simply a system where failure, denial of service, and so forth, could have expensive consequences. Expensive consequences could include loss of life, a loss of business, lost property or financial interests, and so forth. Interestingly enough, the fault injection methods presented in chapter 6 are also relevant to those persons involved in building systems from off-the-shelf (OTS) components, and we discuss in chapter 9 how to use some of these techniques even when source code is absent. Finally, the methods described in this chapter also apply to maintenance problems, specifically today's mega testing/maintenance problem and the Year 2000 problem; we will save the discussion of how to do this until chapter 9.

Before we get started, let's define a few terms used throughout this chapter. Software systems are said to be fault-tolerant if the systems are able to recover from faults during operation. Formally, the Institute for Electronics and Electrical Engineers defines *fault tolerance* to be:

> *(1) The ability of a system or component to continue normal operation despite the presence of hardware or software faults. (2) The number of faults a system or component can withstand before normal operation is impaired. (3) Pertaining to the study of errors, faults, and failures, and of methods for enabling systems to continue normal operation in the presence of fault.*

Our notion, *software failure tolerance,* differs from the traditional meaning of fault tolerance in electrical and computer engineering [Marciniak 1994]. Traditionally, fault-tolerant design refers to building subsystems from redundant components that are placed in parallel. Here, software is deemed as *failure-tolerant* if and only if:

1. The program is able to compute an acceptable result even if the program itself suffers from incorrect logic.
2. The program, whether correct or incorrect, is able to compute an acceptable result even if the program itself receives corrupted incoming data during execution.

The key to this definition is deciding what is "acceptable." The criteria for acceptance can include characteristics as correct behavior and "safe" behavior. Accomplishing failure tolerance requires adherence to a combination of the principles of "safe software" and robust design.

Technically speaking, all software is safe. Software by itself cannot harm you, but software that controls "something else" can cause the "something else" to harm you. Software is considered to be safe if its behavior is safe, meaning that all outputs from the software are such that no harm can occur. Clearly to demonstrate this for all outputs requires that every possible output from the software be studied with respect to the system state when the output is released, and naturally this is generally computationally infeasible. Hence, there are degrees of safety, just as there are degrees of reliability.

For software where safety is a concern, there are three classes of output states that can be produced from a program execution:

1. Correct
2. Incorrect but acceptable (nonhazardous)
3. Hazardous

Software failure tolerance refers to the ability of the software to produce "acceptable" outputs regardless of the program states that are encountered during execution. What constitutes an acceptable output is defined by the system-level requirements. *Software safety* refers to the ability of the software to produce nonhazardous outputs regardless of the program states that are encountered during execution. Once again, what constitutes an output hazard is defined by the system-level safety requirements. By our definitions, software safety is simply a special form of software failure tolerance. Failure tolerance is based on a class of outputs that can be tolerated, and software safety is based on a class of outputs that cannot be tolerated.

We have mentioned several times that safe outputs are defined by the system-level requirements. This is a very important point. Software safety cannot be viewed like reliability, where we can assert what is desirable in terms of software correctness and leave it at that. Even correct software can put a system into unsafe states; for this reason, software cannot be deemed as safe until that entire system is considered, as well as the impact that different outputs from the software could have on the system.

We say that software is *failure-tolerant* (or *anomaly-tolerant*) if the software is able to produce acceptable outputs no matter what anomalies manifest themselves in the states of the executing program. This does not mean that the anomalies have no impact, only that the impact is acceptable. The difference between software failure tolerance and software fault tolerance is that software fault tolerance is generally concerned with programmer faults, whereas failure tolerance is concerned with a broader class of anomalies including corrupt information that originates externally to the application software and is fed into the software as input. Naturally, we desire that software be able to overcome all classes of anomalies during execution. Unfortunately this lofty goal is unrealistic.

Most of the literature on fault-tolerant systems describes design approaches for increasing software's fault tolerance, and thus we spend some time here in chapter 6 discussing the most basic of several of these approaches. After all, the goal of fault injection in this section is mainly to assess software's tolerance, and thus to better understand software tolerance we should discuss the traditional approaches for making software tolerant. Many such approaches employ either redundancy or recovery. In real life, however, most fault-tolerant designs do not conform strictly to either paradigm, and are instead a combination of the two. In sections 6.1.1 to 6.1.3, we discuss several different design approaches for building software that is more resilient to anomalies. Then, we discuss the role that fault injection can play in helping to measure resilience as well as provide insights into how to boost resilience. (See section 10.2.2.)

6.1 Making Software More Tolerant of Faults

There have been a variety of approaches proposed for making software more fault-tolerant. Here, we discuss the more popular of these approaches.

6.1.1 Recovery Blocks

Software recovery has occurred successfully when a piece of software is able to produce acceptable output even when the software somehow gets into an erroneous state. This can happen by getting the software from the erroneous state to an alternative state that is not erroneous. There are two approaches to building recovery mechanisms into software: forward and backward. *Forward recovery* mechanisms enable a program to repair a corrupted state and continue execution. *Backward recovery* mechanisms require that the program roll back in time to an earlier state that was not corrupt and then begin executing forward again. Clearly, rolling back in time can be a difficult, if not impossible, process. The difficulty stems from the impossibility of determining how far back to go in time, as well as the possibility that inverting the computation and going backward depends on nondeterministic events. For this reason, forward recovery is easier to implement.

One of the earliest fault-tolerant software schemes was called "recovery block" [Randell 1975]. A *recovery block* is a fault-tolerance improvement technique that consists of two or more software versions and a single acceptance test. *Acceptance tests* are essentially executable assertions. It is also fair to think of acceptance tests as being the likelihood checks which are traditionally used in process control. Multiple versions of a system are available. The versions are ranked, with the first version called *primary* and the other versions deemed *alternates*. Ideally, the primary will be the version most likely to produce correct output, meaning that executing the alternates will be less likely to occur—something that is certainly better if real-time performance issues must be considered.

The primary version and alternates are independently developed. When a recovery block is executed on an input, the primary version gets executed first and its output is evaluated for acceptability by the acceptance test. If the acceptance test fails for the primary, or any other version for that matter, rollback recovery is attempted by calling the next alternate version on the same input vector. This process of repeatedly moving on to the next succeeding version is continued until either a version produces an acceptable output to the acceptance test, rollback recovery does not succeed, or until all versions fail to produce an output that is accepted by the acceptance test.

Several problems occur with the idea of recovery-block fault tolerance. The first is the sequential nature of the execution of the versions. For example, what if one version were to get stuck in an infinite loop and fail to return a value to the acceptance test or return a value at a time too late to benefit the system? For real-time systems, this could be disastrous [Belli 1991]. Ideally, in the case of real-time systems, the ordering of the alternatives will be set up so the primary is the most likely to satisfy the acceptance test, the final alternative is the least likely, and those in between the extremes are ranked in descending order of reliability. The other key problem is finding a highly reliable acceptance test. After all, if the acceptance test is faulty, then it is possible to reject correct results from the versions or accept incorrect results from the versions! In fact, the acceptance test can be as complex as the individual versions, and should really be thought of as yet another part of the code.

The pseudocode showing the typical layout for a recovery block with K versions follows:

```
guarantee acceptance test
        by primary version
        else by alternate version 2
        else by alternate version 3
        ...
        else by final alternate version K
else fail
```

After the last else clause, where no alternate produces acceptable output to the acceptance test, the recovery-block scheme fails for that input vector. An infamous example of where recovery failed was the Ariane 5 Flight 501 disaster [Lions 1996]. (See chapter 7 for more details.) There were many problems that contributed to that disaster, one of which was that the primary and single alternate version were not distinct, but instead were identical. Thus when the primary failed and the alternate was called, it failed in the same manner less than one second after the primary failed—a multimillion-dollar mistake!

6.1.2 N-Version Programming

N-version programming (NVP) is another approach to making software systems more tolerant to the logical faults that can occur in software [Avizienis 1977]. This approach is based on redundancy and diversity. N-version programming employs the idea of building multiple *diverse* copies of a specification, executing all of the versions in parallel, and then deciding among the outputs of the versions as to which output to use. The purpose here is improved reliability of the total system through a kind of democratic process. Diversity stems from the independent creation of different versions by different programming teams, all starting with the same specification. Although multiple versions are executed in parallel, there is no communication between them. Therefore anything that goes wrong in one version cannot deleteriously impact the computations of others. The theory is that if one or more of the components fails, there will still be enough other components that don't fail that the system will still receive the correct output. N-version programming is currently in use aboard commercial aircraft. Frequent travelers will have bet their lives on it when traveling on the Airbus A-300 and A-310.

N-version programming can be seen as a form of recovery block where all versions are executed in parallel, and the acceptance test is replaced by a *voter* that adjudicates among the outputs and determines which outputs are correct. One problem with all strategies based on voting is that situations can arise where there is an insufficient number of agreeing versions and voting fails simply because the voter can't make a decision. In Figure 6.1, we see a three-version system. The outputs of the versions are fed into the voter, which then makes the final decision as to what the output will be for a specific input vector to the system. Clearly, the correctness of the voter is of enormous importance in an N-version system. Because of this, much attention is given to assuring correct voter behavior. Often the voter is formally proven to be correct. In fact, the quality of the voter is so important to the success of this scheme that it is not completely inconceivable to think of having multiple distinct voters, except that you still need a "meta-voter" for the voters.

There are many different algorithms for software voters. The default voting scheme is called *major voting,* where 50 percent or more of the versions must agree on a result in order for the voter to go with that result. In a *mean voting* scheme, the result is simply the average. For example, if three versions produced

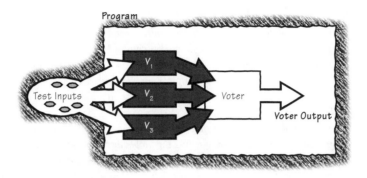

Figure 6.1 *N-version system.*

results 54, 55, and 56, then the voter would select 55. In *median voting,* if three versions produced the values 50, 52, and 60, the voter would select 52. One significant problem occurs for voters that are required to make floating-point comparisons. For example, if the voter receives 123.45678 from one version, is that the same result as 123.4568 produced by a different version?

The concept of N-version programming was first defined by Avizienis and Chen in 1977; however, there were suggestions for multiple versions that appeared in the literature prior to 1977. Avizienis and Chen defined N-version programming as follows [Avizienis 1977]:

> *N-version programming is defined as the independent generation of N ≥ 2 functionally equivalent programs from the same initial specification. The N programs possess all the necessary attributes for concurrent execution, during which comparison vectors ("c-vectors") are generated by the program at certain points. The program state variables that are to be included in each c-vector and the cross-check points ("cc-points") at which the c-vectors are to be generated are specified along with the initial seed.*
>
> *"Independent generation of programs" here means that the programming efforts are carried out by N individuals or groups that do not interact with respect to the programming process. Wherever possible, different algorithms and programming languages (or translators) are used in each effort. The initial specification is a formal specification in a specification language. The goal of the initial specification is to state the functional requirements completely and unambiguously, while leaving the widest possible choice of implementations to the N programming efforts. The actions to be taken at the cc-points after the exchange of c-vectors are also specified along with the initial specification.*

N-version programming as an approach to improving the fault tolerance of software came about because of the success of the two main characteristics of independence and redundancy in improving hardware's fault tolerance. Any value added by employing more than one version of the software is directly dependent on the relationship between the faults in different versions as noted by Avizienis [Avizienis 1977]:

> *The second major observation concerning N-version programming is that its success as a method for on-line tolerance of software faults depends on whether the residual software faults in each version of the program are distinguishable. Distinguishable software faults are faults that will cause disagreement between c-vectors at the specified cc-points during the execution of the N-version set of programs that have been generated from the initial specification. Distinguishability is affected by the choice of c-vectors and cc-points, as well as by the nature of the faults themselves.*
>
> *It is a fundamental conjecture of the N-version approach that the independence of programming efforts will greatly reduce the probability of identical software faults occurring in two or more versions of the program. In turn, the distinctness of faults and a reasonable choice of c-vectors and cc-points is expected to turn N-version programming into an effective method to achieve tolerance of software faults. The effectiveness of the entire N-version approach depends on the validity of this conjecture, therefore it is of critical importance that the initial specification should be free of any flaws that would bias the independent programmers towards introducing the same software faults.*

As we discuss later, the possibility that enough versions contain the same flaw, due to a flaw or an ambiguity in their common specification, is the Achilles' heel of this approach.

Common–Mode Failures

The great problem for N-version programming is common-mode failures. NVP has been attacked in many studies since fault independence cannot be guaranteed. Nevertheless, Avizienis argues that independence is the objective of N-version programming, not an assumed condition necessary for it to be successful. *Common-mode failure* occurs when two or more software components are affected by faults in exactly the same way and at the same time [Johnson 1989]. This means the faults are not independent. Common-mode failures are said to occur when there exists at least one input combination for which the outputs of two or more versions are erroneous, as well as being identical for some input combination. Thus, if two or more versions respond to all inputs in the same way, and there is at least one combination that causes the versions to respond incorrectly, common–mode failure has occurred. Note that this definition is really not talking so much about common failures, but is really talking about common behavior between the versions, because of the restriction added into the definition that requires that the version be in agreement for all inputs. Although the definition requires agreement for all inputs, in practice it is impossible to demonstrate that for all inputs two programs behave in exactly the same way unless this demonstration is done using all possible inputs (which takes us back to the problem of exhaustive testing).

Common-mode failures are generally a result of specification errors, not simple programmer errors. Simple programmer faults are less subtle than are specification errors and can usually be detected and fixed more easily. Whenever specification errors are present, they are likely to result in faults that cause outputs to occur satisfying the definition for common-mode failure. If we could ensure that specifications were complete and correct, most of the flack that NVP draws would go away.

Diversity and Various Perspectives

Although software systems made of redundant software components are somewhat uncommon in the United States, they are looked upon more favorably elsewhere. Airbus uses diverse software components for the A320/A330/A340 electrical flight controls systems. There are two types of computers (SECs and ELACs) for the flight controls system of A320, designed and manufactured by different equipment manufacturers. They have different microprocessors, different computer architectures, and different functional specifications. Each of these computers has a control channel and a monitoring channel. This leads to four different software packages; each program on each channel is distinct. So diversity occurs at more than one level [Traverse 1989; Briere 1993]. The airbus controller is unique among aircraft controllers because it uses NVP.

Unlike the airplane control business, redundancy is universally prevalent in the nuclear power industry. Digital instrumentation and control systems in nuclear power plants employ independent protection systems to detect system failures in order to isolate and shut down failed subsystems. These protection systems usually employ a voting scheme that uses a two-out-of-four logic where, if one channel fails, it is taken out of service and the system goes into a two-out-of-three logic and continues operation. This type of system is deemed *single-failure proof*. The U.S. Nuclear Regulatory Agency has developed a position with respect to diversity, as stated in the technical position "Digital Instrumentation and Control Systems in Advanced Plants" [USNRC 1994]:

> *1. The applicant shall assess the defense-in-depth and diversity of the proposed instrumentation and control system to demonstrate that vulnerabilities to common-mode failures have been adequately addressed. The staff considers software design errors to be credible common-mode failures that must be specifically included in the evaluation.*
>
> *2. In performing the assessment, the vendor or applicant shall analyze each postulated common-mode failure for each event that is evaluated in the analysis section of the safety analysis report (SAR) using best-estimate methods. The vendor or applicant shall demonstrate adequate diversity within the design for each of these events.*

The Canadian Atomic Energy Control Board has also developed a position on this issue. Their draft guide C-138, "Software in Protection and Control Systems," contains the following language [AECB 1996]:

> *To achieve the required levels of safety and reliability, the system may need to be designed to use multiple, diverse components performing the same or similar functions.*

For example, AECB Regulatory Documents R-8 and R-10 require two independent and diverse protective shutdown systems in Canadian nuclear power reactors. It should be recognized that when multiple components use software to provide similar functionality, there is a danger that design diversity may be compromised. The design should address this danger by enforcing other types of diversity such as functional diversity, independent and diverse sensors, and timing diversity.

The U.S. Federal Aviation Administration has a different perspective on redundancy. Their position is that since the degree of protection afforded by design diversity is not quantifiable, employing diversity will only be counted as additional protection beyond the already required levels of assurance [FAA 1992]:

The degree of dissimilarity and hence the degree of protection is not usually measurable. Probability of loss of system function will increase to the extent that the safety monitoring associated with dissimilar software versions detects actual errors or experiences transients that exceed comparator threshold limits. Multiple software versions are usually used, therefore, as a means of providing additional protection after the software verification process objectives for the software level have been satisfied.

The U.S. Office of Device Evaluation of the Center for Devices and Radiological Health of the U.S. FDA has issued a report, "Reviewer Guidance for Computer Controlled Medical Devices Undergoing 510(k) Review" [FDA 1991]. This report applies to the software aspects of premarket notification submissions for medical devices. The FDA does not dictate any particular approach to safety, nor does it dictate specific software quality assurance and development procedures. Because there is no specification on how safety is to be achieved or demonstrated, the FDA provides no guidance on redundancy and diversity.

In summary, N-version programming's goal was to develop independent versions that each suffered from distinct programmer flaws. If this could be achieved, then design diversity should be a programming paradigm that would afford us more reliable software systems. But as we learned, NVP suffered from the commonness of the specification, as well as the strange phenomenon where uncorrelated programming faults in different versions were such that they still produced common-mode failures. This was an unexpected event indeed. But regardless of the flukelike strange events that can occur, NVP is widely touted in the safety-critical community as a prudent way to improve software quality.

6.1.3 *Consensus Recovery Block*

The consensus recovery block (CRB) scheme is a fault-tolerance design paradigm that combines features of both recovery blocks and NVP [Scott 1983]. The method requires two or more independent versions to be developed, a comparator for the results, a modified recovery block, and an N-version voter. In the

CRB approach, the boundaries of the consensus recovery block are established by selecting logical checkpoints. At these locations, the results of the N versions are compared. If a majority of the N versions agree then the voter selects that output and propagates it out of the block. If the comparator decides that there is no agreement or consensus among the versions, a modified recovery block is entered. In the modified recovery block, an acceptance test is applied to the result of the primary version. If this result is accepted, it is propagated out of the block. If the primary version fails the acceptance test, the test is applied to the result of the next-best version. Testing proceeds in this manner until a result is accepted or all alternatives have failed. In this last case, the block fails and an "error" result is returned.

CRB addresses one of the criticisms of NVP: the inability to handle dissimilar but equally correct outputs. In NVP, dissimilar outputs are treated like errors by the voter. When this occurs, it is possible that the voter will fail to select a correct output. In CRB, the acceptance test can validate multiple outputs and avert the problem. As an example of a problem that CRB addresses well, suppose that a piece of software's function is to determine a route to get an airplane from point A to B. It is possible that the different versions decide on different routes, but nonetheless they all succeed in finding paths from A to B. In a traditional NVP system, path diversity would force the voter to decide that, since different solutions were found, bad processing was going on, when in fact all solutions were equally correct.

6.1.4 Analyzing Software for Fault Tolerance with Fault Trees

Now that we have outlined several approaches to improving software's tolerance to anomalous events, let's discuss a common method for assessing the tolerance of complete systems—static fault-tree analysis. *Static fault-tree analysis* is a design/development technique that was developed in the '60s by Bell Laboratories. Static fault-tree analysis is a way of assessing the causal relationship between particular events in a process. It was originally developed to evaluate the possibility that the Minuteman Launch Control System might force an undesirable rocket launch. Since that time, fault-tree analysis has been imported to software from systems safety engineering. Systems safety analysis techniques attempt to ensure safety by using a "backward" approach: first determine catastrophic output events (hazards), and only then work backward from the hazards to show either that the undesired output events cannot occur or that the probability that they will occur is low. Fault-tree analysis is designed primarily as an approach to rooting out the causes of undesirable events.

In a backward analysis, the designer attempts to show that hazards are not possible or, in the worst case, only very rarely possible. By contrast, in a forward safety analysis, the designer tries to show that all output events are noncatastrophic. For a backward approach to be practical, the set of hazards must be small, otherwise the time required to perform the backward analysis will be intractably long. For a forward approach to work, all inputs must be guaranteed to result in nonhazardous outputs. This is also intractable since most applications have huge input spaces.

Software safety can be viewed as a subset of the larger problem of *system* safety. (Hardware fault tolerance is an example of a different subset.) Assume that a physical system has a fixed set of functions that it performs: $F = \{f_1, f_2, f_3, \ldots, f_N\}$. Further, assume that for each subset of F, there are zero or more hazards that must be protected against. Given that the software directly or indirectly controls some percentage of F's functionality, the goal of software safety assessment for this physical system is to show that the software cannot affect a subset of F in a manner that could lead to a physical hazard. Before software safety can be demonstrated in a backward manner, system hazards must be enumerated. So system safety must be completely and unambiguously defined before software safety can be demonstrated.

A fault tree is a graphical representation of events. The graph is a tree-data structure. The root node, sometimes called the *top node,* represents a hazard or class of hazards. It represents the final dangerous and undesirable event in a sequence that hopefully cannot take place within the system. The bad event must be predicted using some other technique before fault-tree analysis can ensue. In other words, fault-tree analysis does not have to define what this event is. The remainder of the tree represents a set of parallel and sequential events that have the potential of causing the hazard to occur. Nodes immediately under the top node are intermediate events. They are combinations of the lowest events in the fault tree. These lowest nodes, called *leaf nodes,* are primary events that can actually occur in the system, whereas the intermediate events are abstract events. Leaf-node events represent a variety of sources: programming faults, design errors, human errors, malicious attacks, or hardware failures. Thus a fault tree represents all types of events that have the potential to set off a domino effect in events that eventually lead to a hazard. In this analogy, if the last standing domino falls, the hazard has occurred. The goal in safe software development is to ensure that even if the domino effect begins, there are some dominos standing in the line that are so large that even if they are hit by a toppling neighbor, they do not fall.

Figure 6.2 shows the relationship between the top event, the leaf nodes, and the intermediate events in a fault tree.

Fault trees are conceptually simple. They are composed of two major parts: events, and logical event connectors including OR-gates, NOT-gates, and AND-gates. Nodes in the tree can be events that are expected to occur under normal circumstances (leaf events) and intermediate events created from combinations of

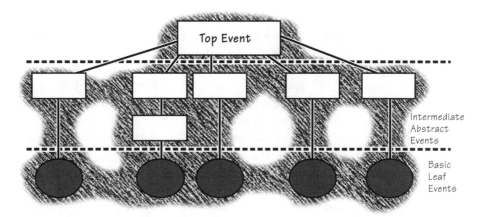

Figure 6.2 Basic fault-tree hierarchy.

lower-level events. Other node types represent conditions that must occur in order to produce outputs from gates, and other fault events that are not considered consequential. Any given nonleaf-event node has children that represent the necessary preconditions that could cause that event to occur. These preconditions can be combined in any number of combinations using logical OR-gates and AND-gates. Events in the tree are continually expanded, creating subtrees until leaf events are created for which we can assign a probability, or until leaf events are created that cannot be decomposed into subevents. Events in a fault tree can describe different levels of system abstraction. Typically, nodes higher on the tree are at a higher level of abstraction, and nodes lower on the tree are at a lower level of abstraction, more precise and refined than the higher nodes. For example, a hazardous event for an auto-land system might be "plane lands before runway is reached," and a lower intermediate node might be "flaps fail to lower," with the leaf nodes from this intermediate node being all actual events that might hinder the flaps from lowering, like "pilot fails to lower flaps," "plane at excess speed," or "flaps are stuck." Once a system state and top event for a system are identified, a fault tree can be constructed by a safety analyst who writes down all of the causal events related to the top event plus the logical relationships between them.

Conventional software safety is typically performed during the design phase of the software life cycle. This happens for two important reasons:

1. Other engineering fields have applied fault-tree analysis to design long before the expense of building the system is authorized. This is prudent: Imagine building a fleet of aircraft and then discovering that the design resulted in a fleet of aircraft that cannot be flown.

2. Catching problems in the design phase before coding begins is cost-effective.

For software, the downside of applying fault-tree analysis only to designs is the possibility that the code will not reflect the original design, and therefore not provide adequate safety. Although fault trees can certainly aid the software-design process, building code-based fault trees and then performing mitigation analysis can also be applied to software safety [Leveson 1995]. In [Leveson 1995], each source-code construct used in a program is represented in the fault tree by a template (which is simply a subtree) that represents the different ways in which the construct could fail. When fault-tree analysis is applied to an entire program, it shows the calling hierarchy and the interrelationships between the actual software components and the top event of interest, which represents undesirable software outputs. The objective of code-based fault-tree analysis is not to replace design-based fault-tree analysis. Both have benefits. But for the purpose of showing whether software can produce certain classes of undesirable output events, fault-tree analysis at the code level is a good idea with the following benefits:

1. The code is a more precise definition of exactly which computations are doing what than a software design document usually gives.
2. Potential sources of hazards can be more exactly decomposed and analyzed when the code is used.
3. A fault tree that is automatically generated from the code can be compared to fault trees previously generated from early versions of the code and compared to see if the system is becoming "safer" as the system evolves.
4. A fault tree that is automatically generated from code can be compared to a fault tree that is manually generated from the design to indicate whether original intuitions about what can or cannot lead to a hazard were accurate—substantiating or disproving the original safety hypotheses.

The downside to code-based fault trees, though, is that each modification of the software can result in a different fault tree, and reexamination of the fault tree may be necessary because of the code modifications. Also, for systems that contain more than a few thousand lines of code, the size of these fault trees can become enormous, and it can become nearly impossible to visually see all of the components of the fault tree. Thus, even though code-based fault trees are an interesting approach to demonstrating safe software behavior, they are rarely applied on a statement-by-statement level through the code.

State of the Practice in Fault-Tree Mitigation

The goal of fault-tree analysis is to find all events that might contribute to a hazard, and then show that they cannot. Clearly life is usually not quite this cut-and-dried. In life, there are various probabilities associated with certain events occurring, and there are certain hazards that are possible but with low frequency. Thus it will often be the case that instead of using fault trees to show that hazards cannot occur, we will instead step back and show that they are unlikely to occur. One such metric that can be used to demonstrate this is mean-time-to-hazard.

Mean-time-to-hazard is an estimate of the average amount of time before a hazardous output event will occur. An example may be helpful in showing how fault trees are currently used to create assessment metrics such as mean-time-to-hazard. As you will see, current practice is heavily laden with assumptions about anomaly distribution. This serves to call the practice into question. For the purposes of this example, assume that the fault tree has events that are time-dependent.

Each leaf node has a mean-time-to-occurrence and a mean-duration associated with it. Each leaf node starts out in the normal state. From time to time each leaf transitions to a nonnormal state (for example, it fails and is down for a while). The interval between transitions from the normal to the nonnormal state is modeled by an exponential distribution whose parameter value is the mean-time-between-occurrence. The amount of time spent in the nonnormal state before transitioning back to the normal state is modeled by an exponential distribution as well, controlled by a parameter known as the *mean-duration*.

Each leaf alternates between a normal state and a nonnormal state. As normal, the higher-level nodes (nonleaf nodes) are Boolean functions of the leaf nodes. The states of each of the leaves pass through the AND-gates and OR-gates of the tree and determine the state (normal or nonnormal) of each nonleaf. Evaluation of the state of the nonleaves proceeds in a bottom-up fashion. When all the output nodes feeding into an AND-gate are in the normal state simultaneously, then the input node is in the normal state; otherwise, the input node is in the nonnormal state. An input node to an OR-gate is in the normal state only if all its output nodes are in the normal state simultaneously; otherwise, it is in the nonnormal state.

The simulation that will eventually provide the mean-time-to-hazard estimate is event-driven. An event is the transition of a leaf node's state from normal to nonnormal (an *occurrence*) and a transition from nonnormal back to normal (a *restoration*). A queue of upcoming events is maintained. This queue is always maintained in chronological order, with events that happen sooner than others at the head of the queue. Because only discrete events are modeled, simulated time passes very quickly, making it possible to run millions of years of simulated time in a few minutes. Every time a leaf node changes state, the higher-level nodes are evaluated as to their state. For every node, a running mean time between occurrences and a running mean duration are calculated and stored. The mean time between occurrences of the root node, then, is the mean time between hazards (MTTH). More technically, each leaf is a two-state Markov model. One state is normal, the other is nonnormal. When a leaf changes state, the nonleaf nodes may change state, too. Each nonleaf node is a Boolean function (nested AND-gates and OR-gates) of some leaf nodes. The state of the root node is a Boolean function of all the leaf nodes. The mean-time-to-hazard is simply the average amount of time that the root node spends in the nonnormal state. What this then shows is not that the software is fully safe, but that portion of the time in which you can expect unsafe behavior. This then is one way to show the level of safe behavior afforded by a particular software program.

In summary, fault-tree analysis is generally applied for one of two reasons: (1) to assess and define the causal relationships between events in a fault tree, and (2) to quantify metrics such as mean-time-to-hazard after various assumptions are made concerning how long events occur and how frequently events occur. Fault-tree analysis has been applied quite successfully and for many years in the hardware world, namely because independence between various events can be guaranteed. In the digital world, these assumptions are more questionable, and hence software fault-tree analysis has not gained the same widespread acceptance.

6.1.5 Software Wrappers

A relatively new software safety idea currently gaining wider appeal as a way of reducing the possibility of misbehaving software is that of *software wrappers*. A wrapper is a piece of software that surrounds another piece of software with the purpose of limiting the outputs that the "inner" piece of software can produce. The intuition behind wrappers is quite similar in nature to the idea behind voters and acceptance tests: Software that has too much functionality (for whatever reason, say, the software has been purchased and has a lot of unnecessary generic functionality) will have its functionality forcefully reduced by either limiting the inputs that the "inner" software can receive or forcefully reducing the output events that the "inner" component can produce.

Limiting the number of different inputs is a clear and unambiguous way to reduce the functionality of the software, but the software still might produce the same undesirable output events for any input case accidentally not filtered. No matter how clever the designer, it is quite likely that filtering all dangerous inputs that the software should not receive will unintentionally result in some dangerous inputs being allowed to slip by. The same thing holds for output filtering. Once again, designers can filter only those events that they remember to filter out. Unintentionally letting some output events by the filter may be a problem. This problem is particularly difficult for executable components, because there may be undiscovered functionality embedded in a component. Without knowing about such functionality, it is impossible to filter it properly.

One other problem with wrappers can be their complexity. Simply determining how to filter the outputs can be a very fault-prone process due to the complexity in the decision-making process. For example, there might only be certain situations where an output value of "6" is not desirable, and so you must decide if you want to disallow all "6"s from being produced, or if you want to build a more complex filter that disallows "6"s only in certain situations. Interestingly, it is often the case that the software that we rely on for special events, like exception handlers, winds up being the code that is the least reliable and most prone to cause problems. Wrappers that are placed around software output are subject to suffer from similar problems and thus are not a panacea for improving the quality of software.

Interestingly, fault injection can be used to test software wrappers. This can be done by injecting corrupted information into a component and then observing whether the component produces outputs that the component was not supposed to. This can be applied in parallel with regular black-box testing to see if certain classes of events that are specified not to occur actually do.

6.1.6 Safety-Critical Partitioning

It is very common in safety-critical systems to attempt to ensure fault tolerance of the safety critical portion of a software system by partitioning the software system such that the functionality of the software that is deemed as noncritical cannot negatively impact that functionality that is deemed as safety-critical. This is sometimes referred to as "firewalling" or partitioning of the software, and almost every set of software standards for safety-critical software has some set of requirements for ensuring that software partitioning is done correctly.

In Figure 6.3, we observe this process in action. In this example, a system-level safety analysis is performed that identifies hazards, and then fault trees are created according to those hazards, where the hazards are the top nodes in the fault trees, as discussed earlier. From this analysis, a set of software requirements is generated which differentiate the critical requirements for the safety-critical functionality. A firewall or partitioning is built between the functionality that is deemed as critical and the remaining functionality. One common way that this can be enforced is through data encapsulation.

Once the partitioning is decided upon, the critical functions and noncritical functions are designed and the code for these functions is written. In Figure 6.3, the critical code is on the left in the shaded box, and the noncritical code is on the right in the unshaded box. The role that fault injection can play here is as follows: At the system level, we can place our hazard monitors on the outputs of the safety-critical functions, and place the fault injection on the non-safety-critical functions, and see if "propagation across" from noncritical to critical occurs; that

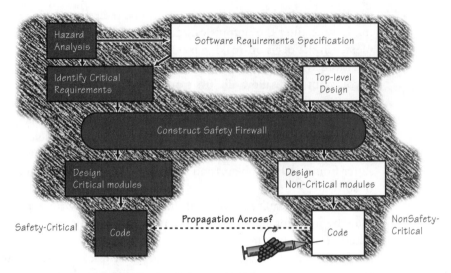

Figure 6.3 *Testing safety-critical firewalls.*

is, do the anomalies we inject into the noncritical functions affect the critical functions? Recognize that the entire reason that we employed firewalling in the first place was to keep this from occurring. If the results of fault injection demonstrate that this is possible, then the partitions that we have built into the system have been breached and are not functioning properly.

There are several software safety standards that are highly concerned with partitioning of those software components that perform the most critical of the system's function. An example is the FAA's DO-178B that defines partitioning:

> *Partitioning is a strategy for providing isolation between software components to contain and/or isolate faults and potentially reduce the effort of the software verification process.*

Section 2.3.1 a.1 of the same document talks about the types of entities that could potentially compromise a partition that should be avoided:

> *Potential breaches of the partitioning that should be considered when designing partitioning protections are:*
>
> *1. Hardware resources: processors, memory devices, I/O devices, interrupts, and timers.*
> *2. Control coupling: vulnerability to external access.*
> *3. Data coupling: shared or overlaying data, including stacks and processor registers.*
> *4. Failure modes of hardware devices associated with the protection mechanisms.*

Although fault injection cannot simulate all of these classes of defined partition breaches, the fourth class is clearly one that fault injection, as we define it later in this chapter, can handle.

6.2 Software Tolerance Measurement with EPA

We have discussed a handful of techniques for improving fault tolerance through different design schemes. Now that we've filled in the background, we can address the use of fault injection in anomaly tolerance assessment.

Software Fault Insertion Testing, sometimes referred to as Software Fault Injection Testing, led the charge in early fault injection–based assessment of software system tolerance levels [Segal 1988; Arlat 1990; Dilenno 1991; Arlat 1992; Avresky 1992; Echtle 1992; Voas 1992; Kao 1993; Rosenberg 1993; Solheim 1993; Clark 1995]. Generally speaking, early SFIT work shares a common theme, specifically, injecting undesirable events into an executing system. The main differences between approaches include the types of systems to which fault injection is applied, fault classes injected, instrumentation methods for performing the injection, and the types of postconditions that define acceptable behavior. System types investigated with SFIT include: safety-critical applications, distributed systems, and operating systems. Fault classes include: source-code modifications, memory bit faults, communication between processor faults, and processor faults.

Software fault insertion testing is not traditional software testing. The idea is not to test software in its normal state, but instead to analyze the effects of injected faults. Injecting faults into program states is the most popular form of fault injection. There are four main methods for state-based fault injection:

1. *Message-based.* This approach corrupts the messages between components as they execute.

2. *Memory/Storage-based.* This approach corrupts the value of information stored either in a database, in memory, or on a disk.

3. *Debugger-based.* This approach uses a debugger to inject errors into a running process.

4. *Process-based.* This approach affects the state of the system by manipulating processes, for example, by having a high-priority process affect system state.

In this chapter, we focus our attention on methods (1) and (2).

6.2.1 Extended Propagation Analysis (EPA)

Extended propagation analysis (EPA) is a memory/storage-based approach to fault injection. This chapter covers several propagation analysis algorithms, and includes information about transforming propagation analysis into a technique for assessing the impacts of broader classes of anomalous states. This chapter also offers a postcondition language for assessing whether a corrupted state "does something" to a piece of software's behavior. This is related to but slightly different from the information provided in chapter 5. This postcondition language is necessary if we are able to use fault injection to assess safety, since to do so we will need a way to define "unsafe."

Software must protect against three major classes of problems before they qualify as failure tolerant: faults in the software itself, the effects of failures in other software subsystems that feed into the software (either implicitly or explicitly), and inputs from hardware that has failed. (Hardware failures are sometimes called "hardware faults.") At the software level, inputs from hardware that has failed can be modeled as erroneous data coming into the software.

Recall that our problem space diagram in chapter 3, partitioned the "all problems" space into the existing faults and external problems that could "attack" the software. To determine the tolerance of the code to existing faults, we only need to execute the code according to the operational profile with a postcondition checker turned on. But for those anomalies outside of the existing faults partition, we must employ modified fault-injection instrumentation procedures.

Our approach for injecting such anomalies is a technique termed "Extended Propagation Analysis" (EPA) [Voas 1994; Voas 1997a]. Extended propagation analysis is a dynamic fault injection–based technique that instruments source code so that it can simulate all three classes of problems. EPA could be thought of as a type of software fault-insertion testing that is applied at the source-code level. EPA allows us to assert with confidence what the net impact of the hardware and software failure simulated by EPA is on output variables. We can also estimate the probability that these failures, which are represented as corrupt data states by EPA, will result in catastrophic outputs from the software.

Just as in propagation analysis in chapter 5, extended propagation analysis requires the unique identification of specific syntactic software constructs as well as the internal data states created during execution. To uniquely identify syntactic constructs, EPA defines a *location* to be either an assignment statement, an input statement, an output statement, or the <condition> part of an "if" or "while" statement. A *program state* (sometimes called a *data state*) is a set of mappings between all declared and dynamically allocated variables and their values at a particular point in the software's execution. Note that a program state also includes both the test case used during the software's execution and a pointer to what the next source code location to be executed will be. Program states exist between consecutive locations. The purpose behind EPA is to modify the contents of program states of software and see what impact such modifications have on the software's output. EPA can be applied at any place in the source code where it is possible to add a syntactically legal assignment statement.

If location *l* is an assignment statement, then lhs(*l*) is the variable that is being assigned at *l*, and rhs(*l*) is the expression being calculated at *l* (lhs is short for left-hand side and rhs is short for right-hand side). If location *l* is a conditional statement or loop-termination expression, then lhs(*l*) is the next source-code location to be executed, and rhs(*l*) is the Boolean expression being evaluated at *l*.

It is necessary to understand the relationship between successive program states. Let *C* denote a program, *x* denote a program input, Δ denote the set of all possible legal inputs to *C* (that will come from the system in which *C* is embedded), *Q* denote the probability distribution of Δ, *l* denote a program location in *C*, and *i* denote a particular execution of location 1 caused by input *x* (what we define as an "iteration"). Furthermore, let A_{lCix} represent the program state produced after executing location *l* on the *i*th execution of *C* from input *x*.

It is useful to group program states into sets with similar properties. For instance, assume that location 1 is executed m_{xl} times by input *x*. Now consider the set of all of the program states that are created by this input immediately after *l* is executed:

$$A_{lCx} = \{A_{lCix} \mid 0 \leq i \leq m_{xl}\}$$

We further group these sets for all $x \in \Delta$ into a superset:

$$\alpha_{lC\Delta} = \{A_{lCx} \mid x \in \Delta\}$$

A'_{lCix} denotes the program state A_{lCix} after a modified value is injected into A_{lCix}. The key here is that A'_{lCix} *must* be different from A_{lCix}. Methods employed for altering program states can be as basic as: randomly modifying an existing value in a data state; using a different value somehow based on the original value; or if a particular failure always results in some specific value, that value. Each of these possibilities defines new values that can be used for A'_{lCix}. We do not modify type definitions of those *l*s (when they are defined), nor do we attempt modifications of values that represent different types. For example, if the current value is an integer value of 400, we might alter the value to an integer of 500, but we would never try to alter the value to be a string with contents 'abc'. Depending on the source language, decisions about how to do this will differ.

Program state mutations can lead to potentially disastrous software outputs—outputs that violate the postconditions. One might ask why program states that change during execution in a manner unrelated to the existing source-code statements would be of any use. The answer is that both faulty hardware and external software failures—of other software subsystems and subsystems that comprise the software's environment—can affect states. Since we cannot imagine all of the reasonable ways that external failures can affect program states, we simply simulate corrupt program states throughout the software in hopes of discovering those places in the code where corrupted states lead to undesirable outputs.

The following extended propagation analysis algorithm employs data-state perturbation to allow observation of the impact of different classes of bad states on the output of software. The following algorithm determines the proportion of outputs that satisfy a logical predicate, $PRED_C$, where $PRED_C$ defines which outputs from C are unacceptable for each input to C. $PRED_C$ is the postcondition for C. What constitutes unacceptable output from software is defined with respect to the system S, in which C will be embedded. Of course, if S is unknown, this will not be possible.

Extended Propagation Analysis (EPA) Algorithm
For each l in C:

1. Set **count** to 0.

2. Randomly select an input x according to Q. If C halts on x in a fixed period of time, find the corresponding A_{lCix} in α_{lCA}. Set Z to A_{lCix}.

3. Alter Z, and denote the new data state as Z'. Execute the succeeding code on Z'. (If by chance l is executed more than once because of the value we placed into Z', alter each state that occurs immediately after l.)

4. If the output satisfies $PRED_C$, increment **count.**

5. Repeat steps 2–4 $n - 1$ times (the greater n is chosen to be, the greater the confidence in the statistical validity of the results as well as the greater the costs).

6. Divide **count** by n yielding ψ_{alCQ}. The numerical value, $1 - \psi_{alCQ}$, is a measure of failure tolerance, and the value ψ_{alCQ} is the proportion of times C's output was of the undesirable type. (If C fails to halt, a time limit can be imposed.)

It is important that this algorithm be applied for every syntactic statement in C that satisfies our definition of a location. If locations are instead selected with a hit-or-miss scheme, this will result in a reduced capacity for generating recovery assertions. Recovery assertions are intended to have the ability to thwart dangerous forms of error propagation, but this works only if all possible candidate locations for assertions are considered.

Distributed Fault Simulation

In step 3 of the preceding EPA algorithm, fault injection occurs at a single location l. This provides information concerning C's sensitivity to problems in the state at l. This algorithm simulates the class of errors known as *single-point faults* (also sometimes termed *simple faults*). Not all problems that arise during execution can be so nicely isolated to certain specific places in the code. It is quite possible that events at a combination of different ls are actually responsible for a particular state corruption which, in turn, affects multiple portions of the data state and ultimately results in $PRED_C$ being satisfied. This class of anomaly is referred to as a *distributed fault* or a *complex fault*.

In the case of programmer-fault simulation, instrumenting for distributed fault simulation becomes too difficult because of the combinatorial-explosion problem. If the instrumentation is simulating corrupt information coming in from the outside, then for certain types of systems the combinatorial-explosion problem is not as severe. For instance, suppose three external values are read in at different points of a program. Call these points locations h, t, and v. It would be realistic to alter step 3 of the EPA algorithm to consider altering A_{hClx} and A_{tClx} in combination, A_{hClx} and A_{vClx} in combination, A_{vClx} and A_{tClx} in combination, and A_{hClx}, A_{tClx}, and A_{vClx} in combination. This simulates all possible kinds of situations in which different combinations of corrupted information come into C. This is better than assuming that only one type of failed information can ever come into C during an execution.

Program Counter Fault Simulation

One interesting class of failure that we will want to perform to assess the tolerance of systems relates to the software taking a wrong subpath during execution. One reason that programs sometimes take a wrong subpath is related to faulty conditions that determine which branch is taken or when a loop terminates.

This idea admittedly is quite simple; however, its implementation involves software mutation principles as opposed to data-state mutation principles. For example, except for explicit goto commands, the programmer does not have explicit control of what statement is executed next. The statement that is executed next is a function of the state of the program at some point and the code that is being executed. For example, if the current value of some variable a is "1" and the statement is reached that says:

```
if (a > 10) then
```

then the software will take the FALSE branch. To simulate the failure of a condition, we have several choices: (1) inject a perturbation function that adds a label to a location and performs a goto, (2) negate the condition:

```
if ¬(a > 10) then
```

(3) modify the condition itself:

```
if (a ≤ 10) then
```

or (4) modify the value of variable *a* before this condition.

Either way, the software will be forced to exercise the wrong subpath from that point forward, and we will have simulated the situation where the software is exercising the wrong code, which is frequently the reason why software systems fail. And when software systems do not fail from the anomalous event of exercising the wrong subpath, that phenomenon is termed *coincidental correctness*. Note that coincidental correctness may also include simpler things like what happens when an ordinary data-state error does not result in failure.

Timing Failures and $PRED_C$

Chapter 5 discussed ways of simulating timing faults in time-dependent systems. Another interesting class of software failure that we want to detect is timing failures. This requires the ability to observe system time in order to determine how quickly certain output events occur. This is a very difficult problem, because added instrumentation will only serve to slow the system down. We can, however, build assertions that are based on polling the operating system to see what time it is and when certain output events occur. This can be done in $PRED_C$ quite easily, and will be meaningful if the only instrumentation used is instrumentation that corrupts data coming into the program. For example, suppose that information coming in at location v is corrupted. It might be of interest to know whether the time interval between when that occurs and when the program halts is greater than Y units of time. This can be done by observing the system clock.

Fault Durations

Fault duration measures the amount of time that a corruption in program state actually exists. Only if a fault exists for an entire test execution is it possible for $PRED_C$ to be violated. In electrical engineering, there are three classes of faults related to how long faults are active. The question is whether the three categories can be applied to software data corruption. The three electrical engineering fault classes are: permanent, transient, and intermittent. A *permanent* fault is one that exists indefinitely; a *transient* fault is one that can appear and disappear in a very short period of time; and an *intermittent* fault is one that appears, disappears, and then reappears repeatedly.

For software, the electrical engineering notion of fault duration will be taken to mean how many succeeding data states are still corrupted because of some initial state corruption. A permanent fault for software then would be one that forces a state corruption that does not clear itself up. In this case, every succeeding data state from the initial fault point forward is corrupted.

Transient faults are those that come and go within a very short period of time. A transient fault is essentially a data state corruption that, for whatever reason, does not propagate. Suppose we had the code:

```
x = x + 1;
x = x div 1000000000;
```

but we should have had

```
x = x - 1;
x = x div 1000000000;
```

It is fair to say that the state of *x* is wrong, but because of the "integer divide by one billion" computation, it is safe to say that the corruption will likely get cleaned up quite quickly. This is an example of a transient fault.

Intermittent faults in software are a bit more complicated. Thus, an example of a state corruption that continually keeps popping up and disappearing is a little harder to imagine. But consider the following example:

```
loop
     x = x - 1;
     x = x div 1000000000;
endloop
```

Essentially, this is a transient fault in a loop. Here, the corruption appears, then disappears, and this process repeats continually. Whether that fault will propagate depends on whether the state is corrupted at the time when the loop is exited.

Defining *PRED$_C$* with Respect to the Complete System

Ultimately, software safety is a system property, not solely a software property. Therefore, there must be some correlation between events that the system is not ever to perform and outputs that the software is never to release. What constitutes unacceptable software output can be: (1) backed out from a forward hazard analysis of the system *S*, or (2) determined from *C*'s specification. If (1) is the manner by which *PRED$_C$* is determined for *C*, then there are two forms of unacceptable behavior, one with respect to *S*, and one with respect to *C* without regard for *S*. What constitutes undesirable system behavior will, in part, drive the definition of *PRED$_C$*.

To get a feeling for what fault injection can simulate that traditional testing's results do not tell us, consider the situation where *C* outputs a value of "5" for an input of "6", and outputs a value of "60" for an input value of "30". Suppose that this behavior meets the specification for C. Also assume that system-level hazard analysis for the system that C will control has shown that for an input value greater than "25", no output value can be less than "50". If, when the program gets an input value of "30", it somehow reads the value in as a "6", what will happen? C will, of course, output a value of 5 as its specification said, but if the system is in a "30" state and not a "5" state, then C forced a hazardous output into the system. This happened not because C was incorrect, but because the incoming data to C was "faulty." When fault injection is employed as a measurer of safety, we need to corrupt data coming into C and employ the system-level hazards (that we will want defined in $PRED_C$) as opposed to using C's "correctness" specification says should be output of C (for $PRED_C$).

On a final note here, one interesting class of software failure is run-time errors, and run-time errors may or may not need to be defined in $PRED_C$. For many systems, run-time errors are problematic and unacceptable; however, for certain safety-critical systems, run-time errors are not problematic. In train transport systems, for example, when the central control system fails from a run-time error, it is expected that all trains will slow down to a halt at a constant, safe rate such that no safety hazard—such as the trains plowing into each other—arises. This is referred to as *fail-safe* behavior, where failure is allowed to occur, but the type of failure is of the "safe" variety. So it is vital that, when you define $PRED_C$ with respect to the system, you account for whether run-time errors have safety ramifications or not.

It is necessary that run-time errors be detectable via the fault-injection tool if run-time errors are defined by the user in $PRED_C$. This requires that the fault-injection tool be capable of detecting that the instrumented code is about to crash. This can be handled with a fairly sophisticated execution manager utility that receives the results from the operating system, traps the run-time error before a crash, and instead allows the instrumented version to continue executing for different locations and different test cases.

$PRED_C$ Is Violated without Fault Injection

An interesting problem can occur during EPA that can be accounted for before EPA is performed, but which adds to the computational expense of this analysis. If you recall, we said at the beginning of this chapter that there is no need to run a copy of the software without the fault-injection mechanisms in it in order to get the software's outputs to then compare with the outputs after the code has fault injection applied to it. This is true, but there are cases where the code, in its original form, creates outputs that satisfy $PRED_C$ even though no fault injection has been performed; that is, there is something wrong in the code even before this analysis occurs. If this occurs, the user of EPA has three options: (1) throw out that test case and not use it during the analysis; (2) debug and fix the code and then perform EPA; or (3) use the test case with the code as it is, knowing that the code already produces outputs that satisfy $PRED_C$. Option (3) makes little sense, and thus what we typically do is to print out a warning to the user that there are test cases that the software is producing hazards for before fault injection has occurred. Only someone highly knowledgeable with the software should attempt to start modifying the code, and since our expertise is only in the fault injection, not in the domain of the application, it is not our place to start modifying code that we did not originally write.

6.3 Simulating Diverse Faulty Components

As mentioned earlier in this chapter, software-design diversity via N-version programming is still a popular approach to developing high-assurance software systems, particularly for safety-critical applications. In section 6.3, we explore what EPA can do for these classes of systems. Note that this is a slightly different implementation of distributed fault injection than that referred to in chapter 5. Here, we are distributing anomalies in separate programs that run in parallel. In chapter 5, we were distributing different anomalies at different points in the same program. But, from a theoretical standpoint, they are essentially the same.

Fault injection can provide some benefit when predicting how likely it is that a specific N-version system will suffer from common-mode failures. The goal is to predict whether problems that manifest themselves in the states of the individual versions can propagate out of the versions. By becoming inputs to the voter, these outputs can force the voter to fail. Fault injection can be used to simulate defects in the versions using state mutation. Figure 6.4 shows our approach. In that figure, we see a system made up of three versions. Fault injection is first applied to version 1, and will also be applied to version 2 or version 3 or both. What we are interested in measuring is how often sets of simulated faults in those two versions produce identical output results that can confuse the voter. Given two incorrect but equivalent outputs, the voter will pick a result that is different from what it would have selected had fault injections not occurred.

An interesting combinatorial problem arises with this approach. The problem is: Which combination of N versions should fault injection be applied to? From mathematics, we know the number of combinations of N distinct objects taken r at a time is given by:

$$\frac{N!}{(N-r)!r!}$$

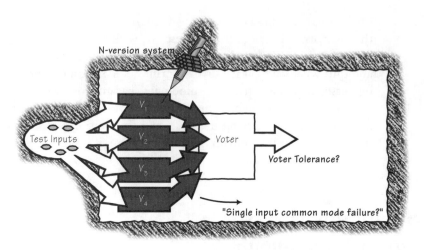

Figure 6.4 *Fault injection applied to different versions in an N-version system.*

For an N-version system, there are:

$$\sum_{r=1}^{N} \frac{N!}{(N-r)!r!}$$

total patterns. This total should not be too large since N is usually a small odd integer, such as 3, 5, or 7, but it will be substantial enough that as N grows, the ability to perform the analysis for all combinations and for all locations in the different versions will be reduced.

Since we are interested in different versions being faulty, we will apply this process to only two or more versions at once, and not to individual versions. The algorithm for performing fault injection on two or more versions simultaneously follows. Note that the fault-injection method in the algorithm can employ mutation instead of state perturbation.

```
for X = 2 to N do
      for each combination of X components do
              set counter to 0;
              loop K times; (K is user-defined.)
                      fault-inject each component of the
                      combination;
                      execute system with system-level test
                      case i;
                      if outputs from "fault-injected"
                      versions are identical
                              and different than without
                              fault-injection then
                                      increment counter;
```

```
divide counter by K;
if counter > 0 then
            provide 'WARNING' for subset.
```

What this algorithm provides are warnings each time the output is a "single-input" common-mode failure. A *"single-input" common-mode failure* is a common-mode failure, but for only *one* input case. This definition drops the additional requirement that the versions produce identical outputs for *all* inputs. The total number of warnings divided by the number of fault injections can be used to predict how often defective versions could cause "single-input" common-mode failures. Of course, this does not guarantee that any common-mode failures would ever really manifest.

Fault injection is not the only method by which we may be able to predict the likelihood of common mode failures occurring for an N-version system. From testability studies using the PIE approach discussed in chapter 5, we have learned that faults are more likely to hide when the specification for a program involves a very tiny output space [Voas 1991]. By "tiny output space," we mean only a handful of distinct output values, such as occurs with a Boolean function. What that suggests, then, is that for systems that employ design diversity, the likelihood of two or more versions suffering from common-mode failure increases when the cardinality of the set of possible outputs from a version is small. If fewer different outputs are even possible from a given version, then the likelihood increases that the versions will agree on all outputs. But by the same token, if there are few distinct output values, then faults are more likely to hide and result in single-point failures from a single version.

To reduce the likelihood of single versions hiding faults, when the versions are tested in isolation it would be wise to force the versions to produce greater amounts of output, hence revealing more about what is occurring in their internals. This can easily be accomplished through the use of software assertions. Given that most NVP efforts involve very elaborate and thorough specifications, it should not be that difficult to derive software assertions for various computations in the code, and software assertions afford us the immediate ability of producing more output information during an execution. In fact, if we were to force the versions to produce more information to the voter, that would increase the likelihood that the voter could not find a majority vote, as there might be slight differences in internal values. Clearly this is not advised—the voter should be given only the information that it needs in deciding on an output. But since the smaller output space of a version has already increased the likelihood that versions will suffer from common-mode failures, it would be smart to test each version more thoroughly by also testing the internal states of a version.

Also of issue are the types of faults that should be simulated if we are interested in predicting how identical faults in multiple versions might affect the reliability of the system. Recognize that in these types of systems the individual versions are generally quite reliable, and hence there are probably few, if any, programmer faults. If there are programmer faults, which are not specification errors, they are likely to be independent. This implies that diversity should be able to compensate for them because of their independence. But in N-version systems, programmer faults are not the overwhelming concern; specification errors (simple errors, omissions, and ambiguities) are. Here, the likelihood of all versions containing the same specification error is much greater. In this case of anomaly, the likelihood that the voter will not be affected cannot be as easily dismissed.

6.3.1 Simulating a Faulty Specification for N-Version Systems

To get the most bang for the buck in terms of common-mode failure prediction, what is truly desired is not only for the fault injection mechanisms to simulate programmer faults, but also for them to simulate specification errors. Voas and Kassab have reported on a technique for doing this that is described here [Voas 1997b].

Specification errors result from specifications that are either incomplete, ambiguous, or wrong. It will not be possible to simulate missing specification directives, but it will be possible to simulate wrong and ambiguous specifications within individual versions. Simulating these classes of anomalies provides a prediction of how robust the voter will be to classes of anomalies that are embedded in each version and that have a common source—the specification. As an example, suppose that the specification defines that the ALTITUDE variable is a function of $f_1 + f_2$. Suppose that this is wrong, and the specification should have stated: $f_1 - f_2$. A specification error-based fault injection scheme could force a corrupt value of ALTITUDE in each version for a particular test case.

We recommend that the perturbation functions applied to the different versions force the ALTITUDE values to be reduced or increased by an equivalent amount, which is what would happen if the error in the specification were all correctly implemented by the programmers. By perturbing the value of ALTITUDE in each of the versions for a particular test input, we can determine how sensitive the system will be to that part of the specification that defines ALTITUDE. Once those portions of the specification that force single-input common-mode failures often are discovered, it will be prudent to go back to the specification and closely examine those requirements in order to ensure that the requirements that are defined are indeed what is wanted. If software fault injection demonstrates that single-input common-mode failures are difficult to observe even if the versions are forced to suffer from common logical errors, then we have observed that single-input common-mode failures are rare via simulated specification errors, and will have to predict then that such will likely be true for real specification errors. Naturally, there is no way to ensure this, short of proving that the specification is correct and that each version is correct with respect to the specification.

Here is one algorithm for simulating a single specification error to a numerical data type. This is one class of perturbation function that can be used for this purpose; however, it is not the only type of perturbation function. Other possible perturbation functions might choose to determine their offsets as a function of some percentage of the current value. So, for example, a different perturbation function could be employed that takes the current value for some common variable in each version and multiples it by 0.95. Thus each value in each version is decreased by 5 percent, and this perturbation also preserves the natural diversity in the different values.

Algorithm

1. Select a computation C from the specification that is expected to be implemented in each version, that is, select some variable X that receives the results of C in the program.

2. For some test case i, apply a default perturbation function to X in some randomly selected version from the N-version set at location l in that version where X is defined.

3. Calculate the offset between what the unaltered value of X is at l and the value it has after it is perturbed; denote this offset as φ.

4. For each other version in the system that has not been perturbed, find where the variable holding the result of C is defined, and force an offset from its original value equivalent to φ.

5. Perform the rest of the analysis for determining "single input" common-mode failure as defined previously.

Once this is completed, we have the situation where a precise "off-by-something" error was made in C in the specification, and that was forced on the data states in every version. By using an offset, and not just forcing the identical perturbed state into each version, we still allow for other diversity that may exist in the different versions. For example, suppose that for test case i, X has a value of 20 in the version where the perturbation function is applied (step 2), and suppose that X is reassigned a value of 10. Then φ is -10. And suppose that in a different version, X had a value of 40; then with the offset of φ, X will be given a value of 30. The fact that one version had X at 25 and the other had X at 40 represents natural diversity created by the different programmers, and if we were to force both versions to have the perturbed value for X of 10, because that is the value we gave the first version to be perturbed, then we eliminate some of this natural diversity, which is not desirable.

The possibility exists that C is not executed when i is selected in all of the versions. If this occurs for all versions, then ignore i and select another input. Otherwise, perform the algorithm as explained, and perform the offset injection into the versions where C is exercised. If versions are executing different calculations than their counterparts for the same input i, then it is certainly possible that the system will fail for reasons other than common-mode faults. An example here would be specification ambiguities, which we discuss in the next section.

This algorithm simulates the situation of a precise "off-by-something" error ($\pm\varphi$) in directive C affecting the data states in each version at the appropriate place. By using an offset, and not just forcing a constant value into each version, we do not disturb other "natural" diversity that may already exist in the different versions. For a fixed C, this algorithm will be applied for many different is and different φs. This suggests how sensitive the N-version system is to C in the specification.

6.3.2 Simulating Ambiguous Specifications for N-Version Systems

To simulate an *ambiguous specification* directive, where a directive could be interpreted one way or another (but only one of these interpretations is actually correct), we need to make only a small change to the previous algorithm.

Algorithm

1. Select a computation C from the specification that is expected to be implemented in each version, that is, select some variable X that receives the results of C in the program.

2. For some test case i, apply a default perturbation function to X in some randomly selected version e from the N-version set at location l in that version where X is defined.

3. Calculate the offset between what the unaltered value of X is at l and the value it has after it is perturbed; denote this offset as φ.

4. For some random number r (where r is in $[0..n-2]$), randomly select r versions, none of which can be e. Take this set of r versions, find in each version where C is implemented, and force an offset equivalent to $\pm\varphi$ into the internal result from those implementations of C.

5. Perform the rest of the analysis for determining "single input" common-mode failure as defined previously.

This algorithm assumes that a computational directive C could be interpreted in one of two ways. This could be modified for three or more different interpretations of C. This algorithm randomly picks which versions will go with the first interpretation for C, and leave the rest alone.

In summary, to perform this type of analysis, it is necessary that perturbation functions are employed that simulate "identical" errors in each version. What *identical* should mean is still an open question: a fixed offset? a fixed percentage of the current value?, and so forth. So far, it has been difficult to fully automate this application of fault injection, because different programmers often use different variable names and may have designed their versions quite differently. Finding the precise place in the software where a particular C is implemented can be difficult, and in some cases impossible, particularly if some programmer failed to implement a particular directive. Nonetheless, using perturbation functions to simulate this additional class of anomaly, specification problems, does hold promise.

6.4 EPA-Based Fault-Injection Tool Architecture

It is useful to lay out a generic framework for building a source code-based fault-injection tool that perturbs data states. Though this particular architecture is not the only possibility, many of the key components we describe are necessary in any architecture. We begin by giving a general overview, and then focus in on the architecture of one commercial fault-injection tool that implements the EPA algorithm—the WhiteBox SafetyNet Tool™ from Reliable Software Technologies. Due to proprietary concerns, Reliable Software Technologies has limited the amount of information that we can provide here; however, this information will be invaluable for those who are interested in building automated fault-injection tools. The CD-ROM that accompanies this book includes a running demo version of the SafetyNet, complete with a thorough HTML-based tutorial.

Fault injection can be implemented by performing the four functions outlined in Figure 6.5. Instrumentation that defines how and where data should be perturbed in the program is specified in the source code by the user of the tool. The user can specify as many locations to receive the data perturbations as there are locations in the code, or the user could simply identify a handful. The instrumentation is inserted directly into the source code, which is then built into an executable program. Next, the instrumented program is executed repeatedly. Finally, when the execution is completed, the results are processed and interpreted.

As we mentioned in chapter 3, source code instrumentation is the process of inserting additional code into the original source code to accommodate fault-

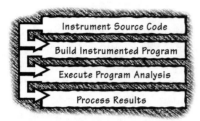

Figure 6.5 *Steps for performing fault-injection analysis.*

injection analysis. Faults are injected into the program by data-perturbation code inserted at locations in the source code. This instrumentation specifies random or constant data perturbations. For instance, a perturbed value may be randomly selected from a given probability distribution, or it may be assigned to a fixed value. Fault simulation for the analysis can be specified in any manner through the insertion of instrumentation. When a location that has been instrumented with data-perturbation code is executed during analysis, the current values at that location are overwritten by newly selected values.

Another necessary form of instrumentation is assertion placement. Assertions test whether unacceptable states are reached during program execution analysis. They are the code tests for $PRED_C$. For instance, in safety analysis, assertions that detect catastrophic states are inserted into the source code. When a catastrophic condition is violated during execution, the instrumentation records the event and forces termination of the program on that test case.

Instrumentation for the fault-injection mechanisms can be performed manually or through an automated code-generation utility. Instrumentation for the $PRED_C$ assertions requires a human to define the assertions in a logical language; then, an automated utility can translate the definitions directly into code. The translated assertions are inserted into the source. Manual instrumentation of the fault-injection mechanisms requires explicit localization at the locations in the source file. This is a time-consuming task for large source-code files. Since the original source code is getting modified, careful configuration management should be applied to maintain the original and instrumented versions. The ability to run a variety of fault-simulation scenarios is limited by using this manual approach to instrumenting source code.

For these reasons, we recommend instrumentation for the fault-injection mechanisms with an automated code-generation utility. Instrumentation is externally specified for locations throughout the source code, based on a set of default rules that understand the semantics of what is occurring at each location. An appropriate fault-injection mechanism is then inserted. The specified instrumentation is inserted directly into the code without requiring manual intervention.

The idea is to make possible something as simple as the user command "perturb everywhere possible". Such an automated utility must have the ability to parse the source code, read the externally specified default-instrumentation rules, and identify the locations in the parsed code at which to add the instrumentation to inject corrupted states. A new source-code file is then generated that includes the original source code plus the inserted instrumentation.

After instrumentation with fault-injection mechanisms and $PRED_C$ assertions, the new source-code program must be compiled and linked into an executable program. This is called the *instrumented executable* or instrumented program. From an implementation standpoint, it is convenient to instrument source code by adding function calls defined in a library. This technique allows the reuse of data-perturbation code, with customization accomplished by varying function parameter values. If an external library is used, the instrumented executable must be built by linking in the library.

Once the instrumented program is built, analysis can begin. Analysis begins with repeated executions of the instrumented program. A separate execution of the program occurs for each simulated fault and for each test case. Different perturbations at different locations for the same test case can occur. A utility to manage all of the different situations being tested by the instrumented program is clearly necessary. This utility will also record analysis results.

Results from all these executions can be postprocessed. The processing of this data is analysis-specific. For propagation analysis, the data collected during all the runs is compiled into propagation estimates for each fault-injection location, which represents the percentage of faults at that location that propagated to the program outputs. Similarly, for safety analysis, the data is accumulated into fault-tolerance estimates per location that can be interpreted as the percentage of faults that did not lead to a catastrophic state during program execution.

The tool has been developed to provide a flexible and rapid application of the fault-injection technique for assessing failure tolerance via the EPA algorithm. (This tool has also been modified as a way to assess the vulnerability of security-critical applications as covered in chapter 8.) Comprised of four main components, the tool contains the core capabilities required to perform general purpose data-state perturbations in source code. These four components roughly correspond to the four main steps described earlier in the high-level architectural layout. The components have been further divided into core capabilities that are included in the diagram illustrated in Figure 6.6. The core capabilities of each of the four components are now described in greater detail:

Source Code Annotator. The Source Code Annotator allows the user to specify data-state perturbations and assertion tests (in $PRED_C$) using a graphical user interface. The interface allows the source code to be loaded and browsed by the user. The Generic Parse Module is a lower-level com-

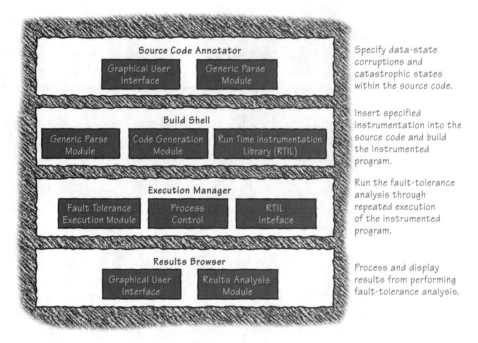

Figure 6.6 *Components of the WhiteBox SafetyNet™ tool.*

ponent of the Source Code Annotator. It is responsible for parsing the source code and maintaining parse-tree and symbolic information about the source code that is used to tag locations where instrumentation for fault injection and assertion tests can be defined. Through this mechanism, default-data perturbations can be automatically assigned to locations if the user wants to define customized perturbation functions or wants to specify a limited set of locations to receive the corruptions. The parse-tree approach allows the Source Code Annotator to control how and where the instrumentation is specified, to ensure that the user is not allowed to specify ill-defined instrumentation or specify instrumentation at invalid locations within the code. (The parse capability in the Source Code Annotator has been designed to apply generically to source code, independent of the development language. Though this is not necessary for fault injection per se, it is a nice way to ensure that new languages can be quickly and easily encompassed.) Once the instrumentation has been adequately specified, it is saved to an external data file and can be accessed later during the instrumented program build step. The advantage to using an instrumentation file approach is that the original source code never gets modified when specifying the instrumentation to insert. That way the original version is always available unaltered for final postanalysis deployment.

Build Shell. The Build Shell component is a command-line utility designed to be easily incorporated into any build environment. The shell is called with arguments that specify the compiler and linker commands used to build the original program. For each source file to be compiled using the given compiler command, the shell reads the instrumentation already specified with the Source Code Annotator and generates a new instrumented source file containing the original source code with the inserted instrumentation. Again, this process avoids the undesirable side effects that come with direct modification of the original source file. Intermediate map files are also generated for each instrumented source file, in order to provide information needed to process analysis results later and display the data to the user in a meaningful format. When the linker command is passed to the shell, the shell links in the Run Time Instrumentation Library (RTIL), which is a key part of the tool. The RTIL contains object code that defines the functions called in the inserted instrumentation. The RTIL functions are reusable blocks of code that perform specific fault-simulation tasks and provide an interface between the executed instrumented program and the Execution Manager. Upon completion of the link command, an instrumented program is built.

Execution Manager. The Execution Manager is responsible for actually performing the failure-tolerance analysis. The Execution Manager sets up inputs for performing analysis with a defined set of test cases. In order to efficiently manage the repeated executions and handle inputs and outputs, this component contains an advanced process control module. The Execution Manager interfaces with the running instrumented program using an interface defined in the RTIL. Through a minimal amount of message passing between the instrumented program and the RTIL, the Execution Manager specifies the location where state will be perturbed for each different data corruption and for each different test case. Results from evaluation of catastrophic state conditions are also sent to the Execution Manager using the RTIL interface. Raw data from each execution that runs are collected during the analysis. These results are written to an external results file when the analysis is completed.

Results Browser. The Results Browser supports visualization of results obtained from the execution process. It contains a results-analysis module that processes the raw data collected and saved by the Execution Manager. During processing of the raw data, the results-analysis module reads in the appropriate map files created by the Build Shell as the instrumented program was built. The map data is stored and used to compose fault-tolerance scores at the application, source file, source line, and location levels. The front end provides the user with the ability to view these fault-tolerance scores in both textual and graphical formats.

6.5 Mutation-Based Fault-Injection Tool Architecture

We have just described in detail the components necessary for a fault-injection tool that simulates anomalies in source code and observes whether certain classes of undesirable output events ensue. Now, we briefly discuss what components are necessary for a fault-injection tool that does syntactic mutation as opposed to data-state mutation.

The processes defining a mutation-based fault-injection tool are very similar to the process just described for a propagation-based utility. The key differences are: (1) *where* are the effects of the mutation going to be monitored; and (2) the fact that code mutations will be employed, as opposed to data perturbations. If the mutation tool is looking for the effects of the mutants in the program's output (as strong mutation does), then the tool that we just mentioned for propagation analysis will contain almost all of the same components. One exception is that the fault-injection mechanisms will have to be based on the *syntax* at the location, whereas in the propagation tool the fault injection mechanisms were based on the *semantics* of a location. For example, if the location to receive fault injection is "x=(x+1)", then propagation analysis cares only that a numerical value is being modified, whereas a mutation tool is concerned that the expression is "(x+1)" as opposed to something like "(x+1−1+1−1+1)".

If the effects of a source-code mutation are monitored immediately after the location (such as is the case in weak mutation and infection analysis in the PIE model), then the assertions to detect the impact of the modifications will be placed in the same place as the mutations. This makes for an interesting problem.

6.6 Process-Based, Debugger-Based, and Processor-Based Fault Injection

We mentioned early on that there are four basic types of fault injection. This chapter deals mainly with messages and memory/storage. For completeness, we now explore how processor-based and debugger-based fault injection are employed.

Process-based fault injection is primarily implemented by forcing a high-priority process to affect the system state. Since low-priority processes have a relatively limited impact on a system (assuming they stay low-priority jobs), it is clear that problems caused by such processes will have a less harmful effect on the system than problems caused by higher-priority processes. In this form of fault injection, high-priority processes deliberately are made to send malicious or anomalous requests into the system, and the impact of those requests on the system is observed.

Debugger-based fault injection uses a debugger to inject errors into a running process. For example, the debugger XXGDB shown in Figure 6.7 allows the user to stop execution of a program at any point, observe what value a particular variable contains using the print command, and modify the contents of the variable using the set *variable* = *expression* command. To make this concrete, with a debugger it is possible to do things like set $x = 4$, and the state of the program will reflect that. Once things are set up, the debugger can continue execution forward with the new state in place of the old. The debugger also allows the user to stop execution at any later point to see what impact that change to the variable has had on later states. When used in this way, it is reasonable to consider debuggers such as XXGDB tools for performing fault injection. The downside to doing fault injection in this manner is the large amount of manual effort required. The labor-intensive aspect of fault injection by debugger means that only a handful of injections can be performed.

Another form of fault injection common to the computer industry is *processor-based* fault injection. This form of fault injection deals with the failure of hardware components in a network. Processor-based fault injection is similar in nature to process-based fault injection. In fact, processor-based fault injection is the hardware counterpart of software-related process-based fault injection. In processor-based fault injection, one node in a distributed system might be disconnected from the rest of the system to see if the distributed system is able to continue to function. Another variant involves disconnecting a vital disk from a network to see if the network can continue operations without the disk. For systems where availability is a key concern, processor-based fault injection is a valuable tool for determining how hardware failures in one part of the network affect other hardware components on the network.

6.7 Electromagnetic Radiation Perturbation Functions for EPA

Not all software systems are Earth-based. Many critical software systems are destined to spend their lifetimes outside of Earth's atmosphere. Because of this, there is another interesting class of failure that we would often like to simulate—the impact of electromagnetic radiation. Although this class of anomaly is not directly tied to a failed hardware unit, the impact of such an anomaly is often very

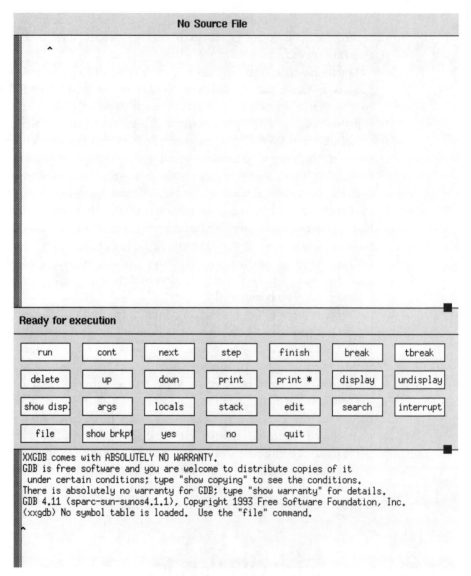

Figure 6.7 *XXGDB basic menu.*

similar to a failed hardware unit. Actually, the anomaly—cosmic radiation or any other form of radiation for that matter—should be classified as an *external environmental failure.*

Space-based systems can experience cosmic bombardment. Cosmic radiation causes two kinds of failures. The first kind can be attributed to the charge carried by the ionized atoms in cosmic rays. These charges lodge into the semiconductor lattice and can create other charges in the lattice by ionization, an avalanche phenomenon. Regardless of whether they migrate or stay in the region of the lattice where they arrive, charges can change the state of a memory cell or create a transient-state change on a semiconductor device. These are called *upsets.* The second kind of failure is cumulative and permanent. If cosmic ray particles are of sufficient energy, they can create a lattice imperfection by knocking lattice atoms out of their positions. Sufficient numbers of these imperfections change the characteristics of the semiconductor device. For example, they can increase the impedance of the device. Since semiconductors are built with very small geometric structures (<0.5 microns), they tend to fail much faster than larger devices.

Avionics systems can experience noncosmic forms of radiation as well. Ironically, the Voice of America (VOA) signal on its frequency is so strong, in order to broadcast over long distances, that its main towers can actually interfere with the navigational systems of aircraft. This is a prime example of noncosmic radiation affecting navigational computations.

An embedded program can reside in contiguous memory and have its data stored in another memory block. Cosmic radiation can affect memory even while leaving the CPU and other hardware alone. That is, cells holding the program and the data can be corrupted. Or the opposite may happen: Memory may remain intact while a transistor ruins the logic of a chip.

There are two main ways to engineer protection against radiation for space-based computer systems. The first is shielding with heavy metals. This is neither cost-effective nor desirable for space-based systems, since the weight restrictions impose tight constraints on a spacecraft's total weight. The second approach to protecting against radiation involves the way the circuits are designed and manufactured. This approach is composed of a multitude of techniques of which large geometry and silicon-on-insulator techniques are the most useful. These techniques are applicable to any chip, processor, or memory. Silicon-on-insulator techniques are extremely expensive and cause manufacturing expenses to be 10× to 100× normal. None are foolproof. They do increase the life span of exposed systems by orders of magnitude, but they eventually fatigue under constant bombardment.

Redundancy and error-detection-and-correction codes (EDCC) are also used to enhance the reliability of the spacecraft software systems. But, without one of the protection techniques mentioned earlier, redundancy and EDCC do not add much to the reliability of the systems. For example, if the probability of failure for each component is 0.9 per week, then a quad redundant system won't even last a month and EDCC would be swamped with multiple bit failures.

The perturbation function flipbit is capable of simulating the effect of random bits being toggled in memory. (See chapter 5.) As such, this perturbation is a start toward developing fault-injection mechanisms for radiation-based software failure. To date, the electrical phenomenon of radiation bombardment is still an open research concern that is being addressed more readily by hardware designers than software designers. But for those systems where random bit-flipping is a concern, fault-injection techniques can play a role.

6.8 EPA as a Redesign Heuristic

There are many design methods for trying to determine what impact a proposed component will have when added to a system. So far, we have covered fault-tree analysis, recovery, redundancy, diversity, and so forth, as methods for reducing the negative impact of failures in one part of a system on another part. Here, we briefly mention how software fault injection is useful not only as an assessment tool, but also as a *system* design tool, even after the systems have already been developed.

Suppose that for a software system it is known that the output value must be within ±0.1 percent of the correct value. Further suppose that the software system is highly dependent on input signals from a variety of external hardware and software sources. Once the software is built, fault injection can be used to simulate imperfections in the external information sources. If they are so unreliable as to force the software's output to be outside of the ±0.1 percent range, then the hardware components must be made more reliable, or the software must be modified. (See chapter 9.) In either case, a redesign of the intended system is needed, because the software is not tolerant enough in its current form to anomalies in the external components. Admittedly, at this point, it is late in the development life cycle to be making serious changes to the design. But it is still better to know about problems before code is put into operation than after.

6.9 Summary

This chapter dealt with the topic of software tolerance to anomalies. We have specifically addressed using fault injection as a way to assess the behavior of software when the software was injected with a variety of different anomaly classes. Ultimately whether software fails, how often it fails, and how severely it fails are all key questions concerning how software behaves. Software fault-injection techniques such as EPA can improve our ability to observe the software in the most stressful of circumstances, and gain insight into how the software will behave in the future should anomalous problems arise. The anomaly classes that we have discussed in this chapter have been capable of simulating specification errors, programmer faults, hardware and sensor failures, input anomalies, and failures of other information sources upon which the software depends. Although simulated programmer faults are not usually needed for this analysis because we are using software with its real faults in it during analysis, if programmer faults are simulated, the potential exists that simulated programmer faults can reveal real errors. How this can occur will be illustrated with several real case studies in chapter 7.

Software recovery and ways to develop systems that are tolerant to the "unknown" are continually sought. It is vital that the systems deployed today can tolerate tomorrow the kinds of problems that we have never even imagined. It is one thing to develop systems that are tolerant to anomalies that we expect will occur, while it is another thing to develop systems that are tolerant to the unimaginable. The fault-injection techniques that we have discussed in this chapter allow the luxury of simulating some of unimaginable events, but clearly it is infeasible to simulate all possible unimaginable events.

After simulating both imaginable and unimaginable events, we can take the appropriate steps to improve the tolerance of the software if the results from the simulations are unacceptable. In this manner, fault injection is playing a testing role. For example, if the software already has safety monitors built into it, yet our fault injection is able to surpass the safety monitors, then that proves that the safety monitors are insufficient.

There are a variety of other applications of the technology that we have described here, such as testing N-version systems, mitigating software fault trees, and testing safety partitions that aide to ensure that the non-safety-critical software in a system cannot negatively affect the safety-critical side of the system. In short, any class of failure and any class of anomalous event can be used with fault injection to allow us to play what-if games, and the answers to those what-if games do stand as predictors of how future events may unfold.

References

[AECB 1996] Atomic Energy Control Board. Draft Regulatory Guide C-138, 1996.

[Arlat 1990] J. Arlat, M. Aguera, L. Amat, Y. Crouzet, J.-C. Fabre, J.-C. Laprie, E. Martins, and D. Powell. "Fault Injection for Dependability Validation: A Methodology and Some Applications." *IEEE Trans. on Software Engineering,* 16(2):166–182, February 1990.

[Arlat 1992] J. Arlat. Fault Injection for the experimental validation of fault tolerant systems. In *Proc. Workshop Fault-Tolerant Systems,* pp. 33–40, 1992.

[Avizienis 1977] A. Avizienis and L. Chen. "On the implementation of N-version programming for software fault tolerance during execution." In *Proc. of IEEE COMPSAC '77,* pp. 149–155, November 1977.

[Avresky 1992] D. Avresky, J. Arlat, J.-C. Laprie, and Y. Crouzet. "Fault Injection for the formal testing of fault tolerance." In *Proc. 22nd International Symposium on Fault-Tolerant Computing,* pp. 345–354, 1992.

[Belli 1991] F. Belli and P. Jedrzejowicz. "Comparative Analysis of Concurrent Fault-Tolerance Techniques for Real-Time Applications." In *Proc. of the International Symposium on Software Reliability Engineering,* Austin, Texas, 1991.

[Briere 1993] D. Briere and P. Traverse. "AIRBUS A320/A330/A340 electrical flight controls—a family of fault-tolerant systems." In *Proc of FTCS-23,* pp. 616–623, Toulouse, June 1993.

[Clark 1995] J. A. Clark and D. K. Pradhan. "Fault Injection: A Method for Validating Computer-System Dependability." *IEEE Computer,* pp. 47–56, June 1995.

[Dilenno 1991] T. Dilenno, D. Yaskin, and J. Barton. "Fault tolerance testing in the advanced automation system." In *Proc. 21st Int'l. Symp. on Fault-Tolerant Computing,* pp. 18–25, 1991.

[Echtle 1992] K. Echtle and M. Leu. "The EFA fault injector for fault tolerant distributed system testing." In *Proc. Workshop on Fault-Tolerant Parallel and Distributed Systems,* pp. 28–35, 1992.

[FAA 1992] Federal Aviation Authority. Software Considerations in Airborne Systems and Equipment Certification, 1992. Document No. RTCA/DO-178B, RTCA, Inc.

[FDA 1991] U.S. Food and Drug Administration. Reviewer Guidance for Computer Controlled Medical Devices Undergoing 510(k) Review, 1991.

[Johnson 1989] B. W. Johnson. *Design and Analysis of Fault Tolerant Digital Systems.* Addison-Wesley, Reading, Mass., 1989.

[Kao 1993] Wei-Lun Kao, R. Iyer, and D. Tang. "FINE—a fault injection and monitoring environment for tracing the UNIX system behavior under faults." *IEEE Transactions on Software Engineering,* 19(11), pp. 1105–1108, November 1993.

[Leveson 1995] N. G. Leveson. *Safeware: System Safety and Computers.* Addison-Wesley, Reading, Mass., 1995.

[Lions 1996] Prof. J. L. Lions. Ariane 5 flight 501 failure: Report of the inquiry board. Paris, July 19, 1996.

[Marciniak 1994] J. J. Marciniak. *Encyclopedia of Software Engineering.* Wiley, New York, 1994.

[Randell 1975] B. Randell. "System structure for software fault-tolerance." *IEEE Trans. on Software Engineering,* vol. SE-1, pp. 220–232, 1975.

[Rosenberg 1993] H. Rosenberg and K. Shin. "Software fault injection and its application in distributed systems." In *Proc. 23rd Int'l. Symp. on Fault-Tolerant Computing,* pp. 208–217, 1993.

[Scott 1983] R. K. Scott, J. W. Gault, and D. F. McAllister. "The consensus recovery block." In *Proc. of Total Systems Reliability Symposium,* pp. 74–85, 1983.

[Segal 1988] Z. Segal et al. "FIAT—fault injection based automated testing environment." In *Proc. 18th Int'l. Symp. on Fault-Tolerant Computing,* pp. 102–107, 1988.

[Solheim 1993] J. A. Solheim and J. H. Rowland. "An Empirical Study of Testing and Integration Strategies Using Artificial Software Systems." *IEEE Trans. on Software Engineering,* 19(10):941–949, October 1993.

[Traverse 1989] P. Traverse. "Dependability of digital computers on board airplanes." In *Proc. of DCCA-1,* Santa Barbara, Calif., August 1989.

[USNRC 1994] U.S. Nuclear Regulatory Commission. Draft Branch Technical Position, 1994.

[Voas 1991] J. Voas. "Factors That Affect Program Testabilities." In *Proc. of the 9th Pacific Northwest Software Quality Conf.,* pp. 235–247, Portland, Ore., October 1991.

[Voas 1992] J. M. Voas. "PIE: A Dynamic Failure-based Technique." *IEEE Transactions on Software Engineering,* 18(8):717–727, August 1992.

[Voas 1994] J. M. Voas and K. W. Miller. "Dynamic Testability Analysis for Assessing Fault Tolerance." *High Integrity Systems Journal,* 1(2):171–178, 1994.

[Voas 1997a] J. Voas, F. Charron, G. McGraw, K. Miller, and M. Friedman. "Predicting How Badly 'Good' Software Can Behave." *IEEE Software,* July 1997.

[Voas 1997b] J. Voas and L. Kassab. "Simulating Specification Errors and Ambiguities in Systems Employing Design Diversity." Reliable Software Technologies Technical Report, May 1997.

7

Applied Safety Assessment

EPA Meets the Real World

Fault injection, when implemented in the form of the EPA algorithm, is well suited for application to control software. This section covers some case studies showing what information can be derived and how that information can be applied. The systems where EPA has been applied include:

1. The Magneto Stereotaxis System (medical)
2. Advanced Automated Train Control System
3. Code from the Halden Nuclear Reactor Project [Voas 1997a; Voas 1997b]

Also, we are interested in determining what if anything fault injection could have done to avert several infamous disasters: the Therac-25 and the Ariane 5 [Voas 1997c]. This analysis of what fault-injection analysis could have done to avert known disasters is based on the best information available from the individuals or groups that diagnosed the disasters and announced to the public what the software problems were [Leveson 1993; Lions 1996].

Software automation is becoming ubiquitous. Nevertheless, some industries are not as enthusiastic about the results of automation as they are about the results of time-honored manual effort. In an interesting article in *U.S. News & World Report* (Dec. 23, 1996), Toyota announced that its newest factory, Kyushu, has less automated equipment than past factories. Automation at the plant was cut 75 percent, compared with Toyota's most automated factory. In the process, Toyota reduced defects by 80 percent, raised productivity by 10 percent, and decreased by roughly half the number of jobs the company classified as physically strenuous. The plan for the Kyushu factory was the outcome of an intense debate within Toyota over the merits of factory automation.

Computer-controlled assembly robots in most factories function mainly as substitutes for high-cost workers. "The old approach to automation was to use machines wherever it was easy to replace men on the line, and let workers do the rest," says Takashi Matsuura, general manager of production engineering. The result, however, was that line workers were often left with the most difficult tasks. The machines also were expensive, inflexible,

and hard to maintain. So instead of replacing workers, Toyota designed machines to make
them more productive.

Although this is an isolated case, it does show the need to build systems that are more robust and reliable. As you will see in the following example, the control software in these systems likewise lacks a degree of reliability. In some cases the lack of reliability is inexcusable.

7.1 Ariane 5 Flight 501

On June 4, 1996, the maiden flight of the Ariane 5 launcher ended in disaster. This Ariane 5 launch represented an investment of $500 million, and this launch was not insured. A mere 40 seconds after initiation of the flight sequence, at an altitude of approximately 3700 meters, the launcher veered off of the expected flight path, at which point it exploded [Lions 1996]. A team of investigators from the Ariane 5 project teams were assembled to investigate the failure. The director general of the European Space Agency and the chairman of the CNES set up an inquiry board to investigate the problem further. Our conjecture is that fault injection could have played an important role in preventing this disaster.

The flight control system of the Ariane 5 is of a fairly standard design. The positioning of the launcher and its movements in space are monitored and measured by an inertial reference system (SRI). The SRI has its own computer, in which angles and velocities are computed-based on incoming data from sensors. Data calculated by the SRI are then sent through a databus to the on-board computer (OBC), which executes the flight program.

The Ariane 5's design contains redundancy. It has two SRIs operating in parallel, with identical hardware and software. One SRI is active, and the other is in standby "hot swap" mode. The Ariane 5 also has two OBCs, and certain parts of the flight control system are duplicated. Interestingly, the software design of the SRI for the Ariane 5 is very similar to that of the Ariane 4's design.

In the design of the SRIs, there was a requirement in the specification stating that in the event of any kind of software exception, "the failure should be indicated on the databus, the failure context should be stored in an EEPROM memory, and finally the SRI processor should be shut down." Hence any software exception was expected to shut down the SRI computer upon which it occurred. This might seem like a strange requirement, but since there were two SRIs, it was allowed. With that in mind, we can cover the particular sequence of events that led to the Ariane 5 disaster.

Much of the SRI design for Ariane 5 was taken from Ariane 4. In the software on each SRI was an internal alignment function called horizontal bias (BH) that returned a 64-bit float. For Ariane 5, the value returned by BH was much higher than what had been expected, probably because the early part of the flight of Ariane 5 differs significantly from that of Ariane 4. This difference led to much higher horizontal velocity values for the new rocket. After liftoff, SRI 1's software reported an operand error while trying to convert the BH value from a 64-bit float to a 16-bit signed integer. Because the value was too large, the operation failed, setting off an exception. This led to the immediate shutdown of SRI 1. Almost immediately thereafter, 72 milliseconds to be exact, SRI 2 tried to perform the same conversion, and it also failed. However, when SRI 2 failed, it sent incorrect attitude data to the OBC, which was controlling the flight. Part of the data that the OBC received from SRI 2 appears to have contained diagnostic bit patterns, as opposed to proper flight data. This forced the OBC to change the angle of attack in such a way that the high aerodynamic loads caused separation of the boosters from the main stage. This in turn triggered the self-destruct system of the Ariane 5. In short, the immediate cause of the disaster was a software exception, but that is not the full story.

The question arises as to why a type conversion was allowed to occur when any exception in the conversion was specified to shut down the computer. Part of the reason for this was that the computers on Ariane 5 were not to exceed a maximum workload of more than 80 percent of capacity. Protecting all conversion calculations might have contributed to exceeding this threshold, thus conversion protection was never carried out. During design, the engineers identified seven variables that were at risk for leading to an operand error. Ironically, one of them was the BH. Four of the seven had been protected, but BH and two others were, for whatever reason, deemed not in need of protection.

The reasoning behind the decision ran as follows: For any variables that were left unprotected, a review had determined either that it was physically impossible to overflow the range of the variable in question or that there was a large enough margin of safety built into the system that an operand error could be accommodated. Following this reasoning, BH and two other variables were left unprotected. It appears that based on what was known from experiences with Ariane 4, this thinking is plausible. We speculate that the engineers probably thought that as far as the BH in Ariane 5 went, an operand error was physically impossible to achieve. In hindsight, it is clear that this rationale was incorrect.

Fault injection could have played a major role in avoiding this disaster. First, if the reasoning used for not protecting BH was that there was an adequate margin of safety already built into the system, then fault injection could have quickly shown otherwise. All that is required is a perturbation function that throws the 64-bit float to a high value, and an exception would be triggered. Given that both SRIs run the same code, any such test would have shown that both SRIs would fail. This information could have been immediately available for the designers. Second, recall that the OBC received corrupted data via the databus; that data appeared to have diagnostic bit patterns in it as opposed to correct flight data. Fault injection can easily simulate corrupt data going into the OBC's software. Since we have no way of knowing whether this was done during testing of the OBC, we assume it was not. Whether simulated corruptions employed by fault injection would simulate diagnostic bit patterns depends on the classes of corruptions tried when fault injection is employed. We assume that the designers knew that when SRI 2 failed, a test pattern was the type of information that would have been put on the databus, particularly because of the requirement: "the failure should be indicated on the databus; the failure context should be stored in an EEPROM memory."

It appears that the Ariane 5 design team was convinced that the BH variable could never have been as large as it was. In the findings of the inquiry board, there was no evidence that actual, expected trajectory data were used to analyze the behavior of unprotected variables. Even more alarming is the fact that it was agreed early on not to include Ariane 5 trajectory data in the SRI requirements and specification. What this means is that the domain of the trajectory data for the expected environment of the SRI software were not included as a part of the SRI specification, even though this specification appears to have been partially reused from Ariane 4. Whether that information did make it into the test plans for the software is not known to us, but it appears that even if it did, the test cases that would have demonstrated this problem were not used.

There are many lessons to be learned here. In our view, the key lessons are as follows: First lesson—when code is reused in a new environment, it is essential to consider the environment thoroughly before deciding what can or cannot happen in the new environment. In the case of Ariane 5, it appears that because it was physically impossible for the value of BH to be so large in Ariane 4 as to cause an exception, it was assumed that this would not be a problem for Ariane 5. Since trajectory data was neither a part of the specification nor the requirements, it would have been very hard to argue that BH could indeed become large enough to cause the operand error. Second lesson—fault injection determines levels of safety. In the report from the inquiry board, it was stated that members of the project team had simply decided that safety was great enough to leave three variables unprotected. Since the engineers were not considering Ariane 5 trajectory data as part of the specification or requirements, they had little evidence upon which to base their intuition. With only a few perturbation trials, fault injection could have easily checked the accuracy of this belief.

7.2 Therac-25

Therac-25 was a medical linear accelerator designed to send electrons at high speeds into tumors, with the goal of destroying tumors with minimal impact to the surrounding tissue. The Therac-25 was first released for commercial sale in 1982. Eleven Therac-25s were installed. Five were installed in the United States and six were installed in Canada. Six massive overdoses to patients occurred between 1985 and 1987, three of which resulted in death.

Like the Ariane 5, the Therac-25 was based on a predecessor—the Therac-20. But unlike the Ariane 5 that was heavily based on Ariane 4's software design, the Therac-20 had little software if any. Instead, the Therac-25's software was intended to replace some of the hardware functionality of the Therac-20. For example, the Therac-20 had hardware interlocks that checked to ensure that illegal overdoses of radiation could not be administered. The Therac-25 did not have hardware interlocks, and did not even have equivalent software interlocks to perform this functionality.

Leveson and Turner [Leveson 1993] provide an in-depth diagnosis of the history of problems that plagued the Therac-25. We reprint only a tiny portion of the information here. We focus our attention on the main software problem and see what, if anything, fault-injection analysis could have done in predicting this problem before the Therac-25 was released in 1982.

To make our reasoning understandable to the reader, we need to show the pseudocode that Leveson and Turner published in their paper in *IEEE Computer*. This is not the actual Therac-25 code, but a pseudocode representation of the main control-flow features of the software. To make the ensuing discussion easier to follow, we added line numbers to the code.

```
1.  Datent:
2.  if mode/energy specified then
3.    begin
4.      calculate table index
5.      repeat
6.        fetch parameter
7.        output parameter
8.        point to next parameter
9.      until all parameters set
10.       call Magnet
11.       if data entry is complete then set Tphase to 3
12.       if data entry is not complete then
13.         if reset command entered then set Tphase to 0
14.   return
15. Magnet:
16.     Set bending magnet flag
17.     repeat
18.       Set next magnet
19.       Call Ptime
20.       if mode/energy has changed, then exit
21.     until all magnets are set
22.     return
```

```
23. Ptime:
24.     repeat
25.       if bending magnet flag is set then
26.           if editing taking place then
27.               if mode/energy has changed then exit
28.     until hysteresis delay has expired
29.     Clear bending magnet flag
30.     return
```

The software just shown controls the hardware and configures it to administer the correct energy levels based on operator inputs to the Therac-25. After an operator inputs the dosage levels in Datent (data entry), the function Magnet is responsible for physically getting the bending magnets into place for administering the dosage. This process takes approximately 8 seconds to set each magnet, and so while a magnet is physically being set, the software calls another function Ptime that sits and waits in a repeat loop for a time interval of hysteresis delay (8 seconds) to see if the operator modifies the prescription that was entered. If the operator does, and Ptime detects that a different energy level and mode was entered, the software's logic forces control flow immediately to exit Ptime, then exit Magnet, and then exit Datent. This basically amounts to restarting the system from scratch.

Notice that in the Ptime function, the software will look to see if editing has taken place (line 26) only if the bending magnet flag is set. Notice also that at the end of the Ptime function, this flag is cleared (line 29). The only place that the bending magnet is set is on line 16 at the beginning of the Magnet function.

The problem is as follows: At the end of the first iteration of Ptime, which is executing when the first magnet is physically being set by function Magnet, the magnet bending flag gets cleared. The bending flag cannot ever be reset, because the only place that it gets set just happens to be outside of the repeat loop in Magnet. The inner condition in Ptime is the only place where modified operator input is monitored. Since the Ptime repeat loop executes for about 8 seconds for each magnet, the only time that the Therac-25 will consider modified input data from the operator is during those moments when the *first* magnet is being set. After that time, when succeeding magnets are being set, Therac-25 will ignore any modifications to the energy and mode parameters from the operator console.

At this point, you might be wondering why this problem was not "tested out" of the code. After all, there are several different classes of test cases that should be able to "shake out" this bug. Recognize that if test cases are used that never test the edit prescription condition on line 26—meaning make it evaluate to TRUE—then this bug cannot be detected via testing. If test cases are not used that exercise this condition only a second or two after the calling of Ptime, the bug cannot be detected. This means, to detect this bug during testing will require "time-dependent" input cases, and possibly many of them, because it may not be the case that all incorrect commands to the Therac-25 result in a miscalculation of the dosage to an observable level.

So what about these time-dependent inputs? *Time-dependent* inputs are data events that are entered at very specific points in time during execution of the software. Stress testing is a form of testing where many work requests are sent to a system simultaneously to see if the system can handle greater workloads. Recognize that trying to do 100 jobs in one hour is very different from trying to do 1 job per hour over a 100-hour period of time. Though the amount of work being requested may be the same in these two scenarios, the timing of the requests will likely impact the likelihood of the system to fail.

Observing the effect of the Therac-25 problem via fault injection, that is, being able to know a priori that this software could result in an unacceptable output dosage level, requires the following:

1. Test cases that include the scenario where an operator is editing a prescription while the bending magnets are being set (note that we do not require these test cases to have the editing occur at any specific time).

2. A hazard assertion that acts as the hardware interlock did on the Therac-20.

3. Fault injection applied to the result of line 16 (that is, clear the flag setting).

Thus the precise perturbation function that we would employ is the perturbation function that flips Boolean variables from T to F or F to T. Note that these three requirements are the normal parameters that we would employ for any fault injection–based analysis of this software. The test cases that we need must exist for proper coverage and feature testing, otherwise the inner code in Ptime could not be exercised. In addition, the fault-injection approach that we use always perturbs flags at the places where they are set or unset. For this particular system, the hazardous event that we would not want the software to be capable of causing would naturally be a radiation overdose. By perturbing this Boolean variable, we would not have allowed the code to be exercised which handled the event where an operator was changing a dosage.

Given this setup, the hazard assertion will at some point be triggered. How many test cases (trials) it will take before the dosage calculated by the software is out of the acceptable range is unknown, but as has been tragically demonstrated in the field, this event will at some point occur. Had fault injection been applied before the Therac-25 went into service, this anomaly would likely have been detected. Of course, these tragedies could also have been avoided by simply having a hardware interlock on the Therac-25 similar to what was on the Therac-20. That solution would have required modification of the code. Fault injection would have detected the problem with the code in its current form.

7.3 Magneto Stereotaxis System

In our previous two cases, we analyzed what fault injection could possibly have done had it been employed. The previous two cases were high-visibility software-related tragedies, where loss of life and property occurred. But our analysis is simply a conjecture. Now we take a look at several case studies where fault injection has been employed *before* the code was released, and highlight the benefits it provides.

The first case study involves a real-world control problem from the medical domain—the UVA Research Prototype Magneto Stereotaxis System (MSS) [Yam 1996]. MSS is an experimental device for performing human neurosurgery being developed in a joint effort between the Department of Physics at the University of Virginia (UVA) and the Department of Neurosurgery at the University of Iowa. (See Figure 7.1.) The system operates by manipulating a small permanent metal seed that is moved throughout the brain using an externally applied magnetic field. By varying the magnitude and gradient of the magnetic field, the seed can be moved, positioned at a site requiring therapy (e.g., a tumor location), and used for ablation and/or cauterization of the diseased tissue. The magnetic field required to move the seed is extraordinarily powerful. The field is produced by six superconducting magnets that are located in a chamber surrounding the patient's head. Dr. John Knight of UVA provided us with access to the source code for an early version of the control software for the MSS; what relationship, if any, our code has with the code to the real system that is slated to undergo FDA approval is unknown [Yam 1996]. The version we used is not the production-software system. At one point during the very early development of this code, there was only a single version of this control software, but several parties involved in the early development split, each taking a copy of the code.

In our analysis, fault injection was applied to a portion of the MSS code responsible for controlling the current level in the coils. In the MSS, the coil current is adjusted by the controller subsystem in order to create a magnetic field that will move the seed to a specified location in the brain. The coil-controller code contains functions that communicate with the hardware, reading and setting coil parameters. It is critical that when a new current level is set by the coil controller, it falls within a specified range. If the current-level limits are exceeded, the consequences could be fatal for the patient, as a metal seed could very well fly from the center of a patient's head with the velocity of a bullet. If any one of the six electromagnets or one of the six power supplies fails, a distorted magnetic field around the brain could occur. In this case, the software has been designed to instantaneously shut down the other electromagnets in order to halt the seed and prevent patient injury.

The coil control subsystem is written in C++. A test program for the coil controller was built, and these source files were instrumented for failure-tolerance

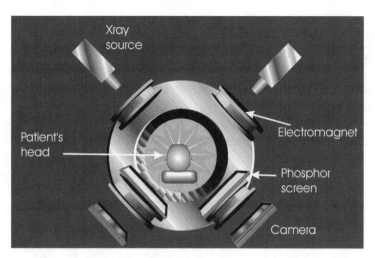

Figure 7.1 *Overview of the MSS.*

zard condition was specified in the set_current subroutine, by defin-
bound on the 12-bit integer representation of the current value
the coil hardware. If this upper limit is exceeded, patient safety is
d. Test cases were generated and then supplied to the coil-control
am for the failure-tolerance analysis.

ntial hazard in the MSS system is setting the current in the magnetic
ve the seed within the brain of the patient. If the current is set in-
r if the change in current is too great, then the potential for life-
injury is real. The function illustrated next takes as an input parameter
that is calculated to move the seed in the proper position. This current
rgoes digital-to-analog (DAC) conversions before being written to an
rt. The example illustrates how a hazard can be detected through fault

ntering this function, a global-status variable is checked. If this variable
that the MSS is not in a safe state, then the program will exit out of the
Next, the safety bounds on the current are checked. If the current
he maximum safe amps or is less than the minimum amps (same ampli-
naximum current, but opposite polarity), then an error is noted and the
is exited.

ded the requested current setting is in an acceptable range and the status
MSS is OK, then the process of converting the current amps to a digital-
og conversion value is started. First, a DAC variable which will be used to
ne DAC value is declared. Next, a function is called which takes the cur-
units of amps and converts it to a 12-bit digital-to-analog conversion
The current value and the DAC value are both stored in memory. Next,

the DAC value is written to the output port. This will cause the coils to charge up according to the current sent by this function. Finally, after the current has been set, the OK status is returned to the calling function.

A hazard in the system, then, would occur if the current exceeded its maximum bounds. We code this hazard in the form of an assertion, and evaluate it right before writing the current to the output port. Next, we inject faults in all possible locations. For example, we corrupt the result of the Boolean assertion that checks if the current is within bounds upon entering the function. We also corrupt the result returned from the function call to convert the amps to its 12-bit DAC representation. We also corrupted the assignment statements for the current and the DAC value.

The results from our analysis showed that 45 percent of the time faults corrupted the "if" condition, and the hazard was triggered. This makes intuitive sense. If the current was out of bounds to begin with, then the Boolean expression would not have allowed the current to be set to the output port. However, since we corrupted the Boolean condition, it would have allowed unsafe currents to be written to the output ports, thus triggering the hazard. While the result from this fault injection is intuitive, it points out the criticality of that expression. Our results also showed that 91 percent of the time that the function call to the DAC function was made and corrupted, the hazard was tripped. This result is somewhat significant, since it shows that a flaw in the conversion function could end up causing a hazard. The results from this example shows the safety-critical portions of this code.

```
function set_current(double current)
{
 if status is not OK {
   if current is out of safe bounds then
       note "ERROR: Requested current of" <<current<<" amps is not
in
bounds";
  else {
    declare DAC_val;
       function(convert current to DAC value);
       store current in current_setting;
       store DAC_val in DAC_setting;
       write the DAC value to the output port;
       return(OK);
    }
 }
else {
    note "ERROR: could not set current value--servoamp status is
bad"
       }
}
REAL CODE:
```

```
int servoamp::set_current(double current)
{
if(!status) {
   if((current>MAX_CURRENT) || (current < MIN_CURRENT))
        cerr << "ERROR: Requested current of" << current <<" amps is
not
in bounds\n";
   else {
        float dac_val;
        dac_val = amps_to_dac(current); // Convert amps to a DAC value
        current_setting = current;        // store the current
        DAC_setting = (unsigned) dac_val;   // store the DAC value
        write_value(DAC_setting,SetAmpCurrentAddress); // write the
DAC
value
        return(AMP_OK);
   }
 }
 else {
   cerr << "ERROR: Could not set current value - servoamp status is
bad\n";
   cerr << "    Servo Amp Status is: " << status << "\n";
 }

return(AMP_FAULT);
}
```

After discovering this mistake in the code, a fix was easily implemented by moving the current-value assertion down in the code so that it occurs after all value transformations have been made. Tests on a version of the MSS coil controller code that had been "patched" in this way resulted in fault-tolerance scores of 100 percent. The magnitude of the difference in score values is not important and can be ignored. What is important is the relative improvement from one iteration to the next of the actual safety of the code under analysis. The safety measures show objectively that improvement has been made.

An additional benefit that stems from performing our failure-tolerance estimation method on the coil-control subsystem is that the failure tolerance of the software in the event that corrupt data is received from the hardware can be assessed. Perturbations applied to values returned from the hardware can be used to determine the ability of the subsystem to tolerate the occurrences of invalid data from hardware.

In summary, the results from this case study isolated a potential weak spot in the coil-controller code [Voas 1997a]. Specifically, a region of the code was isolated that allowed the current level to be sent to the coil hardware without a check on the hazardous current levels. If the current level is corrupted and is not checked prior to being sent to the coils, then a hazardous situation appears imminent. After discovering this error with fault injection, we easily applied a "patch" that objectively improved the safety of the software. In addition to this impressive result, fault injection identified several locations in the code that were not exercised by the approximately 400 boundary-value test cases that we employed, hence suggesting that simple test coverage analysis would have provided useful results. This information could be of use in the development of a more thorough set of tests.

7.4 Advanced Automated Train Control System

Our next case study involves another real-world control problem. This study involves a transportation control system—the Advanced Automated Train Control (AATC) system. Hughes Aircraft Company, El Segundo, California, in partnership with the San Francisco Bay Area Rapid Transit (BART) district and Morrison Knudsen Corporation, has produced a new train control technology with partial funding from the U.S. government's Defense Advanced Research Projects Agency (DARPA). In this innovative control system, the head and tail cars of each BART train are equipped with spread-spectrum radios. Additional radios are situated along the trackside and at stations. The trains in a station's "control zone" form a wireless local area network with time-division multiplexing. This wireless network provides not only data communications between the trains and the station but also provides, through radio ranging techniques, information about the location and speed of the trains. A computer at the station uses this information to calculate safe speed commands, which it sends to the trains via the wireless network. The system provides BART with the ability to increase the throughput of trains through BART's Transbay Tube from the current 16 trains/hr to a minimum of 30 trains/hr. The new system will enable BART to locate the position of trains with an accuracy of ± 15 ft and support control algorithms that will allow the train service to operate with greater throughput and reduced braking, which in turn will result in more efficient use of energy and a higher quality of service to patrons. The system being replaced was able to detect train locations only within 350 feet of their actual location.

While almost all previous control systems have been primarily hardware-based, the AATC is primarily software-based. This presents both opportunities and vulnerabilities. The software is written in a restricted subset of the C++ programming language. Hughes has incorporated software fault injection into its assessment methodology for developing safety-critical software and is using automated fault-injection tools from Reliable Software Technologies, Sterling, Virginia, to analyze the station computer software. For BART, hazards were identified and a fault tree was developed that depicted all credible ways that a hazard could occur from the causal and logical interrelationships of system events and conditions. Certain leaves of the fault tree related to particular software output being incorrect. These hazardous output conditions were expressed in terms of output program variables. Software fault injection assisted Hughes in identifying locations where additional safety preconditions, postconditions, and assertions were inserted to mitigate identified hazards. The terms "preconditions" and "postconditions" are used in an informal sense here; they are safety assertions that are evaluated upon entry to and exit from a safety port function. *Safety port functions* are a small subset of the modules' function which provide the interface to other modules.

In running one test scenario (on a subset of the code responsible for initializing the system's databases, controlling the local area network, and processing the data from the trains), Hughes analyzed about 2000 locations. The analyzed locations resulting in poorer failure-tolerance scores (about 26) were subjected to a larger number of test cases. Fourteen of the 26 locations caused core dumps as their failure mode. This is considered a safe state in the context of the AATC system, although undesirable for performance, since trains are designed to revert to a backup system or stop safely when they stop receiving speed commands. Hughes was able to take corrective actions at the remaining 12 code locations, bringing the failure tolerance score to 1.0. Many of these locations had not been qualified as potentially harmful by any other software safety methodology that was being employed. The fault-injection tools used were able to uncover these potential problem areas early in the development and validation phases—in the Integration Test phase—where corrective action could take place relatively inexpensively. Fault injection also provided Hughes with a double-check on which software functions were safety critical.

This case study contains a review of results from four different analysis points which resulted in failure-tolerance scores of 0.0 [Voas 1997a]. At analysis point 1, the perturbation function caused a routine to be called with unexpected input parameters. This resulted in the train position being off by one track segment. The mitigation was to perform a precondition check to further validate the input parameters and report errors and/or stop processing of the data if necessary.

At analysis point 2, the perturbation caused the software to process a range report as though the trains were located before gross position location had been achieved. The result was that the train position was off by many track segments. The mitigation was to perform a precondition check that gross positioning has been performed prior to processing the report as located.

At analysis point 3, the perturbation function caused the lead radio set ID to change. Since validation had already been performed earlier in the code, the program assumed that if the train radio set ID was not equal to the first radio set ID, it would be equal to the second radio set ID. This caused the second radio set ID to be the front of the train, resulting in the train position off by the length of the train. The mitigation was to add an assertion to the conditional location to verify that the train radio set ID equals the second radio set ID before making the second radio set ID the lead of the train.

At analysis point 4, in the database initialization code, fault injection pointed out five areas in the code where data read in during database initialization should be protected with an error-detecting code. A cyclic redundancy code (CRC) check was added to protect this data.

Note again that these situations do not represent actual faults in the code. Software fault injection detects locations in the code only where undesirable outputs could occur, that is, if anomalies hypothetically existed and were triggered during execution. But this allows developers to place additional mechanisms in the code to improve its robustness in case these anomalies do happen to manifest themselves during operation. When lives are at stake, such a maneuver is easily justified.

7.5 OECD Halden Reactor Project, Norway

The OECD Halden Reactor Project, located in Halden, Norway, is an international research organization with member organizations representing 19 countries. The main objective of the research performed by this research group deals with safe and efficient operation of nuclear power plants. The current research direction of this group is to study the PIE testability model from a theoretical nature, and determine how accurate it is for use with this highly critical application. The work is progressing by all accounts and is going smoothly.

A portion of the software built by the Halden researchers has been delivered to the U.S. Nuclear Regulatory Agency for consideration. The piece of software that was under EPA analysis is the "Departure from Nucleate Boiling Ratio (DNBR)" algorithm [Voas 1997b]. The specification for this program was originally made for a diversity experiment, but was later simplified and reprogrammed to be used as a closed-circle experiment in the SOSAT project. The software reported on here, though realistic, is not in use in any nuclear power plant.

The DNBR code was developed for the purpose of doing research on software; it was not developed for use in a nuclear power plant. Functionally, the DNBR code uses synthesized sampled plant data as input, such as reactor coolant (water) temperature, pressure, and axial core neutron flux sensor readings. These sampled signals are processed and then used to compute DNBR.

The computed DNBR is then compared to a set point and a reactor trip signal is issued upon violation of the set point. The trip circuit selected concerns nucleate boiling. In English, this means the amount of steam in a channel is so high that parts of the fuel are no longer in contact with water. This prevents cooling of the fuel and will lead to a burnout. The program evaluates the amount of steam (quality) at various locations in a set of instrumented channels, and examines whether it is reasonably below a limit where the nucleate boiling will start. This limit is evaluated as a function of the mass flow and the heat flux in the channel. The reactor consists of a set of fuel channels in a plenum with excess pressure used to obtain forced circulation of subcooled water. A subset of 40 of these channels, in which the test is performed, is instrumented with neutron detectors. However, this program uses merely one channel in order to simplify the task.

Input data to the DNBR program is randomly generated. The seed used to initialize the random number generation is fixed within the program, so that at startup of the DNBR program, the initial state is always the same. The randomly assigned data falls within certain ranges. The following table is a listing of the input variables, their types, and the allowed ranges for their values.

Variable	Type Input	Range
input_space.pressure	int	[14400, 17600)
input_space.pressure_difference	int	[13300, 20000)
input_space.temperature &	int	[16400, 17200)
input_space.channel[i][j], 0<=i<4, 0<=j<3	int	[7730, 10450)

The main steps the DNBR software goes through as it executes follow:

1. Input variables are assigned random values at startup.

2. These values are copied into the current state fields of variable DNBR_data.

3. Limit checks are performed on the data for this first time. If they fail, then the program terminates. Otherwise, it continues.

4. In the DNBR_data variable, it saves the current state field values in the previous state fields.

5. New data is randomly generated for the variables previously listed.

6. The current state fields of DNBR_data get assigned this data, and this time no limit checks are performed.

7. The DNBR program does its main processing.

8. In the DNBR_data variable, it saves the current state field values in the previous state fields.

9. When the main processing step is completed, DNBR waits for the user to supply a <Return> or an "e" followed by a <Return> via stdin. A <Return> tells it to repeat the main loop starting at Step 5, and an 'e' followed by a <Return> tells it to stop.

To observe whether code can output unsafe states after anomalies are injected, unsafe output states must first be defined. For DNBR, two classes of unsafe (hazardous) output states were identified: (1) Burnout, and (2) Drastic time check. We now discuss these hazardous states and the data we collected telling how often we were able to observe unsafe output.

The first hazard is tested for internally by the software via burnout code, which is simply a safety monitor that is implemented via software and embedded in the nuclear application. Burnout occurs during a transition from a nucleate boiling state, a safe condition of operation, to a film boiling state, an unsafe condition of operation. In the code, there already exists a safety monitor for this condition:

```
if (Q[j] > (0.7*QBO))
    gbl_data.trip_signal = TRUE;
```

If this condition is true, the system is said to be in a hazardous state. (The multiplier 0.7 is used in the DNBR code to provide a safety margin to the actual crossover threshold.) Using the preceding hazard with the 0.7 multiplier, we did not observe hazardous output after fault injection inserted anomalies. With 0.7 as the multiplier, the code demonstrated high fault-tolerance.

As an experiment, we then decided to try to find a multiplier and hence a new hazard such that the new hazard could be triggered. To do this, we started decreasing the multiplier to obtain the sensitivity of the DNBR program to multipliers that were smaller than 0.7. The multipliers tried are in the following table, and as we continued to decrease the multiplier, we were finally able to force a hazard to trigger.

Replacement Hazards

```
(Q[j] > (0.29*QBO))
(Q[j] > (0.28*QBO))
(Q[j] > (0.27*QBO))
(Q[j] > (0.26*QBO))
(Q[j] > (0.25*QBO))
(Q[j] > (0.24*QBO))
(Q[j] > (0.23*QBO))
(Q[j] > (0.22*QBO))
(Q[j] > (0.21*QBO))
(Q[j] > (0.20*QBO))
(Q[j] > (0.19*QBO))
```

```
(Q[j] > (0.18*QBO))
(Q[j] > (0.17*QBO))
(Q[j] > (0.16*QBO))
(Q[j] > (0.15*QBO))
```

What was actually occurring here is this: For a fixed value in Q[j], and by gradually decreasing the multiplier, we were increasing the likelihood of a hazard warning occurring (from our embedded hazard observer). Interestingly, the "modified" hazard tests that we injected, which employed a multiplier of 0.27 or greater to check for burnout, were never triggered by any injected corruption. Given the test cases and injected anomalies, this suggests that if the multiplier is greater than or equal to 0.27, the program is very tolerant to anomalies.

For multiplier values between 0.27 and 0.21, we observed a small handful of hazard warnings being triggered, but not until the multiplier was 0.21 or less did hazard warnings occur frequently. With smaller multipliers, the calculations made in dnbr_MAIN are much more sensitive to our injected anomalies. This indicates that if the actual multiplier in the safety monitor of DNBR were to be modified to a value around 0.21, then failure-tolerance assertions and data checks should be made at the intermediate calculations in the dnbr_MAIN code, because at the lower multiplier values, hazard warnings will frequently be going off. By adding failure-tolerance assertions to trap anomalous internal states, those states will not be allowed to propagate through the succeeding calculations to the burnout condition (hazard). This will help eliminate the number of false positives and false negatives reported by the DNBR program's actual burnout check.

Recognize that there is nothing wrong with a multiplier value of 0.7 in the burnout hazard. Since we could not trigger the burnout hazard in its original form, we simply "played games" until we were able to find hazards where our anomalies started having an impact. In short, this was a purely academic exercise, but what it did do was to test the sensitivity of different defined hazards to anomalies. If it were the case that it was unsafe to have bogus hazard warnings going on, an analysis like this can help find the multiplier threshold where that is likely not to occur.

The second hazard is tested for internally by the software via drastic time check code, which is simply a safety monitor that is implemented via software and embedded in the nuclear application. There are tests within the DNBR program to test the magnitude of changes in each input variable from previously measured values. The purpose of this monitor is to ignore input variable data if they exceed a physical limit of change from the last time step. Tests for this are performed in the drastic_time_check routine. When the program's state is tested, if a value fails the check, a global variable pass_drastic_time_check is set to indicate that a hazardous situation has arisen.

The basic control flow of the drastic time check implementation is detailed in the following pseudocode: During fault injection, a specific hazard was instrumented at each line where a star appears in the pseudocode.

```
FUNCTION: _drastic_time_check_
INPUTS: int_value_, int_type_
{
  IF (_type_ == PRESSURE) {

    IF (_value_passes pressure drastic time check) {
      SET a flag
    ELSE {
      PRINT error message
      DO error handling
    }
  } ELSE IF (_value_ == PRESSURE_DIFF) {

    IF (_value_passes pressure difference drastic time check) {
      SET a flag
    ELSE {
      PRINT error message*
      DO error handling
    }
  } ELSE IF (_value_ == TEMPERATURE) {

    IF (_value_passes temperature drastic time check) {
      SET a flag
    ELSE {
      PRINT error message*
      DO error handling
    }

  } ELSE IF (_value_ == NEUTRON_FLUX) {

    IF (_value_passes temperature drastic time check) {
      SET a flag
    ELSE {
      PRINT error message*
      DO error handling
    }
  }
}
```

When the results were analyzed, it was discovered that the code portions responsible for the drastic time checks for (1) pressure difference, (2) temperature, and (3) neutron flux, were not exercised. In contrast, the drastic time check for pressure was exercised. This unusual circumstance immediately raised suspicions.

After further analysis, a programmer fault was discovered in the conditions that determine which type of drastic time check to apply. In the preceding pseudocode, you can see that there are four different types of drastic time checks: (1) pressure,

(2) pressure difference, (3) temperature, and (4) neutron flux. The pressure difference, temperature, and neutron flux conditions that test for hazardous data were executed based on comparisons using _value_, whereas the pressure test is executed based on a comparison using _type_. This is an error for the pressure drastic time check. The programmer introduced a fault by comparing _value_ instead of _type_ in order to determine which drastic time check to use. Various consequences of this error will now be detailed.

It is very unlikely that the value passed in _value_ will be equal to the correct value of its associated type parameter (i.e., PRESSURE_DIFF). In fact, it is more likely that _value_ will contain a value that does not match any of the four types, in which case _drastic_time_check_ fails to apply any checks, that is, the software mechanisms provided in the code to check for safety will act as dead code. Since the input data is rarely checked for pressure difference, temperature, and neutron flux measurements, invalid data will likely go undetected. This defeats the purpose of having those checks in the code, and this is the case where checks that are needed are not being performed.

The pressure difference check tests the input variable _value_ for excesses to the physical limits defined in pressure difference. The physical limits specific to the other types are tested in their respective drastic time checks. A value that is acceptable according to the drastic time check of its associated type may be unacceptable according to the drastic time check of a different type.

As an example of this, suppose that _drastic_time_check_ was called to perform the (TEMPERATURE) drastic time check. The error in the expression

```
(_value_ == PRESSURE_DIFF)
```

may cause the pressure difference (PRESSURE_DIFF) drastic time check to be applied instead. The incorrect type check may result in the detection of some truly invalid values; however, it is also possible that the check will result in falsely firing a failure signal for a valid (_value_, _type_) pairing. Therefore, it is possible that _value_ can enter _drastic_time_check_ in such a way that it is valid according to _type_, but is determined to be hazardous because of this fault. So this represents the case where checks that are not needed are being performed.

One other useful application of fault injection that we have been championing is to measure software's sensitivity to incoming sensor data. In this effort, that was performed. In the dnbr.c code there is a statement where we can do this:

```
tsat = 1804 + (DNBR_data.pressure/30.0);
```

tsat is the saturation temperature for water and is a function of sensor data, DNBR_data.pressure. Simply stated, tsat is the temperature at which water boils and in this program. If the water entering the reactor is near the boiling point, the flow is low, and heat by the reactor high, then the conditions are ripe for burnout and film boiling.

The value assigned to tsat is a function of the current data pressure value. By simulating the pressure sensor making inaccurate measurements due to calibration errors, fault injection can be used to quantify the degree of sensor error that could lead to burnout warnings occurring if tsat is incorrectly calculated.

7.6 Summary

This chapter has presented several real-world case studies. The results from EPA can be significant, even to the point of revealing that the software safety mechanisms embedded into the software devices are not working. In the MSS and Halden examples, the software safety monitors were defective and were not protecting against hazardous outputs.

Generally speaking, though, EPA will not be capable of detecting errors. Fault injection does not require access to an oracle, and so other than what is defined in, fault injection does not know correct versus incorrect. The role of fault injection is to warn us when we are able to put the software into simulated anomalous states and undesirable output events still occur. From that information, we can take the appropriate recovery actions to ensure that those types of anomalous states do not occur in practice.

So in summary, EPA asks a lot of "stupid" questions of the software when it forces the software into unusual states. If the software answers back with "stupid" answers, then we can ignore this exercise and move forward. If however the software answers back with serious, hazardous outputs to those "stupid" questions, then we must stop and mitigate in our minds that the anomalies we injected can never occur during software operation. If we cannot do this, then fault-tolerance improvements are warranted and, as you will see in chapter 10, we can even use the results from EPA to guide in building these fault-tolerance improvement mechanisms.

References

[Jones 1996] R. C. Jones. "An Experiment Using Fault Injection on the Collision Avoidance System (CAS) Logic II." Technical Report TR-96-10. Reliable Software Technologies Corporation. December 1996 (availability restricted).

[Leveson 1993] N. G. Leveson and C. L. Turner. "An Investigation of the Therac-25 Accidents." *IEEE Computer,* 26(7):18–41, July 1993.

[Lions 1996] Prof. J. L. Lions. "Ariane 5 flight 501 failure: Report of the inquiry board." Paris, July 19, 1996.

[Voas 1997a] J. Voas, F. Charron, G. McGraw, K. Miller, and M. Friedman. "Predicting How Badly 'Good' Software Can Behave." *IEEE Software,* pp. 73–83, July 1997.

[Voas 1997b] J. Voas and F. Charron. "Error Propagation Analysis Studies in a Nuclear Research Code." RST Technical Report, April 1997.

[Voas 1997c] J. Voas. "Software fault injection: growing 'safer' systems." In *Proc. of the IEEE Aerospace Conference,* February 1997.

[Yam 1996] P. Yam. "Magnet on the Brain." *Scientific American,* 275(2):32, August 1996.

8 *Information Security*
Simulating Attacks with AVA

This chapter describes a fault injection–based software assessment method still in research and development. Adaptive vulnerability analysis (AVA) is designed to *quantitatively* assess information system security and survivability. This approach exercises software in source-code form by simulating incoming malicious and nonmalicious attacks that fall under various threat classes. AVA is a new approach to information security. AVA computes a metric by determining whether simulated threats undermine the security of the system as defined by the user according to the application program being analyzed. This approach stands in contrast to common security assurance methods that rely on black-box techniques for testing completely installed systems. AVA does not provide an absolute metric, such as mean-time-to-failure, but instead provides a relative metric, allowing a user to compare the security of different versions of the same system, or to compare nonrelated systems with similar functionality. To our knowledge, AVA is the only fault injection–based approach to security assessment.

The original computer security defense strategy, circa 1970, was appropriately termed "penetrate and patch." At that time, defense was entirely reactive—something that happened only after an attack was detected and some damage had already been inflicted. Penetrate and patch was followed by a series of more advanced defensive techniques (e.g., formal analysis, real-time intrusion detection, and auditing tools). Unfortunately, a recent proliferation of sophisticated threats has caused defensive security schemes to come full circle, back to where they began twentysome years ago. Penetrate and patch has once again become the status quo.

The AVA research applies technologies originally developed for software engineering—specifically, for failure-tolerance assessment—to perform software-security assessment. Related work includes [Beizer 1983; Spafford 1990; Aslam 1995], though the fault injection–based approach taken in AVA is novel.

Problems in information security are more difficult to understand than those of other certification/assurance disciplines such as software safety or failure tolerance. The fact that a security threat is malicious adds subtleties and challenges that are different from what we have already seen in chapters 6 and 7. There, we did not have to account for the fact that the anomalous events we were concerned about could include very rare malicious attacks from experienced attackers.

It is obvious that an unsafe event has occurred after an aviation disaster; but security intrusions are far less observable and often go undetected. In a recent keynote address at the Eleventh Annual Computer Security Applications Conference (ACSAC '95) held in New Orleans, Louisiana [Werner 1995], Paul Strassman stated that only between 1 in 400 and 1 in 1000 attacks are detected. Because security violations are so hard to detect, there is a shortage of good data about them.

The detection of malicious threats is one complication. The nature of those threats is another. Unlike real military intrusions, software intrusions are "virtual." Counterintuitive though it may seem, an unsuccessful software offensive almost always strengthens the attacker (by way of gained knowledge), and does not strengthen the site attacked (by way of weakening the attacker). In traditional military intrusions, an unsuccessful offensive usually weakens the attacker at least as much as the site attacked. Furthermore, in traditional war strategies, the potential for retaliation provides an important deterrent to attack. On the information battlefield, however, the fear of retaliation is minimal at best, and does not affect the balance of power. Most information security techniques used today are based on either the outdated tactics of twenty years ago or tactics that apply only to conventional warfare, not to information warfare. As a result of these shortcomings, the information infrastructure is left weakened and ill-prepared for defense.

This chapter describes a new quantitative measure for computer security that is based on the same principles covered in chapter 6. We seek to measure a program's security weaknesses in terms of both known threats and unknown threats that may occur in the future. Security defenses can be more sharply honed and security strategies more objectively compared and contrasted if the vulnerabilities of a system can be scientifically measured.

Throughout this chapter, we define a *security attack* as a dynamic event that occurs during the execution of a piece of software. Security attacks are the anomalies that we wish to use fault injection to simulate. An attack is made possible by a combination of two things. First, weaknesses (or defects) must exist in the system under attack. Second, some particular sequence of weakness-exploiting input signals to the system is required. An attack is a particular event at a particular time. Like an attack, a *vulnerability* comprises two parts: a potential defect or weakness in an information system together with the knowledge required to exploit the defect. An attack is an active attempt to exploit a system vulnerability. A *threat* is an agent outside of a software system that works to exploit a vulnerability through one or more attacks [White 1996]. "Outside the software system" does not imply that the agent is necessarily outside of the organization being attacked.

This chapter is devoted to adapting EPA to security measurement. (EPA is covered in chapters 6 and 7.) Here, we provide the theory that underlies the new security-assessment methodology called *adaptive vulnerability analysis* (AVA), which provides a relative measure of software security. Though AVA may fail to account for especially clever intruders who create new malicious threats from scratch, it will certainly be capable of simulating many important previous security threats and, with some luck, will also be able to detect some unknown vulnerabilities. Our approach will allow information system vendors to know a priori whether their systems are secure against a predefined set of threats $T = \{t_1, t_2, \ldots, t_n\}$, where T includes recurrent threats that are commonly encountered. T will be open-ended in the sense that when novel intrusion schemes do surface and are analyzed, T can be augmented so that they are included during security assessment. Since the evaluated metrics will vary with different sets T, we label the method "adaptive."

AVA attempts to simulate novel threats as well as known threats during analysis. The likelihood of success via injection for novel threats is less certain than the success we have had using known vulnerabilities. However, the knowledge to be gained through the discovery of even one potential vulnerability using fault-injection techniques is significant.

8.1 The State of Security Assessment

The state of the art in commercial security assessment is penetrate and patch. Usual security-defense methods involve testing a site by applying common security attacks against it and determining if such attacks are successful. If the result of any attack is an intrusion, then an appropriate patch for the software is devised and applied to the vulnerable site. Such patches may prevent further exploitation of a particular known vulnerability, but they provide no assurance that other vulnerabilities in software will not be exploited in the future. Furthermore, the patches are usually applied to only one site, leaving other sites open to the same attack until they, too, are patched.

Computer Emergency Response Teams (CERTs) have been devised to try to coordinate the patching of multiple sites throughout the Internet. Each time a vulnerability is discovered and a patch is devised, CERT broadcasts this information publicly throughout the Net. The assumption is that patches will be applied large-scale throughout the Internet. Unfortunately, many sites choose to ignore CERT Alerts until they have been successfully attacked. (This is a result of the common don't-fix-it-if-it-ain't-broke phenomenon that is pervasive in Computer Science.) Often, sites that have been invaded patch only the security hole that allowed the attack to succeed, leaving themselves open to other attacks.

Empirical vulnerability methods generally center around dynamic software testing that takes place *after* a system has been installed. One such method (briefly alluded to earlier) is tiger-team penetration testing. In *tiger-team testing,* a group of experts in the design and weaknesses of operating systems attempts to break into an installed system. Tiger-team penetration testing is aimed more at uncovering the presence of anomalies than at showing the absence of anomalies. Thus it could be argued that this form of testing is actually a specialized form of *stress testing.*

One major disadvantage of tiger-team penetration testing is that deciding exactly what the results of this testing mean is a highly subjective undertaking. Tiger teams all have different strengths and weaknesses, and often use dissimilar approaches. In other words, there is no standard in place for tiger teams. Furthermore, vulnerabilities that actually exist in a system may not be discovered since they are so novel that they are nearly impossible to detect through standard penetration techniques.

Tiger-team testing is the traditional procedure that is used to demonstrate resistance to intrusion. However, quantifying security via tiger-team penetration testing is far from statistically reproducible, since there are many factors in a manual process that may not be reproducible at a later time. In addition, as we mentioned previously, tiger teams vary in their levels of expertise and their approaches. It is often difficult to put together a tiger team.

The Orange Book and similar evaluation schemes provide a rough measure of trusted computing base (TCB) security. Unfortunately, this criterion is an evaluation of the process that some piece of software undergoes during development, and does not involve any evaluation of the software itself. Therefore it is possible for a software-developing organization to jump through all of the right hoops but still end up with a system having inadequate security. Models such as the TCSEC and the Systems Security Engineering Capability Maturity Model (SSECMM) [SSECMM 1995] all suffer from this weakness—a weakness that comes as a result of process versus product verification. (See chapter 1 for more on process versus product assessment.)

A number of security tools that have automated the process for tiger-team testing are currently available in the public domain. Among these tools are the TAMU system [Safford 1993], COPS [Farmer 1990], Tripwire [Kim 1993], ISS [Klaus 1995], SATAN [Farmer 1993], and Crack [Muffett 1992]. These defensive security tools, as well as related tools that are on the market or in the public domain, attempt to assess vulnerability using the tiger-team approach. These tools are summarized as follows:

> **TAMU.**   The TAMU system [Safford 1993] is a collection of tools developed at Texas A&M University that is used to provide security protection and intrusion detection. The TAMU package includes three related sets of tools: the "drawbridge" packet-filtering package, the "tiger" scripts used to attempt to penetrate machines, and the "netlog" set of network monitoring tools.

COPS.   The Computer Oracle Password and Security system [Farmer 1990] is a collection of about a dozen programs and shell scripts that each attempt to detect different problem areas in UNIX security (e.g., easily cracked passwords or system files with loose permissions). Part of COPS works by creating a summary of the system information that it can use for comparison purposes at a later time.

Tripwire.   Tripwire is a UNIX file system integrity checker [Kim 1993] that uses message digest algorithms to detect file tampering that may have been caused by an intruder or a virus.

ISS.   The Internet Security Scanner [Klaus 1995] is a package that allows remote scanning of a network domain for misconfiguration errors.

SATAN.   The Security Analysis Tool for Auditing Networks [Farmer 1993] probes sites locally or remotely and reports bugs and weaknesses in network services and windowing systems.

Crack.   Crack [Muffett 1992] attempts to guess passwords using a dictionary, a set of rules for guessing, and a brute-force matching scheme. Default rules are provided and more rules can be added using a Crack-defined language. Additionally, the dictionary used by Crack can be expanded by a user's own entries or by downloading dictionaries placed on ftp sites.

SPI.   Security Profile Inspector combines programs such as COPS and Tripwire to provide greater security assessment for a site. SPI is available only to certain U.S. government agencies.

The defensive security tools just listed attack a site through well-documented and common security holes. By contrast, the fault–injection–based approach that we present here tackles the same problem from a completely different angle. Instead of trying to "break" existing software that has already been installed and is in use, AVA is applied before a program is released in order to predict how strong a system is and where the weak points are. The fault–injection–based approach rests on the (very reasonable) premise that all software has defects. For security-related software, any defects may engender significant security problems. The goal is not to try to get out all of the defects, but to find out what effect defects might have when they are combined with exploit attempts.

In addition to the penetrate-and-patch method of improving system security after systems have been installed, there are two other security-defense measures that are widely implemented: firewalls and data-communication encryption. *Firewalls* are gateway machines interposed between a local site (often a LAN) and the larger network outside the site (e.g., the Internet). Often, a user must first log into the firewall itself in order to access a machine on the other side of the firewall. Firewalls serve to filter data packets based on their source and destination addresses. While firewalls are effective at thwarting some security attacks, they provide almost no protection against problems in higher-level protocol applications [Cheswick 1994]. Firewalls can also be powerless in preventing attacks that aim to exploit vulnerabilities in applications executing at a higher level than that of the network protocol stack. For example, bugs in sendmail once permitted unauthorized remote users to execute programs on local machines protected by firewalls by placing actual commands in mail headers [CERT 1993].

Encryption is generally used to ensure confidentiality in data communications and to authenticate a message's author. The primary drawback with relying heavily on encryption algorithms is, as in the firewall case, the strong possibility that the implementation of the encryption algorithm will be flawed.

The AVA technique tackles the problem of assessing security from a completely different angle. Instead of trying to "break" existing software that has already been installed and is currently in use, our method is applied during the software development phase before a program is released in order to predict how strong a system would be if an attack were to occur.

As Cheswick and Bellovin state [Cheswick 1994]:

> . . . *any program, no matter how innocuous it seems, can harbor security holes. (Who would have guessed that on some machines integer divide exceptions could lead to system penetrations?) We thus have a firm belief that everything is guilty until proven innocent.* (p. 7)

The realization that bugs in software can lead to security intrusions is a prime motivation for applying fault injection. In this sense, fault injection is designed to find potential security-related bugs in software before the software is put into use. Historically speaking, buggy software is responsible for most security vulnerabilities.

Cheswick and Bellovin have pointed out that the most effective safeguards in the Orange Book would have done no good at all against this kind of attack [Cheswick 1994]. Unfortunately, all of the good software-engineering processes mandated by the Orange Book and similar process-oriented guidelines are ineffective against these sorts of attacks. This is because even the most assiduously developed code will still have bugs that can be exploited by malicious intruders. The Internet worm illustrates a case where a single component failure can lead to systemwide shutdowns in service. It also clearly illustrates the critical need for using unexpected or malicious inputs to programs during program testing. Not too surprisingly, many vulnerabilities are a direct result of what happens when a program processes "garbage" input that the program's author never anticipated [Cheswick 1994].

In summary, the state of the art in software security *assessment* is lacking in three fundamental ways. First, there seem to be few or possibly no metrics. Second, most methods in common use take the process-versus-product approach. Third, vulnerability assessment for the most part relies on postinstallation tiger-team testing of known vulnerabilities.

8.2 AVA Theoretical Model

The AVA software vulnerability metric is based on observing the impact of incoming hypothesized threats on an executing system. AVA is a dynamic software analysis algorithm adapted from the extended propagation analysis technique discussed in chapter 6. Threat simulation in AVA is accomplished through a combination of fault-injection and test-case generation methods. Intrusion detection is accomplished using a predicate-based intrusion specification language. More specifically, the basic $PRED_C$ language discussed in chapter 5 is used, but with a few additions needed in order that security violations can be specified.

Some researchers in the software security assurance community oppose the introduction of measures of software security. It is easy to contend, however, that some way of measuring software security is required before programs with demonstrably better security can be developed. Just as some in the security field warn against using metrics, there is a vocal group of researchers in software engineering who crusade against placing numbers on software quality. These researchers hold that any such numbers either cannot be believed or are inaccurate. It is the contention of the authors of this book that the only thing intrinsically wrong with numbers is that their meaning is often oversold. If we remain realistic about the true worth of metrics, they provide an important scientific tool. Numbers are the only way to assess anything meaningful about software quality, provided that any such numbers are used as relative measures of quality and not as absolute measures of quality.

Many software professionals rely on the theory that if the right processes are followed during development, then a secure product will result. We have termed this the process-versus-product problem. As we spelled out earlier, we find this exclusive emphasis on process misleading and even dangerous. Nowhere is the problem more evident than in the SSECMM [SSECMM 1995]. The SSECMM comprises a set of development processes that, in theory, should improve security. While good software-engineering processes may result in higher-quality software, good processes alone are not sufficient. Knight [Knight 1995] warns of the complacency brought on by an overestimation of the impact of employing standard software processes in developing safety-critical software. Common sense demands enhancing the process approach with a good product approach. This is entirely feasible since quantitative product-based assurance and process-based assurance can play complementary roles. Consider the fact that AVA could be used as a tool to demonstrate whether a system developed according to the SSECMM actually does decrease vulnerability when compared with a system developed that does not adhere to SSECMM. AVA provides the possibility of objective comparisons of products.

AVA is a concrete way to rate the vulnerability of a software system. Because it is an adaptive measure, the AVA vulnerability-measuring technique can be specialized to assess different kinds of threats. The AVA environment can be tuned to better assess a particular piece of software based on vulnerabilities that similar pieces of software revealed in the past. For example, if httpd programs have proven to be particularly open to specific attacks, new versions of httpd should be tested using such attacks.

EPA's success as a safety-assurance technique suggests its application to other closely related fields. Adapting the basic EPA fault-injection methodology to a security-assurance tool requires three major activities:

1. Strengthening the ability to simulate code weaknesses through fault injection
2. Implementing automatic test-case generation
3. Creating a language for specifying intrusion predicates

Next, we describe each activity.

8.2.1 Simulating Code Weaknesses

Step 1 in adapting EPA to AVA is enhancing EPA's primitive means for simulating code weaknesses or flaws via fault-injection mechanisms.

The underlying AVA fault-injection algorithm is simply the EPA algorithm specialized for malicious threats. Because the class of potential, future threats is unknown, any set of default threat classes may not adequately reflect how future threats will affect internal program states. In addition, the user of the perturbation function template may not have the foresight to envision certain classes of threats. To address this weakness in the technique, any prototype that implements the AVA algorithm should have a set of default perturbation functions that do not necessarily simulate threats, but simulate random corruptions in the state of the executing program. Because we cannot know exactly what attacks may be levied against a piece of code, it is prudent to try a wide variety of unusual anomalies. These "weird" random corruptions, which may include things such as intentional buffer overflows, are forced into the software after which program behavior will be analyzed to see whether $PRED_C$ is ever satisfied (assuming that $PRED_C$ now defines security policy violations).

Since future threats may be so novel that they are unknown, we will simulate as many anomalous events as possible using the perturbation functions already provided in chapters 5 and 6. It is plausible that some of the future threats will have signatures on the states that are at least similar to the random corruptions that were employed in these earlier chapters. We recognize the theoretical weakness of this argument.

8.2.2 Test-Case Generation

Step 2 is test-case generation. In order to exploit code weaknesses, a means for defining expected input profiles as well as unusual input sequences is necessary.

Input sequences come in many variations. We denote the set of all inputs to a system by Δ. In the vulnerability analysis algorithm to follow, the user will define either a file of input sequences or a distribution of input values. Q represents the normal operational profile of inputs that some system is expected to receive and Q^{-1} represents the inverse operational profile. (More on profile inversion is provided in chapter 10.)

During testing according to some distribution Q, the majority of the test cases that are chosen at random is made up of cases that are the most likely to be selected. This is true even if testing over an enormous number of runs. As more and more samples are picked according to the assumed operational profile and run, the potential for repeating particular test cases, or at least running test cases that do not exercise any novel functionality or forge new paths, becomes greater. Running more and more test cases according to the same distribution does improve the chances of selecting an "infrequent test case" (from an area of the input space which we term the *ultra-rare region*), but only slightly. In some cases (e.g., if the distribution has a small variance), selecting members of the ultra-rare region Q^{-1} may require sampling an intractable number of test cases. When an operational profile is inverted in order to sample rare test cases, the rareness of these cases stems solely from the infrequency with which they are sampled during operational use. This does not mean that such cases are necessarily a small subset of Δ. In fact, it is possible that the rare test cases represent a substantial portion of Δ.

Sampling from the input space rarely used in practical operation may prove to be useful for detecting security vulnerabilities. That is, processing unexpected, rarely used but legal inputs may result in a program state that compromises the security of the system. These ideas suggest that it will be meaningful for AVA to combine the modified-for-security EPA algorithm with test cases that represent the ultra-rare region of an input space. Such inputs, when employed, will help predict how secure the software will be during unusual operational events. When the software does not perform securely during experiments with unusual inputs, chances are that it will not perform securely if unusual events occur after deployment. Likewise, if the software does behave securely, this suggests that the software may be sufficiently hardened against anomalous events and threats. Such indicators are not guarantees of future secure behavior of the code, but they clearly suggest that such behavior will occur.

8.2.3 Specifying Intrusions Using Predicates

The third major requirement for the AVA assurance tool is a clear definition of what kinds of events represent security breaches. Security intrusions are the events that any tool implementing the AVA algorithm must detect. A security intrusion can include: (1) unauthorized read access, (2) unauthorized write access, (3) denial of service to the system under attack, and so on. The vulnerability assessment method simulates threats by injecting faults into an executing program and then asking the question: Has a particular type of intrusion occurred? Intrusions will be defined via logical predicates using a predicate-specification language powerful enough to specify a range of different intrusions.

In analyzing an *ftp* daemon program, $PRED_C$ may specify, for example, that user *anonymous* is not allowed to own any files or directories within the ftp file partition. Depending on the layer of the protocol stack at which the program under attack operates, the intrusion classes will vary. At the application layer, having a program create a shell with *SUID* may constitute an intrusion, while at the operating system kernel layer, creating root shells will most likely be acceptable.

Care is required in the definition of intrusions. The more ambiguous the description, the more potentially insecure events will be marked. The more specific the description, the fewer potentially vulnerable events will be generated and the more precise the ability to localize regions of vulnerability will be. These two characteristics of intrusion descriptions are not necessarily at odds, but both should be considered in the development of $PRED_C$.

8.2.4 Limiting the Information Available from AVA

In the AVA algorithm, there are two pieces of internal information that could be made available from the algorithm but probably should not be: (1) the default simulated threats used in the algorithm, and (2) the locations that received these default simulated threats and were identified as vulnerable. Also, the locations where execution estimates are small are a mixed blessing: On the one hand, these locations are unlikely to affect the computation of the executing system, and hence threats that use them for this weakness are unlikely to be successful; on the other hand, these are locations where threats (perhaps in the form of Trojan horses) can remain hidden for longer periods of time.

Limiting the amount of internal information provided to the user will be of paramount importance to the long-term success of AVA if the technology moves into widespread use as a software-security certification scheme. Consider this analogy: A student who gets an advanced copy of a test is more likely to get a good grade than a student who does not. The precise manner in which AVA simulates threats and measures vulnerability, if known by attackers or unscrupulous developers, can be used to their advantage. For instance, suppose that a system X received a very "high" rating according to AVA. Since the algorithms are white-box and assess the vulnerability of each region of a system, they inform a would-be attacker where the weakest points are in a system. If attackers have the source code being analyzed, they have adequate information to test the effectiveness of old and new intrusion schemes on the weaker regions, allowing for fine-tuning for decreased detectability. This allows AVA to be employed as an offensive weapon, assuming the source code to the simulated threats was published providing hints as to how to code new threats.

Another argument for limiting the internal information is that revealing the default threats allows lazy developers a means of providing enough security to protect against just the class of threats that AVA considers. If a developer does not have this information, and the product receives a low vulnerability score (e.g., not vulnerable), we have both an intuitive and statistical confidence that their system is not only secure with respect to the classes of threats AVA considers, but additionally to other threat classes AVA does not explicitly consider. For these reasons, it is vital that the methods AVA uses to assess security for the default threats are not used as tools for improving the opportunity for intrusions. With respect to the perturbation function template, the user is still able to test various theories as to what constitutes a successful threat.

AVA is not a foolproof assurance approach. No security assessment will ever be comprehensive. Previous security measures have focused more on manual effort and human judgment. By contrast, AVA concentrates software experimentation and computer power on the problem of assessing security.

AVA has several clear advantages:

1. It can be continually modified to simulate additional classes of threats. New threat classes can be quickly linked into the system without disturbing the processing of old threats.

2. It can be customized (by the user) for application-specific classes of intrusions without requiring any changes to the assessment measures.

3. It measures dynamic information (as opposed to static information) in order to determine behavior.

4. It can provide information from which to develop improved design-for-security heuristics.

5. It yields reproducible "numerical" results—meaning that the same analysis parameters will produce the same results at a later time. Tiger-team testing is too subjective to be considered reproducible in this way.

6. It can be used in conjunction with tiger-team penetration testing and other established techniques to better assess software security.

AVA can isolate regions within the source code where further scrutiny should be applied. We believe that this approach to software security will shift attention toward the root causes of information system vulnerability, including programming errors, and thus stimulate a greater interest in secure system design and security assessment.

8.3 httpd Security Analysis
Results

The NCSA httpd Server Version 1.5.2 has been subjected to AVA security analysis. The httpd program is a popular Web server. The analysis attempted to test the basic authentication mechanism to determine if any potential flaws might exist that may affect the security policy of a Web site. The test involved attempting to access a page that required basic authentication. In order to access a page protected by authentication, a user must enter a valid user name and password. The analysis of the httpd server sent a single input over a network socket using the grammar of the http network protocol. The user name entered was correct, whereas the password was not. As a result, in the unperturbed test, the authenticated Web page is never returned. Instead, the server returns a warning message that authentication failed.

The analysis used fault injection to perturb program states throughout the httpd server software. These perturbations corrupted both the flow of data through control branches and internal states assigned to program variables. A security violation assertion was placed at a location in the source code that, if executed, indicated that the authenticated Web page had been incorrectly returned. The source code for the server was instrumented with default perturbation functions throughout. The analysis perturbed over 650 locations in the source code. Each experiment injected only a single fault. The AVA tool recorded the result of each fault injected. If the combination of input used and fault injected triggered a security violation, then the location where the fault was injected was recorded. The security analysis was fully automated.

Based on the experimentation, a significant number of locations were found for which the security of the application—and therefore the Web site—is sensitive to the perturbed states. That is, perturbations injected in these locations resulted in the security being breached and allowed access to a document that should have been prohibited.

We present the results as a real-valued security metric in the range of [0,1]. A rating of 1 indicates no insecure events occurred for every input, while a rating of 0 indicates that an insecure event occurred on every input. Since only a single input was used, the scores for this experiment are always either 0 or 1. The results can be viewed from the source code statement level up to the application level. Low scores propagate up the hierarchy. Thus if a score of 0 was obtained at any statement in the entire application, then this score will be propagated to the module level and finally to the application level. Figure 8.1 shows the scores from the security analysis of httpd at the application level. The score for the overall application was rated at 0, since the lowest scores from each module are propagated up. The modules where fault injection resulted in insecure behavior are denoted by the 0 scores. The sensitive modules include:

- `http_access.c`
- `http_auth.c`
- `http_log.c`
- `http_request.c`
- `util.c`

In the module http_access.c, the evaluate_access function is vulnerable to fault injection. Within this function, fault perturbation on nine different statements each resulted in security being violated. As an example, the following statement when perturbed results in the access-protected page to be illegally retrieved:

```
329 num_dirs = count_dirs (path) ;
```

This assignment statement on line 329 calls the function count_dirs, which counts the number of directories in the path of the requested document. This function is necessary to determine if the document, image, or program requested by the Web client is situated in the document root anywhere under an access-controlled directory. For example, if the requested document is three subdirectories under the document root and the document root is access-controlled, then the document should not be fetched for the Web client without first authenticating the Web client.

The variable num_dirs, which is assigned this value on line 329, is subsequently used in the function to implement the access control. In our analysis, a perturbation function corrupted this variable and ultimately resulted in a security violation. It is instructive to speculate how corrupting this variable may cause a security violation. Since this variable determines the number of directories to search in the path of the requested document, if this number is changed to zero in the trivial case, then no directories will be searched for access control, and the access-controlled page will be delivered without authentication. In the more general case, perturbing this number to any integer less than the number corresponding to the directory where access control is first instantiated will result in a security violation. One interpretation of this result is that if the function count_dirs is incorrectly coded such that it returns an incorrect value, or if num_dirs is assigned or read incorrectly, then the security of the application may be in jeopardy.

The sensitivity of this variable to perturbation is seen later in the same function:

```
372   for (x=0; x<num_dirs;x++) {
373       y=num_sec;
```

When the condition (x < num_dirs) on line 372 is perturbed, a security violation results. In this case, the variable num_dirs itself was not corrupted; rather the

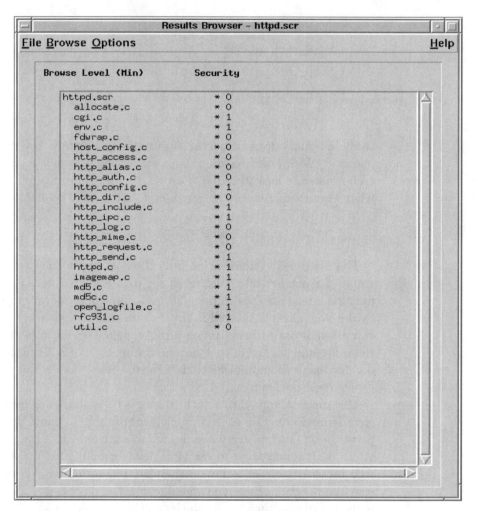

Figure 8.1 *Application-level scores from security analysis of httpd.*

condition that is evaluated in the for expression was perturbed. For example, if (x < num_dirs) evaluated to TRUE, then it was perturbed to FALSE. Speculating on the security implications, it seems likely that if the loop execution is terminated early due to the false evaluation of the condition expression, then the access control features within the body of the for loop may never be executed—thus resulting in a security violation.

On line 373, when the variable assignment for y is perturbed, the security of the application is again compromised. This variable is later used in a conditional expression of a branch statement on line 411 shown next. Perturbing y will affect the result of the branch and may ultimately have prevented some of the access control code from executing.

As an example of vulnerable conditional statements, consider the following statements in the same evaluate_access function:

```
409   if (override [x]) {
410         parse_htaccess (reqInfo,d,override [x]);
411         if(num_sec != y){
```

In this example, when the condition on line 409 is perturbed to the opposite state, a security violation occurs. Likewise, when the condition on line 411 is perturbed, then a security violation also occurs. The results from perturbing these branch conditions indicate the security-critical nature of these branch points. That is, a failure to correctly code and evaluate the branch conditions may result in a security violation. It also indicates a lack of fault tolerance on the part of the program design. Since only a single fault is injected per experiment, each of these branch conditions is a single point of failure. The security of the application can be improved by adding multiple checks of the branch conditions. Several other conditional statements that were perturbed in the evaluate_access function also resulted in security violations.

Consider the check_auth function in the http_auth.c module. The following if conditional:

```
569   if(strcmp(real_pw, (char *)crypt (sent_pw,real_pw)){
570         sprintf (errstr, "user %s: password mismatch",
              reqInfo->auth_user);
571         auth_bong(reqInfo, errstr,reqInfo->auth_name,
              sec->auth_type);
572   }.
```

When the condition on line 569 is perturbed, the security assertion of the system is violated. This example is fairly intuitive. The code compares the password sent from the browser client to the password that exists on the server host for accessing the protected page. If a mismatch results, then an error is noted and an authentication window is launched which notifies the client of authentication failure. During the execution, the condition on line 569 would have evaluated to TRUE since the passwords were different, except for the fact that the fault perturbation forced the statement to be FALSE. This result can be interpreted to mean that the condition evaluated in line 569 had better be coded correctly and the functions executed within the condition (strcmp, crypt) had better perform correctly, or else a security violation will occur.

The last module we describe, util.c, has a number of functions that result in security violations when perturbed. Figure 8.2 shows the results at the function level from security analysis of the util.c module. The functions where fault perturbation resulted in security violations are:

- no2slash

- make_dirstr

- count_dirs

- strncpy_dir

- getword.

Note the following code from the make_dirstr function. This function is used to convert the path to a protected directory into a parseable string.

```
468    for (x=0, f=0; s[x] ;x++) {
469        if((d[x] = s[x]) == '/')
470            if((++f)==n){
471                if (x == 0)
```

Line 468 provides four opportunities for fault perturbation. When x=0 and s[x] were perturbed using the default perturbation functions for integer and Boolean types, respectively, the security assertion was violated. Perturbing these variables resulted in the body of the for loop not being executed. As a result, the path of the access-controlled resource would never be available to the other security-critical functions that process it. Fault perturbations in for loop variables in the count_dirs, strncpy_dir, and getword functions had similar results. That is, the variables that index the path string of the protected directories are of a security-critical nature.

When the Boolean condition on line 469 of the make_dirstr function was perturbed, *no* security violations were detected. Conversely, when the Boolean condition of line 470 was perturbed, the Web page was illegally accessed. Finally, perturbing the Boolean condition on line 471 did not result in the violation of the security assertion. This example illustrates the sensitivity of some statements and structures to the security policy that is coded for a particular application.

It is difficult to statically analyze structures and source code to determine which structures are most dangerous and which are not. Certainly, the example previously given, where the password is checked and compared, can be intuitively understood as security-critical. But in the example just given, it is difficult to realize a priori that the condition on line 470 is security-critical while the one on line 469 is not, given our particular violation assertion. Bear in mind that for this experiment only a single input scenario was used, only the default set of perturbation functions were used, and only a single security assertion was coded. The results will vary with different inputs, different perturbation functions, and different assertions of security.

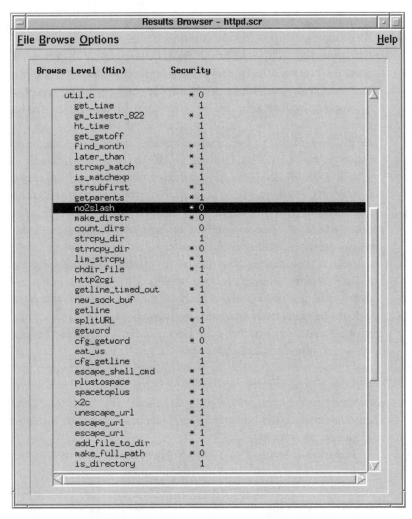

Figure 8.2 *Security analysis results of util.c module.*

8.3.1 Discussion

The analysis of the NCSA httpd server shows a number of features of fault injection that are attractive for designing and analyzing security-critical applications. It is important that the results from fault-injection analysis be interpreted for what they represent, and nothing more. The results from fault injection do not reveal *if* flaws in the source code exist or *where* flaws in the source code are. Rather fault injection shows only the potential for anomalous behavior in an executing application to violate the security policy of the application.

In this case study, the security policy coded for the httpd server stated that the access-controlled Web page should not be revealed to a client without proper authentication. The role of the AVA security analysis prototype tool is to automate the process of perturbing states throughout the software. Because of the size and complexity of a piece of software such as the httpd server, the human mind cannot at any one time think about all relevant critical factors, including the number of ways in which software can fail; the security-critical nature of all statements; and the ways in which statements, functions, and modules interact to cause potential security violations. AVA permits automated instrumentation of source code for continuously executing programs such as network servers. This type of analysis reveals the potential for a program to violate the security of a system in the face of anomalous events. Even further, the prototype notes the locations where, if code imperfections exist or if anomalous behavior results, the security of the system may be compromised.

Armed with this information about where potential anomalous behavior can violate security, what is a software designer to do? The designer/developer of the software is most knowledgeable about the intricacies of the software. Once individual functions and statements are identified as security-critical, the developer may be able to determine if the potential fault scenarios that resulted in security violations could occur in practice. If a flaw is found, then it can be fixed. While it is certainly the case that the developer of the software is most familiar with the code, it is wise for another developer or engineer to perform the inspection of the code to determine if security flaws exist. This is similar to what occurs during software design reviews in organizations that implement mature software engineering processes.

The problem with this approach, however, is that it requires a deep level of manual intervention and human judgment. An alternative is to automate a design-for-fault-tolerance approach where results from analysis are automatically fed back into design in order to produce more robust software. For example, the results from fault-injection analysis determine where potential anomalous states can violate the security of the application. These results can be used to code assertions or other fault-tolerant software structures to mitigate potential anomalous behavior at their source. This is similar to discovering a flaw and placing a wrapper around it, so the anomalous states can never propagate to the outputs of the software—where security violations in fact occur.

8.4 Buffer Overflow with AVA

Possibly the most common general class of software engineering errors are *buffer overflow* anomalies. Here, we show how we are able to create perturbation functions capable of simulating this error class.

8.4.1 Buffer Overflow

Program inputs should always be checked to ensure that they are well formed. If the birth date field in a Web form should not exceed 6 characters, then the program interpreting the birth date input must make sure that it actually doesn't exceed 6 characters. It is not enough to simply limit the size of the field on the form, since these data can either be entered directly in the URL field of the browser, or they can be posted to the server by a custom-written program which does not abide by form-field limits. Similarly, if the number of arguments read should be exactly 10, then it is essential to make sure that exactly 10 arguments are received. If each of the arguments is supposed to fit within some range, then the interpreting program should make sure that each argument does so. Finally, and most important, the length of the input should always be checked and limited before it is copied into a program *buffer*. A buffer is simply a contiguous portion of memory that stores data used by a program. A buffer *overflows* when more data is copied into the buffer than the space allocated for the buffer in memory.

Buffer overflows are a very popular hacker target. Overflowing a buffer results in overwriting memory that is not assigned to the buffer. The consequences range from no discernible effect, to aborting the program execution, to executing possibly malicious instructions contained in the input that caused the overflow. If no adverse effects result from an input buffer overflow, then the program is tolerant of this common type of attack. It may be difficult to verify this through standard testing, since programs behave differently for different input streams. We include a buffer-overflow perturbation in AVA to address the buffer overflow problem and help grapple with the difficulty of testing for it.

In the second case of overflowing buffers, it may be possible to crash an executing program. Consider the TCP/IP network program, ping. This program is often used on many different platforms to determine if a remote host is "alive" or not. The ping network daemon responds to a network packet which is usually 64 bytes in length, but can be up to 65,536 bytes in length—the maximum packet length allowed by an Internet Protocol (IP) datagram. Using TCP/IP, the standard protocols for sending messages over the Internet, it is possible to send several IP datagrams and reassemble them at the ping server as a single input with length greater than 65,536 bytes. Unfortunately for many servers, the ping network daemon does not respond very well to input this large. Rather than limiting the length of the buffer it will read, the ping server attempts to read the entire input and ends up choking on it. On some machines, the ping server shuts down, while on others, the entire system shuts down or reboots. This is a particularly easy way of launching a denial-of-service attack to machines that are vulnerable to the ping attack. This kind of attack has been commonly seen in the last few years.

The third case of overflowing buffers can result in the most serious security problems for a site. Overflowing program buffers with unconstrained input is a technique widely employed by hackers to attempt to execute commands embedded in the input. Depending on where in memory the buffer is allocated, it is possible that overflowing a buffer may result in overwriting a special section of memory called the program stack. The *stack* is the section of memory that is used to restore the state of the executing program after returning from a function. During the execution of a program, whenever a call is made to a function, the current state of the program, including all program variables and internal registers, is saved on the stack. In addition to the program state, the address of the next instruction to be executed after returning from the called function is "pushed" on the stack. This address is known as the *instruction pointer.* So, when the program is finished executing the called function, the next instruction to be executed is "popped off" the stack and loaded in the *program counter* to execute the next program instruction.

By overwriting the stack with data overflowed from an input buffer, it is possible to change the instruction pointer to another address. In the case of many program crashes caused by buffer overruns, this is exactly what happens. That is, the instruction pointer is overwritten with random or garbage data that does not correspond to a legitimate instruction address for this program. Upon return from the called function, the processor will attempt to execute an instruction from a section of memory outside of the program's address space and a serious error called a *segmentation fault* will result. If a segmentation fault occurs during the execution of a program, the program will normally abort and create a file on the disk called a core file. Most users of UNIX systems have experienced the frustration of having a core file dumped on their file system. In addition to being useless for people who are not developing or debugging the code, a core file can take up a very large amount of disk space. These files should be limited in size, since consuming large amounts of disk space is one possible means of implementing a denial-of-service attack. In some cases, core files have been known to contain passwords which were stored by an authenticating program (such as a Web browser) before crashing. This is a good reason to prevent core files from being created on the file system altogether.

If the input stream that overflows a buffer is carefully crafted, it is possible that the instruction pointer can be overwritten in a principled manner. That is, a specific address can be written into the instruction pointer so that upon return to the calling function, the next instruction to be executed is located at an address of the malicious user's choice. This technique is known in the hacker underground community as "smashing the stack." It is also possible to construct the input stream so the address written in the instruction pointer points back onto the stack frame instead of to some other portion of the program memory. By pointing back onto the stack, it is possible to execute any instructions embedded in the input stream that have overwritten the stack. This technique is as effective as being able to access and modify the program source code, recompile it, and execute it on the server without ever having access to the source code! Smashing the stack is one of the primary attacks launched against SUID root programs. The implications are that an attack launched by an unprivileged remote user over the Internet can potentially execute arbitrary commands on a machine with super-user privileges.

One of the most notorious cases of exploiting a buffer-overflow flaw occurred in 1988 and was implemented by a program known as the Internet Worm. The Internet Worm was written by Robert T. Morris Jr. to exploit a flaw in the fin-ger server which runs on many networked machines. The finger server provides information to remote clients about the local users. Normally the finger server is queried using a command of the following format:

```
finger userID@machinehost.domain.com.
```

The information returned by the finger server may include the identity of users that are logged on to the queried machine, how long the user has been idle at the terminal, the last time the user read mail, the status of mail received, and sometimes additional information that users will provide about themselves such as phone numbers, office hours, public encryption keys, and the occasional philosophical statement about life. The finger server can also provide information about which users are currently logged on to a host machine. While this infor-mation may reveal more information than is necessary, the Internet Worm did not exploit any of this information in its attack. Rather, the Internet Worm exploited a flaw in the finger server that allowed it to overflow an internal buffer.

The finger server allocated an array in memory (the buffer) of 512 bytes to store the argument of the finger client command. The argument to the finger client command is normally just a user ID and machine name, or simply the machine name itself. The function the finger server used to read the argument did not check the length of the buffer it was copying into, nor did it limit the length of the argument to the limit of the buffer. As a result, if the argument the finger client sent was greater than 512 bytes, then the buffer allocated in mem-ory would be overwritten. This flaw is exactly what the Internet Worm exploited to overflow the buffer and overwrite the stack on many machines it attacked. By overwriting the stack, the Worm was able to execute its own code that it sent in the argument to the finger command. The code written by the Worm created a shell from which arbitrary commands could be executed. Since many finger servers run with root privilege, the Worm was able to execute its commands as the superuser. The Worm made its point, not by damaging the systems it vio-lated, but rather by launching the same attack on other machines from each suc-cessive machine it conquered through this program flaw. This case has been studied and well documented in the literature [Spafford 1989]. An entire issue of the ACM was devoted to papers discussing the Internet Worm incident. Despite its prominence in the annals of computer security, a very large number of security attacks today exploit buffer-overflow flaws in programs.

8.4.2 An AVA Perturbation for Buffer Overflow

The AVA prototype includes a perturbation capability that can overflow string buffers. This perturbation function, in concert with appropriate assertion placement, is a powerful assessment capability. There are two kinds of string buffer-overflow perturbations in the current prototype: One requires that the user of the tool know the exact size of the buffer being exploited; the other determines this information automatically.

Different platforms implement different forms of program stacks. For this reason, a buffer-overflow perturbation is a platform-dependent entity. The AVA prototypes two buffer-overflow perturbations that work under Linux, SunOS 4.1.x and Sparc Solaris 2.x. Development efforts are under way to support other platforms.

The first perturbation requires the user to specify the length of the buffer to be overflowed. It overflows a string buffer by copying a string constructed in such a way that executable instructions are embedded in it. These instructions are executed given a correct offset.

The second perturbation determines automatically where in memory to embed executable instructions. It requires neither a buffer size nor an offset to determine the correct address at which to place the attack code. Instead, this perturbation walks up the stack frame pointer chain.

Both perturbations have proven to be useful during experimental analysis. In particular, buffer-overflow problems in the UNIX system commands lpr and mount can be simulated with the AVA tool. The tool identifies the fact that particular buffers in the code are susceptible to attack. This kind of information could be used during software development to eradicate buffer-overflow problems. Buffer overflow is currently among the most popularly exploited problems in computer security. The AVA technology should be useful in helping to curb its utility.

8.5 Information Warfare

In sports, ask any offense coach what his or her pregame plan is, and it is often quite simple: Exploit weaknesses in the opposition's defense. Attacking an adversary's weakness is a fundamental strategy. This section explores in a little more detail how the AVA utility can sense what information systems are more vulnerable to. It is not necessarily the case that every possible vulnerability can be exploited by a malicious user, and certainly not every type of fault-injection mechanism can be tried during AVA. It is our contention, however, that AVA provides an immediate, offensive information warfare capability, even though the main research and development focus of AVA remains defensive.

AVA seeks to measure a program's security weaknesses with respect to both known and unknown threats. Unknown threats are those that may occur in the future, but have not yet been observed.

As part of its procedure, AVA injects *random* corruptions in the state of the software, to see if those corruptions, which in some sense represent programmer errors, create security holes that potentially result in security-policy violations. There can be little argument that security defenses could be more sharply honed and security strategies more objectively compared and contrasted if the locality of vulnerabilities in a system could be scientifically measured. AVA tries to make this happen. A secondary benefit of AVA is knowledge about what systems are vulnerable to. It is this secondary information that makes our approach attractive to those thinking about offensive-information warfare.

We have already talked about limiting the information to the user concerning what types of corruptions are injected into a system and where those corruptions are injected. But even if that information were readily provided to the user, it is still insufficient information for the user to turn into a successful attack.

For an attack against an information system to be successful, the sequence of input signals used to exploit a weakness must often be extremely precise. It is usually the case that both a particular sequence of inputs and the timing of the inputs are critical features. To thwart an attack, a system can attempt any combination of three strategies:

1. Compensate for its weakness with monitors or wrappers
2. Detect and deflect malicious input
3. Disrupt the timing of an attack

When devising such strategies, it clearly pays to know as much about "generic" security vulnerabilities as possible. Ironically, such knowledge is hard to come by using legitimate means of research. There is a lack of an organized, central repository that clearly and explicitly explains past vulnerabilities. The idea that researchers can make progress against future exploits when they cannot learn of past exploits is absurd. No other engineering profession makes such requests from its scientists. From such information we can home in more quickly on the classes of threats that are most likely to be successful when we perform our threat simulation to determine existing defensive deficiencies.

Though AVA simulates previous security threats, the strength of AVA is in finding program flaws that can be exploited for malicious gain. This knowledge is useful for offensive- and defensive-information warfare. The problem of defensive security protection of information systems is in some ways more difficult than offensive-information warfare. Finding one vulnerability or program flaw in software may be sufficient to mount an offensive attack. However, fixing just one weakness is not sufficient for ensuring that the system is adequately defended. The knowledge of where vulnerabilities in information systems exist and the means by which to exploit them must be closely guarded since this knowledge can serve as the basis for offensive attack.

Currently, information vital for exploiting vulnerabilities is hidden from AVA users. In the AVA algorithm, the *internal* information that is hidden includes: (1) the simulated threats (both known and especially pseudorandom) used in the algorithm, and (2) the locations that received these default-simulated threats and were identified as vulnerable. This information provides essential data about successful systems' security breaches. These data demonstrate a path of events involving injected anomalous events into a system's state that are capable of thwarting information defense. This provides clues as to where problems can be injected, hidden, and triggered via a similar means at a later time.

Developing a successful offensive capability is a two-step process of assessing the defense and developing an appropriate offense. The novelty of AVA is that it first builds the offense to assess the defense, and if the offense that it builds is successful, then you know where the software is vulnerable and what it is vulnerable to.

When AVA has been performed, results show how frequently artificial, hypothesized corruptions cause events defined as security violations to occur. We also know what those corruptions are. A corruption occurs at the program-state level, and this process takes place when the code executes on some input value i. The quest then becomes to determine what input value j could naturally (without fault-injection mechanisms) cause the same corrupt program state to occur just as it did after fault injection was employed. Once this problem is solved, we have a true security exploit. Until the target software is changed, every exploit discovered in this way is a new offensive weapon.

References

[Aslam 1995] T. Aslam. "A Taxonomy of Security Faults in the Unix Operating System." Master's thesis, Purdue University, West Lafayette, Ind., 1995.

[Beizer 1983] B. Beizer. *Software Testing Techniques.* Van Nostrand Reinhold, 1983.

[CERT 1993] CERT Advisory. Sendmail vulnerability, November 1993. CERT Advisory CA-93:16.

[Cheswick 1994] W. R. Cheswick and S. M. Bellovin. *Firewalls and Internet Security.* Addison-Wesley, Reading, Mass., 1994.

[Farmer 1990] D. Farmer and E. H. Spafford. "The cops security checker system." In *USENIX Conference Proceedings,* pp. 165–170, Anaheim, Calif., Summer 1990.

[Farmer 1993] D. Farmer and W. Venema. "Improving the security of your site by breaking into it." Available by ftp from ftp://ftp.win.tue.nl/pub/security/admin-guide-to-cracking.101.Z, 1993.

[Kim 1993] G. Kim and E. H. Spafford. "The design and implementation of Tripwire: A file system integrity checker." Technical Report CSD-TR-93-071, Purdue University, West Lafayette, Ind., 1993.

[Klaus 1995] C. Klaus. "Internet security scanner." Available by ftp from ftp://ftp.iss.net/pub/iss, 1995.

[Knight 1995] J. C. Knight and K. G. Wika. "Software safety in a medical application." Technical report, University of Virginia, Department of Computer Science, April 1995.

[Muffett 1992] A. D. E. Muffett. "Crack version 4.1, a sensible password checker for Unix." Available by ftp from ftp.cert.org/pub/tools/crack/readme.txt, 1992.

[Safford 1993] D. R. Safford, D. L. Schales, and D. K. Hess. "The TAMU security package: An ongoing response to Internet intruders in an academic environment." In *Proceedings of the Fourth Usenix UNIX Security Symposium,* pp. 91–118, Santa Clara, Calif., October 1993.

[Spafford 1989] E. H. Spafford. "The Internet Worm Program: An Analysis." *Computer Communications Review,* 19(1):17–57, 1989.

[Spafford 1990] E. H. Spafford. "Extending mutation testing to find environmental bugs." *Software Practice and Principle,* 20(2):181–189, February 1990.

[SSECMM 1995] Systems Security Engineering Capability Maturity Model Report, October 2, 1995.

[Voas 1997] J. Voas, F. Charron, G. McGraw, K. Miller, and M. Friedman. "Predicting How Badly 'Good' Software Can Behave." *IEEE Software,* July 1997.

[Werner 1995] B. Werner, ed. *Proc. of the Eleventh Annual Computer Security Applications Conference* (ACSAC '95), December 1995. IEEE Computer Society Press.

[White 1996] G. B. White, E. A. Fisch, and U. W. Pooch. *Computer System and Network Security.* CRC Press, New York, 1996.

9 *Maintenance and Reuse*
Software Life Support

This chapter is devoted to the topics of software maintenance and reuse. Throughout this chapter we survey what role fault injection can play when software is being maintained or if software reuse is being considered.

9.1 Software Maintenance

Software maintenance is usually considered the most expensive phase of the software life cycle. Some estimates suggest that maintenance activities account for upwards of 50 percent of the total cost to develop and support a program. Still others estimate that the cost of maintenance is around 70 percent of the total cost of the system. One clear factor in the large difference between these estimates is a function of how long the software system will need to be maintained and how many changes will be required. As systems age, maintainability decreases, while at the same time confidence in satisfactory behavior increases.

Software maintenance activities generally revolve around two sets of procedures: (1) adding functionality to a system as requirements change, and (2) fixing existing code when failures are observed and the contributing faults are identified. Regardless of which of these activities is being pursued at any given time, it is clear that software testing will always be a large part of the costs of maintenance, since the maintainer must be convinced that his or her modifications to the code do not negatively impact the quality of the existing functionality.

Software maintenance is no less error-prone than any other life-cycle phase. We say this because maintenance is typically performed by someone other than the original developer. Good developers move from project to project. The title "Software Maintainer" is frowned upon as a job description by many who would rather be creating something new as opposed to trying to breathe life back into someone else's mistake-riddled code. Whenever code is modified by someone other than the original team members that understand the specification, requirements, and design, unexpected errors are much more likely to crop up. Major problems occur when people who do not understand the system modify it. The likelihood that they will understand the ramifications of their changes on parts of the system that they are not modifying is very low. These people may have a fair amount of understanding about the little piece of the system they are modifying without realizing the global impact their changes are having on the rest of the system through propagation.

In its most basic form, maintenance is a *propagation* issue. As we have described in chapters 3, 5, 6, and 8, there are many different forms of propagation analysis that may be suitable for solving this problem. In this chapter, we look briefly at what static and dynamic analysis techniques could provide, using the Year 2000 problem as our maintenance exercise.

The basic fault-injection (propagation) algorithms of chapters 5, 6, and 8 can also be used for software maintenance. The original algorithms need a few modifications, however. We will also talk about two static propagation analyses (not based on fault injection) that may be beneficial during maintenance. At the end of the chapter, we discuss how to build perturbation functions for the Year 2000 maintenance problem.

9.1.1 *Program Slicing*

Program slicing is a fairly simple code-analysis technique. Program slicing is a source code–based impact-analysis technique for determining what effect certain input variables have on certain output variables [Weiser 1982]. The original application for slicing was debugging; however, it has since been used as a maintenance technique. It is fair to think of software slicing as static propagation analysis.

There are two forms of slicing: static and dynamic. *Static* slicing traces *backward* from an output variable(s) to all input variables that have the ability to affect the values that the output variables get. Every statement in the program that is traced back during this backwards analysis is considered a part of the program slice. The program slice represents a decomposition of the original program, and should be compilable and executable as a stand-alone program. For maintenance purposes, static slicing provides the valuable benefit of knowing what impacts what.

Dynamic slicing is a forward analysis that starts with a specific input value and traces forward to all computations that can be affected by the input until all output values are computed. This provides knowledge about each computation that occurs given a selected input value. Note that each dynamic slice must be subsumed by some static slice.

Dynamic slicing is better for debugging than static slicing. That's because if the test case for which a failure occurred is known, it is possible with dynamic slicing to determine every computation that was executed on a failing run. If, however, static slicing started from output variables that contained bad information, that could be as useful as dynamic slicing in certain situations. Since chapter 3 covered the theoretical underpinnings of slicing, we will now turn to the complementary nature of slicing and fault injection. Together, these two technologies can help solve several of the main problems of software maintenance.

The relationship between slicing and fault injection is as follows. Slicing can determine a priori whether certain inputs or states in the program can affect a certain output variable or variables. If output variable X is referenced in $PRED_C$, and if static slicing shows that input variable Y cannot affect X, then applying fault injection to Y in order to see if X satisfies $PRED_C$ is a bad experiment and a waste of resources. On the flip side of the coin, if static slicing shows that Y might indeed affect X, this does not mean that it will do so in such a way that satisfied $PRED_C$. Fault injection predicts any such effect more accurately. In short, slicing can be used to guide dynamic techniques that study both program behavior and semantic interrelationships. For PIE, slicing would find assignment statements where perturbing the variable on the left-hand side of the assignment cannot impact any output variable. Knowing such information in advance of a set of experiments can be used to make the PIE propagation-analysis algorithm much more efficient.

It is also possible to statically slice backward from internal states (acting as outputs) to input variables. This sort of exercise could be useful in the situation where fault injection has identified a set of corrupted states (or partial states) that force $PRED_C$ to be true, but it is not clear exactly which inputs contribute to those corrupted states. Static slicing can trace backward to determine which input variables contribute to the suspect computations. This information can be used in combination with automatic test-case generation to determine which input values (if any) will put the software into those internal states that will enable undesirable outputs. A strategy like this would prove very useful in combination with the AVA algorithm covered in the previous chapter.

9.1.2 Parnas's Uses Hierarchy

Software written in "imperative" languages is made up of syntactically sequential compositions of statements and subroutines. The subroutine hierarchy is ordered according to which routine calls which other routine, and therefore defines what it means for software components to be "in series." In general, software components are connected in series so that some component A feeds information into B which returns information to A once B is done processing.

Dave Parnas argues that the analogy between a serial chain of hardware components and a serial chain of software components is flawed. Parnas defines what he calls the *uses hierarchy* to clarify the relationship of subroutines. Routine X that calls routine Y is defined to *use* Y if and only if correct functioning of X depends on correct functioning of Y [Parnas 1974]. Note that "uses" is thus a concept defined in terms of functionality. If routine X can carry out function F independent of routine Y (which it nevertheless calls), then X does not "use" Y for F. One primary example that Parnas gives involves a routine X which is required to find an item in a list. If X does not find the item, it must call another routine Y. X does not "use" Y, because X's finding function is unaffected by Y's possible failure. We should mention that if a called routine can fail to return, then it is "used" by any caller.

The relationship between slicing and the uses hierarchy is not so straightforward. If slicing were applied to a program where procedure calls were replaced with procedure bodies as in-line code, then even if there is no use of the results from Y in X, there might still be statements belonging to X in a slice that traces backward from Y. This distinction can be explained as follows: The uses hierarchy offers a semantic perspective on propagation, whereas static slicing offers a syntactic perspective on propagation. The dynamic propagation algorithms we have provided in earlier chapters demonstrate a way to quantify the amount of use that one part of the code gets from another part. Likewise, if there is no syntactic capability for Y to call X, then Y does not use X. This capability can easily be determined without dynamic analysis, and, in fact, can be determined statically.

9.1.3 The Year 2000 Problem

In order to demonstrate what fault injection can do for maintenance, we turn our attention to the most widely discussed software maintenance problem of all time.

Many programs are ill-equipped to deal with the turn of the century. That's not to say that the algorithms they use are antiquated. The problem has to do with the way the year 2000 is represented in many programs, especially those written in the '60s and '70s. This may, in fact, be the most widespread problem ever in software. If your checks are like most people's, the place where you fill in the date includes a prewritten "19." You had better use all your checks before January 1, 2000. In a computer, a calendar year is simply an integer, and the next century is simply the current century plus one. If you don't use the century as a part of your representation for a year, then the last day of this century, 12-31-99 (MMDDYY), will roll over into 01-01-00. Obviously, the integer 00 is smaller than 99. From a computer's perspective, where time forward means increasing integers, a change from 99 to 00 represents a giant step backwards in time. That is, the computer may actually believe that events that occur after the turn of the century occurred before the turn of the century.

This problem will wreak enormous havoc for financial and billing systems that are time- and date-dependent. Many medical testing and patient record systems are time-dependent as well, and make diagnoses and schedule appointments based on fixed intervals. Here, the Year 2000 problem may not only be annoying, but could be lethal as well.

How will these systems react when events that should be scheduled in the future are considered as the past? Answers to these questions are sparse, and depend entirely on particular systems. There is no general-purpose answer to this dilemma. For example, one developer of part of a large system may have had the forethought (or the extra memory) to use century fields in their year representation, whereas another developer working on another part of the same system may have decided to leave out the often redundant century field to save space. Thus, even in the same system, some parts may be affected by the Year 2000 problem, where other parts are not.

So what might fault injection have to offer in such a case? Fault injection can be used to separate the parts of the system that need modification from those that do not.

Exacerbating the whole problem is the fact that no one actually knows which systems may have problems. Nor does anyone know precisely how affected systems will react. The fact is that as we continue to get closer to the inevitable date change, more uncertainty and more errors are likely to occur. This is the reason that solutions to the Year 2000 error are often touted as imperative if businesses are to continue to operate smoothly into the century change. To get an idea of the magnitude of the problem, consider grocery store checkout lines. Ever been in a line where the scanning technology is on the blink, or where the card payment system is not functioning properly? Such an occurrence leads to pandemonium very quickly. Tempers flare. Now imagine what could happen in the year 2000 in offices and stores worldwide.

Interestingly, the Year 2000 problem has already affected grocery store checkout lanes. Some credit cards issued in 1997 have an expiration date that falls in the year 2000. Many point-of-sale credit card terminals have software that cannot deal with expiration dates in the next century. These terminals reject purchases from credit cards that, as far as their poor programs can tell, are 94 or more years expired. The Y2K problem—as it is sometimes called—is already here.

According to a notice from the United States House of Representatives' Committee on Science, Representative Constance A. Morella, chair of the Committee on Science's Subcommittee on Technology, along with several of her colleagues sent a letter to the Clinton administration in early 1997 requesting information on the Year 2000 problem. "We initially thought the problem affected just computer software and programs, but we are now learning that the magnitude and scope of the Year 2000 challenge seems to be growing beyond just computers," Morella stated. "If consumer products which contain microchips are affected, we need to know whether agencies are addressing this fact and whether the American public is being adequately informed." Congress is slowly becoming aware of the problem.

The Gartner Group claims that 90 percent of the applications in use today will be negatively affected by the Year 2000 problem. Experts expect to begin seeing system crashes prior to 1999 because of the problem, as computers start scheduling future events that begin to appear as past events. It is estimated that today, there are 180 billion lines of COBOL code on MVS, with a maintenance workforce for that code of around one million employees. To attack the Year 2000 problem during 1996–1998, an additional 200,000 new employees are needed *just for this body of code.* How many new programmers do you know that are all hot to drop Java and move on to COBOL? But COBOL is only the tip of the iceberg—there is much more code that suffers from this problem. Since it is unlikely that such a huge number of highly trained people will ever be found to tackle the problem, the need for automated maintenance technologies which do not require more manual effort than they save is huge. The demand is there. In reaction to the demand, many companies have started to hawk their Y2K solutions. The Year 2000 conversion technology marketplace, where a variety of vendors with different approaches all promise fast, accurate, and inexpensive solutions for your code, is here. Buyer beware.

One of the current approaches for solving the Year 2000 problem revolves around impact analysis. *Impact analysis* (for example, slicing) involves scanning statically through the source code to see where variables are defined and where they are used. One problem that results from a purely static approach to the problem is that impact analysis can lead to an overestimate of problem magnitude. That's because it is not necessarily the case that every place that a year variable is defined or used there is a problem. Many date fields may already conform to the four-digit ISO 8601 standard: YYYY-MM-DD. Another problem involved with impact analysis is that of date fields that are overlooked, but still need to be changed because they are subject to the two-digit problem. Tracing tools can miss date infections, because of their limited understanding of what a date is not. For example, suppose that some programmer stores year information in a variable X_X_X, and suppose that this is undocumented. No impact-analysis tools could be expected to know this; they follow only def-use information, which is syntactic, not semantic. Problems such as these are known as false negatives.

Impact analysis will also find a lot of places in the code where variables like "costs_to_date" variables are defined. Though these variables may not in any way have anything to do with dates per se, they make the mistake of having the string "date" in their name. These are false positives, which can result in a lot of unnecessary concern over the problem and a possible overestimation of how big the problem really is for a specific application.

Fault injection provides a very nice benefit, at least if you know the correct names of the date variables. Fault injection can be applied in a postimpact analysis role. By taking an existing system without any Year 2000 modifications, we can simulate inputs of future events after Year 2000, and we can immediately study the impact of those events via assertions that are also placed throughout the code to increase observability. Impact analysis will quickly locate where the fault-injection perturbation functions should be applied, and can even aid in determining where the observability points should be. Impact analysis, however, will not help us determine what we should be looking out for. That is the role of a good regression test suite or an oracle.

Fixing the Year 2000 Problem

The fundamental solution to the problem is to use four-digit years and include the decade. To do this for systems that employ two-digit years involves database changes, changing data types, and changing files and parameters that are passed throughout systems. Note that this forces changes in the syntax of the software. There are also many semantic considerations that must be taken into account— we address them in the following paragraphs.

The Year 2000 problem is the simple result of software developers not designing systems to last a long time. In the late sixties and early seventies, it was incomprehensible that programs would live to see the twenty-first century. They have. These systems are hardwired to assume that the first two characters in any year field are "19." Only the last two characters in the pattern "19YY" can vary. This was done mostly to decrease the amount of memory (on disk and in RAM) required to store dates. "Why store a bunch of redundant 19s," went the thinking. Imagine a database of financial transactions, which naturally must record when a transaction occurs. In the imaginary database, each transaction required 2 bytes of storage to store the "19" part of the year. (This assumes the 8-bit integers of the old days.) For millions of transactions, storing lots of extra 19s gets very expensive, especially taking into account the value of memory twentysome years ago. The problem is that the software that operates on highly optimized databases expects the year to be in a YY byte of the database. The number 2000 won't fit in the field. Plus the date arithmetic is based on an assumed "19."

The first step toward solving this problem is identifying where in the affected systems date (year) information is set and used. One solution to the problem is to let the computer think that 2001 is 1901, but whenever output data contains year information such as 1900, 1901, ..., a quick postprocessing step would be immediately invoked to correct the obvious problem. This is clearly a cheap fix and will not work for all systems. Note that even this quick-and-dirty fix makes use of propagation analysis to determine where all the output points are. In this case, impact analysis is partially applicable.

A more thorough approach to solving the problem is to actually fix the software to understand dates of the form "20YY." This can require major changes to the database in terms of the offsets where data is stored. For example, if the data is stored as:

Figure 9.1 *Graphical representation of database fields. The "xx year" field contains only two positions.*

then the offset for where payment method will need to be shifted if we decide to store this now as:

Figure 9.2 *The same representation partially shifted to make the date field longer.*

A change in date representation requires that the offset where "amount" is stored to be shifted to accommodate the change.

It is prudent to decide how much of an impact a Year 2000 problem has on the existing software *before* modifications such as the one just shown are attempted. Fault injection is perfectly suited to such a task. We can easily force internal states to hold years greater than 1999 in them and then see how such dates propagate through the system. This is one way that fault injection can be applied to a legacy system to see what impact the Year 2000 problem has before maintenance even begins.

9.1.4 COTS and Life Expectancy

Another serious maintenance concern exists when safety-critical systems rely on executable software subsystems that were not created by the developers of the rest of the safety-critical code. We consider this maintenance problem to be one of the most grossly overlooked problems facing software development today. But because fault injection is not immediately applicable, we will only briefly touch on this issue. Later, we discuss maintenance problems that fault injection can address for executable software.

When source-code access does not exist, maintenance is virtually impossible. The problem is analogous to trying to fix a car's engine without being able to open the hood. In today's ever-changing marketplace, it is not unrealistic to fear that a vendor of off-the-shelf software may soon be out of business. Most safety-critical systems have life expectancies of 25 years or so. It is almost certainly the case that once market demand decreases for a specific off-the-shelf offering, support for the users of the offering will also falter. This presents serious problems over a system's operational lifetime. In fact, this problem is so serious that it immediately raises issues concerning whether saving money today on a fly-by-night vendor will not end up costing more in the long run. One way to protect from this problem is to require a copy of the source code before agreeing to license the executable, in the event that the vendor decides to discontinue the product. Of course, this solution simply changes the kind of problem into one requiring the ability to maintain someone else's software.

9.2 Software Reuse

Shrinking budgets and corporate downsizing require innovative approaches to reusing existing software systems. Starting from scratch is no longer an attractive option. Think of how many times a day around the world programmers are recoding binary searches! This is a monumental waste of time and effort. There exist tried-and-true software components that perform many important common functions. These components should be reused, not reimplemented.

For the U.S. government, software reuse has become an important national imperative. U.S. Defense Secretary William Perry mandated this in his infamous speech on using off-the-shelf computer products for Defense information products. Two technical conditions must be satisfied in order for software reuse to be trivial and immediate: (1) Any reused code must properly compute the expected function it was designed for, and (2) the reused code must have an acceptable reliability in each new environment. The first condition is obvious and not worth elaborating on, but the second condition is an often-overlooked problem that plagues widespread software reuse. Without the second condition, immediate reuse is really a game of Russian roulette, where a developer can never be sure whether the bullet chamber is empty or loaded.

As we have seen, maintenance is a propagation-based issue. Maintenance can also be thought of as a special case of software reuse. There are several reuse-related applications for fault injection that are closely related to the one we discussed for the Year 2000 problem.

Software reuse involves employing software functionality in an application that may not exactly mirror the original application for which the software was designed. Successful software reuse allows for systems to be developed rapidly and at lower overall cost. There are many different issues with software reuse that cause it to be more problematic than appears at first blush. For example, the fact that the environment may change can cause serious overprediction regarding how well the software will perform in its new environment. In addition, a commercially bought component that is reused may have too much functionality, which can cause serious concerns as well.

What can software fault injection do to improve the prospects for successful software reuse without greatly diminishing the cost benefits of reuse? After all, if it costs more to employ reuse than it does to build the functionality from scratch, reuse cannot be justified.

9.2.1 *Applying Fault Injection to Legacy Code Testing*

Software reuse can be more readily enabled if the results of testing the code in the original environment (E_1) still apply in the new environment (E_2). An environment for a software system includes all other systems that directly feed inputs into the software, like user inputs, information that comes in from the operating system, or input that comes in from other systems upon which the system depends. The issue is whether the code will work as well in E_2 as it did in E_1. The reusability of previous verification efforts is an important parameter is assessing the "immediate" reusability of the code. The PIE testability assessment approach can be used as a measure of the reusability of the previous testing according to E_1.

The ability to reuse testing results is a factor to consider in determining the reusability of code even if $E_1 = E_2$. Without considering this, a fair determination of how much money is being saved by reusing code will not be made. For example, suppose that a piece of code worked fine given limited usage in E_1, and suppose that it will get reused in the same environment elsewhere, but the new environment is much more critical in terms of importance. What does the limited usage according to E_1 really buy?

The methodology that we now describe has been applied to a large NASA supersonic software simulation slated for reuse and facing this exact question. The application was the High Speed Civil Transport (HSCT). The results of using PIE to predict reusability for the HSCT simulation will be condensed here.

The development costs of critical systems can be significantly reduced if existing control code can be reused. An example of where this was not the case was the Ariane 5 disaster, where code from the Ariane 4 rocket was reused, resulting in disaster. (See chapter 7 for an analysis of what fault injection could have done to foretell the likelihood of those events.) Input distribution changes can significantly impact (both positively or negatively) the reliability of a component. Thus, to reuse software cost-effectively, components must be reverified in their new environment.

A software component is termed *dependable* if the component is reliable at some level X regardless of environment. It is quite common to make reliable software components for a fixed operational distribution. But to make dependable components that can be plugged into any environment and still give reliable functionality is still an art. There are no cookbook-type rules for how to do it. Ironically, even if we do manage to do it, we still don't know how to assess that we did it.

Software testing today consumes from a minimum of 50 percent of the labor content of development to a maximum of 90 to 95 percent for life-critical software. Testing is the single biggest factor in software development costs and time to market. This creates a problem in software component reuse technology. Software builders should be able to create effective, dependable, software systems based on components selected from preexisting libraries. To increase the cost advantages of software reuse, it is necessary that the original testing be applicable for the component in its new environment. If subsequent testing is necessary before components can be reused, the cost benefits of reuse are severely discounted.

On an interesting side note, there are those who would argue that systems today are more likely to be overtested than undertested. They would argue that if we did intelligent testing in place of brute-force, unintelligent testing, resources could be applied to other development tasks or even to additional forms of validation. Because there are few techniques (like PIE) that tell how much testing is enough and tell how good that testing is, these arguments are hard to refute.

Software that has not failed during nonexhaustive software testing is considered both a boon and a curse. Software testing that does not result in failure is termed *successful*. Such software is a boon for the manufacturer since no defects are known to exist. Yet the user inherits the risk of discovering any defects that are unknown but still exist in the software. Complete success in testing makes it difficult to assess whether the inputs that are being selected have an acceptable ability to reveal existing faults. Thus successful testing is problematic from the standpoint of being able to put a number on the reliability or mean-time-to-failure of the system. If successful testing is a problem for assessing the quality for E_1, imagine what it means (if anything) for E_2!

Unlike other software systems, simulations present additional challenges for software testing, particularly because they are based on models (which are likely to be flawed themselves), and these models serve as specifications. The purpose of a simulation is to test the model under various conditions. This implies that if a simulation is incorrect, it is difficult to determine whether the model or the simulation is flawed. Also note that simulations are often tested using a human oracle, who supposedly is an expert on the model, so the possibility of a flawed oracle is very real. In short, verifying simulations is a very hard problem, and more troublesome than most other software classes. This was another problem relevant to the NASA HSCT software, because no one really knew how good the mathematical model was on which the code was based.

Fortunately, the software testability approach presented in chapter 5 can be used to assess whether the amount of testing done according to E_1 was sufficient for E_1. Recall that for a given environment, some number of test cases must be used in order to be confident that faults are not hiding from testing according to E_1. This approach cannot say whether the testability of the code will also be sufficient for E_2. To do this, testability analysis would have to be reperformed according to E_2. However, for the HSCT effort, the only question was whether the testing was adequate for E_1, because the code was being reused in an environment E_2 that should be the same as E_1, $E_1 = E_2$.

Recall that the PIE model is based on the code and the test cases (or if one exists, the test distribution Q). After testing with some number of test cases according to input selection technique Q and observing no failures (with the a priori knowledge that the testability of the software was high), we assert with confidence that faults are not hiding. However, if after testing according to input selection technique Q, we observe no failures and are told that the testability of the software is low, we gain less confidence that faults are not hiding. This suggests that we need to test more to gain greater confidence. This view of software testability provides a way of quantifying the risk associated with critical software systems that have demonstrated successful usage and are candidates for reuse based on prior behavior. PIE allows testers to determine when testing can stop with an acceptable confidence that no faults are hiding. This is important information to have if it is known that a particular component is likely to be reused in different environments.

PIE can be used to quantify whether prior and/or planned testing will be sufficient. This can be carried out both for the original testing environment, E_1, and for the new testing environment, E_2. If $E_1 = E_2$, and the testing according to E_1 was sufficient according to the testability scores produced by sensitivity analysis, then no further testing according to E_2 is necessary for an equivalent confidence in the code. If an increased confidence is desired even though $E_1 = E_2$, then additional testing will be required. (A model exploring the reverification costs of reused software components can be found in [Voas 1993].) If $E_1 \neq E_2$, it is prudent to use fault injection to assess the value of the previous testing according to E_1 when determining whether new testing should be performed in E_2. According to theory, since $E_1 \neq E_2$, testing according to E_2 should be performed, but this is an idealistic perspective that is often not practical.

By quantifying any value added by testing with testability analysis, we immediately know whether the original verification is sufficient. If it isn't, then continued verification is necessary, and immediate reuse is not justified. To demonstrate this approach, the immediate reusability of an existing aircraft simulation system, High Speed Civil Transportation (HSCT), was assessed for use in NASA's High Speed Research (HSR) program [Voas 1995]. Clearly, all software can be reused if enough effort is put into reverifying the reliability of the code in the new environment. Code is said to have "immediate reusability" if there is no need for any additional reverification and the software requirements are equivalent, that is, the needed functionality matches the specification for the existing software component.

HSCT was written in Fortran-77 and was based on the AST-105 supersonic aviation model. This model came out of the first generation of supersonic transport work performed at NASA. The AST-105 simulation was developed in 1980 and the HSCT simulation was derived from the AST-105 model in 1990. This project focused on whether the previous testing performed on HSCT was adequate to assure that the simulation will be reliable in future environments without further verification, or whether additional verification was warranted. To perform this analysis, a Fortran-77 PIE prototype tool was built and applied to all modules that NASA requested be analyzed.

According to NASA officials, the HSCT code operated satisfactorily in its original application. Unfortunately, to what extent the code was used in the original environment was not actually known. In the experiment on HSCT, two different test suites were used to represent the original test suites. Note that neither experimental test suite contained the tests used in years past when HSCT was built and originally applied. Nevertheless, the experimental test suites were thought to be representative of the ranges on parameters that were employed for original test case generation. It turned out to be impossible to unarchive the original suite of tests. Not only was the original test suite unavailable, but it was also unknown how large the original test suite was.

This can be important, because even if the original distribution might not have been a distribution with a high mean fault-revealing ability, if enough test cases were employed, then this concern could be somewhat discounted. In any case, the input distributions that were used to generate the two experimental test suites were, in terms of distribution, as close to the original tests as possible. After careful analysis and consultation with NASA, one experimental suite was selected for analysis.

PIE was applied to 94 subroutines of HSCT source code using this experimental test suite. The conclusions from the PIE analysis using this suite suggested that the HSCT program should be subjected to additional verification. The results were not attractive enough to give us confidence that if the same number of test cases had been used as were used for our analysis (and from the same distribution), that adequate testing had been performed. It is, of course, possible that the test suite we used in the experiment was less rigorous than the original test suite, but since that information was not available, we gave a conservative recommendation, which, although saying nothing about the goodness of the HSCT (in terms of correctness), did talk about the quality of the test cases that were generated and used. Indirectly, however, it did say something about the fault-hiding ability of the HSCT code. If high testability is considered a measure of code quality, this code did not pass muster under the given experiments.

9.2.2 Applying Fault Injection to COTS Systems

We now shift our focus away from the problems of determining whether original testing is effective for a software system, toward the reuse problems associated with systems for which source code is not available. Up to this point, our methods have assumed that source code is available. PIE was applicable to HSCT only because the source code existed. Our Year 2000 solution also assumes source code availability. But what if we relax that assumption and consider only executable code?

Modern information systems include distributed hardware and distributed software components, and also involve interactions with other machines and humans. The interconnectedness and amount of coupling in today's systems is staggering. The original reason for *divide-and-conquer* strategies in engineering was to reduce huge problems to a set of smaller, more understandable problems. The idea was that once the smaller problems were solved, their solutions could be combined with other small-scale solutions, eventually to provide the desired larger solution. In today's information systems, we have clearly succeeded in dividing up the problem, but it is not clear that we have succeeded in conquering these unbelievably complex systems by conquering their parts.

Software subsystems, hardware subsystems, and humans are all aspects of today's information technology. All play a part, directly or indirectly, in any information system. The number of different failure modes for just one of these components can be intractably large. When all components are considered in combination, the number of different ways that a system failure can occur becomes effectively *infinite*. For example, consider the failure modes for a human operator of a nuclear power plant when five different warnings occur simultaneously. Or consider all of the possible combinations of failure modes for the components of a complex telephone switching system that is distributed over many states, and processes millions of calls daily.

Software reliability theories often make illogical assumptions (e.g., assuming failure-independence or completely known failure modes). The weakest link in most systems is never known. Furthermore, the weakest link can vary from component to component with the slightest deviation in the environment. This makes the problem that much harder.

These problems are exacerbated by modern computational concepts such as object-oriented programming and Web-based development. New technologies like these introduce the possibility that programs may no longer be monolithic. Instead, modern programs are likely made up of thousands or millions of little parts distributed globally, executing whenever called, and acting as parts of one or more complex systems. These distributed technologies create a scaleability problem for virtually all existing software quality-assessment approaches. It is somewhat telling that it's impossible to exhaustively test a simple program which takes in two 32-bit integers and adds them, because there are 2^{64} combinations. Testing all possibilities would take more time than has occurred since the big bang.

Commercial-off-the-shelf (COTS) software offerings are a large part of this problem. It is true that they have become a cost-effective method for rapid prototyping of complex software systems. It is also true that they provide significant cost savings. But it is not clear that COTS reuse provides any measurable increase in quality. Until recently, software reuse amounted to cutting and pasting chunks of source code from file to file. Object-oriented design put an end to that bad habit, and has forced current thinking to consider building generic enough components that reuse is conceivable. After all, why reinvent the wheel—and an expensive one at that—for every new development?

The greatest impetus for using component-based technology is the potential resulting gain in productivity. Today, organizations tout modern product-cycle times of 3 to 4 months—a four-fold decrease over the usual 12 to 18 months of the past. Speeding the product cycle requires enormous success in making reusable components of fundamental objects. Such components can be reused in a large number of future software-development projects. To make this happen, a development manager must be confident that fundamental objects constructed throughout an organization (and perhaps outside an organization) are compatible and reliable for his or her application. Surprisingly, almost 50 percent of bugs are detected *after* component integration and not during component development and testing, a number cited as industry standard. The key issue here is whether a product that is developed more quickly and more cheaply but is totally untestable because it makes use of executable objects is going to remain inexpensive over time, particularly during maintenance.

Because of Secretary Perry's mandate, nowhere is the shift to COTS objects more noticeable than in the United States Department of Defense. Previous DoD procurements of computer systems always involved contracts with dozens of pages of military specifications. Today, these dozens of pages have been reduced to a few paragraphs; and the paragraphs detail performance requirements, not mil-specs [DoD 1994]. This paradigm shift toward COTS has an important impact on national security, however, because any adversary of the United States can now access the same off-the-shelf technology that the DoD can. Enemies can analyze security-critical software for vulnerabilities. That is not good.

Therefore it is paramount that we develop a fault-injection capability for systems that are heavily reused and are delivered in executable format. The executable fault-injection analysis technique that we describe next has several advantages. The main advantage is that COTS fault-injection analysis can be used to analyze executable COTS components for which source code is not available. As we have shown, this is a very broad capability, since the set of executable COTS components in the marketplace today is already large, and growing rapidly. EPA is an effective approach to failure-tolerance assessment. COTS fault-injection analysis brings the power of EPA to bear on executable code, where failures may appear to be far more random when the opportunity to debug the problem is not afforded us.

There is no formal definition for what COTS software is; COTS components are essentially any software component that is not *bespoke* (custom-made). For the past thirty years, most software systems have been one of a kind. Today that is changing, as the percentage of the costs of doing business representing software development has steadily increased. It has become imperative that as much reuse and cost-sharing as possible occur to decrease rising software costs. If a generic software system can be sold to 1000 customers, then they can all share in the cost of developing it. If the cost burden is borne by only one customer, that customer will pay dearly.

Executable COTS software components come in many forms, ranging from low-level dynamically linked libraries (DLLs) to full-blown complete applications. Because the methodology described here is general in scope, it can theoretically be applied to any component in executable format. Some idea of the breadth of this range can be garnered from the following list, showing a progression in COTS components from lower levels to higher levels:

1. **Dynamic link libraries.** These are commonly known as DLLs. There are many different kinds of DLLs. Some are used to define the Win32 system call interface, such as KERNEL32.DLL, USER32.DLL, and GDI32.DLL. Some are used as libraries by applications, such as MSVCRT.DLL (the Visual C++ runtime library) and MFC40.DLL (the Microsoft foundation classes library). In addition, a number of applications divide up their code into DLLs. For example, the Microsoft PowerPoint directory contains eleven separate DLLs.

2. **Low-level user programs.** These include standard commands like xcopy.exe and format.com.

3. **OLE components.** These are also known as ActiveX controls. These components make up a potentially distributed object protocol similar to CORBA.

4. **Executable scripts.** These run on an interpreter. These sorts of programs (which are by definition not made up of machine code) include Java, Perl, and Tcl/Tk scripts.

5. **Servers.** These run behind the scenes. For example, a Web server intended to support electronic commerce.

6. **User applications.** These include Web browsers.

Generally speaking, true COTS components are delivered without source-code access. Thus developers that employ COTS components will have access only to the interfaces to the executable files in which they reside. The common way for developers to interface with such components is through application program interfaces (APIs). For this reason, COTS components are typically considered black-box systems. This is in contrast to public domain software (or what is sometimes termed freeware), which usually includes a distribution with the source code. There are, however, restrictions that often limit how the source code can be reused. For example, certain GNU offerings cannot be used directly in military systems or other commercial tools.

When we talk about COTS components, we are usually talking about two different types of components: operating systems and application libraries. When people talk about the *COTS operating system problem,* they are more often than not talking about the fear that the OS will return garbage information to the application software via a system call. When people talk about the *COTS application problem,* they are concerned with the information returned from some other application component for which source-code access is not permitted. For example, a dynamically linked library (DLL) contains a wealth of routines that a developer may wish to call, but the source code to those routines is proprietary. What is the developer to do for the sake of robustness if a call to a library function in a DLL fails?

As industry moves toward COTS-based systems, assessing the inherited risks found in a shrinking pool of COTS components gains urgency. Because of standards and moves towards interoperability, there are fewer and fewer choices in the marketplace, instead of more and more. Who would really care if a better word processing package than Microsoft Word were released?

We have spent most of our time up to this point talking about assessing the impact of anomalies using source-code fault injection. We now look at what we can do to determine the impacts of anomalies on software systems when no source code is available.

Fault injection can help us gain confidence that a system can withstand the following three different failure-related "COTS" scenarios:

1. When the application source code is calling an OTS executable component, like an operating system call, and a failure of the called executable returns corrupt information (or no information) to the application

2. When the code under analysis is itself in executable format, and external subsystems that are responsible for feeding information into the executable component fail

3. When a system is simply a composition of multiple COTS components, that is, there is no source code for the system.

Each of these scenarios is amenable to study by fault-injection mechanisms. One approach requires a fancy "corrupt"-input generator, and the other requires a way of trapping calls to other executables, grabbing the returned information, and then perturbing it.

Scenario 1: Source Code Applications Making Operating System Calls

We begin by looking at the situation of application source code making calls to executable functions of the operation system. Our solution involves the perturbation of the return parameters from a system call or a call to another external information source. Here, we use UNIX system calls as our examples, but this approach is not limited to operating system calls. This section walks through four examples of applying fault-injection perturbations to the output of operating system calls and measuring the impact of propagation across the calling programs.

Software with embedded UNIX system calls can encounter problems, especially when the calling software uses the output returned by the system calls in subsequent computations throughout the program. The output from a system call may get corrupted for a variety of reasons, not the least of which is just a simple failure of the system software. It is not uncommon for developers today to spend an increasing amount of their time trying to write software workarounds for failures in the software that others have developed, but upon which their software depends. Bugs in UNIX system calls have been well-documented and could cause such calls to return unexpected output [Miller 1990; Miller 1995]. Corruptions can occur within the stack of the program if memory resources have been exhausted. Physical failures in the computer could be responsible for noisy returned values as well. The following are all examples of the impact that corruptions in the return values of calls to the operating system could potentially have on the calling application programs.

As a first example, the usage of the vmstat command is explored. A program may contain a vmstat system call to determine the amount of real and virtual memory currently available. Such a program may attempt to allocate a large block of memory on condition that a sufficient amount of memory is indeed available. If the output from the vmstat command is perturbed numerically, a value indicating a larger amount of available memory than currently exists could potentially be returned to this program. The result could be disastrous for the program, which would fail to successfully allocate the needed amount of memory.

A second example involves the usage of the mkdir system command, which attempts to create a directory with a given name if possible. The mkdir command is representative of a large number of UNIX commands that output only a new-line character if successful, and an appropriate error message if unsuccessful. For the mkdir command, error messages begin with the string "mkdir". A program that has not been carefully designed might test the resulting output assuming that output can be returned in only these forms. For instance, it could test whether the output from a mkdir call begins with the "mkdir" string, and determine whether the attempt to create a new directory failed or was not based on the result. A corruption of a single character in the "mkdir" string at the beginning of a resulting output error message would be misinterpreted as an indication that the mkdir command succeeded. On the other hand, a test based on the expectation that all successes will be indicated with a single newline character would encounter similar problems for the same class of perturbation. A single-character perturbation causing a newline character to be at the beginning of a mkdir error message would result in the incorrect determination that the mkdir command succeeded, when in fact it had failed.

A program that uses the printenv system command to determine an environment variable value would be susceptible to corruptions to the returned output. The result from a printenv command might be the path name for a directory in which to locate certain configuration files for that program. If the printenv output is perturbed such that extraneous characters appear at the end of the returned string, the returned directory path name would be invalid.

Another case involves the usage of the find system command. Imagine a program that uses the find command to determine the full path name of a file it wishes to delete. If the file is located, and its full path name has been corrupted to the name of another file that exists, the wrong file would be deleted by the program. For example, a file called critical_program.OLD is to be located using find and then deleted. Suppose that it is located in the file system, having the path name /home/apps/critical_program.OLD. If the output from the find becomes corrupted in such a way that it is truncated to the path name /home/apps/critical_program, the program will attempt to delete the file named critical_program in the same directory. In the event that critical_program exists, the program will inadvertently delete it.

One last example is the case where the date system command is used in a program. The program might use the date command to determine whether its associated license has expired. A combination of numerical, character perturbations or even arbitrary bit flipping in the representation of the output in memory could result in an invalid assessment of the license status. "Jun 1 1996" could be corrupted to "Jan 1 1996", or "Jun 1 1996" could become "Jun 1 1997", or a nonsensical date could be returned, so the program is unable to determine the license status.

A UNIX/COTS fault-injection tool has been built by Reliable Software Technologies (Sterling, Virginia) allowing the user to define functions that perturb data values during execution of the program. The tool can be applied to software on the AIX platform; it perturbs the results of those calls in order to determine the impact that a failure of AIX will have on the software. To do this, the source code can be instrumented such that the data states associated with the returned output from the system calls are perturbed. The tool supports hardware-fault perturbations, standard random numerical perturbations for both discrete (integer) and real (floating-point) values, and assorted character-string perturbations. Currently, this tool is being used on commercial air traffic systems.

Scenario 2: Testing an Executable Component in Isolation

The solution for the problem where all that exists are executable components involves looking at incoming component interfaces and applying fault-injection instrumentation directly to the interface's data. It is at the interfaces that corrupt data coming into a component will be simulated. From a theoretical standpoint, there is no difference between perturbing a state that already contains input information and perturbing the information in the same manner before it gets read into the software's state.

The fault-injection methodology that we will use for executable components has two key components which are very similar to the key steps of the EPA algorithm: a "corrupted" input generator and a postcondition checker (that acts like $PRED_C$ did in the EPA technique). The input generator is a tool for generating inputs according to expected user profiles—something also needed for traditional testing. In order to test outside the normal user profile, however, the input generator must be capable of creating corrupted inputs that mimic all sorts of unusual events, even including malicious attack scenarios. By including malicious input generation capabilities, we will enhance the usual and expected user input stream. (Recall that the same strategy was applied in chapter 8 where we showed how AVA could be used for security assessment.)

The postcondition checker monitors the system for unacceptable events. Such events satisfy predicate-based definitions specifying those events that are unacceptable output behavior. The postcondition checker tool considers the software application's functional correctness as well as the output of the software and its effects on the system environment to determine if systemwide anomalies occur. The postcondition checker takes a global perspective for determining which output events from the component are undesirable. (The user of the tool must define these events.) All observation is automatically and dynamically performed by a tool, and the results are presented to the user. Without a doubt, the most critical part of this methodology is the postcondition checker. If that is incorrectly set up, then the entire value of the analysis is nil.

Three fundamental components embody the stand-alone executable component fault-injection methodology: (1) the Input Generation and Perturbation module, (2) the Postcondition Checker, and (3) the Execution Manager. Given the four basic types of fault injection defined earlier, this falls somewhere between a message-based and a memory/storage-based approach because, in this case, information coming into a component is corrupted.

The input generation and data perturbation component can be developed as a stand-alone tool supporting generation of expected and unexpected input streams through an extensible language of predefined functions. The postcondition checker can also be a stand-alone tool that can comprehend undesirable output events for a software component in relation to its system environment. As in the input generation and perturbation tool, a specification language consisting of a number of predefined functions, extensions, and operators should be provided in the postcondition checker. The execution manager links the input generation and perturbation module with the postcondition checker to provide fully automated collection and analysis of vulnerability information. The execution manager can be configured to perform any desired amount of testing. Thus it can be set to run as many tests as are required to achieve particular levels of assurance. The execution manager also provides a crude offensive information warfare capability by determining which input stream causes which particular undesirable events.

Executable Component Fault-Injection Tool

A schematic diagram showing the architecture for an executable component fault-injection analysis tool (based on this three-part architecture) is provided in Figure 9.3. This tool is currently under construction. The input generator creates inputs from a definition of the expected user input distribution. The perturbation capability employs data perturbation functions to enhance the input stream. This simulates corrupt incoming data to the component. The output from the input generation and perturbation capability generates all of the data that will be thrown at the executable component. The individual executable receiving analysis is then fed the resulting input stream. The behavior of the executable is monitored by the postcondition checker which contains information about the systemwide specification as it relates to the executable. For example, if the executable is not allowed to make certain actions against the system, then those behaviors need to be defined in the postcondition checker. The postcondition checker monitors both the well-defined outputs of the executable as well as the system state to determine if system irregularities have occurred. The automation and collection of the analysis and the synthesis of corrupted inputs are performed by the execution manager. We describe each of the modules needed for performing this analysis in more detail in the next three sections.

Component 1: Input Generation and Perturbation   The input generation and data perturbation module is used to generate both expected user input distributions and corrupted inputs. In EPA, inputs are generated by instrumenting software source code with calls to mathematical functions that perform pseudo-random number generation. The software code—that is, the instrumented version of the original code—provides the software needed to assign random values to programmer variables. This approach is possible in theory for executables, but it would be extremely difficult. Therefore, we do not consider it a viable option. In order to analyze how robust executables are to externally supplied anomalous events, a stand-alone module is used that employs a simple input definition language. The language allows users to combine predefined input functions, by way of operators, into sophisticated input specifications. The language is also powerful enough so that once coded in terms of the input language building blocks, most operational profiles can be automatically generated. This capability is crucial for determining how robust a given piece of software is, and how easily the software can be forced to exhibit undesirable behaviors.

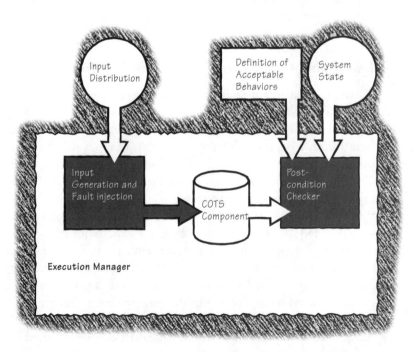

Figure 9.3 *Basic fault-injection tool for an executable component.*

The generation of an input stream can be conceived as sampling from different input spaces. Most software application testing samples input from the expected user input distribution, or *operational profile*. In cases where the operational profile is unknown, the input generation functions provided will support sampling from a wide range of potential user profiles. Generally, the most glaring and perhaps most dangerous intolerances by the executable will be detected by generating unexpected input distributions and forcing them into the executable.

A fundamental difference between standard testing of an executable and applying fault-injection analysis to the inputs of an executable is the ability to test explicitly for robustness. Standard testing, which occurs in good software development labs, generally tests for functional correctness. Robustness is another story. Software can be correct yet still be unsafe. The Postcondition Checker (described in the next section) provides the ability to determine if a system hazard policy violation has occurred as the result of input sampled from the expected user distribution.

A critical additional capability of the input generation and perturbation component is the ability to enhance the expected input stream with data sampled from malicious input space. (This becomes very important when we talk about using fault injection for security-critical applications as in chapter 8.) The *malicious input space* is the space of incoming information into a component that forces the component to perform some operation that violates the security policy concerning what the component is allowed to do. One way to do this is to throw large quantities of random input strings at the component, much as would be done by a large set of very dumb hackers.

Analyses that use perturbed inputs can be thought of as a variant of stress testing. *Stress testing* typically refers to measuring the performance and availability of operating system and other multiuser capabilities in times of heavy workload requests, where the heavy workloads in this case represent classes of the more unexpected inputs. Many vulnerabilities result from design errors where a developer does not properly account for unexpected inputs. These errors are amenable to discovery by fault injection, although there is some degree of dumb luck that is needed to succeed.

The malicious input space consists of the inputs that may be used to try to subvert an executable component. This space will vary from application to application; however, certain characteristics will prevail. For example, the list of system commands that can be executed on the operating system platform may form a subset of the malicious input space. Another example is a list of nonalphanumeric control or "meta" characters that can potentially result in the execution of shell commands. The input stream of a component is enhanced with malicious input using perturbation functions. These functions must include the ability to truncate input streams, to overflow input buffers, to append garbage input and malicious commands, to perturb numerical constants, and to garble strings.

The input generation and perturbation module is capable of generating random data that includes nonalphanumeric control characters as well as strings of arbitrary length. This utility also supports the ability to sample inputs randomly from an input file. Such a file might include, for example, a set of potentially dangerous inputs. Finally, the input definition language supports the creation of carefully crafted combinations of input functions to create any desired malicious inputs that may potentially exploit vulnerabilities in software. The module must be capable of generating inputs independently of the software application under analysis. However, any generated input must abide by constraints defined by the input types accepted by the program being analyzed.

The input generation and perturbation module is designed to accept user specification from a graphical interface. The user defines which input functions to use in order to generate the input stream. The functions include the ability to generate expected user profiles as well as to perturb the stream with malicious input. The user also needs to specify the output format for the generated stream.

Component 2: The Postcondition Checker   The Postcondition Checker is responsible for detecting undesirable output events that may propagate across the executable under analysis. It must also be capable of gauging other environmental changes the software may produce as side effects. Interestingly enough, if this component is designed properly, it can also serve as a system-monitoring tool.

The Postcondition Checker should be flexible and capable of detecting complex events. In order to make the Postcondition Checker extensible, it is configurable in two different ways. First, a number of predefined postcondition functions are supplied that allow the analyst to select which anomalies to check during analysis. These functions are grouped according to application area. For example, one set of functions will enable checking of system file input/output (I/O) functions to the local disk drive. Another set may check for unauthorized port access. Determination of process and file ownership are also supported in the postcondition checker, to track whether new shells or processes running at a higher privilege level may have been started.

Implementation of the Postcondition Checker can require some access to operating system–level functionality. Tracking global environmental events requires the ability to keep tabs on the entire system. For example, it is useful to monitor DeviceIoControl function calls. Not only will such calls need to be tracked, but isolating exactly who (or what) is doing the calling is also required.

Component 3: The Execution Manager   The Execution Manager serves to tie the functionality of the two previously described stand-alone components together, forming a COTS fault-injection analysis utility. The Execution Manager is responsible for automating the analysis of a COTS software application. Once the input generation and policy assertions have been coded in their respective components, the Execution Manager exploits the power of automation and high processor speeds to perform the high volume of testing necessary to rigorously test executable systems. As a result, high-confidence statistical analysis is made possible by extensive use of the tool over time.

The Execution Manager controls the Input Generation and Perturbation components to drive the execution of the software application under analysis. The Execution Manager also collects results from the Postcondition Checker in order to determine how often and in what conditions a violation occurs during experimentation. This information is displayed dynamically during the analysis as output anomalies are detected. A running percentage of testing completed can be displayed.

FUZZ   Together, the three components of the COTS fault-injection analysis prototype make a powerful tool for analysis of COTS software and other executables. The executable component fault-injection analysis tool just described is similar to the FUZZ model of Miller, et al. [Miller 1990; Miller 1995]. The FUZZ model has proven to be a powerful testing tool for software reliability even though its criteria are coded at the grossest of levels. FUZZ works by generating completely random input, feeding that to a UNIX system function, and watching for core dumps. Though certainly crude, FUZZ has proven effective.

FUZZ provides a low-resolution approximation of the robustness of particular UNIX utilities (e.g., ls). Watching for a program to dump core (that is, watching for a program to crash) is a very crude way of determining whether something bad has happened. FUZZ is capable of tracking events only at that unsophisticated level. FUZZ causes core dumps by feeding completely random noise to an application. Once again, crude but effective. The Input Generation and Perturbation module provides a more effective way of testing application robustness. Finally, FUZZ was designed solely to test reliability. Executable fault-injection analysis, if designed properly, can provide an added benefit for assessing the security risks associated with an executable.

Scenario 3: Systems of Executable Components

Consider a system composed of multiple executables as shown in Figure 9.4, which shows a system composed of six executable components, A, B, C, D, E, and F.

The approach that we take in this case is very similar to the approach that we took in scenario 2. We will once again send corrupted information into executable components, again simulating the situation of where a different executable component has failed and has output corrupt information. But unlike the technique used for scenario 2, in this case the Postcondition Checking utility can reside anywhere in the system between components and can also exist at the exit point of the system. Therefore, instead of corrupting only the input coming into

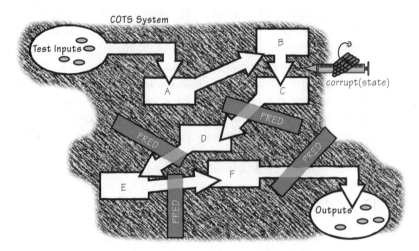

Figure 9.4 *Interface Propagation Analysis for COTS-based system.*

a component and looking at the output of the component, this approach corrupts the outgoing information produced by a component. By placing postconditions at any interface between other components that are executed downstream from the point of corruption, the effect of the corruptions can be observed. The degree of difficulty in writing a post-condition is directly tied to how precise the system-level specification is.

The current analysis is geared toward injecting anomalies into the interfaces between components and determining if predicates are violated at a later point in the system. As we mentioned early on, it is possible that a violated predicate might have been caused without any injected anomaly. Because we do not run another copy of the system without the anomaly to see if it also violates the predicate, we cannot know whether the corruption is the precise reason. The expense involved to run two versions of the system makes it better to ignore this possibility.

Legacy software or massively large-scale software systems require concentrating on analyzing aspects of behavior at large, not small, scales. The solution for assessing the tolerance of large-scale systems (that will almost certainly be built from distributed objects) is to assess the robustness of the interfaces between the objects in order to predict how the software will behave if malicious or nonmalicious anomalies arise. This is an alternative to trying to apply fault injection to the code itself. We have already described a fault injection–based approach for assessing the weaknesses of executable components in isolation. Here, we are talking about using fault-injection techniques to assess the weaknesses of systems in the large. This can be done by injecting corruptions into the interfaces between components, in order to simulate the failure of components.

Today's complex systems are made up of two kinds of entity: (1) components and (2) interfaces. In her book *Safeware* [Leveson 1995], Leveson acknowledges the necessary role of interfaces in composing complex systems:

> *One way to deal with complexity is to break the complex object into pieces or modules. For very large programs, separating the program into modules can reduce individual component complexity. However, the large number of interfaces created introduce uncontrollable complexity into the design: The more small components there are, the more complex the interface becomes. Errors occur because the human mind is unable to comprehend the many conditions that can arise through interactions of these components. An interface between two programs is comprised of all the assumptions that the programs make about each other. . . . When changes are made, the entire structure collapses. (p. 36)*

Later in the same work, Leveson succinctly describes the importance of thwarting the propagation of failures through the many interfaces that complex systems employ:

> *A tightly coupled system is highly interdependent: Each part is linked to many other parts, so that a failure or unplanned behavior in one can rapidly affect the status of others. A malfunctioning part in a tightly coupled system cannot be easily isolated, either because there is insufficient time to close it off or because its failures affect too many other parts, even if the failure does not happen quickly. . . . Accidents in tightly coupled systems are a result of unplanned interactions. These interactions can cause domino effects that eventually lead to a hazardous system state. Coupling exacerbates these problems because of the increased number of interfaces and potential interactions: Small failures can propagate unexpectedly. (p. 410)*

Our recognition that the quality of today's systems is highly dependent on the quality of their component interfaces suggests it will be useful to have a fault-injection methodology that zeros in on software interfaces. Assessing the failure tolerance of the interfaces with respect to component failures and problems that may enter the system from external sources is beneficial.

Interfaces are the mechanisms by which information is passed between components during system execution, with the *final interface* being the mechanism through which any output passes to the user. Fault injection can be designed to observe the way that interfaces behave when we intentionally corrupt data passing through them. The robustness of an interface under simulated stress provides valuable information about the likelihood that the interface will produce acceptable results when the stress is real (i.e., in real everyday use after release). System robustness is inferred from the likelihood that malicious or nonmalicious anomalies from software components or external sources will result in a loss of mission.

As we have already seen, software *propagation metrics* measure the dynamic properties of information corruption through the software code. Applying the same principles to interfaces between software components is equally beneficial and, for large-scale systems or legacy systems, presents the only viable approach. The fact is that until we are capable of demonstrating interface failure tolerance, the goal of composing high-assurance systems from COTS components will remain unsatisfied.

In the system-level interface analysis that we are about to describe, the exact manner by which the states on either "end" of a propagation chain are corrupted is not necessarily important. We say that if component *A* sends information into component *B,* then *A* is the *predecessor* of *B* and *B* is the *successor* of *A.* For a component, its *entrance interface* is the interface that reads information into the component, and its *exit interface* is the interface that passes information out from the component.

9.2.3 Software Component Composition

Software components can be combined in *series* and *parallel* just as mechanical systems are. The most common way to combine components, whether physical or software, is to connect them one after another in a series. When physical components are connected in a series, the quality of the whole is necessarily less than that of the worst component (e.g., a chain is only as strong as its weakest link). However, in the case of software, this may not be true—sometimes the interactions between two or more faulty components may actually make the system more reliable, since faults may have the effect of canceling each other out. This is one of many reasons why hardware reliability models do not apply to software.

Another way of composing systems from components involves connecting components in parallel. Parallel component construction of physical systems is employed as a mechanism for increasing overall quality through redundancy (e.g., two chains are better than one). As in the serial case, when the parallel paradigm is applied to software, the expected increase in quality through re-dundancy may not occur—the two parallel components may each break in the same way. In the end, it is apparent that quality-based arguments for designing from components in engineering physical systems cannot be straightforwardly co-opted for use in software systems. Instead, another approach is required. (N-version programming, covered in chapter 6, suggests one method for parallel construction.)

The key benefit of this technique is that it will analyze the failure tolerance of legacy systems that may be composed of COTS software components. This technique also provides a prediction of future failure tolerance in case additional COTS components are added to legacy systems. This prediction can be provided without requiring formal semantics for the components or for the system as a whole. Because of this, interface propagation analysis can be applied to existing systems that often do not have formal specifications—specifications that often require extensive analysis and/or reengineering to develop.

9.2.4 *Interface Propagation Analysis*

System integrators are often surprised when a system behaves incorrectly even though previous unit testing had indicated that the components were all reliable on their own. This disappointing problem is a direct result of the fact that the testing environment is often different from the ultimate integration and user environment. Many times, developers have expectations for software that are unrealistically high. That is, they expect software to work correctly in all environments if they show it works correctly in one. A similar expectation would never be applied in the case of hardware. For example, would we ever expect a computer motherboard to work correctly while immersed in a liquid sodium bath just because it worked correctly in normal atmospheric conditions? Apparently our expectations for software are in need of radical adjustment. We need to more carefully consider the environment in which a software component runs. The environment of a software component encompasses the distribution of inputs that the interface delivers. In addition, a hypothetical test distribution may be dramatically different from the actual use distribution.

The technique described in this section is termed *Interface Propagation Analysis* (IPA) [Voas 1996]. It is applicable to complete computer systems and is applied between the interfaces between the hardware and software as well as interfaces between the operating system, microkernel, middleware, and so on. This approach observes how corruption propagates through component-based systems. The fault-injection mechanism used here is based on the fact that all corrupt information must originate in either: (1) a component, (2) an interface between components, or (3) an interface between a component and the external environment.

In IPA, "propagation across" a component will apply perturbation function(s) to interfaces feeding into components and then analyze component exit interfaces of successor components and determine whether the corruption propagated. It is possible to determine this information for any particular component without knowledge about other system components. Our basic algorithm for finding the proportion of times that a corruption crosses a component C as well as successors of C is as follows:

1. Set temporary variable **count** to 0.

2. Randomly select an incoming parameter set to apply to C from the distribution of data values that are likely to enter it. Global parameters make up part of this data tuple.

3. Perturb the sampled value of some variable **a** in this data tuple if the value of **a** has already been defined, else set **a** to a random value. Execute the component on both the perturbed data set and the original data set. (This can be done either synchronously in parallel or in serial order.)

4. For each set of two outcomes in the output of the component and its successors resulting from executions using the perturbed input set and executions using the original input set, determine if the outcomes are different. If so, increment **count.** Note that count may also be incremented if an infinite loop occurs and the component does not terminate in either of the two cases. (We suggest simply setting a time limit for termination. If execution is not finished within the given time interval, we can safely assume that an infinite loop has occurred.)

5. Repeat algorithm steps 2–4 n times.

6. Divide **count** by $n - 1$ yielding the proportion of times that propagation crosses C when C receives corrupt data.

This algorithm provides a frequency with which the hypothesized interface corruptions cross C and C's successor to a later interface in the system. The quantity derived by this algorithm is a function of three things: component C and its successors; the manner by which the corruption occurs; and the distribution of incoming data tuples that can enter the component. The final quantitative measure will also be dependent on the environment that surrounds C.

To explain the benefit of this approach to the large-scale and legacy system problem, consider the system in the following system S made of two components, A and B composed in a series.

```
Program
        B(A);
    End.
```

Suppose however that a new executable component, D, is needed in S between components A and B, as shown here:

```
Program
      B(D(A));
End.
```

The designer of *S* will certainly want to know whether *D* will seamlessly integrate into *S*. To discover if this is the case, fault injection will help answer the following questions:

> **Question 1.**   If *D* is faulty, will its incorrectness propagate and affect the functionality of *S*?
>
> **Question 2.**   If *D* is correct, but the interface between *D* and *A* is faulty, will that propagate and affect the functionality of *S*?
>
> **Question 3.**   If *D* is correct, but the interface between *D* and *B* is faulty, will that propagate and affect the functionality of *S*?
>
> **Question 4.**   Might *D* exacerbate any existing problems in *A* or *B* that have thus far escaped notice since they did not noticeably degrade *S*'s functionality?

To answer Question 1, IPA can inject simulated anomalies into the outgoing parameters coming from *D*, by instrumenting the main code as follows:

```
Program
      B(fault-inject(D(A)))
End.
```

To answer Questions 2 and 3, IPA can simulate incorrect interfaces between *D* and *A* as well as between *D* and *B* (including such problems such as incorrect parameter orderings and incorrect parameters) by instrumenting the main code as follows:

```
Program
      B(D(fault-inject(A)))
End.
```

and

```
Program
      B(fault-inject(D(A)));
End.
```

Note that the fault-injection functions which answer Question 1 and Question 3 differ in which parameters are tweaked. To answer Question 4, IPA can attempt various combinations of events, using code such as:

```
Program
        B(fault-inject(D(fault-inject(A))));
End.
```

Once answers to all four questions have been established, insight is gained into how likely modified *S* will continue to perform satisfactorily after the addition of *D*.

In summary, IPA offers a scaleable approach to assessing the robustness of large-scale systems based on COTS components. This methodology offers several advantages.

Advantage 1   Once the decision has been made to integrate a new component into an existing system, it is prudent to try to determine what the possible effects of integration will be. The methodology uses a modified type of fault injection to answer some fundamental questions about the integration of new components into both legacy systems and new systems. By abstracting the composition problem to interfaces, we can account for a variety of subcomponent failures, whether they originate in software or hardware.

Advantage 2   This approach takes a *black-box* view of software components. This is vital if we are to develop a plausible component-based software engineering theory without falling back on source-code analysis. Today's information systems are made up of many different layers, from the innermost kernel to the outermost application layer. This methodology predicts interface robustness between application layers.

Advantage 3   Today's systems are increasingly object-based, with message-passing handling object communication. IPA is clearly applicable to this new programming paradigm.

In summary, predictions of component-to-component interface propagation provide a portion of the information necessary to predict failure tolerance and survivability of large-scale information systems.

9.2.5 *Why Not Fault Inject Straight into Executables?*

The IPA approach outlined earlier in no way alters the executable itself. It simply alters incoming information. Since EPA and PIE are code-based fault-injection techniques, it is natural to wonder whether fault injection should take place at the object-code level or maybe at the assembly-code level. To date, there are no known research prototypes that perform fault injection by taking machine code and mangling it. If there were, it would probably be easiest to accomplish this by code mutation as opposed to state perturbation.

One interesting question here is what performing such an analysis might really mean. Clearly, perturbing at low levels does not simulate programmer faults, because programmer faults happen at the source level, not machine or assembly levels. Also, perturbing at low levels does not simulate corrupted incoming data any better than the approach that we have outlined, which does not involve injecting faults into lower levels of code, and in fact might not work as well as the scheme outlined.

What performing a low-level analysis would provide is information concerning how the software behaves if the translation process from source to assembly or from source to machine is faulty. That is, if the compiler fails and produces erroneous machine or assembly code, then essentially what we are doing is similar to a PIE testability analysis, but at the lower code levels. Since the compiler is responsible for producing those lower code levels, it is as if we are simulating errors that it introduces. We could then test the original executable and the modified executable to see how likely it is that the test cases make the low-level mutants observable.

9.3 Summary

This chapter has focused on two primary concerns of most developers today: (1) how to reduce maintenance costs, which some estimates say cost more than 50 percent of the total costs of the software during its lifetime, and (2) how to benefit as greatly from software reuse, whether that is done by cutting and pasting source-code objects or through employing off-the-shelf components.

The key maintenance problem that fault injection addresses is impact analysis. Fault injection can be used to simulate the failure of some region of the code, and then information can be collected elsewhere concerning the impact of that simulated failure. This information immediately suggests which parts of the code are and are not amenable to future maintenance activities. There are the parts of the code where any changes, no matter how minor, are likely to cause problems. Interestingly, however, these are the regions that should require less testing after changes are made, because these regions wear their faults on their sleeves. It is the regions of the code that are more adaptable that are more likely to hide faults. From a testing standpoint this is undesirable, but from a software quality standpoint it is desirable. Latent faults improve reliability, but they are a nightmare to debug when they decide no longer to be latent.

Software reuse is a concept as fundamental as programming itself. We reuse a fixed set of language-provided operations all the time. Software reuse is simply an attempt to take that to a higher level, and reuse developer-defined operations that may include large numbers of language-defined operations. After all, if we can reuse a "+" operation as often as we want, why can't we reuse a binary search?

The largest reuse problems today come to us from reusable functions that are provided only in executable format. Because of this, white-box software quality assurance techniques are not applicable. This opens a serious technology void for those that must know that the executable component that they plan to use is of acceptable quality for their application. It is one thing to suffer from your mistakes; it is something else to have to suffer from someone else's.

Fault injection provides a nice way to observe how tolerant your application is to problems that might be foisted on it by all external factors. It can simulate the failure of OTS software at many different levels. Fault injection can test an OTS component in isolation only by sending anomalies into the component and checking its output. Fault injection can test a component with respect to the rest of the system by simulating the failure of an OTS component, and test for the impact elsewhere in the system. This second capability can be applied for OTS components such as operating system calls, as well as other OTS components that are linked in.

References

[Dahl 1972] O. J. Dahl, E. W. Dijsktra, and C. A. R. Hoare. *Structured Programming.* Academic Press, 1972.

[DoD 1994] Defense Science Board. "Acquiring Defense Software Commercially." June 1994.

[Leveson 1995] N. G. Leveson. *Safeware: System Safety and Computers.* Addison-Wesley, Reading, Mass., 1995.

[Miller 1990] B. P. Miller, L. Fredrikson, and B. So. "An empirical study of the reliability of UNIX utilities." *CACM,* 33(12):32–44. December 1990.

[Miller 1995] B. P. Miller, D. Koski, C. P. Lee, V. Maganty, and R. Murthy. "FUZZ revisited: a re-examination of the reliability of UNIX utilities and services." Computer Sciences Department, University of Wisconsin, November 1995.

[Parnas 1974] D. L. Parnas. "On a 'Buzzword': Hierarchical Structure." *Proc. of the IFIP Congress '74.* North-Holland Publishing Company, pp. 336–339.

[Voas 1993] J. Voas and K. Miller. "A model for improving the testing of reusable software components." In *Proc. of the 10th Pacific Northwest Software Quality Conference,* pp. 353–360, October 1992.

[Voas 1995] J. Voas, J. Payne, R. Mills, and J. McManus. "Software testability: an experiment in measuring simulation reusability." In *Proc. of the ACM SIG-SOFT Symp. On Software Reusability,* pp. 247–255, April 1995.

[Voas 1996] J. Voas, F. Charron, and K. Miller. "Robust software interfaces: can COTS-based systems be trusted without them?" In *Proc. of the 15th Int'l. Conf. On Computer Safety, Reliability, and Security,* Springer-Verlag, October 1996.

[Weiser 1982] M. Weiser. "Programmers use slices when debugging." *CACM,* 25(7):446–452, July 1982.

10 *Advanced Fault Injection*
Icing on the Fault-Injection Cake

This chapter is devoted to a variety of miscellaneous topics related to both implementing and applying software fault injection. We covered much information concerning how software fault injection is performed in chapters 3 through 9. In this chapter, we focus on a set of additional processes that can be employed to improve the value you can get from the algorithms already provided.

We begin by looking at the role that "inverted" or otherwise modified operational profiles can play to enhance analysis. Recall that Q was a central parameter in both the EPA and PIE algorithms. Q represents the probability density function over the domain of the software. In other words, Q is the test distribution and, in the best of all possible worlds, is the actual operational profile for the software. We instrument the software in order to observe events. What we observe is highly dependent on what Q is. Interestingly, we can modify Q in a variety of ways so that different information is captured. This turns out to be particularly beneficial for analyzing and improving safety-critical software systems where the most worrisome inputs are also the rarest inputs.

After we discuss different approaches for modifying Q, we focus on the role that traditional software assertions can play in conjunction with the PIE analysis technique. Assertions modify the meaning of *observability* for our propagation analysis algorithm, and when the definition is modified, so are the results from the analysis. By using assertions to make the definition more liberal, in some situations, we can get an enormous increase in the fault-detecting ability of test cases.

To close the chapter, we discuss a specialized type of software assertion that learns during fault-injection analysis. This kind of assertion helps in trying to recover from corrupted internal states during execution. Such assertions are very specialized and are sometimes hard to create, but they can be powerful software-recovery mechanisms since they are derived from the results of EPA. These assertions are called *cleansing assertions,* and have the potential to truly increase the failure tolerance of many different types of systems.

10.1 Profiles and Environments: The Keys to Good Behavior

Brushing your teeth in your bathroom would be considered as acceptable behavior, but brushing them in a grocery store would not. Although the act of brushing your teeth is the same, the context of where it is done impacts whether the behavior is considered acceptable. The same is true for software. Depending on the environment that the software is in, one behavior may have different implications for the system; here we will look at how the profile and environment for software affect the software.

10.1.1 Operational Profiles

Most dynamic assessment approaches to software quality are operational profile–dependent. Because of this, any modification to the profile almost certainly results in a change in the perceived quality. It is possible for two totally different profiles to result in exactly the same observed quality of the software, but knowing that this is true in advance of extensive testing is generally impossible.

Profile dependence is possibly the most difficult problem in software reuse (one of the stars of chapter 9). There are two distinct things that must be teased out of the general problem of profile dependence: (1) changes in the input domain (Δ), and (2) changes in the distribution of the inputs, but not the input domain. When Δ changes, then all bets are off in terms of the quality of the system, because the environment has experienced enormous modifications. An example of this would be if the original domain were integers greater than zero, but then was changed to include only negative integers.

The case where only the distribution over Δ changes (i.e., Δ remains fixed) is generally regarded as a less drastic change than the one where Δ itself changes. In our example, this might represent the situation where positive integers are still the inputs to the software, but the distribution by which the integers are picked has changed. If the original distribution, Q, were uniform, the new distribution might be exponential. From a quality perspective, observed quality can change as much if not more from a distributional change like this as it can from a domain change. Regardless of which kind of change occurs to the environment, even including a combination of the two changes, any assessment of quality will almost certainly have to be redone.

This problem can be partially alleviated if Δ is partitioned in such a way that the quality of individual partitions is known. So if $\Delta = \{\Delta_1 \cup \Delta_2 \cup \Delta_3\}$, the reliability of Δ_1 is R_1, the probability of selecting a test case from Δ_1 is P_1, and similar relations hold for the other partitions, then the reliability of the software R_Δ for Δ is:

$$R_\Delta = \sum_{i=1}^{Y} \Delta_i P_i$$

when Δ is partitioned in Y partitions. Given this formula, it is easy to recalculate R_Δ whenever the P_is change. Hence, even though the environment might have changed, an assessment of the quality of the software in the new environment can be made without retesting the code.

10.1.2 *Inverted Operational Profiles*

Assessing the failure tolerance of a program by using the rare region of an input space (Δ from earlier discussion) can be beneficial. The *rare* region is the partition of the input space that contains inputs that are highly unlikely to be selected for execution under typical testing and operation. (At this time, we will not concern ourselves with what probability thresholds constitute the class of "highly unlikely." Simply consider our squishy prose as a conceptual notion that can be tuned by the user.) For our purposes, the rare region is not necessarily a small subset of the input space. It is entirely possible by this definition that the rarest portion of the input space actually makes up a larger subset than the subset represented by more frequently chosen inputs.

When we observe a program executing on inputs that were selected from the rare region of the input space, knowledge is gained concerning how *robust* the software will be during unusual operational events. Observing a lack of robustness during EPA or AVA analysis suggests that the software may not perform acceptably if unusual events occur during operation. Likewise, if we repeatedly observe robust behavior, this suggests that the software is sufficiently hardened against anomalous events. This suggestion is no strict guarantee of future failure-tolerant behavior; it is merely an indicator of that desirable property.

Converting EPA into a rare-event failure-tolerance technique still requires using the EPA algorithm provided in chapter 6 [Voas 1994]. The difference is that we will no longer use the operational profile Q. For the adapted version, we will instead use Q^{-1}—the inverse of Q. *Inverse operational distributions* can be derived directly from operational distributions. They cannot often be true mathematical inverses; however, they capture the same intuitive property. In our inverse distribution, elements that occur frequently in the original operational distribution Q occur infrequently in the inverse operational distribution Q^{-1}. Recall that an *input distribution* for a piece of software is the probability density function that assigns to each possible test case i a probability. This is the probability that i will be selected on a random execution of the software in a certain environment. If a particular $Q(i)$ equals 0, then i is not a member of the input space as we previously defined it. The "inverted" input distribution, call it Q^{-1}, assigns a large probability to elements that had a small probability in Q, and assigns a small probability to elements that had a large probability in Q. To use profile inversion, a description of Q is necessary. The more accurate this description is, the more accurate Q^{-1} will be. Note that if a description of Q is unavailable, then our inversion approach cannot be employed.

There is an interesting relationship between software testing's ability to produce failures (when faults exist), Q, Q^{-1}, and failure tolerance, as shown in Table 10.1. Note that when failure tolerance is high, software testing has little ability to produce failures, even when faults exist. Also note that inputs which might have great fault-revealing ability are of little help during testing if they have little or no chance of being selected. So during testing the only hope of detecting problems is to have software that has reduced failure tolerance with respect to the high probability inputs, because those are traditionally the ones selected.

The intuition for what occurs when Q is inverted was first described in a paper on distribution inversion for failure tolerance by Voas and Miller [Voas 1995]. Here is the algorithm described there.

Algorithm

1. Let N be the number of different legal inputs. Let $M = 1/N$, the mean of the probability density distribution over N possible inputs.
2. For each element i, let $g'(i) = 2*M - Q(i)$.
3. Find the minimum $g'(i)$, m. If $m \geq 0$, $g'(i)$ is Q^{-1}. Otherwise, proceed to step 4.
4. When $m < 0$, let $(g''(i) = g'(i) + \textbf{abs}(m))/(1 + N*(\textbf{abs}(m)))$. Then g'' is Q^{-1}.

This algorithm is not ideal for profile inversion, because lower and upper bounds are not specified. This causes the algorithm to result in poor approximations to the original profile Q. Better algorithms that do account for lower and upper bounds have been subsequently published elsewhere. See, for example, [Voas 1996].

Table 10.1 The Likelihood of Software Failure Occurring Given Low and High Probability Inputs and Different Levels of Failure Tolerance

	HIGH FAILURE TOLERANCE	LOW FAILURE TOLERANCE
High Probability Inputs	little	great
Low Probability Inputs	little	little

10.1.3 *Modified Operational Profiles*

For a fixed input domain, Δ, there is a continuous set of different distributions over Δ between the extremes of Q and Q^{-1}, assuming that we are not dealing with an original distribution such as the uniform distribution, which has an inverse that is a reflection of the original. How each member of this continuum alters the quality of the software's behavior cannot be immediately assessed unless testing of the software is performed with respect to test cases sampled from each distribution.

For example, consider the following original and inverted distributions, as well as several intermediate distributions, each of which is a modification of its predecessor. (See Figures 10.1 to 10.5.) In each of these transformations, there is a fixed function F that adds the noise and produces a modified distribution.

The results of fault injection are profile-dependent. Even the slightest change in a distribution can change the actual reliability of the code as well as the estimated reliability. Changes in the distribution can alter software metrics that are derived from the results of fault injection.

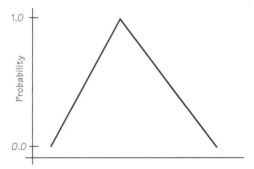

Figure 10.1 *Original distribution.*

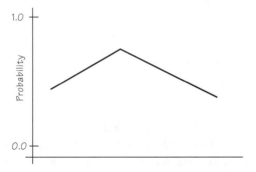

Figure 10.2 *Original distribution with noise.*

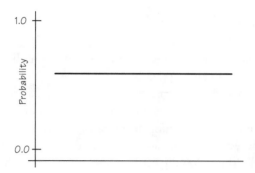

Figure 10.3 *Uniform: "Noisy" original with more additional noise.*

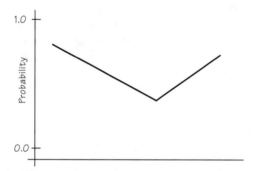

Figure 10.4 *Uniform inverted distribution with noise.*

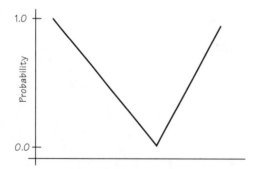

Figure 10.5 *Inverted distribution.*

As an example, suppose that EPA is being employed. If original and inverted operational profiles are employed when EPA is performed, and if the results between these two distributions are drastically different, it is an interesting exercise to generate various members in this continuum and see approximately where in the continuum the EPA results become divergent. There might be one distribution, for example, where the failure tolerance scores go from generally high (using the original distribution) to very low (using the inverted), or vice versa. The value of performing this exercise becomes clearer if you recall that mangled distributions can be thought of as "noise" in input signals. This exercise can find the degree of noise that can be handled before tolerances begin to drastically change. (This is different yet somewhat similar to what we did in chapter 7 with the burnout hazard condition, when we tweaked the multiplier to see where the results started changing.)

10.2 Assertions

White-box software testing involves a conscious decision to consider the code when selecting test cases or when determining whether the testing is adequate. *Black-box* testing, in contrast, could care less about the code's structure, source language, design, and the like. Black-box testing is purely concerned with the input domain to the software, and it uses various partitioning or random approaches to select test cases from that domain.

White-box testing suffers from a general inability to detect certain errors such as missing code errors. Black-box testing suffers from an inability to know how much code was actually exercised. You could, for example, test a piece of code one billion times with that many different test cases, yet still always follow the same path through the code, ignoring all others. Regardless of how software is tested, adding probes into the code that test the state of the program as it executes for various conditions is at once a very simple and powerful technique for flushing out errors. Fault injection can make the process of localizing where to place the probes more effective.

In chapter 5, we discussed how the PIE methodology can be used to assess where faults are more likely to hide. Although that flavor of software testability focused only on the code, software testability actually provides insight concerning how good some properties of your test cases are [Voas 1992]. Another perspective on testability is that it provides information about how easy the software testing process is to perform. This is valuable information for project scheduling and project cost estimation. However, such information provides little insight into how good test cases are at defect detection. Because of this deficit, we argued in chapter 5 that it is much more useful to treat software testability as a measure of how good test cases will be at making defects observable. In general, that is the view we have been espousing throughout the book. Now, we will investigate the use of assertions to make software even more testable.

Software assertions can play an interesting role in increasing software's testability. *Run-time assertion checking* is a programming-for-validation trick that helps ensure program states satisfy certain semantic constraints. Strategic run-time assertion checking presents the opportunity to thwart defect hiding at a more reasonable cost than ad hoc assertion placement. Most software developers place assertions in a nonsystematic manner to increase the efficiency of debugging, with no intention of making testing as efficient as possible, which would occur if assertions were placed only where testing was weak. The widespread appeal of assertions is evident in the recent languages of Anna (Annotated Ada) [Luckham 1985] and Eiffel [Meyer 1992]. Anna uses comments to embed assertions; Eiffel uses object invariants that are inserted as pre- and postconditions to all operations on the object. Unfortunately, the brittleness of the Anna Tool Set has all but killed Anna as a language, and Eiffel is not winning the battle between various OO languages.

The conclusion that assertions are beneficial for testability parallels the comments by Osterweil and Clarke concerning the value of assertions to testing. In 1992, Osterweil and Clarke classified assertions as "among the most significant ideas by testing and analysis researchers" [Osterweil 1992]. Because of our extensive experience with the PIE fault-injection approach, we have some insight as to why assertions work and how their placement can be made more systematic.

Software assertions are Boolean functions that evaluate to TRUE when a program state satisfies some semantic condition, and FALSE otherwise. If an assertion evaluates to FALSE, it will be considered the same as if the execution of the program resulted in failure, even if the output for that execution is correct. Hence it is necessary to modify what is considered failure in the output space: A *program failure* will be said to have occurred if the program output is incorrect or an assertion fails. Also, we will consider assertions as output information when we assess testability, thus modifying a program's observability criteria. This move not only modifies what is considered *failure,* but it also modifies what is considered *output.* The goal here is to use the information provided by fault injection for measuring testability to tell us how to insert assertions in a manner that engenders testing with the greatest defect-revealing ability. The point here is as follows:

> *Why place assertions on program states if it is known a priori that if these states are in error, failure of the software is nearly guaranteed to occur? Instead, place assertions on program states when it is likely that incorrectness in those portions of the state will not be observable in the software's output.*

Correctness proofs can be thought of as formal assertion checking systems that statically test to ensure that the entire program satisfies certain logical constraints for all inputs. By contrast, software testing checks the correctness of outputs only for specific program inputs. Software assertions perform a different function than correctness proofs or software testing; they semantically test program states (or parts of program states) created during execution with program inputs. For example, given a known range of legal values for some intermediate computation in a program, a software assertion could check the correctness of the program state. Or an assertion might be able to test for an exact program state as opposed to just checking for a range of possibilities. Admittedly, assertions are often expensive to write and, if written incorrectly, can produce misleading information concerning quality. Since assertions are able to check intermediate data values, they can reveal when the program has entered an undesirable state. This is vital, because it is possible that the undesirable state will not propagate into a program failure.

Observability is a metric that has long been used in hardware design. Observability describes the degree or ability of a chip to detect problems in its inner logic by looking only at the output of the chip. When observability is poor, built-in self tests (BISTs) are employed to force complex circuits to self-validate. Hardware probes are placed into circuits to increase the observability of the circuit during test. Software assertions can play the role of BIST for software. Assertions can increase observability in software by increasing the dimensionality and/or cardinality of the software's output space. This is precisely what is desired when the goal of testing is to catch defects.

The effect assertions have on the dimensionality and cardinality of a program are best explained through examples. Figure 10.6 illustrates a program that reads in an integer and outputs an integer. In this example, an input value of 5 produces 100, 6 produces 200, and 7 produces 300. Thus, the dimensionality of the output space in Figure 10.6 is *one.*

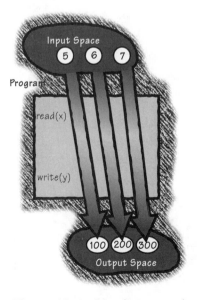

Figure 10.6 *One-dimensional output.*

In Figure 10.7, a conditional branch in the code causes only certain inputs to execute the assertion. The assertion essentially acts as another output statement whose result can be checked by an oracle. Thus, for some inputs, the dimensionality of the output actually increases. In the figure, the inputs 5 and 6 execute the assertion and will therefore have outputs with a dimensionality of two, whereas an input value of 7 will have a dimensionality of one.

Now imagine a slightly different example where two unique input cases result in the same output value. Further, assume this value is of dimension n. By adding an assertion to the code that is executed by both input cases, it is possible that the variable on which the assertion acts will have different values. Thus each input case can be thought of as producing a unique output value of dimension $n + 1$. This example demonstrates how an assertion can increase the cardinality of the output space.

Assertions have an interesting ability that is similar to the ability of oracles. Assertions warn of problems at the point in the code where they evaluate to FALSE. But this warning flag may actually belie a problem at a completely different place in the code, and may not necessarily reflect a problem with the statement immediately preceding the assertion. Determining where an assertion-firing problem may have originated requires reversing an execution trace back to preceding computations. But the main value of assertions still holds—they warn of problems in the program.

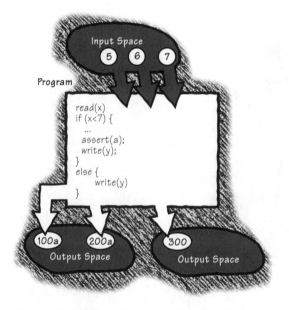

Figure 10.7 *Two-dimensional output from added assertion.*

The key to getting the best return on investment from software assertions is to intelligently place them on those states produced by the program that, if corrupted, are unlikely to cause the program to result in incorrect output. Once testing is completed, the assertions can be removed. The removal of assertions is motivated by the desire for more efficient execution during production runs.

10.2.1 Testability-Based Assertion Localization

To increase the value of testing, it is necessary to pick some middle ground between the extremes of having no software assertions at all—the most common practice—and the theoretical ideal of having assertions on every statement in a program. The compromise is to place assertions only at locations where traditional testing is *unlikely* to uncover software defects.

There are two key reasons why faults hide: Either inputs do not exercise the faults, or infection and propagation do not occur. If faults are not exercised, then it is possible that the assertions won't get exercised either, especially if they are placed in parts of the code that don't get much use. In this case, assertions are as useless as the original test cases for detecting errors in nonexercised regions. If, on the other hand, the reason that testability is poor is a lack of infection or propagation, then assertions may be just what is needed.

PIE tells where in the code infection and propagation are unlikely to happen. This information can be a very useful guide for assertion placement. Assertions can boost the utility of test cases if they are placed at locations where infection and propagation estimates are low. Of course, "low" will be a user-defined threshold. From a cost perspective, balancing infection and propagation scores with the number of assertions that can be placed is a good strategy.

If a propagation estimate is one of the culprits for some assignment location 1, then place an assertion immediately after 1. If an infection estimate is one of the lowest scores for an assignment statement, again assert just after the assignment statement. If an infection or propagation estimate is low for a conditional location, then assert at the beginning of each branch to make sure that the control flow is following the right branch.

Given a statement like:

```
a := (b + c + d) * (b - c);
```

and a weak propagation estimate resulting from a perturbation of a, then placing an assertion at this point:

```
a := (b + c + d) * (b - c);
ASSERT (a);
```

not only tests a but also tests the correctness of those computations that previously assigned a value to b, c, and d. So one assertion not only tests the value of the variable being directly studied, but it also tests other indirect computations that occur before the statement is executed.

Example of the Benefit of Assertion on Error Propagation

We claim that the impact of assertions on error propagation must be either (1) negligible or (2) positive. Greater error propagation increases testability.

Claim   The impact of an assertion on error propagation must be either (1) negligible or (2) positive.

Argument   Assume that for some program P, all programmer-accessible variables are contained in a 10-element array: a[0], a[1], ..., a[9]. Some percentage x of that array, $0 < x \leq 100$, is output from P. All information that is output from P is checked by an oracle O. For any element in a, there is a probability that a defect will cause the element to contain incorrect information; we denote these probabilities: $\Pr\{a[0]\}$, $\Pr\{a[1]\}$, ..., $\Pr\{a[9]\}$. If incorrect information is asserted on or checked by O, then error propagation is 100 percent.

Asserting on an element of a that is already being checked by O cannot decrease the likelihood of error propagation. But if $x \neq 100$, and we assert on a reachable member of array a that is not being checked by O, then the likelihood of error propagation must increase, because of the basic probabilistic laws: A reachable data member does not exist in dead code. Given two events A and B,

```
Pr{A} ∨ Pr{B} ≥ Pr{A}
```

and

```
Pr{A} ∨ Pr{B} ≥ Pr{B}.
```

For example, suppose that a[0] through a[1] are being checked by O; then adding an assertion to a[9] cannot decrease the likelihood of error propagation, because

```
Pr{a[0]} ∨ Pr{a[1]} ≤ Pr{a[0]} ∨ Pr{a[1]} ∨ Pr{a[9]}
```

Detectability and Incorrect Assertions

Greater testability is usually a desirable characteristic, with one caveat. If a piece of code is correct, the code's testability is completely irrelevant. Therefore, somewhat counterintuitively, the value of code with high testability is greatly reduced if the mechanisms that are depended upon actually to *detect* problems (i.e., the assertions and the oracle) do not correctly accomplish their tasks. It is possible that the same assertions that increase defect observability provide no defect detection during testing. But isn't defect detection the return on investment for the costs of instrumenting code with assertions!? Actually, the value added by inserting assertions is directly dependent on two factors:

1. The correctness of the assertion.
2. The amount of detectability the assertion itself provides (i.e., the assertion should be able to determine incorrectness when the state is truly incorrect). Assertions that cannot detect problems are useless, as they never evaluate to FALSE.

Deriving correct assertions is nontrivial, because it is contingent upon both proper assertion placement and the ability to semantically detect program-state defects for all inputs. For any specification, there are an infinite number of correct programs that implement the desired functionality, and an infinite number of incorrect programs that are slight mutations of each correct program. Thus, the process of assertion placement is version-specific; that is, you must consider which correct version is closest to your version before injecting assertions. A reasonable rule of thumb is: One assertion may not fit all purposes! This fact highlights the difficulty inherent in correctly placing assertions.

Semantically correct assertions evaluate TRUE for all inputs if the program state is not defective, and FALSE otherwise. Even if an assertion is not always correct—even if a defective program state is not caught by an assertion for some input—any assertion will likely benefit testability assessments. The goal of assertion injection is not merely to use assertions to increase testability. Rather, the big-picture goal is to employ assertions as windows into the computational state in order to detect problems. When this is done correctly, problems can be corrected and reliability enhanced. Only semantically correct assertions can aid in accomplishing this goal.

There is an interesting relationship between the degree of detectability that an assertion provides and its correctness. The *degree of detectability* of an assertion is a measure of how accurate the assertion is in making its comparison before returning FALSE. An assertion can contain the correct expression, but not contain enough detectability to catch a problem every time. This renders the assertion unable to be correct at all times. A lack of detectability is often related to variables containing too few bits or to round-off or truncation occurring during the calculation of an assertion expression. When an assertion contains the correct logical check and has complete detectability, then the assertion is truly correct. Unfortunately, incorrect assertions can still boost testability, which can give a false sense of security to testing, especially when testing does not detect problems.

Several Hypotheses about Assertions

We have several hypotheses regarding the relationship between software assertions, test suites, and fault revealing ability. These are explained in the following sections.

Reachability   Static testability metrics cannot as easily or as accurately address software reachability as dynamic metrics can. Although collecting data about information loss is useful for assertion placement, reachability analysis is still necessary to know if an assertion will ever be exercised.

Let $T(P)_Q$ represent the testability of program P when tested with test suite Q. And let $(Q \cup \Delta)$ represent test suite Q after it has been augmented with enough test cases such that all statements in P are exercised. There exist software test-case generation tools (Godzilla [DeMillo 1991], WhiteBox™ TGen) that are intelligent enough in practice to find test cases that will exercise previously unreached statements in the code, though this is an unsolvable problem in general. Note that Δ could be empty, in which case $Q = (Q \cup \Delta)$. Since reachability is the first event in the fault/failure model, it is a necessary condition for improved testability, hence

$$T(P)_Q \leq T(P)_{(Q \cup \Delta)}.$$

Changing Test Suites   What happens to the testability of software when a test suite changes? Begin with the case where the code has no assertions, and then consider the case where assertions are added.

For program P without assertions, we just showed regardless of what Δ adds to test suite Q, we know that $T(P)_Q \leq T(P)_{(Q \cup \Delta)}$. Given a new test suite Q' that is not identical to Q where neither test suite is a subset of the other, what can we say about the relation between $T(P)_Q$ and $T(P)_{Q'}$? Quite simply, we cannot say anything confidently without performing a technique similar to sensitivity analysis with both Q and Q'. That is, we do not know whether $T(P)_Q <= T(P)_{Q'}$ or $T(P)_Q > T(P)_{Q'}$.

Now let P_Q^A represent program P with assertions specifically designed to boost the fault-revealing ability of Q. Assertions increase the likelihood that the second and third conditions of the fault/failure model happen. Then according to our lemma,

$$T(P)_Q \leq T(P^A)_Q$$

From there, we conjecture that:

$$T(P)_{Q'} \leq T(P^A)_{Q'}$$

regardless of whether Q and Q' have common members. Our argument in support of this conjecture follows: If the assertions (that are based on Q) placed in P are never exercised via inputs from Q', then $T(P)_{Q'} = T(P_Q^A)_{Q'}$; if as little as one assertion is exercised by some input in Q', then by the lemma it is possible that $T(P)_{Q'} \leq T(P_Q^A)_{Q'}$ will be true.

Christoph Michael's research studying "homogeneous propagation" supports this conjecture [Michael 1996]. When several different forms of program-state corruption impact the same program variable at the same place in the code for the same program input, all of these corruptions may exhibit the identical propagation behavior. If they do, *homogeneous propagation* has occurred. That means that either all of the corruptions propagated or none of them did.

What this suggests about assertions is straightforward. Since assertions directly affect propagation, if propagation is homogeneous for some $i \in Q$, then it is likely that it will be homogeneous for some other $j \in Q$. Whether j is in Q or Q' is immaterial. In general then, assertions appear to have an impact on testability without respect to whether the inputs to the software come from one test suite or another. Since assertions improve the propagation prospects for inputs from Q by increasing the cardinality or dimensionality of the output space, they should also improve the propagation prospects for Q'.

Finally, we conjecture that it will generally be true that:

$$T(P)_Q << T(P_Q^A)_{(Q \cup \Delta)}$$

though there will be cases where:

$$T(P)_Q = T(P_Q^A)_{(Q \cup \Delta)}$$

specifically when $Q = (Q \cup \Delta)$ and/or the assertions placed into P are not exercised.

10.2.2 Cleansing Assertions

DNA is often likened to a complex program. DNA contains a code for performing certain actions based on the molecular sequence of instructions. Though we still have only a limited understanding of DNA, we do know it has one very interesting capability: DNA somehow knows when its molecular sequence (program) has been damaged. In some cases DNA will even attempt to reconfigure itself back to correct code.

Traditional assertions of the usual sort are a boon for software testability. They are also a curse for failure tolerance. Could assertions be adapted to help solve the failure-tolerance problem? An assertion whose job is not only to warn that a dangerous state has occurred, but also to try to recover from that state, may do the trick. This form of assertion is called a *cleansing assertion*.

The inspiration for cleansing assertions stemmed from a real-world analysis of safety-critical software. The dilemma that resulted from EPA analysis was: What is the best method for maximizing failure tolerance and still fitting within real-time constraints? The methodology described here addresses this problem for software components in general.

Ideally, every developer would like to build software that knows when it reaches an undesirable state, and most important, how to recover. The assertion technique described in the following paragraphs is geared toward providing developers with information about candidate locations where instrumenting with forward-recovery mechanisms is likely to be a cost-effective way to lead to acceptable behavior. Making software more tolerant and less likely to core dump, hang, shut down, crash, and so on, is a key characteristic of robust, dependable systems.

Cleansing assertions are forward-recovery software mechanisms that have two purposes: (1) to detect that a state needs modification before program execution continues, and (2) to determine an appropriate state to recover to that will not produce an output satisfying $PRED_C$ (see chapter 5).

The role of fault injection here is as follows:

1. Create a set of corrupted internal states
2. See which ones lead to outputs that satisfy $PRED_C$ and which ones do not
3. Determine what recovery mechanisms to embed into the software to enable the detection and recovery processes

This methodology localizes where recovery assertions, which act somewhat like antibodies in an organism, should be injected into software components to ensure desirable outputs; the second part of our approach defines what the assertions should be for a program. Recovery assertions are *fail-safe* forward-recovery mechanisms that are added to software to detect suspicious states dynamically and attempt to repair them by replacing them with different program states known to result in acceptable system outputs.

The novelty of this problem is twofold: how to decide where to place recovery mechanisms, and how to build the recovery mechanisms themselves. Software recovery techniques can generally be subdivided into two categories: backward recovery and forward recovery. Backward recovery techniques return the software to a previous state (hopefully not erroneous) and continue computing using an alternative piece of software. Forward recovery attempts to repair the damaged state without rolling back the state of the program [Leveson 1995]. This was discussed further in chapter 6.

The approach discussed here assumes no knowledge of all of the different ways in which subsystems can fail. This approach injects corrupt information into the states of an executing software component and, by doing this, stores up information about how to build forward-recovery mechanisms capable of thwarting the effects of the corrupt information. That is what differentiates this approach from the many other forward and backward recovery schemes [Johnson 1989, Leveson 1995]. This approach is not able to thwart all forms of corrupted information, but in some situations it can cleanse a substantial number of corrupted states. This methodology improves the prospects of satisfactory system operation by forcing software components to overcome anomalies during execution. (Here, *overcome* means producing output states that the rest of the system can tolerate, and an *anomaly* is corrupt information that is either fed into a component as input or a corrupt program state created by the component.)

Before we detail this approach, we provide a simple example that illustrates our goals. Figure 10.8 shows a layout of an information system S comprising $N + 1$ components (C_0 through C_N). S receives a variety of incoming inputs, from hardware devices or human operators (shown as H_1 through H_5). It also receives input signals from three external software components: E_1, E_2, and E_3 (which could include commercial off-the-shelf software components). For output, S sends three output signals to H_6, H_7, and H_8.

Focus on C_1. In practice, the following process is done for each component. C_1 gets its inputs from H_4 and C_0, and sends its output to C_2. Here, the goal is to ensure that any anomalies that might exist in the internal program states of C_1 do not cause the output of C_1 to be such that H_6, H_7, or H_8 receive unsafe or vulnerable outputs. Anomalies could arise in the program states of C_1 from a variety of sources, including faulty data from H_4, faulty output from C_0, or defects in C_1 as it executes.

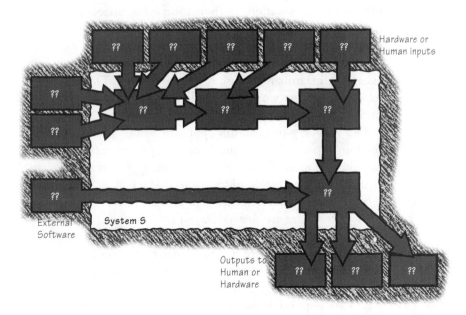

Figure 10.8 *Typical modern control system.*

If the following approach observes events that could cause the output of C_1 to be likely to impact output of S in an undesirable manner, then C_1 is a candidate for modification to improve its robustness. If C_1 cannot be modified to be more tolerant of such anomalies, then improving the *reliability* of C_0, C_1, or H_4 must be considered in order to ensure that H_6, H_7, and H_8 do not receive undependable outputs (unsafe or vulnerable). The main goal of this methodology is to *force* software components to be robust with respect to the sources of potential problems, such that the components do not output events that could cause system-level catastrophic output events. In [Leveson 1995], Leveson makes the following statement which strongly supports the main objective of the approach described for using fault injection to train recovery mechanisms:

> *Software needs to be protected against failures and other events in its environment—including erroneous operator inputs, such as inputs that arrive out of order—and it must be designed to stay in a safe state (and to keep the system in a safe state) despite these events. . . . The code must implement these robustness requirements. (p. 425)*

A secondary goal of this approach is to perform recovery in a cost-effective manner so that it can even be applied to real-time software. The cost of an assertion injection should be estimated (or otherwise calculated) before assertion placement recommendations are made.

This methodology was inspired by work we performed with a real commercial application. After using existing tools for analyzing the tolerance of a safety-critical application to corrupted internal states, the client determined that around 30 locations in their source code needed recovery mechanisms to ensure that particular state problems did not manifest. This situation was exacerbated by the real-time constraints that allowed for a maximum of three to five assertions to be added into the code. As a result, it was critical that the few assertions maximize the improved robustness. This meant that one assertion needed to do the work of several whenever possible. The problem was determining this possibility.

Our recovery-mechanisms approach is four-phased. Figure 10.9 shows how the four phases of the methodology are integrated. First, EPA is performed on the software to determine where data-state corruptions can originate that propagate into unacceptable outputs [Voas 1994, Voas 1997]. (See chapter 6.) The second phase, called *static error flow analysis* (SEFA), analyzes how different program state spaces are dependent on one another, with respect to the different source-code locations that are associated with them. By combining the results of the first two phases into a single metric, we can identify regions in the code where we can effectively thwart anomaly-propagation from multiple source-code locations via appropriate recovery mechanisms. The third and fourth phases are responsible for building the "appropriate recovery mechanisms." The third phase, called *program state classification* (PSC), develops a classifier for program states to determine whether they will likely lead to unacceptable output. The fourth phase, called *recovery assertion injection* (RAI), places a recovery assertion, based on the classifier, at those places in the code identified from the first two phases as most likely to improve the fault tolerance of the component. Recovery assertions attempt to replace existing program states with other states in order to return executing components to states that will result in acceptable component outputs.

As an analogy, consider a complex chain of dominos set in a display. This display corresponds to the dynamic execution of software. Chains of dominos in the display branch out, sometimes reconverge, and result in "outputs" at the last dominos of each chain. Pushing over a domino so that it topples and starts a chain reaction is equivalent in our analogy to introducing an anomaly that propagates through the executing program. Just as sometimes pushing one domino can result in many of the last dominos falling over, introducing a fault in a running program sometimes corrupts many program outputs in unacceptable ways. The objective is to stop all last dominos from falling.

This can be accomplished by inserting an immovable domino somewhere in the chain of falling dominos after the first fallen domino and before the final output domino. In the trivial case, all domino chains reconverge to a single domino chain at the output end. In this case, insertion of only *one* immovable domino just prior to the final domino solves the problem. Trapping all bad program states just before a component halts is the software equivalent of this trivial case. But such a case is unrealistic. Realistic domino displays have multiple domino chains with

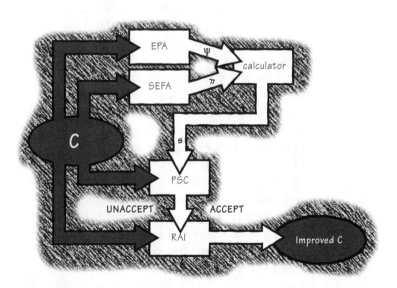

Figure 10.9 *General fault-injection recovery scheme.*

complicated interrelations as well as multiple last dominos. Realizing that inserting immovable dominos before every last domino is too expensive and unrealistic, we are left to determine where to insert immovable dominos in some intelligent way so as to minimize the number of falling last dominos. As part of our approach, we provide a methodology for determining where recovery assertions—corresponding to immovable dominos—can be placed for maximum robustness of the software component at a minimum in performance costs.

Defining $PRED_C$ with Respect to the Complete Information System

What constitutes unacceptable component output can be: (1) backed out from a forward hazard analysis of the system S, or (2) determined from C's specification. If (1) is the manner by which $PRED_C$ is determined for C, then there are two different forms of unacceptable component behavior: one with respect to S, and one with respect to C and without regard to S. The definition for what constitutes undesirable system behavior will, in part, drive the definition for $PRED_C$. For example, in terms of Figure 10.8, we can simulate anomalies exiting C_1, and see if any of those anomalies force unacceptable outputs in H_6, H_7, or H_8. If they do, then we know something about what types of states we do not want to exit C_1 and can build that information into $PRED_{C1}$.

Static Error Flow Analysis (SEFA)

The second phase in the approach, Static Error Flow Analysis (SEFA), is applied to analyze data-space dependencies between the different locations in a component. SEFA is simply a static slicing algorithm [Weiser 1982] in reverse. A *data space* is the set of all program states that can be created by a location l. In the domino analogy, the function of SEFA is to study the domino chains and find the fewest locations where a single barrier halts the most domino toppling. If many different lines of dominos merge into a single line, then placing a barrier in the merged line is more cost-effective than placing a barrier in each incoming line. The role of SEFA is to perform a similar analysis for program-state corruption propagation.

SEFA begins by first assuming an initial corruption in some variable a at location l. Next, SEFA predicts which set of variables might be corrupted after executing subsequent locations w. SEFA creates sets of these variables, called fault sets, that reveal dependencies between data spaces. Intuitively, a *fault set* is simply all programmer variables that are currently corrupted during a particular execution of the program at a specific location in the program. Furthermore, SEFA assigns a metric rating to the domino chains in order to identify critical fault sets. The reason for performing SEFA is to prune the number of locations that are candidates for recovery assertions in order to boost the component's fault tolerance within real-time constraints. SEFA is implemented by the following algorithm.

Algorithm: Static Error Flow Analysis (SEFA)

1. For each assignment statement *l* in program *C*,

   a. Set temporary variable *k* to *l*,

   b. Assume a fault in *l* causes the variable on the "left hand side" lhs(*l*) to be corrupted (*initial corruption assumption*). Set **faultset**$_{l,k}$ to the set containing lhs(*l*). In the notation **faultset**$_{m,n}$ the first parameter *m* represents the location where the initial corruption supposedly occurred, and the second parameter *n* is the location just executed before the fault set is built. Typically, *n* is a location executed after *m* is executed.

   c. Perform a *breadth-first* traversal from *l*, and for each succeeding assignment statement location *w* that is statically reached on this traversal from *l*, BUILD (**faultset**$_{l,w}$).

Algorithm *BUILD* (faultset$_{l,w}$):

1. Set **faultset**$_{l,w}$ to **faultset**$_{l,prior(w)}$, where *prior(w)* is any location that could be executed immediately before this iteration of *w* and only if *prior(w)* does not equal null. If there are multiple *prior(w)*s, then set **faultset**$_{l,w}$ to the union of the fault sets of those multiple *prior(w)*s.

2. If the "right hand side" of *w*, rhs(*w*), references a variable in **faultset**$_{l,w}$ then add lhs(*w*) to **faultset**$_{l,w}$.

The reason that we perform a breadth-first traversal is so that when we get to a node to build its fault set, we already know that these sets exist for each of their predecessors.

The results of this algorithm provide static information needed by the Calculator (see Figure 10.9) concerning the data-flow relationships between different locations and our static predictions as to what can corrupt what else. Given the SEFA algorithm, the *composite* fault set for location *w*, called π_w, is:

$$\pi_w = \bigcup_{\text{for each } k} \text{faultset}_{k,w}$$

This composite set provides a "guess" at the set of all variables that could be corrupted after executing location *w*, assuming that some location executed before *w* caused an initial corruption.

We now wish to provide a single numerical score, s_w, for each location w in the code. s_w represents the degree of failure tolerance of the component if the program state created by w is corrupt, and can be written as:

$$s_w = \sum_{\pi_w} \psi_{aICQ}$$

where we sum over each variable a in π_w using the extended propagation analysis score that was found when a was perturbed at l, and l is executed before w. (ψ_{aICQ} is defined in section 6.2.1.)

The higher s_w is, the lower the predicted failure tolerance. For those s_ws that are large, a recovery mechanism should be inserted immediately after location w to force the variable on the lhs(w) into a range that is unlikely to satisfy $PRED_C$. Let L represent the set of all ws that do so. A single fault-tolerant mechanism of this sort can measurably improve the component's ability to recover from faults originating from every location that added a member to π_w. Later we describe how recovery mechanisms might be derived.

Figure 10.10 illustrates this in action. In this figure, we see that at location l_0, we have an assignment statement that increments variable a by one and we follow this computation done until l_6. Note that we only follow the flow of assignment statements, and do not show the control statements that allow the program to go from l_0 to l_1 or l_2 or l_3. The fault sets are: {a} for l_0,l_0, {a, b} for l_0,l_1, {a, c}

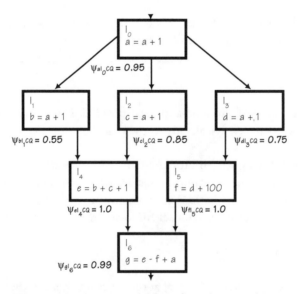

Figure 10.10 *Example data flow diagram from location l_0.*

for l_0, l_2, {a, d} for l_0, l_3, {a, b, c, e} for l_0, l_4, {a, d, f} for l_0, l_5, and {a, b, c, d, e, f, g} for l_0, l_6.

Recovery Assertions

As already mentioned, after the first two phases of this approach are complete (EPA and SEFA), the process of identifying where recovery mechanisms are needed is completed. At this point, exception handlers could be employed instead of the type of recovery assertion we espouse. The purpose of the last two phases of the approach is to determine what repair should occur once we detect that the software is in an undesirable state.

Embedded software assertions are mechanisms that can detect state anomalies. Assertions test current program states for a number of different things: out-of-range variables, the presence or absence of certain relationships between variables and inputs, and known corrupted states. When an assertion fires (and ignoring the possibility of false-positives), a corruption has been detected. Assertions can be made either to halt the execution, which is similar to an exception, or to attempt recovery from the corruption. The exact nature of a recovery mechanism is highly application-specific. The EPA algorithm and the SEFA algorithm do *not* solve the problem of deriving fault-tolerant mechanisms, they merely identify locations in the code where recovery is most likely to be effective at repairing corrupted program states. In this section, we discuss deriving these mechanisms.

Recovery assertions attempt to replace existing program states with other states in order to return executing components to states that will result in acceptable component outputs. This frequently involves replacing the current state with a replacement state that is known to be an acceptable alternative. The difficulty lies not in actually doing the replacement, but rather in knowing that it is an acceptable alternative. Recovery assertions are similar to classical pre- and postconditions which determine correctness but are not formally derived from a specification. Like classical pre- and postconditions, recovery assertions are subject to misuse.

Recovery assertions are similar to traditional assertions, except that recovery assertions attempt to do state replacements when an assertion condition is triggered; traditional assertions produce only warnings. With respect to exception handlers, recovery assertions have the same purpose. What is unique in this methodology is the derivation of where to place the recovery assertions and what the recovery assertions should be.

Recovery assertions boost fault tolerance. They wipe the slate clean so that corrupted output will not result. A recovery could, for example, replace only the values identified as corrupt, or it could reassign all variables, returning the entire state of the computation to some state known to be safe. Recovery does not have to be triggered only by detected anomalies; Parnas advocates periodically resetting most variables in safety-critical real-time systems so that test trajectories are limited in length [Parnas 1990]. Periodic recovery also limits the propagation of corrupt data values.

The model for determining where to put recovery assertions is primarily geared toward keeping a component in an acceptable state at a reasonable cost. For real-time systems, it is not feasible to insert recovery assertions at every location in the code. Nor in general will it be possible to derive the recovery assertions for every point in the code.

There are two tasks that must be performed by a recovery assertion:

1. *Detection* of states that will likely lead to unacceptable events

2. *Substitution* of acceptable states for *probably* dangerous states

The recommended approach here is first to perform the Program State Classification (PSC) algorithm repeatedly at those locations whose s_w was large, and then to implement the Recovery Assertion Instrumentor (RAI) algorithm, that creates and inserts the instrumentation of the recovery assertions into C that is about to be provided. For performance reasons, the number of assertions that we can feasibly expect to inject may be few. Therefore, the threshold defining whether a particular s_w is large may itself be quite large. Thus the number of assertions that are deemed feasible will directly determine where the following algorithm is applied.

This algorithm provides the state classifications needed for detection and recovery at the locations in the component determined to have the greatest "recoverability." Because recovery at w repairs many places in addition to w (i.e., those places directly connected to w by means of variable sets can also be considered repaired

---

Algorithm Program State Classification (PSC)

1. Create an empty set, $UNACCEPT_w$.

2. Create an empty set, $ACCEPT_w$.

3. Randomly select an input x according to Q, and if C halts on x in a fixed period of time, find the corresponding $A_{|Cx}$ in $\propto_{|C\Delta}$. Set Z to $A_{|C1x}$.

4. Alter the sampled value of variable a found in Z, and denote the new data state as Z', and execute the succeeding code on Z'. If by chance w is executed more than once because of the value we placed into Z', alter a in each state that is produced by w.

5. If C's output satisfies $PRED_C$, add Z' to $UNACCEPT_w$. If C's output does not satisfy $PRED_C$, add Z' to $ACCEPT_w$.

6. Repeat steps 3–5 for as many x's as resources allow.

when w is repaired), the process has positive side benefits. The PSC algorithm builds up two sets of states for location w: (1) one set made up of those states that have been observed to lead to unacceptable output, and (2) another set of corrupted states that did not lead to unacceptable output. Once sets of program states that are acceptable (in terms of the outputs they produce) are found, there exists a pool from which to choose any substitution that may be required during deployment.

The recovery assertions that are developed by PSC are a function of Q, and S's output states that are defined as undesirable. This begs an interesting question: "What value, if any, do the recovery assertions added to C have when C is placed into another system S' which might have different definitions for undependable system behavior?" If $PRED_C$ is defined specifically for S, then it is possible that this four-phase process would need to be reperformed for each different S. If, however, $PRED_C$ is defined according to C's specification, then the recovery assertions should be valid for each S that C is embedded in, if C is the correct component for S.

The PSC algorithm is rife with unresolved implementation issues, specifically exploring both direct lookup of previously encountered program states in the *ACCEPT* and *UNACCEPT* sets and alternatives to lookup. One alternative might be to create a classifier based on Hidden Markov Models (HMMs). In addition, many recent AI and Cognitive Science techniques to classification have proven useful: genetic algorithms (GAs), sparse distributed memory (SDM), connectionism, and high-level perception [McClelland 1986; Kanerva 1988; Goldberg 1989; Hofstadter 1995; McGraw 1995]. By learning or otherwise creating a reasonable classifier using artificial intelligence techniques, we may be able to more quickly and accurately determine state classification. One method that applies particularly well to our classification problem is connectionism (i.e., neural network modeling). Another involves the application of genetic algorithms. All of these are reasonable candidates because of their potentially significant value in reducing the costs of state storage.

For each location whose s_w is found to be unacceptably high, the code of C will be augmented with the appropriate instrumentation to implement the following algorithm:

Algorithm Recovery Assertion Instrumentor (RAI)

Immediately after each execution of location w, insert recovery code that performs the following requirements:

1. Test to see if the current state is in $ACCEPT_w$; if so, then no action is required, else if the current state is in $UNACCEPT_w$, then swap out the current state for some other member in $ACCEPT_w$ if and only if it is determined that the current state's system input value is similar enough to the selected state's system input value.

This algorithm is a very high–level description of the functionality of the instrumentation injected into the software. Research into how to give the green light and actually do the right substitution is still needed.

The key problem is in determining when a state is similar enough is a system-state–specific task. Determining whether a substitution will not worsen a situation is dependent on the state of S. For some components, an assertion may be adequate for making this decision. In other components, an examination of the states in $UNACCEPT_w$ may reveal a pattern in the unsafe states that can be captured and codified in a classifier. The transformation of $PRED_C$ and $UNACCEPT_w$ data into some procedure that determines whether states are similar to what we already know about is often a manual process. After more experience has been gained with this transformation, it may be possible to automate the process, perhaps using machine learning techniques to discover and replicate classification patterns. For example, it appears possible to train a connectionist model to provide a useful measurement of similarity using the states $UNACCEPT_w$ and $ACCEPT_w$ as training sets.

If we go back to our example in Figure 10.10, we see that the scores that the locations receive are as follows: l_0 is 0.95, l_1 is 1.5, l_2 is 1.8, l_3 is 1.7, l_4 is 3.35, l_5 is 2.7, and l_6 is 7.04. Since at location 6 we know that if g is corrupted, it frequently propagates; then by placing an assertion on g at this location, we decrease the propagation scores for the other 6 predecessor locations of l_6. Thus the failure tolerance of seven locations is improved by an assertion at only one of those locations.

We have described a fault injection–based approach to cost-guided software recovery. Though the idea of software recovery has been around for decades [Johnson 1989], this approach presents several advantages:

1. It gets the needed information regarding where and how to recover from the observations made during fault-injection analysis.

2. It can be combined with other forward-recovery techniques that prevent single-cycle errors.

3. It recommends recovery mechanisms only at the fewest possible points. (Since recovery is expensive, this is vital.)

4. The user can objectively observe and measure any increase in failure tolerance that the injected recovery assertions provide.

Similarly, there are weaknesses in our approach, mainly the reliance on access to definitions of undesirable system behavior in $PRED_C$ as well as the possibility that a state substitution will occur that worsens the situation. At this point, solutions to these problems are not known.

The four-part technique just described has been successfully (though manually) applied on several small systems. Currently, EPA is fully automated. The utility that implements RAI is near completion. Slated for automation next are

SEFA and PSC. Because these components of the methodology are still being researched and built, we do not yet have industrial-strength results. We do know that the guidance that this methodology provides in not a panacea. Nevertheless, it provides insights useful to both practitioners and researchers who are interested in building systems that can handle the unexpected.

There are limitations to this four-part approach. Primary among limitations is a source-code requirement. Second to that is a limited ability to scale to systems of millions of lines of source code. It should be possible to mold this technique into a mediator that sits at the interfaces between components (even in executable format) for large-scale systems. If this can be done, the approach then will be scaleable. A further problem is storing $ACCEPT_w$ and $UNACCEPT_w$. One potential solution (already mentioned) is to train a neural net to recognize when a state is likely to be in $UNACCEPT_w$. Another potential limitation is that the performance-degradation caused by the recovery assertions will be unacceptable. This problem affects all recovery schemes equally. Related to this point, there may also be more locations that warrant assertions than can be accommodated for performance considerations. Finally, it is possible that a state substitution forced by this approach could mistakenly worsen the situation. Care to prevent this is paramount.

10.3 Summary

This chapter has touched on several important subjects that are directly related to software fault injection: inverted and "noisy" operational profiles, software assertions to enhance testability (i.e., enhance observability), and fault injection–based recovery mechanisms.

Because fault injection is a dynamic technique, the inputs that are used during fault injection are of vital importance. If the results of fault injection are frequencies with which certain events occur, then to use these frequencies as predictors of how frequently similar events will occur in the future, it is necessary to have a reasonable approximation of the operational profile. If the results of fault injection are not being used as probability estimates, then it is not as imperative that the operational profile be available. Of course, whenever a profile is available or some approximation to it is available, using it is always preferable to using a fictitious distribution.

Having access to the operational profile is still only one part of building confidence in the quality of the software's behavior. It is also valuable to show that software will behave as desired when it is forced to deal with unusual operating circumstances. Combining inverted and modified profiles with fault injection is one way of doing this.

We have learned that fault hiding could be predicted by fault injection when fault injection uses either test cases from a testing distribution or samples from the test suite that was used to test the software. The PIE testability model allowed us to pinpoint where in the software the external test cases were unlikely to detect faults; it is these locations where assertions will provide the extra testing capacity that currently does not exist. Hence combining testability assessments with assertions provides for more thorough testing than not using assertions. By using testability to decide where to place assertions, we can ensure that the assertions are not performing redundant work already being accomplished by the test cases.

Finally, we have discussed another fault injection–derived assertion technology that performs recovery. This technology learns over time what types of data-state corruptions result in undesirable output events. From that information, specialized recovery software can be inserted into the software to monitor for those states during execution. If the monitors observe bad states, either warnings can be generated or the software can be designed to attempt forward recovery by replacing the undesirable states with states that are thought to be less harmful.

References

[DeMillo 1991] R. A. DeMillo and A. J. Offutt. "Constraint-based automatic test data generation." *IEEE Transactions on Software Engineering,* 17(9):900–910, September 1991.

[Goldberg 1989] D. Goldberg. *Genetic Algorithms in Search, Optimization, and Machine Learning.* Addison-Wesley, Reading, Mass., 1989.

[Hofstadter 1995] D. R. Hofstadter and FARG. *Fluid Concepts and Creative Analogies: Computer Models of the Fundamental Mechanisms of Thought.* Basic Books, New York, 1995. (FARG is an acronym for the Fluid Analogies Research Group.)

[Johnson 1989] B. W. Johnson. *Design and Analysis of Fault Tolerant Digital Systems.* Addison-Wesley, Reading, Mass., 1989.

[Kanerva 1988] P. Kanerva. *Sparse Distributed Memory.* MIT Press, Cambridge, Mass., 1988.

[Leveson 1995] N. G. Leveson. *Safeware: System Safety and Computers.* Addison-Wesley, Reading, Mass., 1995.

[Luckham 1985] D. Luckham and F. VonHenke. "An Overview of ANNA, a specification for Ada." *IEEE Software,* pp. 9–22, March 1985.

[McClelland 1986] J. McClelland and D. Rumelhart, eds. *Parallel Distributed Processing: Volumes I and II.* MIT Press, Cambridge, Mass., 1986.

[McGraw 1995] Gary McGraw. Letter Spirit (part one): Emergent High-Level Perception of Letters Using Fluid Concepts. Ph.D. thesis, Indiana University, CRCC, 510 North Fess Street, Bloomington, IN 47405, September 1995. Available on the Web at <http://www.rstcorp.com/~gem/thesis.html>.

[Meyer 1992] B. Meyer. *Eiffel the Language.* Prentice-Hall, Englewood Cliffs, N.J., 1992.

[Michael 1996] C. C. Michael. "On the regularity of error propagation in software." Technical report, Reliable Software Technologies Corporation, Sterling, Virginia, 1996. Research Division Technical Report RSTR-96-003-04.

[Osterweil 1992] L. Osterweil and L. Clarke. "A Proposed Testing and Analysis Research Initiative." *IEEE Software,* pp. 89–96, September 1992.

[Parnas 1990] D. L. Parnas, A. J. Van Schouwen, and S. Po Kwan. "Evaluation of Safety-Critical Software." *Communications of the ACM,* pp. 636–648, June 1990.

[Voas 1992] J. Voas and K. Miller. "The revealing power of a test case." *J. of Software Testing, Verification, and Reliability.* John Wiley and Sons, 2(1):25–42, May 1992.

[Voas 1994] J. Voas and K. Miller. "Dynamic testability analysis for assessing fault tolerance." *High Integrity Systems Journal,* 1(2):171–178, 1994.

[Voas 1995] J. Voas and K. Miller. "Examining Software Quality (Fault-tolerance) Using Unlikely Inputs: Turning the Test Distribution Upside Down." In *Proc. of the Eighth Annual Conference on Computer Assurance,* pp. 3–11, NIST, June 1995.

[Voas 1996] J. Voas, F. Charron, and K. Miller. "Investigating Rare-event Failure Tolerance: Reductions in Future Uncertainty." In *Proc. of the IEEE High-Assurance Systems Engineering Workshop (HASE '96).* Niagara-on-the-Lake, Canada, October 1996.

[Voas 1997] J. Voas, F. Charron, G. McGraw, K. Miller, and M. Friedman. "Predicting How Badly 'Good' Software Can Behave." *IEEE Software,* July 1997.

[Weiser 1982] M. Weiser. "Programmers use slices when debugging." *Communications of the ACM,* 25(7):446–452, July 1982.

11 *Inoculating Real-world Software*

*Getting Started Injecting
Fault Injection*

11.1 Selling Management on Fault Injection

Selling management on any new software engineering technique requires many considerations to be satisfied. The following questions must be addressed:

1. Is the new technology already being performed by some alternate technique?

2. Is the value added by fault injection cost-effective?

3. Will the time it takes to perform fault injection delay existing project schedules?

If these concerns can be convincingly addressed, management is more likely to allow fault injection to be employed.

If you are a technical person, the first of these might seem too obvious to require defending, but proving it to management will likely not be as easy. This is particularly true if your organization is already collecting metrics, has a formal test process in place, employs a variety of reliability models, and so forth. If management is already following a government procurement process such as 2167-A, they might consider this analysis an unnecessary tax on resources.

Let's face it: Managers often do not have technical backgrounds. Their backgrounds are accounting, scheduling, and fighting political battles. In such a setting, the advanced nature of fault injection will likely be disregarded due to a lack of understanding of its unique advanced features. To convince management that fault injection is not "yet another metric" that provides the same information as some suite of metrics already in place should be easy. Here are two key facts to cite:

1. Fault injection is dynamic (behavioral), not static.

2. The code is only one of three key parameters in this process, whereas metrics typically only consider the code.

Fact is, fault injection itself is not a metric, although the results can be presented in the form of event frequencies. Fault injection should be sold to management as a tool for testing how well the code responds to anomalies—nothing more or less profound than that. You don't need to be a technocrat to understand that. Traditional testing almost never directly captures the information that fault injection has to offer, that is, unless a code specification explicitly states certain corrupted test scenarios that the code must be tolerant to and how the code must tolerate them. If this is done, then the test plan will almost certainly spell out testing with such scenarios. This is not something we see often in the real world. In any case, recognize that the specification can enumerate only some number of corrupt test scenarios. Because of its built-in stochastic aspect, fault injection can broaden such classes of problems and go far beyond those anticipated by the specification writers.

Fault injection is not a reliability modeling tool. Reliability modeling estimates the likelihood of correct output, usually under the assumption that faults exist and each component of the system fails with some rate. Here again, fault injection can produce a different piece of information. Using fault injection, it is possible to estimate the likelihood of component failure assuming that some other component has failed. That is, fault injection can be used to determine how independent component failures really are. This is something not usually considered in reliability modeling. Such information will enable a V&V team to assess more reasonably whether the predictions provided by a reliability model are valid in light of the way in which the components are composed.

Another problem that is frequently encountered but rarely mentioned in the literature is the "smoking gun" syndrome. All too often, management fears that unsatisfactory code analysis results, coupled with a lack of preventative actions taken after the fact to improve the code, leave a negligence trail that is too volatile. A recent example of this phenomenon that made national news came from the tobacco industry. Tobacco industry executives claim to have no documentation of any of the experiments that proved that cigarettes are addictive and cause cancer. To back up their claims, they ensured that there was no hard evidence of this put into writing. The only claims against them, which state in no uncertain terms that at some point in the past their secret corporate files contained written evidence, are from previous employees. The issue here is whether those former employees are telling the truth or whether they are simply disgruntled ex-employees. It is unfortunately the case that some software managers tend to feel if they do not run code analysis, then they can avoid making a smoking gun. It is likely that software liability concerns will change this attitude drastically.

The long-term costs saved by not running fault injection have to be studied on a case-by-case basis. The argument for and against spending the resources should be weighed by asking the following question:

> *If the analysis showed possible weaknesses in the code that would cost some given amount to improve, but making the improvements resulted in fewer operational problems, would the cost of fixing things in the first place be less than fighting a single claim against a defective system at some possibly larger cost?*

If the results and suggested improvements cost some given amount, yet some operational problem still remained that ultimately resulted in a lawsuit, could the vendor use their proactive employment of fault injection to demonstrate above-and-beyond due diligence? The incentive for using fault injection in this case is to limit or fully avoid punitive damages in the case of a lawsuit. As software professionals, we predict that software liability—bugaboo though it may be—will drive some of these questions in the near future.

Demonstrating cost-effectiveness for any quality-improvement technique simply requires showing that some cost of C percent over initial resources results in either a measurable, nonzero increase in quality or a nonzero increase in confidence. After all, it is possible, though unlikely, that the results of fault injection will reveal no weaknesses that can be improved. If problems are revealed, the percentage of improvement cost need not be linear with respect to the cost increase. If it costs 10 percent more to improve a piece of code, the increase in quality for the system might be only 0.1 percent, but if that 0.1 percent includes fixing a bug like the one that destroyed Flight 501 of the Ariane 5, it is fairly easy to justify this ratio!

When management's key concern is schedule slippage over and above releasing a defective product, something as unfortunate as it is pervasive, selling fault injection to management will be much more of an uphill battle. If this is the attitude from the outset, then the waters may already be a bit too choppy to successfully navigate. The strongest argument that you could make appeals to intangibles such as "corporate reputation." An argument such as this has the best chance to receive a warm welcome if previous products have suffered from a negative image in the marketplace. Management might be inclined to try to undo a poor reputation and leapfrog the competition by trying an advanced approach to predicting future quality out on a new family of products. In such an environment, management might be receptive to the positive press that it would gain by announcing that new technologies geared toward higher quality were being employed on their new product line. We admit that failing to get to market in a timely manner can also kill a product, even if it is of high quality. Hence there needs to be an appropriate balancing of the two concerns.

There is no valid argument against the charge that fault injection costs money and resources—it *will* require both human and automated resources to put a program in place. Again, the question is how great might this cost be relative to reputation, rework, and the hassle of fixing problems after release. When these sorts of problems can be caught before software is released, fault injection starts looking good.

Our recommendation to you: Get started, even with small-scale efforts, to get that first glimmer of evidence for management. Find a project on which fault injection can be piloted. By this, we mean find a system that is not so strapped for resources that three to four days of human effort will be considered a matter of life or death. Then, plan to perform the fault injection manually. It is more costly this way and more ad hoc, but for a pilot this is not unreasonable. The manual process will be quite simple: Instrument the code with the necessary fault injectors and inspect the outputs. This process is as simple as placing a function call such as perturb_int(x) at the place in your code where you want x corrupted, and then placing a monitor such as "if output_value > 20 then print ('warning')." Also, you will need to insert the code for the function perturb_int into your software. The developers can reveal which code regions they are the most concerned about, either from an output standpoint or from a complexity/testing standpoint. If they are concerned from an output standpoint, find out what classes of outputs they want to avoid. Once you have this, you have all the information you need to instrument those regions with assertions to observe the outputs. If developers are concerned from a complexity/testing standpoint, then instrument those regions with fault injectors to see what happens if those regions were to fail or to otherwise contain latent defects. Typically when developers are concerned about complexity, what they are really saying is that they do not feel that they can take complete responsibility for what happens in those regions because they are too complex to understand.

Remember that complexity is a problem for humans, not for computers. Complexity does not automatically imply error hiding or other problems, but rather implies that testing is likely to be less than optimal. Here, fault injection can assess the likelihood of error masking, and help determine whether the complex regions are likely to produce anomalies later that would adversely affect the state of the system.

Fault injection has much to offer. We've shown how it can help analyze software behavior under many different circumstances. But even the best new technologies meet resistance from management. How do successful early adopters do it? We propose a strategy by which you can get fault-injection methods in use in your organization.

As we have shown, fault injection is usually a source-code–based technique. That means there is not a lot of activity that needs to occur early on in the software life cycle in order to set up code for fault injection. It is always good to plan ahead, though. Prior to code development it is a good idea to:

1. Enumerate the fault classes that you wish to simulate.
2. Decide how you wish to interleave fault injection with other V&V activities that are planned.

Once you have completed the first initiative, it is possible to begin building any customized perturbation functions needed for analysis of the application. By taking a look at the plans for using other metrics and V&V techniques—the second initiative—you will find it easier to assess where there are gaps that fault injection can fill. Fault injection is not meant to replace currently employed processes, but rather to augment and complement those activities that are already planned. In fact, even if fault injection might be better than existing approaches at certain measurements, that fact alone is not enough to justify throwing out the existing procedures. Personnel expertise and project schedules should always be factored in to any such decisions.

Nothing results in more confusion and disaster than coming into an organization and trying to completely undo existing processes. Most organizations have already done an analysis of their needs. They know what is available and what they can afford. Undoing current processes is often a politically insurmountable problem—except in the case where management wants a major overhaul—and the costs to an organization can be staggering, even if the processes that fault injection is replacing are inferior. Many V&V personnel loathe having to learn how to implement new metrics and standards. Trying to inject a set of processes that are as rigorous as fault injection into an organization often meets some resistance. Given all this, the best strategy is to ease an organization slowly into any new assessment approach. Later in this chapter, we present a simple five-step plan for familiarizing an organization with fault injection, and getting them up to speed without having to make any changes to the way they are currently doing business.

Automation is another critical selling point. Fault injection is a complicated process, and trying to perform it manually is not very rewarding. Find an automated tool. It is possible, in a very limited fashion, to use a debugger to modify data and then execute the code with that modified information. That is fine if a handful of corruptions at one point in the code and one test case are all that is needed. Together with this comes the requirement to manually check to see if $PRED_C$ is satisfied. If it is important to try many different corruptions and get the results quickly, using a debugger to perform fault injection is not a good approach.

The reality is that there are few commercially available software fault-injection tools. Building one from scratch involves a huge amount of time and effort. We estimate that building a noncommercial general-purpose prototype would take a minimal investment of one to two work years of effort.

As a result, fault-injection utilities command a premium price. There are no shrink-wrapped tools that sell for $500–$1000. Because they are expensive, deciding to use fault injection is a long-term investment decision. Fault injection is a scientifically sound approach based on observing how errors originate and propagate. It is an especially useful technique for mission-critical code.

Today, many organizations are only beginning to standardize on certain unit-testing techniques such as coverage. These organizations are falling behind and are basing their testing on old techniques. Unfortunately, such organizations have a long way to go before they are ready for fault injection.

We include a limited version of the Reliable Software Technologies' White-Box™ SafetyNet tool with this book. This utility is included on the CD-ROM. We include code for multiple UNIX flavors including Linux, SunOs, and Solaris. SafetyNet is a fault-injection tool for C and C++ source programs. We think it is important to get a hands-on feel for how fault injection works. That is why we included the CD-ROM with the book. With the CD-ROM, you have the opportunity to experiment with fault injection yourself. This tool can be used to develop a sound case to your managers as to why fault injection should become a part of your organization's standard software development procedures.

11.2 Developing a Winning Game Plan

Before facing management, it is vital to think through your justifications. There are a variety of standard objections to fault injection that we have observed over the years. Knowing what they are can help in preparing a convincing case. It would be wise to be able to answer the following points.

11.2.1 Avoid the Fruit Mix-up

Most software professionals suffer from the apples-and-oranges problem when it comes to comparisons relating to metrics and software V&V techniques. Managers are particularly guilty of this problem. Much of this confusion is a result of misunderstanding the definitions of common terms such as *reliability, testing,* and *correctness.* The IEEE has developed a 27-volume set of software engineering standards, one of which is nothing but standard terminology [IEEE 1983]. Before pitching management on a fault-injection pilot program, it is imperative to understand the official IEEE terminology and how different terms interrelate. Determine how fault injection compares to any more traditional processes in your organization.

Management is likely to ask if fault injection makes software more reliable. The precise answer is "no." Fault injection's results can be used in tandem with things like assertions to improve the quality of software, but fault injection in and of itself has no direct relationship to reliability.

What about software testing? Is software testing the same as fault injection? Again the precise answer is "no." Fault injection complements testing very nicely, but could never replace it. Testing and fault injection provide different results. Many software professionals, even some who purport to be software testing experts, misuse software V&V terms and end up muddying the water. The take-home lesson is to fully understand these approaches and their interrelations before selling fault injection to management.

11.2.2 Consider the Life Cycle

Another approach to selling management on fault injection is to cast an argument in terms of the software life cycle as shown in Figure 11.1. By looking at the most commonly employed processes, it is possible to develop a sound argument as to why fault injection should be added to a project.

Stepping through this simple and in some ways obvious exercise will help to ensure that you can explain why fault injection is different from anything else organizations currently do. Figure 11.1 shows the general progression from software requirements to maintainable software. In this book, we have glossed over the requirements, specification, and design phases, and have instead focused on the code, test and V&V, debug, and maintenance phases. Fault injection clearly fits within this latter group. That is not to say that applying fault injection to things like requirements, specifications, and designs is impossible. This may well turn out to be a very useful approach. Figuring out exactly how to go about doing such a thing is an interesting open research question, one that we predict will be the next big area of advance for fault injection.

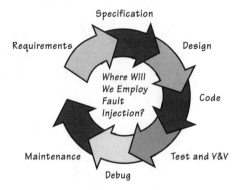

Figure 11.1 *The "general" software development life cycle.*

It is a useful exercise to consider the last four phases of the software life cycle and discover how PIE, source-code AVA, executable-code AVA, and EPA can be used to augment existing and competing procedures. This may give you some feeling for how fault injection fits in with your already existing processes.

Precoding Phases

As we previously pointed out, it is not completely correct to say that fault injection does not or cannot play a useful role early in the software life cycle. A decision to employ fault injection requires the identification and creation of fault classes that must be simulated. It is even more important to begin thinking about $PRED_C$. Both of these actions should take place early in the process.

As far as PIE goes, $PRED_C$ is not an issue, but for source-code AVA, executable-code AVA, and EPA, $PRED_C$ is an issue. Correct specification of observability predicates requires a remarkably good grasp of what a piece of code should and should not do. It might come as little surprise that people rarely consider this issue. More precisely, people usually spend a lot of time deciding what they want the code to do, not what they don't want it to do. A nice side effect of fault injection is that some of its prerequisites turn out to benefit in unforeseen ways. Because the fundamental question of code misbehavior is addressed early on, it is only natural that this information feeds back into the development process and affects the design of a system to satisfy the additional set of requirements. Somewhat ironically but interestingly, nonetheless, even if fault injection never gets performed, the act of defining $PRED_C$ is such an important and powerful learning experience that code quality ends up naturally increasing!

Organizations still exist that believe that coding standards are the key to good quality software. There is no doubt that good writing standards are key ingredients for successful maintenance, testing, and debugging; and there is at least some circumstantial evidence that certain design styles are better or worse from the ease-of-testing perspective on testability (see chapter 5). But the evidence does not support any strong claim that coding standards are good enough to replace dynamic assessment techniques, such as testing and fault injection. Do not fall into the trap of believing that rigorous coding conventions solve the problem of quality! Software can still fail because of someone else's negligence.

Coding Phase

The typical processes and tools that are employed during code development are:

1. Computer Aided Software Engineering (CASE) tools
2. Debuggers
3. Unit testing techniques
4. Compilers

EPA, AVA, and PIE can be applied only after code exists, so at the time that a CASE tool is being used and a specification schematic is being entered, it is too early to use fault injection. But once code exists, fault injection can be applied not only to develop better unit and integration tests by testing the goodness of the existing test cases but also to test for the effect that failures of external subsystems will have on a particular piece of code, and to see if particular fault injections force security violations to occur in the state of the software or state of the system.

No such information is produced by CASE tools, debuggers, unit testing, and compilers. Thus there is no reason that management should feel that applying fault injection in addition to these techniques would be duplicating work. Consider how PIE stacks up against other testing approaches or complexity metrics that might already be in use. No matter which testing approach is used, PIE can help you better decide if that approach is as valuable as you think. If is isn't, PIE can reveal where testing is deficient. There is also no definitive evidence that most other software metrics overlap results produced by PIE. PIE is dynamic and test case–based. Static metrics are not. In our opinion, the avoidance of the test domain on the part of static metrics is their downfall.

In short, any decision should not boil down to fault injection *or* these other methods; it should instead be fault injection *and* these other methods. Given limited resources, a developer must sometimes decide which information is more useful. Admittedly, gathering fault-injection results will always cost more than gathering static metric results or instrumenting code to see how much software coverage has been achieved during unit testing. But the payoff is very large as well.

Static Code Metrics

Just as coding standards often fool people into believing that quality has been achieved, so too can static source-code metrics. A simple example based on complexity demonstrates this point.

Suppose a piece of software has the statement:

```
x = x + 500;
```

This is a fairly simply statement, and that statement could be replaced in the code with 500 copies of the following statement in sequence:

```
x = x + 1;
```

This probably seems absurd from an implementation perspective, as well it should. We make this pedagogical move to emphasize the following point: Static complexity metrics such as Halstead's and a simple source code line count suggest that the latter implementation is going to be far harder to test than is the single-statement implementation. We think this is utter nonsense. The second implementation is a definite loop that changes control flow but does not make it harder to find test cases for coverage. We think it is no more likely to contain errors than "$x = x + 500$." Now it is true that this strange implementation may have an impact on performance, since the executable may be much larger. But from a testing or quality perspective, the programs are equivalent, regardless of what static metrics might suggest.

The point here is that static metrics are far less precise than fault injection. Furthermore they may make incorrect suggestions about quality that are misleading. In their defense, static code metrics can be gathered quickly and very cheaply, and the information produced can give a very quick insight into certain aspects of coding and design styles. In the end, information from static metrics could in no way ever hope to replace the behavioral information produced by fault-injection methods, but for some programs with minuscule quality assurance budgets, they may be the only approach that can be afforded.

Test and V&V Phase

Chapter 5 shows why fault injection is valuable to software testing. This is especially true of the code mutation and state perturbation varieties of fault injection. During the test phase, and particularly at integration and system-level-testing time, it should be clear that a technique such as EPA, where corrupted calls to operating systems are employed, provides more software bang for the buck than generic system-level testing does.

System-level testing is designed for showing that the outputs align with the inputs when the inputs are controlled and follow what is expected. It is a completely different task to determine whether the outputs are acceptable when everything goes wrong in an uncontrolled manner. This is particularly important for safety-critical systems, where the number of external factors can be large, and the number of external failure modes can be even larger. For this reason, no one can rightly claim that fault injection and system-level testing are in any way duplicating each other's work. In fact, it is not difficult to imagine a situation where the results of fault injection are actually more meaningful than the results of system-level testing.

Debugging Phase

We have not talked much about the debugging phase of the life cycle, mainly because debugging is so much a part of both the coding phase and the maintenance phase. But there is an interesting application of PIE results to software debugging that we should take some time to explore.

There are two times when debugging is generally invoked: either during development and unit testing or during maintenance. How might fault injection be used during the maintenance phase after a rare failure has been observed and no code modifications have been made? That is to say, the software system is generally robust and well used, but an unexpected failure has ensued. The real question is: Where is the bug?

Recall from the PIE model that the results for individual sections of code can be used to predict the minimum fault size that might be hiding at that location. The predicted minimum fault size for a location in the code is a prediction of the smallest probability of failure that could occur for the software if there was a fault at that location. In the situation where a rare (read small fault size) failure has occurred, then it is quite possible that those locations deemed insensitive to fault injection are the culprits that have caused this failure. So those are the regions of the code that should be considered first during debugging.

If it is suspected that a system failure is the result of something other than a code defect, this scheme will not work. Instead, some of the results from EPA might be applicable. For example, if we know that a system failure results from faulty input coming from some external source, and if the external devices fail regularly, then the results predicted when EPA simulated external failures might be useful for tracking down which subsystem is the culprit. However, if the external subsystem fails only intermittently, then this approach may not be beneficial.

Maintenance Phase

Chapter 9 was devoted to the benefits of using fault injection for maintenance, and thus we will not explore that further here. We should add that impact analysis tools may give a good low-resolution view of maintenance impacts. Using results from such a tool, it is possible to get even more precise information by employing fault injection to see what the real impact of state modifications are throughout.

11.2.3 Software Standards

Many software practitioners have placed all of their eggs in either the ISO9000 or the SEI-CMM basket, and are hopeful that the recommended software engineering processes will improve their final products. If standards for software production are properly followed, they should be pleased with the results, because the standards should result in better code. The concern here, however, is that the standards say little about problems such as what to do with respect to anomalies that could occur outside of the software application, or how to find test cases to detect the most troubling "tiny" faults.

It is these types of concerns for which fault injection is best suited. Note that these types of concerns cannot be easily handled by vague international software standards. For this reason, it is quite straightforward to be able to assert to management that fault injection does not overlap with the basic functionality provided by development standards. But it must also be stated that performing fault injection will in no way win you any brownie points when you apply for certification, as it truly assesses the product, and international standards are much more geared toward the processes. (For our views on process versus product in software development, see chapter 1.)

11.2.4 Regulations and Certification

The cry for the government to become more involved in software certification and regulation seems to grow louder by the year. Vendors are frustrated by the potential of unreasonable liability. Industry is confused by the hundreds of standards that have been published, almost none of which provide guidance that would help with compliance, and almost all of which seem to subsume other parts of other standards. The costs of developing and testing software is stretching beyond the limits of smaller companies, many of which can no longer afford the burdensome costs that software brings. Consider the quandary that smaller medical device companies find themselves in. They can barely afford the costs of embedding software into their products, without which their products become unusable! The complexity that has resulted from the Web and distributed systems, in general, has overcome any ability to logically determine quality. Our ability to test these systems to even a small level of thoroughness is not great.

The interesting fact about software developers is that a 14-year-old could be writing the critical software that controls the brakes on your car. Unlike disciplines such as medicine, there are no professional standards of conduct for software. Software has long been viewed more as an art and a form of self-expression than as science. This has resulted in many rumblings over the need for software engineering certification—something that occurs in every other engineering discipline. How such a certification program would be put in place is a tough problem, but standardized tests would probably be warranted. This sort of thing takes place in other engineering, piloting, legal, and medical disciplines, so why not software?

It would be ideal if there were some minimum level of software quality. If your code satisfied this level, then your software received a professional standard ranking that could be attached to your product. Fault injection could very well play a role here, but probably not as a stand-alone means of certification, since anomalies—as we have learned—are simulated with respect to each individual program. That means it could be possible if two distinct programs are up for certification from two different organizations, that one receives a much more thorough testing, because of the set of anomalies, than the other. Of course, if the simulated anomalies all represent external problems, then a fixed suite of external corruptions could be developed and used against all versions undergoing certification.

11.2.5 Liability

The most convincing case for fault injection involves something software practitioners will come to be painfully aware of any day now—liability. The liability card may be the surest way of getting management to buy into a fault-injection pilot. The current Information Revolution is having as strong an effect on society as the Industrial Revolution did in the early 1900s. But today's revolution carries with it challenging new problems (e.g., how do you ensure that the new currency of information is not lost, incorrectly computed, or maliciously mangled?). If the correctness and authenticity of information cannot be guaranteed, information consumers will be left vulnerable and information system developers may find themselves liable. For these reasons, the prospect of seemingly unbounded liability hangs over the heads of today's software developers and suggests that we are entering a new age where haphazard development and assurance philosophies will be met with severe penalties. So many people have become dependent on software that it is only a matter of time before lawsuits over information and its quality become commonplace. This an argument that any high-level manager should relate to rapidly.

Consider the fact that the phrase "software engineer" is illegal in 48 of 50 states because the term "engineer" is reserved for persons who have passed state-sanctioned certification examinations to become professional engineers. There is a perverse advantage to this situation. It appears that the less competent a person portrays himself or herself to be, the lower the standard of professionalism to which he or she will be held. Taking this principle to an extreme, we might suggest that a disclaimer be included in a comment at the top of each program, stating: *This software was developed by an incompetent person trying to learn how to program and it probably does not work.* The degree to which this tongue-in-cheek disclaimer actually reflects reality is a sad commentary on the state of our industry.

For most software practitioners, 1986 was probably not a particularly noteworthy year in the software industry. However, 1986 was the year of the first court case ever to result in a software development company being found guilty of software engineering malpractice [Data 1986]. It is not unreasonable to foresee the day when even public domain software, provided freely without compensation or warranty, will result in litigation against its developers. Legal precedence has been set according to the Hill-Burton Act that allows patients to sue medical personnel that volunteer their services in free health clinics. It is foolish to believe that developers of freeware will be immune to this type of unwanted attention. Of course, most attention will probably be focused on companies with deep pockets that are developing and selling code for a profit.

State-of-the-practice rules, which differentiate code that meets professional standards from code that does not meet professional standards, are nonexistent. However, some guidelines do exist to help differentiate good software development processes from bad software development processes (e.g., the Software Engineering Institute's Capability Maturity Model and ISO9001). But as we have pointed out repeatedly, good processes do not necessarily result in good code. Thus, there is a real need for techniques that can assess how well a piece of software can handle internal problems and external problems over which the programmer may have no control. Knowing better how a particular piece of the information-processing puzzle fits with other pieces can only serve to strengthen the legal protection of that piece. Software liability is strikingly hard to predict. Fortunately, the sort of information that software fault-injection methods can provide makes such prediction attainable.

Software liability issues are characterized by two key questions:

1. Who is liable when a piece of software fails?
2. What is the probability that a liability event will occur (in other words, what is the *risk* associated with using a piece of software)?

The obvious answer to the first question is the developing organization; however, the answer to the second question is more subjective and is our current focus.

Questions of liability are legal and ethical quagmires that in the case of software also happen to introduce technical questions. We argue for employing fault-injection methods that simulate the effects that real faults will most likely have—as opposed to simulating the faults themselves—as a means of quantifying the risks created by the software component of a system. If we can accurately and scientifically measure said risks, we will have a means for probabilistically bounding liability.

If software never produces undesirable outputs, then questions of liability should not arise, although given today's litigious atmosphere even this is not guaranteed. But determining a priori that software will never fail is, in general, impossible. In order to quantify the liability risks of software failure, we need to know the *probability* that the software will fail in a manner that is consistent with a resulting loss. After all, not all failures translate into losses.

Generally speaking, risk can be divided into two types: speculative and pure. *Speculative risk* can result either in a loss or a profit (e.g., investing in company stock may or may not pay off). With *pure risk,* the only potential consequence is loss (e.g., automobile collision insurance pays off only if an accident occurs). Risk is not problematic if it is either too small or if affordable insurance can be obtained to offset the potential loss. Insurance gives companies that produce goods and services an opportunity to order their business affairs so that a certain cost, a *premium,* is substituted for an uncertain potential cost, specifically, a disastrous loss of unacceptable magnitude. The ability to acquire insurance provides some degree of security, and thus continued economic activity in an environment containing risk. Failure to substitute risk through the payment of premiums means retention of the potential adverse consequences. Few prudent businesses are willing to assume such a risk.

Software risk assessment is still a black art. Thus far, insurance companies have purposely opted not to insure software as a stand-alone entity apart from the entire information system. Before insurance companies as assumers of risk can offer the security that comes with insurance, they must quantify their risk. Risk quantification evaluates uncertainties and places a dollar amount on the risk to be assumed. *Perils* are the cause of pure risk. Examples of perils include floods, fire, and disease. Underwriters also look beyond specific perils to the causes of such perils, that is, hazards which precipitate the resulting loss. Examples of hazards include bad weather patterns for the peril of flood, poor electrical wiring for the peril of fire, and poor health habits for the peril of disease. Thus the providers of insurance need tools to measure the risk and assess hazards so that they can mathematically calculate premiums. Without such tools, the insurance provider cannot prudently assume risk and accurately set premiums.

The early writers of marine insurance estimated the risks of ship and cargo loss by taking into account weather patterns of specific routes at specific times, patterns of known pirate activity, and the success and failures of key crew members, such as the captain, as well as the particular vessel. Underwriter accuracy in assigning a premium/risk ratio is enhanced if a large database of previous shipping experiences is available. For example, suppose that an underwriter assigns risk numbers from 1 to 10 (smallest risk to greatest risk) on each of the assumed equal categories of the perils: weather, pirates, previous crew/ship experiences. Next assume that a winter voyage calls for a weather rating of 9, pirate activity calls for a 2, and the crew/ship have an excellent rating of 1. In this case, 12 is the combined risk out of a possible total of 30. A premium of 12/30 of the insured value would be assessed, as well as some value for underwriter profit. The relatively high premium for this proposed trip could be justified if the shipper anticipates inflated profits due to a winter delivery. However, the shipper might decide to sail later when the weather peril decreases. Another option is for the shipper to sail without protection and retain all risk. The concept of seeking data to turn total uncertainty into reasonable certainty is the main impetus of both those who seek and those who provide insurance.

Insurance companies can "play the percentages" when they have extensive prior experience that is directly relevant to a certain risk. Prior knowledge allows for prediction with reasonably high confidence. In the software domain, however, extensive prior experience is not applicable because each piece of software is one of a kind, and a reasonable amount of prior experience with a particular piece of software will almost certainly not be built up until the life span of the software is essentially complete.

In terms of the preceding definitions, software is a pure risk. Software is expected to work correctly even though failure occurs often in practice. But, as we mentioned earlier, even correct software can carry risks. This problem is compounded by the fact that correctness is defined with respect to the requirements/specification. If the requirements or specification are not correct, as is too often the case, it is foolish to expect that the software will perform properly in all circumstances. When a problem related to correct code from incorrect requirements/specification occurs, the issue of who is liable becomes even muddier. This is because it is the customer who uses the software, not the developer, who is often tasked with writing the requirements.

Software presents a relatively novel form of risk—particularly software that is capable of triggering loss of life. There has been no lengthy historical time frame over which software systems can be evaluated in order to accumulate prior knowledge, and thus each disaster must be viewed anecdotally. Each software system is unique, hence generalizing risk assessments from previous projects will not necessarily be beneficial, although it might. This is the case even if factors such as application domain and personnel are very similar. A good example here is the Ariane 5 rocket disaster (see chapter 6); the code that caused the disaster on the Ariane 5 had not caused problems for the Ariane 4, and because the code had worked properly for the Ariane 4, it was assumed it would work well for the Ariane 5 [Lions 1996].

Software fault injection provides a unique opportunity to probe deeper into the question: *What is the probability that a liability event will occur?* It cannot provide a direct answer, but it can provide some insights. By observing how bad things get from our hypothesized future anomalous events, we can get a partial feeling for how bad the future *might* actually get. Then, we can begin to search for bounds on the degree of liability being risked before software is deployed.

11.3 Five Steps to Getting Started with Fault Injection

The *first step* in getting started is to assess your current testing processes. Make sure that your organization has a reasonable way to store the suites of test cases that it generates. After all, dynamic processes that study behavior require inputs. Show management that this information is readily available and can be used when fault injection is employed. It is always a plus for management to hear that they already have some of what they need to do! Also, make sure to find out what testing schemes are currently employed. This question may come from a test manager, who will immediately see fault injection as part of his or her turf.

The *second step* is to study the types of output events that should never happen, and formulate the types of anomalies to simulate. This can be done early in the software life cycle; you don't necessarily need to wait till you have code. In fact, the results from a hazard analysis for a specification for the system can be used as soon as the spec is available.

The *third step* is proving to management why fault injection is different and necessary. This book has shown why there is really nothing comparable to fault injection, so this step should be easy. Management needs to know that the information that results from fault injection is meaningful and that it adds tangible value.

The *fourth step* is to pick a pilot project. Start by having a handful of key employees trained. One good way to do this is to find an expert on fault injection and invite him or her to consult for a few days, in-house, and teach your personnel the basics. This can be done quite inexpensively. Training has the added benefit of being a decision point. If, after training, no one is convinced of the value of fault injection, a good stopping point will have been reached.

Finally, the *fifth step* is to experiment with the SafetyNet tool that is provided in this book. If you do not have Linux on your personal computer, install it. The tool includes two HTML tutorials that show how to use it. Within a few hours of studying the installation documentation and studying the manual, you can be injecting corruptions into real software and seeing how things propagate. It is just that simple. And do visit an accompanying Web site for this book that will have updates and new releases of this tool at http://www.rstcorp.com/fault-injection .html.

11.4 What's the Bottom Line?

Building a fault-injection tool from scratch will take several work-years of effort. Even buying a fault-injection tool off the shelf costs in the tens of thousands of U.S. dollars. Customization of such a tool can run into an additional tens of thousands of U.S. dollars. Added to these costs are the costs of training personnel to use the tool and be able to make sense of its results. This will take weeks or months. Finally, actually using the tool on a specific project incurs some cost, but relatively speaking these are minimal.

In the end, this technology is much more expensive than a static metrics package or a software coverage tool. Determining whether it is cost-effective to use fault injection really boils down to a determination of how critical it is that your software is well tested and works properly with other parts of a system that may not have been built by you. If you plan to sell thousands of copies of your software, then the cost per copy of applying fault injection is really relatively minimal. If your software is embedded into a safety-critical application such as the Ariane 5, then although there will not be thousands of copies sold, the one copy had better work as advertised. In comparison with billions of dollars in liability, a few thousand dollars pales to insignificance.

11.5 Conclusion

Throughout this book, we have described the myriad benefits to be realized by injecting anomalous, simulated states into a running program. Fault injection can be used to predict what events might occur in the future, as long as the future contains the same anomalous circumstances that fault-injection analysis employs. Fault injection is not a perfect approach. It is only as good as the anomalies simulated. But it does allow us to observe how bad the future could get. In other words, it allows us to build up a body of knowledge about probable future behavior. Such a capability is arguably the next best thing to having a fortune-teller's crystal ball, and it certainly beats facing the future with no predictions at all.

Fault injection as a process does not explicitly state how good software is per se. Rather, fault injection provides forward-looking, worst-case predictions for how badly a piece of code might behave and how frequently it might misbehave. This frequency is a relative metric, not absolute. Nevertheless it manages to provide a means for observing how often undesirable outputs occur after we have injected corrupt information into executing software. By contrast, software testing explicitly states how good software is. But even when testing can be successfully applied, correct code that has been thoroughly tested can have "bad days" and not work as desired because of external influences. For example, a workstation might be in good working order, but if the network server is not functioning, the workstation's user may find it so unusable that it might as well be broken, too. Simulating these sorts of events falls under the rubric of fault injection, and understanding the impact of these events is our justification as to why fault injection should be a part of software assessment.

Today, software developers are living in a liability grace period ironically afforded them by the legal profession. This is most likely because the legal system does not yet understand how software works and the insurance sector does not understand how software's potential risks can be assessed. Furthermore, the courts have not demanded of software practitioners the absolute level of professionalism that is required of other engineering disciplines. As the aphorism says: "All good things must come to an end." It is prudent to recognize this unusual period of nonliability in our profession's history for what it is—temporary. Furthermore, it is advisable for our profession to develop honest and objective risk metrics so we can all share the risk of software ventures through insurance. Not having access to such protection is like jumping out of an airplane without a parachute—maybe you will land in a big bale of hay, and maybe you will not.

It is our contention that software fault injection is a promising technology in software quality assessment. Even if only a small fraction of all possible anomalies are explored during analysis, the results still provide useful information about how well-behaved a software system will be. The key to a successful experience with software fault-injection methods is the proper interpretation of the results. When satisfactory outputs are observed after injection occurs, it is very tempting to rush to the premature decision that the software is incapable of ever producing undesirable outputs. Nothing could be further from the truth. The correct interpretation is that the software is known to be resilient only to those anomalies tried; nevertheless, it is likely that the software is also resilient to many other anomaly instances. Somewhat counterintuitively, the greatest benefit from fault injection occurs when a piece of software does not tolerate injected anomalies. Any interpretation here is less likely to be oversold because the only honest claim is: *The software presents risks.*

References

[Data 1986] *Data Processing Services Inc. v. L. H. Smith Oil Corp.,* 492 N. E. 2d 314 (Ind. App. 1986).

[IEEE 1983] *IEEE Standard Glossary of Software Engineering Terminology,* IEEE Std 729-1983. IEEE, 1983.

[Lions 1996] Prof. J. L. Lions. Ariane 5 flight 501 failure: Report of the inquiry board. Paris, July 19, 1996.

Appendix

The CD-ROM includes two packages for experimenting with fault injection: the WhiteBox SafetyNet from Reliable Software Technologies, and MOTHRA, a software mutation tool. The CD-ROM is written in Unix ISO9660 standard format and can be read by a variety of different Unix systems.

To check out the CD-ROM, you must first mount the CD-ROM drive on a local file system. This assumes, normally, that you have a mount directory called "/cdrom" that the CD-ROM is mounted on.

- Most Solaris systems will automatically mount the CD-ROM when you insert it. If not, use the following command:

  ```
  % mount -o ro /dev/sr0 /cdrom
  ```

  This assumes that your CD-ROM drive is attached to the normal Solaris SCSI ID.

- For SunOS, use the following command:

  ```
  % mount -r -t hsfs /dev/sr0 /cdrom
  ```

- For Linux, mount the CD-ROM using the following command:

  ```
  % mount -o ro /dev/hdc /cdrom
  ```

  This assumes you have a standard IDE CD-ROM that appears as hdc on your computer. Consult your system administrator if your computer is configured differently.

Once you have successfully mounted the CD-ROM, you can peruse its contents and read the README files. We have reproduced both the Toplevel README file and the README file for SafetyNet. Along with SafetyNet is an HTML Tutorial explaining how to run the demo that you can view with a Web browser such as Netscape Communicator or Microsoft Internet Explorer.

The Toplevel README Contents

```
Demonstration directories:


./SafetyNetDemo
------------


Demonstration of WhiteBox SafetyNet, a commercial software
analysis tool that employs fault injection to perform fault
tolerance assessment of safety critical systems.

To run the SafetyNet demonstration, please look at the README
file in the ./SafetyNetDemo directory. You may also use a Web
browser to view the 'index.html' file in this directory and
follow the links properly.

For more information on WhiteBox SafetyNet, contact


        Reliable Software Technologies Corporation
          21515 Ridgetop Circle, Suite 250
          Sterling, VA 20166  USA
                      703-404-9294
          www.rstcorp.com
                    info@rstcorp.com


./Mothra
------


Demonstration of the Mothra II software testing package, an
academic research tool that employs fault injection to perform
mutation testing analysis of FORTRAN 77 programs.

To run the Mothra demonstration, please look at the README
file in the ./Mothra directory. You may also use a Web browser
to view the 'index.html' file in this directory and follow the
links properly.


For more information on Mothra, contact
```

The Mothra Group
c/o Professor Gene Spafford
Dept. of Computer Sciences
Purdue University
W. Lafayette, IN 47907-1398
317-494-7825
mothra-support@cs.purdue.edu

Contents of the SafetyNet
README File

WhiteBox SafetyNet
Demonstration Version
July 1, 1997

Reliable Software Technologies Corporation
21515 Ridgetop Circle, Suite 250
Sterling, VA 20166   USA
www.rstcorp.com

Support: 703-404-9294
support@rstcorp.com


```
===============================================================
Contents


1. Introduction
1.1 Summary of Demonstration Version modifications
1.2 System requirements
1.3 Contacting technical support


2. Installation on local host


3. Running the SafetyNet demonstration


===============================================================
```

1. Introduction

This is a demonstration version of WhiteBox SafetyNet, one of
the tools in the WhiteBox Software Assurance product line of
Reliable Software Technologies (RST). SafetyNet is a software

analysis tool that uses fault injection technology to assess
the fault tolerance of safety critical systems written in C and
C++. For more information on other tools within the WhiteBox
suite, please contact RST via WWW, email, phone, or fax.

```
WWW:      www.rstcorp.com
Email:    whitebox@rstcorp.com
Phone:    703-404-9294
Fax:      703-404-9295
```

1.1 Summary of Demonstration Version Modifications

The WhiteBox SafetyNet Demonstration Version has been modified
from the standard WhiteBox SafetyNet version. Many key capabilities provided by the standard version have been disabled
for this version. Some of the differences are described below:

* Only runs via the provided Demo Framework GUI.

* Only supports the 2 tutorial applications provided with the
  demonstration.

* Limitation on available perturbation functions for symbols.

* Only supports numeric data perturbation.

* Single perturbation definition per symbol.

* Analysis execution accepts only 2 options: the number of
  perturbations to perform at each location for each test case
  and the master seed used to seed the random number generation used in the data perturbation during the analysis.

1.2 System Requirements

WhiteBox SafetyNet Demonstration Version is available on the
following platforms and operation systems:

```
Platform    Operating system and Version
-------     --------------------
SPARC         SunOS 4.1.3 - 4.1.4, Solaris 2.4 - 2.5.1
x86           Linux 2.x
```

The SafetyNet demonstration can either be run from the
CD-ROM or installed on a local host. When running from CD-ROM,
SafetyNet will require approximately 10MB of space for installation of some sample source code that can be modified and
compiled. To install SafetyNet on your local host's hard
drive, you will need approximately 50 MB of disk space, plus
an additional 20 MB of disk space during installation.

1.3 Contacting technical support

If you have difficulties installing or running the software,
please contact WhiteBox technical support between the hours of
8:00 AM and 5:00 PM EST.

```
Email:   support@rstcorp.com
Phone:   703-404-9294
Fax:     703-404-9295
```

==

2. Installation on local host

If you wish to install SafetyNet on your local host system
instead of running it from the CD-ROM, please follow the steps
below. If you wish to run SafetyNet from the CD-ROM, please
skip to the next section.

To install the software, follow the steps below.

* Mount the CD-ROM drive on a local file system. This assumes
  that you have a mount directory of "/cdrom" that the CD-ROM
  is mounted on, normally.

        - Most Solaris systems will automatically mount the
          CD-ROM when you insert it. If not, use the follow-
          ing command:

              % mount -o ro /dev/sr0 /cdrom

        This assumes that your CD-ROM drive is attached to
        the normal Solaris SCSI ID.

        - For SunOS, use the following command:

              % mount -r -t hsfs /dev/sr0 /cdrom

- For Linux, mount the CD-ROM using the following
  command:

        % mount -o ro /dev/hdc /cdrom

    This assumes you have a standard IDE CD-ROM that
    appears as hdc on your computer. Consult your sys-
    tem administrator if your computer is configured
    differently.

* Change your working directory to the CD-ROM's SafetyNetDemo
  directory.

Example:
        % cd /cdrom/SafetyNetDemo

* Run the installation script to unpack and install the software.

        % ./INSTALL

This step will go through, ask you to accept the legal license,
ask for a directory to install the information into, then
unpack and install the software.

Upon completion of the INSTALL script, WhiteBox SafetyNet
should be installed properly on your system.

===

3. Running the SafetyNet demo

Prior to running SafetyNet, you must make sure that you have
either installed it on your local host's hard drive (i.e. in a
directory such as "/usr/local/safetynet"), or have the CD-ROM
mounted (i.e. in "/cdrom").

Execute the program named 'safetynet' in the 'bin' subdirectory
of the installation (or CD-ROM) directory subdirectory. For a
local installation, this will be the 'bin' subdirectory of the
directory that you specified during the INSTALL program. For
the CD-ROM, this directory will be /cdrom/SafetyNetDemo/<arch>/
bin. '<arch>' in this case will be

```
linux           - for Linux platform
sparc-sunos4    - for SunOS 4.x platform
sparc-sunos5    for Solaris 2.x (SunOS 5.x) platform
```

The 'safetynet' demo framework can be invoked in a number of ways. Here are 2 examples of ways that it can be invoked, given that the installation directory is /usr/local/safetynet:

Example 1: Invoke using full path name.
```
>/usr/local/safetynet/bin/safetynet
```

Example 2: Invoke using PATH environment variable (csh assumed in this example).

```
>set path = (/usr/local/safetynet/bin $path)
>safetynet
```

Step through the tutorials described in HTML format in the 'docs' subdirectory of the installation directory. The top level document is contained in filename 'docs/title.html'. To browse the tutorial, load this file in your HTML browser of choice (i.e. Netscape Navigator).

Example:
```
netscape /usr/local/safetynet/docs/title.html
```

Index